ONE HUNDRED

D1098816

ONE HUNDRED DAYS

The Memoirs of the Falklands
Battle Group Commander

ADMIRAL
SANDY WOODWARD

With Patrick Robinson

HarperCollins*Publishers*

HarperCollins*Publishers*
77–85 Fulham Palace Road,
Hammersmith, London w6 8jb

www.**fire**and**water**.com

This paperback edition 2003
1 3 5 7 9 8 6 4 2

First published in Great Britain by
HarperCollins*Publishers* 1992
Copyright © Admiral Sir John Woodward and Patrick Robinson 1992

The Author asserts the moral right to
be identified as the author of this work

isbn 0 00 713467 3

Set in Postscript Linotype Janson by
Rowland Phototypesetting Ltd,
Bury St Edmunds, Suffolk

Printed and bound in Great Britain by
Clays Ltd, St Ives plc

All rights reserved. No part of this publication may be
reproduced, stored in a retrieval system, or transmitted,
in any form or by any means, electronic, mechanical,
photocopying, recording or otherwise, without the prior
permission of the publishers.

This book is sold subject to the condition that it shall not,
by way of trade or otherwise, be lent, re-sold, hired out or
otherwise circulated without the publisher's prior consent
in any form of binding or cover other than that in which it
is published and without a similar condition including this
condition being imposed on the subsequent purchaser.

CONTENTS

ILLUSTRATIONS

Midshipman Woodward, at 19.

HMS *Sanguine* off Malta in 1954.

Wedding Day, 9 April 1960.

HMS *Warspite* coming into Cardiff docks, 1969.

With Lord Carrington aboard HMS *Warspite* at Faslane, Scotland, in 1969.

An old Navy ceremony, HMS *Warspite*, 1970.

With my staff on HMS *Glamorgan* – The Flag Operations Room.

Ascension Island, with HMS *Hermes* at anchor in the foreground.

Captain Mike Barrow of the destroyer HMS *Glamorgan*.

Captain Paul Hoddinott of the destroyer HMS *Glasgow*.

Captain David Pentreath of the frigate HMS *Plymouth*.

Captain Sam Salt of the destroyer HMS *Sheffield*.

Captain Kit Layman of the frigate HMS *Argonaut*.

Captain David Hart-Dyke of the destroyer HMS *Coventry*.

Captain Lin Middleton of the aircraft carrier HMS *Hermes*.

HMS *Hermes*, June 1982.

Captain Brian Young of the destroyer HMS *Antrim*.

Commander Alan West, Captain of the frigate HMS *Ardent*.

Captain Jeremy Black of the aircraft carrier HMS *Invincible*.

Commander Christopher Wreford-Brown, Captain of the nuclear submarine HMS *Conqueror*.

Captain Mike Harris of the destroyer HMS *Cardiff*.

Commander Tony Morton, Captain of the frigate HMS *Yarmouth*.

Captain John Coward of the frigate HMS *Brilliant*.

Captain Bill Canning of the frigate HMS *Broadsword*.

Commander Christopher Craig, Captain of the frigate HMS *Alacrity*.

Ian North, Captain of the container ship *Atlantic Conveyor*, with Captain Mike Layard, the senior Royal Navy officer on board.

Commodore Mike Clapp.

Captain Peter Dingemans and Captain Jeremy Larken, the two Captains of the amphibious ships HMS *Intrepid* and HMS *Fearless*, respectively.

Captain Hugh Balfour of the destroyer HMS *Exeter*.

HMS *Exeter* in Carlos Water.

HMS *Exeter* opens fire.

With Admiral Sir John Fieldhouse, the C-in-C, at Brize Norton, 4 July 1982.

With Char, Andy and Tessa.

> The drawings in this book are all done by Sandy Woodward, some of them drawn at night in his cabin in the waters off the Falklands in the spring of 1982.

Admiral Woodward's last signal to the Task Force before his Flag was lowered from HMS Hermes off Port Stanley, Falkland Islands, 4 July 1982.

As I haul my South Atlantic flag down, I reflect sadly on the brave lives lost, and the good ships gone, in the short time of our trial. I thank whole heartedly each and every one of you for your gallant support, tough determination and fierce perseverance under bloody conditions. Let us all be grateful that Argentina doesn't breed bulldogs and, as we return severally to enjoy the blessingss of our land, resolve that those left behind for ever shall not be forgotten.

FOREWORD TO THE FIRST EDITION

It is not very easy to take a decision which commits your country to fight a war eight thousand miles from home. At such times it is impossible to clear the mind of the inevitable heartbreak of war – of all wars – and the grief of those families who suffer loss.

But on Friday, 2 April 1982, Argentina invaded the Falkland Islands.

On the previous Wednesday evening, John Nott, Secretary of State for Defence, had hurried into my study at the House of Commons, anxiety in his face, tenseness in his every movement. He told me that the Argentine Fleet had set sail, whether for another exercise or to invade the Falkland Islands, he knew not.

As the news hardened, I called several people together, ministers and advisers. If the islands were invaded, I knew exactly what we must do – we must get them back. Their people were our people. Their loyalty and devotion to Queen and Country had never faltered. As so often in politics the question was not, *what* should we do? But, *how* could it be done? The Falklands were three weeks' sailing time away – three weeks' warning to the enemy – the seas were inhospitable and there would be no British air base on land. The Chief of Defence Staff was in New Zealand on an official visit. Other advisers were not very optimistic about our chances. But appeasement? Britain? Never. Admiral Leach joined us.

'First Sea Lord, if this invasion happens, precisely what can we do?' I enquired. I shall never forget the quiet, calm, confident answer.

'I can put together a Task Force of destroyers, frigates, landing craft, support vessels,' he said. 'It will be led by the aircraft carriers HMS *Hermes* and HMS *Invincible*. It can be ready to leave in forty-eight hours.'

Once again, the hour had produced the man. It was to produce many more throughout the campaign – Admiral Fieldhouse, whose warm humanity and sureness of touch never failed him or us; Admiral Lewin, Chief of Defence Staff, a tower of wisdom and strength; Admiral Woodward himself, who saw the risks, knew and felt every loss, and who raised morale day by day by day. There were many others, some known heroes, others whose valiant deeds are written on the scroll of life. Eventually we sent a hundred ships and twenty-five thousand men, but we were not to know that at the beginning.

The issue, from the start, was one of purest principle. Foreign governments all over the world waited, some of them anxiously, for our reaction. But British people, everywhere, knew there could be but one answer.

And, when finally the Royal Navy put the land forces ashore in Carlos Bay in the early hours of 21 May, one island farmer summed up, in a sense, what it is about us which so often sets this nation apart. Asked by an officer of the Parachute Regiment whether he was surprised to find the Task Force anchored in the Bay, the farmer replied, 'No, not a bit. We knew Maggie would come.'

He said 'Maggie'. But he meant Britain. He meant all of us. Because he knew that we, as a people, believe in the Rule of Law, in fair play and decency. We will not accept military hooliganism against us and I am perfectly certain that many small countries felt that much more secure when, in 1982, the British Lion again made his stand against a tyrant and for the rights of the citizens of the tiny, remote Falkland Islands.

This book, *One Hundred Days*, is written by a man whom, at the time, I had never met, but who was constantly in my thoughts throughout those dreadful weeks of the spring of 1982. He was then, to all of us, Rear Admiral Sandy Woodward, Commander of the Task Force. Later he became Admiral Sir John Woodward, Commander-in-Chief, Naval Home Command. But he will always be remembered as the senior British commander on the spot who bore the major responsibility for the recapture of the Falkland Islands.

As they have done so many times in past conflicts, the Royal Navy once more chose the right man to accomplish an extremely hazardous task. The tall, rather stern, former nuclear submarine commander sailed to the south with the highest academic and practical qualifications – in naval strategy and operations, nuclear engineering, anti-aircraft missile defence systems, computer technology, and senior naval planning and management techniques. There were those who considered him the cleverest man in the Navy. French newspapers called him 'Nelson'. He was precisely the right man to fight the world's first computer war.

In this book he tells, finally, his own story as seen from the Admiral's Bridge of the 29,000-ton carrier HMS *Hermes*. As a narrative, it is historically important because the Admiral allows us to follow his thoughts, his plans, his fears and, as a life-long career officer, his expectations of those who would fight with such high courage under his command – sometimes against a near-suicidal enemy. He takes us into the heart of fierce actions fought by the Royal Navy both in Falkland Sound and on the high seas. When the British Fleet steamed through the night and passed silently below the Argentinian gun positions on Fanning Head as they made for the landing beaches, the tension must have been unbearable for the commander. In Chapter Thirteen he takes us with them, behind the guns of HMS *Antrim*.

In the end, Sandy Woodward shows himself to be not only a very great patriot and a superb sea-going admiral, he demonstrates to us who were not there the inevitability of his actions, how so many hard, critical decisions ultimately made themselves.

But I do believe his book, perhaps unknowingly, reveals the massive sense of justice that was ever-present in the minds of the men who fought in the South Atlantic. Some of them never came home. To them and their families, we owe an enormous debt of gratitude which we can never repay. I doubt if either the Admiral or I will ever be entirely free of that private, lonely responsibility.

I believe that all who read this very personal account of the war, will feel some pride in the kind of people we are, and in the country which gave us birth. We have a long heritage of freedom and in 1982 it was most nobly upheld by all of our armed forces who took part in the battle for the Falkland Islands.

MARGARET THATCHER, 1992

PREFACE TO THE FIRST EDITION

I have tried to write this book as if I were telling my story to a close friend. And to help me in this task I selected Patrick Robinson, who was thus obliged to sit very quietly, very patiently and do a great deal of listening – none of which are his strong suits. I chose him because he is not a serving officer in the Royal Navy; indeed has never been in the Royal Navy, and so far as I know does not intend to sign on now. He is what you might describe as a layman – an author who has written bestsellers about yacht racing and, in calmer waters, the University Boat Race.

But, in his own words, battleships had thus far eluded him. Which in one sense clarified my task (to him I would have to explain just about *everything*). But in another sense it made the entire project more onerous, in that I would be permitted to take nothing for granted on behalf of my readers. If there is one sentence I shall remember from Patrick for all of my days it will be the first time he felt he had to say: 'I have not the *slightest* idea what you are talking about – and neither I suspect will anyone else!' This occurred on Day One.

Why, you may wonder, did I not dispense with all of that heartache and self-inflicted grief by hiring a proper naval historian to assist me? Because, I suspected, it would be the kiss of death for a book such as this, for four principal reasons:

a) just about every historian I know has already written a book about the conflict in the South Atlantic;

b) historians are inclined to write for each other, and for other 'experts', other specialists;

c) they would, in their entirely proper search for 'the truth', have found the temptation to argue with me quite irresistible – perhaps the only thing we would have agreed upon was that no one would ever have heard of me but for the events of 1982;

d) I did not, in any event, want to write a formal history. It is too soon for that. I sought only to document the thoughts and opinions of the senior naval Forward Commander, from first to last. And for that I needed a professional writer with an entirely open mind.

As it was I ended up with this extraordinary man to help me. Putting it as kindly as I can, he has a keenly developed sense of drama. This led him to badger me mercilessly into describing things I considered both boring and commonplace. He practically had apoplexy when I attempted to dismiss the first sinking of a Royal Naval warship for forty years with the short phrase from my diary: 'They blew my old ship *Sheffield* away last night . . .'

But together we somehow sailed the course. And we have tried to restrict ourselves to revealing, as plainly and honestly as possible, what went on in my mind throughout those weeks, how I planned things, how I saw things, and how events affected me. This entailed careful adherence to the essentials of my diary and letters of the time, with the addition of much extra material to put it in proper context.

You must judge for yourself whether or not I am capable of such honesty. By definition this book has to be uncomfortably self-revealing, but I am fairly well prepared for any consequential discomfort. For I have been variously accused by the media: not least, of cowardice – indeed it was the highly reputable one-time editor of the *Daily Telegraph* Max Hastings who repeated the charge, made of course by others, that I should have been awarded the South Africa Star, because I positioned HMS *Hermes* so far back to the east of the action.

They said I had no idea how to treat the media. That I was over-confident in April, over-cautious in May. That I failed to understand amphibious warfare, or air warfare. That I was in fact 'out of my depth' (*Sunday Telegraph*). As for personal descriptions, the too-aptly named *Times* Insight Team, reported my 'flaming red hair' as matching my character. They may or may not have got the character right, but their lack of a capless colour photo led them well astray on the colour of my hair in their search for catchy phrases.

If, after reading this book, you happen to agree with the most critical of the commentators, that I am a coward, an incompetent, and arrogant to boot, then so be it. In any case, a leader has to have an element of all those things in him, and I am only trying to give you a glimpse into the mind of a bloke who found himself in charge, in the front line of the war.

I think the aspect of the book which most surprised my editors and publishers, and indeed Patrick, was the inescapable conclusion that, one way and another, it was a bit of a close call.

There have been those who went as far as to describe Britain's battle to recover the Falkland Islands as 'A damned close run thing', as the Duke of Wellington was moved to do after Waterloo. I don't quite go that far – but, like the late but timely arrival of Blucher's army, there were several critical turning points which could have gone either way. Most of them, I was glad to note at the time, turned in our favour.

It should also be recalled that there were several entirely competent organizations which initially suspected the whole operation was doomed. In no particular order they were:

a) the United States Navy, which considered the re-capture of the Falkland Islands by British forces alone to be a military impossibility;

b) the Ministry of Defence in Whitehall, which assessed that a tolerable air situation could not be achieved and that therefore the battle could not be won;

c) the Army, which considered it to be ill-advised, for lack of a 'proper' advantage ratio in land force numbers;

d) the Royal Air Force, which, seeing little role for themselves on account of the vast distances, and no chance of a navy surviving in the face of an air force, was inclined to agree;

e) the Secretary of State for Defence, Mr (now Sir) John Nott, who firstly represented the views of his ministry and possibly also since success in it would probably overturn his 1981 Defence Review.

There were certainly very many more people calling 'BACK!' than there were calling 'FORWARD!', and most of the ones calling 'BACK!' sat in high places. But the principal voice calling 'FORWARD!' was that of the First Sea Lord, Admiral Sir Henry Leach, the professional head of the Royal Navy, my ultimate boss. And he was the man whose voice had to be listened to, whatever his innermost thoughts. If he said the Navy *could* do it, that was essentially that. Not least because that was what Mrs Thatcher and the majority of British people wanted to hear.

In addition he had an extremely powerful supporter across the Atlantic Ocean in the person of Mr (now Sir) Caspar Weinberger, America's Defence Secretary, who took a solid stand in Britain's favour in the face of every kind of local opposition. Cap Weinberger cast aside the hitherto pro-Argentina stance of the Reagan Administration – arguing his President and the Pentagon into giving much support to America's staunchest military ally. In his own excellent book, *Fighting for Peace*, Sir Caspar outlines his firm and inviolate instructions to his military subordinates that 'Britain be given every possible assistance in terms of hardware and intelligence'.

All of us have reason to be extraordinarily grateful to a very good friend for offering assistance in times of need; perhaps I owe a debt greater than most. For the newest version of the American Sidewinder air-to-air missile was one of the decisive weapons in the combat above the ground, and over the ocean. Also, without US co-operation in allowing us access to Ascension, we would not have had that vital forward base for our forces in the south. Never mind the other ways that help was provided, lack of these two alone would probably have reversed the outcome. I am thus doubly grateful for Cap Weinberger's generous assertion, that 'The War in the South Atlantic was won by the indomitable will of the British armed forces'.

In general terms the British victory would have to be judged anyway as a *fairly* close run thing in matters of timing, land forces and air forces. There was also the inescapable truth that the Argentinian commanders failed inexplicably to realize that if they had hit either of our aircraft carriers, the British would have been finished. They never really came after the targets that would surely have given them the best chance of victory.

As it was, we fought our way along a knife-edge, I realising perhaps more than most (and certainly more than Max Hastings's informant), that one major mishap, a mine, an explosion, a fire, whatever, in either of our two aircraft carriers, would almost certainly have proved fatal to the whole operation. We lost *Sheffield*, *Coventry*, *Ardent*, *Antelope*, *Atlantic Conveyor*, and *Sir Galahad*. If the Args' bombs had been properly fused for low-level air raids we would surely have lost *Antrim*, *Plymouth*, *Argonaut*, *Broadsword* and *Glasgow*. And we were very lucky indeed that *Glamorgan* and *Brilliant* were still floating in mid-June.

Basically it was all a bit tight, and I hope this book will illuminate what a searching test the Royal Navy underwent.

I have tried to be graphic, where necessary, and I have tried to convey something of the professionalism required in sea warfare. I have also quoted shamelessly from personal letters home to my wife, and also from the diary I kept each night – a diary which displays not only my frequent ill-temper and occasional insecurities, but also my impatience, my tensions, my lack of tact and understanding, and most of the other failings of the human race. That diary, like many others, was more a safety valve and confessional, than any attempt to record facts.

I have begun the book with the *Sheffield* because it gave me an opportunity to bring you right into the Operations Room with the men who formed our 'Picket Line' in the three Type 42 guided-missile destroyers, none of which survived the war unscathed. Also, it is important to have such a picture in your mind, as a backdrop of the dreadful reality of war, if you are to share the experience of the commander. Because he, above all, must act in the face of those realities, never taking counsel of his own worst fears.

I cannot and do not pretend to know all that went on. Nor can I possibly do justice the inshore naval, amphibious and land force commanders and their operations. So I could never pretend to be giving you the truth, the whole truth and nothing but the truth. I doubt I even knew as much as half of what went on in my own particular area of responsibility first hand – much less anyone else's. But throughout the book we have picked out most of the key ingredients from many other sources: from friends, colleagues and, in some instances, from strangers who fought the war with me, in other ships, in other places, but nevertheless, with me.

My story swings inevitably through the sagas of the weather, the sea conditions and sudden, intense, short-lived action, with its persistent reverberations, that kept the adrenalin flowing and rendered boredom a permanent outcast. Patrick and I have tried to make it real. We have tried not to exaggerate, and I have tried not to defend myself. If you do not think much of me at the end, that's just another risk I have to take.

Meanwhile we may as well take the plunge, get into some of those 'dreadful realities' I mentioned, and transport ourselves back to the cold grey waters off the Falkland Islands, May 1982 – watching, waiting, for the Argentinian missile strike we more or less knew was due, on this day.

April 1991   SANDY WOODWARD

PREFACE TO THE SECOND EDITION

In the preface to the first edition, published in 1991, I wrote that I did not want to try and write a formal history of the Falklands War, believing it to be too soon for that. In 2002, it is still too soon – there are many events and stories that may not yet be told for all sorts of good and perhaps not-so-good reasons. However I find I cannot just leave the first edition unamended, stuck in the mists of 1991, when so much more *has* emerged and been revealed since then.

Sailing south in the April of 1982 I jotted down in my diary a phrase to help me plan ahead: 'What is it today, that tomorrow, I will wish I had done yesterday?' Sadly, there seem to be many things concerned with the battle for the Falklands which fall into that category now that it is already the 'tomorrow' of twenty years later. No doubt, we could all have done better, had we known better, at the time. The same may be said of the historiography of the war and our first accounts of the events, as we saw them. Amongst these there were groups who, though satisfied at the overall outcome, were variously distressed at the way the outcome was achieved. Some were very much justified: at the top of that list are all those who lost relatives and friends, and those who were disabled. Lower down that list, other areas of anxiety existed, unknown to me, two of which can come under the heading of 'professional contention'.

It was only when I read the accounts of my two fellow

Commander Task Groups (CTGs) for instance, after the publication of my own book, that I realized that serious contention between us existed – such reports as I previously had, I put down to the normal behaviour of the press and/or the natural 'exuberance' of the time, often recorded in personal diaries. It was also only then I realized I had failed to share with them many of the factors which drove my decisions, both at the time and in the first edition. Had I been aware of their concerns, I would have taken more care to examine the causes of them, to explain, even justify their dissatisfactions in my book.

Now that I have been able to read and reread their accounts, I have tried, in this second edition, to reduce the level and range of contention between us, the three front-line CTGs; myself, the Battle Group Commander; Commodore Michael Clapp, the Amphibious Group Commander; and Brigadier Julian Thompson, the Landing Group Commander – and have incorporated their comments and perspectives into this revised account. But I still cannot possibly know even half of what went on in my own Battle Group, much less any one else's. This can only be another short step towards clarifying those 'professional contentions' on the way to what may come to be written as 'definitive history' many years ahead.

However, several matters can only be covered in a new preface since they would cause major distortion of the run of the book. Firstly, a personal apology: the quote from a letter by Field Marshal Lord Bramall on the first edition flysheet was gravely offensive to the Amphibious Group. It was a direct quote, but it was incorrectly informed. It should be made quite clear that the choice of San Carlos as the landing place was a corporate decision, and most certainly could never be claimed as my own. The decision was governed primarily by amphibious considerations, but there were many non-amphibious factors of considerable importance. The final decision between all the various, often conflicting inputs lay with the Task Force Commander, the Commander-in-Chief, at his headquarters in Northwood, the only place where all the factors could be balanced. The quote should not have been used. I unreservedly apologize for letting this through the net.

Secondly, and as a lead-in to several other matters, the Task Force command structure – known as the Task Organization – in the South Atlantic proved to be a major concern for the Amphibious and the Landing Group commanders, and was consequently discussed at some length in both their books, *No Picnic* by Julian Thompson and *Amphibious Assault Falklands*, which Mike Clapp co-wrote with Ewen Southby-Taylor a Royal Marine major. Both books are of high quality and make essential reading for students of the campaign. But like my own, neither should be taken as Gospel when they comment on other commanders' business. Both Mike and Julian told me that they had deliberately avoided reading my account before writing their own for fear of it influencing their opinions. That is entirely understandable – my own opinions have certainly now been influenced by their books – as will readily be seen. This is how history is written and is a reminder that individual first-hand accounts of any event, taken in isolation, can be misleading.

But it does suggest that their judgements of events and people outside their own immediate experience should be taken strictly as their opinions of the time, not as objective post-event analysis. This judgement must include my own book, of course. Mike's book, excellent in almost every way and illuminating in its detailed account of Amphibious Group business, is notable also for singling out colleagues and superiors as occasional targets for criticism without telling his readers whether the opinion given was culled from his direct memories and records of the time, or given with the benefit of hindsight, made unemotionally with many later 'facts' available to hand. Where their criticisms are quoted directly from diaries, I have no complaint – we all let ourselves go in diaries, it's what diaries are for, I believe; but they are worth some comment from me. I have tried here to present the extra information needed for a balanced assessment of the criticisms which they have made with a degree of hindsight. It has been a learning process for me, extending right up to the present day.

Some of Mike's criticisms appear to be born of his perception of the command structure issue. Others, particularly Julian's, stem from our meeting in mid-April. It is my aim to distinguish between their recorded impressions and my own understanding in the light of all the evidence available so far. Thus I hope these matters may be put to rest. But let me say that these misapprehensions are good examples that the well-tried phrase – the 'fog of war' – was plainly alive and kicking in the war of 1982.

War-fighting is an exceptionally intense activity, totally engrossing to those involved. Command in war is governed in high measure by communications facilities, and the management and interpretation of the information which is their product. However good, no commander in war has instant and complete knowledge of what is going on. Modern electronic communications (even video links, not available in 1982) remain imperfect, despite major improvements in the technology. There is still nothing to equal routine workaday face-to-face communication to resolve most problems – provided always that important points discussed are recorded and disseminated to all others who need to know.

One result of less than total intercommunication is that command centres become like islands occupied by close associates. Within each such centre, the combination of isolation, intensity of work, abundant adrenalin and stress, and the comradeship such pressures can generate, may create insular states of corporate mind. The malady is commonplace and it certainly affected all Falklands campaign headquarters, which includes all ships, and all the various centres of command, right down to gallant corporals in the land forces ashore. Mike and Julian, indeed, record some of the stresses between each other and their own people, even though their staffs were co-located in HMS *Fearless* until after the landings took place.

War is fought by a matrix of such teams. They all strive for the common objective, provided that has been clearly established to all. Without a clearly stated objective, the chances of success become less likely. It is important to remember that such common objective, 'to repossess the Falklands', was only finally established and fully promulgated on 12 May 1982, nearly six weeks after the operation was put in train, some twelve days after the Battle Group had 're-started the war' and just eight days before the actual landing. Small wonder that different perceptions between the front-line commanders continued until that date.

The disparity of perception between command centres, great and small, was aggravated by poor communications and the pace of events. Substantially different pictures developed for each in the different areas of action, and only with lulls and the passage of time can the complete picture emerge. There were also elements of information which were shared only between certain commanders and command centres. This was usually because conversations between different commanders or staffs, even when intended to convey common information, took different paths, or were not fully recorded or sufficiently widely shared. Whenever required and if time permits, therefore, staff should follow up with hard copy signals which record conclusions and actions, effectively the minutes of all such conversations. Any organization that fails to observe this basic management habit is heading for danger; the 'fog of war' can descend here, as everywhere. But ignore it, we did, from time to time, as is now all too apparent.

So we in the South Atlantic suffered our ration of such fog. This has led some, who wish to find dissension among us, to fuel a sad culture of implicit distrust, even mutual disloyalty, between groups of the Task Force, perhaps in hope of retaining some newsworthiness up to the present day.

The amphibious commanders had good reason for their opinions of the time on the command organization. There were many sources and clues on the subject which, taken individually, did not all point in the same direction. The first four are quotes from Mike's book. The last clue is my own experience, not available to either of them until I had read their books and realized the need to try and reconcile the widely differing perceptions:

a) 'The first formal Task Organization signal originated by the CTF in Northwood [2/4/82] showed us, all four, as Commanders Task Units (CTU's), Battle Group (Rear Admiral Woodward), South Georgia Group (Captain Young), Amphibious Group (Commodore Clapp) and Landing Group (Brigadier Thompson) – all at the same level, but with me doubling as the Commander Task Group (CTG) to whom the

CTU's report. As CTG, I would report to the Task Force Commander (CTF). This is a common enough formula, suitable for the initial operational plan, such as it was, up to mid April and perhaps, thereafter until the arrival of General Moore.'

b) 'This was overtaken by a second formal Task Organization signal [10/4/82] which showed us, all four, at the same level of command eg as CTG's. The CTG for South Georgia reverted to my TG on his return to the Battle Group after the S Georgia operation had been successfully completed.'

c) 'The outline plan for Operation Sutton, the Landing Plan, had me down as "The Commander Combined Task Force."'

d) 'A formal amplifying signal to b. above, specifically described me as being the "Senior Task Group Commander" in the South Atlantic, without defining precisely what that actually meant.'

e) 'The Commander-in-Chief's Fleet staff, from Admiral Fieldhouse personally downwards, often but by no means always, seemed to treat me as the front-line Area Commander, at least until the time General Jeremy Moore went ashore in late May and after he left in late June. Indeed, at one stage, the C-in-C personally told me to go ashore and order the Landing Group Commander to advance out of the beachhead. I refused to do so, telling him it was neither within my competence nor my authority, but that's another story.'

It should be remembered that once the Amphibious Group started its final approach to the landings at San Carlos, my most important task was to try to provide whatever Mike and Julian and their staffs might require and call for. But at the same time, my Battle Group had to ensure that our overall dominance of the Falklands area – land, sea and air – though it could never be absolute, remained adequate to maintain us all in the South Atlantic for an indefinite period. That period extended several months beyond the completion of any land battle itself. To this end, I had the broader strategic, tactical and logistic considerations to reconcile and plan – indeed my Group was the ultimate shield for our forces in San Carlos and deploying forward from the beachhead. I believe I was also in closer (but still less than complete) touch than Mike and Julian with at least some of the overlying issues, as seen by the Commander-in-Chief, the Ministry of Defence and the Prime Ministers War Cabinet. I, like Mike, did not consciously think too much about it at the time. We strove, within our apparent responsibilities, to do whatever seemed necessary as best we could and to keep each other appropriately informed. Usually, following an important and necessarily one-to-one conversation on the secure satellite telephone (DSSS) with Mike, for instance, I would follow up with a confirmatory hard-copy signal for those who would need to act in accordance with what we had agreed and as a check that we had properly understood each other on that 'strangled duck' machine. On other rare occasions, events seemed to require me to ensure that my Group's interests were fully kept in mind by those uncomfortably busy inshore. There were additionally whole sectors of information, important to my broader horizons and decisions, which, since they only impinged marginally on the Amphibious and Landing Groups' activities, were not shared by me with those already engaged in the battle inshore and on shore. The fog pervaded throughout, often leading to unhappy tensions.

The timing and manner of *Hermes* boiler cleaning is a note-worthy example. Had I shared my long-term carrier roulement problems with Mike in detail, he would not have been so critical, at least the fog would have thinned. The outcome would have been the same, but without the aggravation.

My two colleagues both record taking strong exception to my attitude towards them at our first meeting in *Fearless*, the circumstances of which I have now enlarged on in this edition. It was only on reading their books that I became aware of the strength of their feelings, the very intensity of which distresses me on several counts. We all have our faults, but mine did not include any failure at any time to support them to the utmost of my ability and, while I could not presume to try and tell their stories, I hope I gave them due credit for their eminent successes. Those who know me better, for instance, would scarcely tease me for a tendency to 'clear my yardarm', as does Mike more than once, in comment on some of my signals sent as 'Minutes' of our DSSS conversations. 'Yardarm clearing' is a serious accusation in naval terms. It is described in Commander Rick Jolly's entertaining and scholarly lexicon of naval usage, *Jackspeak*, as 'the process of taking precautionary steps to ensure that no blame will attach if something goes wrong'. While my CTF's report of his conversation with the Defence Secretary, John Nott, made it all too clear where any major 'blame' would attach, this was no motivation for any of my signals. But fog of war was of course, the true culprit at the time.

Mike's belief in 'coequality' at the CTG level also appears to have been a contributor to his concerns. But any concept of strict 'coequality' makes poor sense in the front line: a committee meeting of equals is unlikely to reach any agreed decision in the required timescale, particularly if sheer geography makes the meeting an impossibility in the first case. 'Flexible interdependence' would be a better phrase than some ritual, arbitrary 'coequality'. They gave the appropriate lead down there on Amphibious and Land force matters: I, with a lot of help from specialist advisers, gave the lead down there on just about everything else. All three of us had inputs to each others' specialist areas. But at least we all agreed on the fundamentals of this matter. Someone was required to be officially 'in charge' in the South Atlantic.

At the simplest possible level of argument and completely separate from the Falklands situation we faced, I was a Two Star officer and they were both One Star, until General Moore arrived. It would follow that barring specific instructions to the contrary from higher authority, 'coequality' did not exist. But that *is* much too simple. Priorities between commanders at similar levels with similar tasks are bound to vary with time and event, even if co-located. It is almost a *sine qua non* that someone is placed in authority over them if only as the local arbitrator. Whether an overall commander down south should have been me, or a Three Star officer appointed over me or in my place, or even in place of COMAW, remains an open question. The fact remains that no such Three Star was so appointed. The CTF probably thought that b and d, above, sufficiently met the requirements of the situation, but clearly Mike did not – he remains a firm believer that 'coequality' was in force. And the end result was that he frequently found my signals, comments and advice on what he considered to be strictly his personal and coequal business to be insufficiently sympathetic or supportive, too yardarm squaring or excessively directive according to the mood of the moment. But he could know very little about the pressures driving me to comment on our mutual business, nor how I tried, at all times, to avoid doing so.

On a quite different subject, there was another large area of professional contention which only came to my attention when I read Commander 'Sharkey' Ward's fascinating book *Sea Harrier over the Falklands*. I have to say that I found his book revelatory on the capability of the Sea Harrier at that time, particularly as to the operational use and value of its radar and navigation systems. As CO of the Sea Harrier Intensive Flying Trials Unit, he had initiated operational night flying from the deck for his aircraft only nine months before the start of the Falklands War and directly contrary to the considered advice of the test pilots at Boscombe Down. By April 1982, he had pioneered so much of the new air combat manoeuvering, air intercept and instrument flying techniques that his aircraft had developed from a very limited 'day/visual' fighter to an 'all-weather' interceptor. But it *was* pioneering. By April 1982, there appear to have been only three operational pilots in the entire Sea Harrier force (Ward, Mortimer and to a lesser degree, Curtis) who were actually qualified for night flying of the Sea Harrier off a carrier's deck. They were all three, naturally enough, in Ward's 801 squadron of six aircraft, formed in mid-1981. By contrast, at this early stage of the Sea Harrier operational development programme, even the CO of 800 Squadron on board *Hermes* could only claim one full-night sortie from a carrier's deck. Within two weeks of sailing for the south, Ward had managed to bring his other squadron pilots up to the night flying standards he had personally set, despite the many other calls on the embarked Sea Harriers for other trials and training tasks, not least providing the newly and very lately (mid-April 1982) formed Battle Group with its first, 'better-than-nothing' opportunities to exercise force air defence.

Unfortunately, his efforts and time were so extended in the process of bringing his own squadron up to the newly discovered standards that his knowledge and skills could not be transferred more widely to 800 Squadron much less to the 'Flag' – a word he frequently used as his generalized target for anyone who disagreed or appeared not to be listening to him as he hurried on.

I was not aware of much that went on in the naval aviation world, virtually all of it one or two levels below me. I suspect it was deliberately hidden from me, probably on the sensible basis that I should not be troubled about such intraprofessional arguments, not least because I was not an aviator and would be likely to jump to the wrong conclusions. Until I read Sharkey's book, I had absolutely no idea that there had been any kind of a problem between the Sea Harrier squadrons in *Invincible* and their senior aviation management in *Hermes*. Indeed, the only argument I remember having personally with *Invincible* concerned the relative stationing of the two carriers, recorded in my first edition. In all other respects, I, naively perhaps, believed our relationship to have been entirely amicable and co-operative. How can two such stories coexist, you might well ask?

But I am not the one to explain it in detail, only the then captain of *Hermes*, Lin Middleton, is in a proper position to do so. In his capacity as my senior naval aviation adviser throughout the campaign, it was his advice I had to listen to first and last. The conflicts were not usually allowed to come up to me. I seriously questioned his professional judgement only four times, and two of those occasions appeared in my book. The other two are best left between us. Of those four occasions, I was once completely right but for the wrong reasons, the second we were both wrong but probably for the right reasons, and the other two, I am not talking about, nor is he. Make of that what you like!

All I wish to say is that Sharkey Ward's account seems largely correct, except where it occasionally presumes to know what went on in the management's minds (usually referred to as 'the Flag' – a very loose term, actually meaning variously Admiral Reffell, [FOF3], Captain Middleton [CO *Hermes*], me [from about 17th April], and the professional naval aviation staff officers under delegated powers from all three of us). Nor did he appreciate the limited basis of information such 'management' had to make its decisions on, namely the capabilities of the fairly basic aircraft Sharkey had started to work on so intensively only months before. In that process, he virtually created another, very different, much more capable, all-weather fixed-wing jet aircraft for the Navy, but had no time to transfer or apply directly his knowledge beyond his own squadron. No substantial blame attaches here on either 'side', the plain fact is that the Royal Navy had to go to war with its only fixed-wing assets in the early stages of a fast-moving development programme. His book essentially tells us about the many frustrations of the few 'fast-movers'.

However, his appreciation of the value of the airfield in the Falklands is particularly accurate, I believe. Having arrived at almost exactly the same conclusions myself in 1986, I proposed to the then Chief of the Defence Staff, Admiral of the Fleet Sir John Fieldhouse, that at the very least we should install disruption munitions under the runways, *à la* World War II. Thus the airfield would be of no use to either side, should a re-enactment of 1982 threaten, since the airfield could be wrecked even in the face of a *coup de main* operation from Argentina. CDS told me that if I thought he was about to tell Mrs Thatcher he was planning to blow up her favourite airfield, I had another think coming. I persevered and said we didn't actually *need* to do the job, just make it look as though we had, to deter the Argentinians from trying in the first case. As a poor second best option, that was understandably not accepted either.

'Maverick' he may have been, I know he enjoys the description, but if I were able to change anything in Sharkey's book, it would be to say that the short but complimentary quote of his captain, JJ Black, greatly understated Sharkey's contribution. And if I were to add anything in the way of general comment on Sea Harrier performance in 1982, it would be to say 'Land forces usually claim that they are the only people who can win wars, but without the Sea Harriers, the land forces wouldn't have even have been given a chance to win the land battle in 1982'.

And as to this second apparent 'area of professional contention', I have to conclude that the differences of view were entirely understandable, reasonable, and excusable at the time. Given another six months, maybe, just maybe, it would have been a different matter – but by then Operation Corporate would probably have been impossible to mount for lack of carriers and amphibious ships, whatever had happened to the Sea Harrier development programme meanwhile.

I can only add that if you do not agree with my conclusions on these two contentious areas, then I must live with that – in one case for being excessively 'arrogant, insensitive and interfering' with my amphibious colleagues, and in the other for failing to be sufficiently so with my aviation advisers. But that's life in a blue suit with rather too many stripes on your arms.

Major Ewen Southby Tailyour, Royal Marines, in his book, *Reasons in Writing*, tried to find mistakes and errors in my book. I have no problem with that, there were many errors and omissions, now mostly corrected. He eventually managed, for all I know after careful study and determined effort, to find exactly one. He recorded his view that 'this important historical fact really must get into the history books of the world'. I have corrected it in this edition. Correcting it involved the removal of three words. There is a prize of a pint of beer for the first person, other than Southby Tailyour, to spot it. Either way, I would judge that history is unlikely to be affected greatly. Finally, I have to tell you that the changes in this edition seek to illuminate some of the cross currents more recently revealed to me. I believe that they may now be better understood, and that historians, coming late to the scene, can be more widely informed in their judgements. So, in addition to being a first-hand account of what it felt like to be the Battle Group commander, it now contains a fair amount of 'hindsight'. None of the issues raised this time affect the outcome of a war that was won together. It remains a huge credit to the British armed forces that a highly complex amphibious operation, on a scale we had not practised since Suez in 1956, was such a success. Think back to Gallipoli! My own conclusion, bearing in mind that the entire operation was a 'first' for all involved, at home and down south, is that the Task Organisation for the Falklands War worked well enough and the Sea Harrier force was a truly critical factor in our success – something plainly completely forgotten by the present government in their decision not to take the vastly improved and up-dated AMRAAM Sea Harrier out of service in 2006 without any replacement.

However, the manner in which success was achieved may

not be as pleasing to all as they would have liked. Several elements of the fog of war might perhaps have been thinned. As it was, we managed quite adequately, if not without the odd case of frayed edges and misjudgement of each other under difficult circumstances ... *Plus ca change*.

2002   SANDY WOODWARD

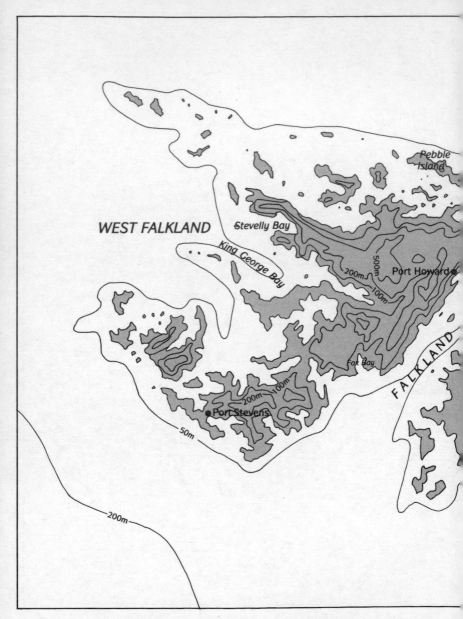

WEST FALKLAND

Pebble Island

Stevelly Bay

King George Bay

200m

500m

100m

Port Howard

Fox Bay

200m

100m

Port Stevens

50m

FALKLAND

200m

THE FALKLAND ISLANDS

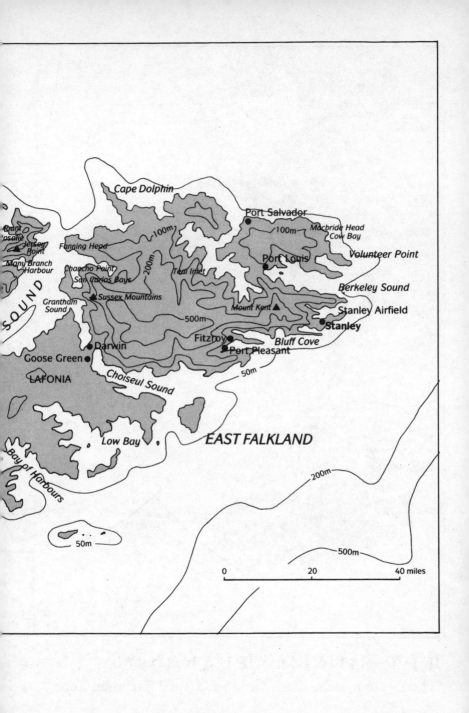

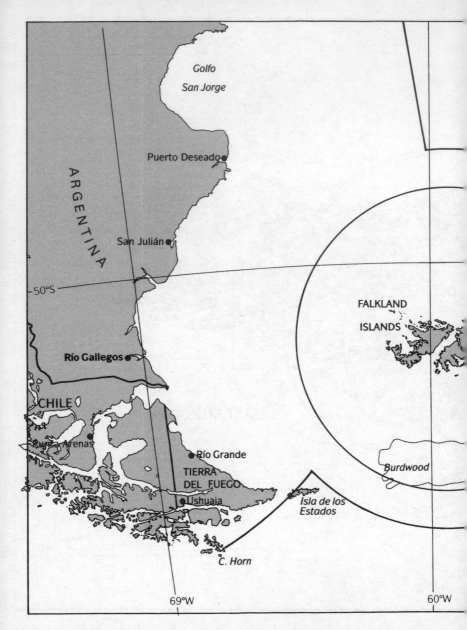

THE SOUTH ATLANTIC
The Position of the Battle Group and Total Exclusion Zone

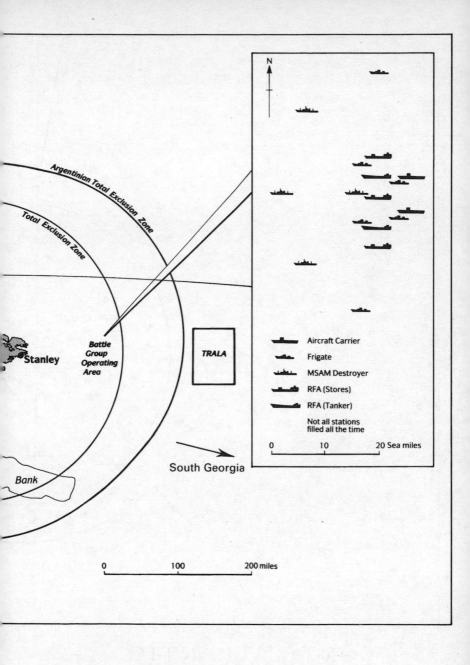

N

Argentinian Total Exclusion Zone

Total Exclusion Zone

Stanley

Battle
Group
Operating
Area

TRALA

Bank

South Georgia

Aircraft Carrier

Frigate

MSAM Destroyer

RFA (Stores)

RFA (Tanker)

Not all stations
filled all the time

0   10   20 Sea miles

0   100   200 miles

SHEFFIELD

1

The Day They Hit HMS *Sheffield*

They flew in radio silence, climbing to five thousand feet above the white banks of cloud and fog which covered, partially, the rocky, almost treeless coastline they were leaving behind. The jet engines of the two single-seat naval attack aircraft were throttled back to a speed of around 400 knots to conserve fuel. They flew in close formation, heading due east, with radar switched on but not transmitting.

Disappearing swiftly with the slipstream was their last contact with their Argentinian homeland, the air control officer at the Rio Grande Air Base on the island of Tierra del Fuego, the legendary 'Land of Fire' which sits south of the Magellan Straits. Home of Commander Jorge Colombo's 2nd Naval Fighter and Attack Squadron.

The two pilots, Lieutenant-Commander Augusto Bedacarratz and Lieutenant Armando Mayora, were members of a group of senior naval aviators specially selected to undertake these critically important missions, using the Etendard/ Exocet system, a system regarded as the most serious and immediate threat to my aircraft carriers. Now, after a succession of technical problems, they were airborne, and on their way.

The planes they flew were French-built Dassault Super Etendards, and beneath the port wing were fixed extra tanks of fuel, every litre of which they would require if they were to complete their 860-mile round trip. Beneath the starboard wing of each aircraft was slung the similarly French-built, radar-homing, sea-skimming, anti-ship missile Exocet, weighing half a ton, with a 364-pound warhead. Its 650-knot impact velocity could cause very major, possibly terminal damage to any ship.

It was ten o'clock in the morning, on Tuesday, 4 May 1982. Britain was at war in the South Atlantic.

The hour of day, however, was different on either side of the battle lines: it was ten o'clock in the morning for Bedacarratz and Mayora, but for us, in the British Battle Group, it was officially one o'clock in the afternoon. Which may seem odd, but wars can be won and lost on matters of timing: British Battle Group time was deliberately set to coincide with the 'Zulu time' of our military High Command back in the UK.

'Zulu time' is the time code normally used to identify British military communications messages. It ensured that we were all in the same time slot wherever we were working – Britain, Ascension, or the Falklands. What on earth for, you may ask? Who wants to get up at four in the morning or go to bed at seven at night. It was simply *intended* to minimize the errors of programming which can so easily be caused by conversations between planners far apart and in different domestic time zones. It may not have been all that good an idea, but it turned out to have one major advantage: it meant that we had completed three hours of battle preparations before the start of the Argentinian day. Thus when Bedacarratz and Mayora lifted through the fog from Rio Grande early that morning, it was 1000 local time for them, but 1300Z for us, and several thousand British sailors, temporarily in residence 400 miles off the shores of South America, had already had their lunch.

Our ships were ranged in fairly standard formation to deal with air attack. Our objectives for the day were relatively simple. I wanted us well inside the south-eastern sector of the Total Exclusion Zone. I was in no particular hurry since we did not need to be in position until last light for the evening's main activities – inserting reconnaissance teams of SAS and SBS by helicopter into the islands. For this we needed the cover of darkness and the ships to be as close in as possible to minimize the choppers' time in transit. We were 'probing' forward, feeling our way towards the enemy.

So we continued on course, largely unaware of the position of the enemy surface fleet – which had been curiously elusive since the tumultuous events of the previous Sunday afternoon and the sinking of the *General Belgrano*. We were particularly watchful of the western skies which might, at only four minutes' notice, reveal the precise effectiveness of the Args' Etendard/Exocet combination. Privately we still hoped that they did not yet have this complicated weapons system ready for front-line service.

But even to gain a critical, perhaps life-saving, four minutes, we needed all the radars and the inter-ship communications active, to provide us with the best possible picture of what was going on in the skies, and on the sea surrounding us. While the enemy did not have particularly good direction-finding equipment, there was a serious gap in our air defence. We lacked Airborne Early Warning. I therefore assessed the balance of advantage lay with comprehensive communications between the British ships and aircraft, despite the risk of the Argentinians charting our whereabouts from them.

The British Battle Group's Commanding Officers were fully aware of our situation. All were agreed that air strikes against us were imminent, given that the sinking of the Arg cruiser was probably being viewed in Buenos Aires as a bit embarrassing, particularly in the absence of any countervailing good news for the Argentinian public.

That morning I had spoken to three or four of my captains on 'encrypted voice' UHF radio. This circuit was given the appropriate code-name 'Cackle' (as in 'Captain, sir, the Admiral wants to speak to you on Cackle'). Our feeling of expectation of attack was not specific – more a matter of heightened alertness for whatever the next minute might bring. This was only the fourth day of the war for us and the Royal Navy had not experienced conflict at sea on this scale since the Second World War.

Basically, we all thought we might be facing up to an attack from the Etendards, each armed with one Exocet. 'Still,' I noted in my diary, 'they have only about five of them altogether. Let's just hope that one is unserviceable, two of them miss, and the others don't hit anything vital.' This is what is known in my trade as 'Threat Reduction', a mental process which usually makes you feel better while you wait to see how it actually turns out for real. In general terms we assessed that the Argentinian pilots would come in low, 'pop up' (climb from 50 feet to about 200), take a very short radar look, and then, if they got nothing, dive back down under our radar again. We then assumed they would come in a bit further and 'pop up' for another look – taking the risk that we might intercept their attack radar on *our* direction-finding equipment or get a couple of sweeps on them on our own radar before they could get down again. This should give us the four-minute warning we need for the deployment of our defensive radar decoys, called 'Chaff'.

The trouble with that whole scenario is, however, that on a day such as this, when we all actively expect an attack, everything that finds its way on to our radar screens, a flock of seagulls, an albatross, even a whale blowing, can start to look like a missile launch to anxious radar operators. Two single flocks of sea birds, totally unrelated, seen on separate sweeps, can look like an air track coming at you at 500 knots. And every other squeak of radar intercepted on an unexpected bearing can sound like the one you fear. In war, you cannot afford to ignore such things in case it really is a missile.

And all that morning, since before first light, we had a stream of reports of contacts of various kinds. Over in *Invincible* the brains that deal with our Force Air Defence system were becoming understandably sceptical of these warnings of attacks which did not materialize. 'Confirm'. 'Say again'. 'Check'. 'Verify'. 'Disregard'. It was the staccato language of uncertainty.

Every couple of minutes, something. Every half hour, something of concern. Every hour, something to make the chaff-button finger twitch. War, particularly in the early stages, has this effect on its participants. But nothing, absolutely nothing happened all morning in the way of enemy action. As far as we could tell, the skies, bright and sunny over a calm sea, were also clear of threat.

Bedacarratz and Mayora climbed to a cruising height of fifteen thousand feet for their first rendezvous. This was with a KC-130 Hercules tanker, a converted transport aircraft, to refuel them 150 miles out from home. Still in radio silence themselves, they were talked into position by radio from the navigator of an old Argentine Air Force Neptune maritime patrol aircraft, which was also trying to locate the British fleet.

Without a lot of practice, air-to-air refuelling is a difficult manoeuvre, as the planes try to match speeds precisely, and to hold position closely while the long fuel line locks in from above. The last Argentinian long-range mission, two days previously, had been aborted at exactly this stage of the proceedings. But today it was successful.

Bedacarratz and Mayora pressed on to the east, towards HMS *Hermes*, the 29,000-ton British aircraft carrier, from which I was attempting to conduct the local war, and which I regarded as indispensable. It had already been agreed between Northwood and myself that major damage to *Hermes* or to *Invincible* (our equally vital, but slightly smaller, 'second deck'), would probably cause us to abandon the entire Falkland Islands operation.

The two Argentinians began their gradual descent for the final approach and attack. They were two hundred and eighty miles from the British Battle Group and every five minutes brought them thirty-three miles closer to our radar cover. They were, as they say on the golf course, 'there for nothing', with full tanks and still in tight formation, heading down into the clouds and rain, trying their hardest to level off just fifty feet above the waves. There they could gain the protection of the curvature of the earth from the line-of-sight sweep of our forward radars. At that speed and height, nearly all of their concentration was devoted to avoiding flying into the sea; while they sometimes caught a glimpse of each other, mostly they were entirely out of contact, never daring to open up on their own radios. I have no doubt it was a tough, nerve-wracking and lonely flight.

There are other kinds of loneliness, however, and one in particular, known to warship commanders only, is that of the captain of a 'Picket Ship', one of the three or four warships that form the first line of defence, well up-threat from the main force. Out there, you really are on your own. It is quiet: deceptively peaceful. You are not covered by the main weapons systems of the rest of the force, other than a Combat Air Patrol (CAP), if you are lucky. And you find much time to contemplate the likely fate of your ship, your crew and your friends. No one has ever enjoyed picket duty very much, principally because history tells us they tend to be the first to get sunk by the opposition, because they are deliberately placed in harm's way. The classic anti-carrier tactic is to hit the picket with a few aircraft and then push the main raid through the hole you have just made in the defences. And should attack come from the sea, any picket is a sitting duck to a well-handled submarine. Single ships usually are especially vulnerable. Groups of two or three are much more effective in weight and variety of defensive systems and particularly in subsequent counter-attack. All submarine commanding officers know this. As a breed, whatever their nationality or training, they are bound to prefer a single-ship target.

In our case, on that morning, we fielded a picket line of three Type 42 guided-missile destroyers, quite small ships each displacing 4000 tons. Far to my right, was the tall, rather patrician Captain David Hart-Dyke's HMS *Coventry*. Out to my left was HMS *Sheffield*, commanded by Captain Sam Salt, at five feet four inches physically the opposite of Hart-Dyke but another experienced officer whom I had known, liked and respected for many years. In the centre was HMS *Glasgow*, placed to ensure the three ships presented a very wide surface-to-air missile defensive front. *Glasgow* was commanded by Captain Paul Hoddinott, the forty-year-old former Commander of the Polaris submarine HMS *Revenge*, and a man likely to make as few mistakes as any.

I trusted all three of them implicitly. I knew them all personally and professionally, and I knew what was involved in their unenviable task from my own time in command of the *Sheffield* five years before. I spoke to each of them, individually, every now and then on Cackle. Paul subsequently told me cheerfully that it gave his Operations Room staff great comfort – to see that he had a direct line to the boss. They even drew cartoons showing him on the line in conference with me: 'Speak up, sir!' someone is calling, and the ears of all his Ops Room team are drawn about four times natural size, two men hanging upside down from the overhead electric cabling above Paul's desk.

In fact, I spoke to several of the commanders on a daily basis, particularly those in highly vulnerable positions, and while it did not really occur to me that in doing so I would be, somehow, boosting morale in various ships, it always boosted mine to hear the crisp, confident tones of the man at the other end. Crisp, confident – whatever he may actually have been feeling.

Paul Hoddinott was typical of them. In a way, he was a real sea-dog, going back generations, and he believes some branches of the family served in the Spanish Main. To this day one their most treasured possessions is a grandfather clock which still shows the times of high and low water at Plymouth Hoe. His father was an engineering commander in destroyers in the Mediterranean during the Second World War. One of his grandfathers had been a naval lieutenant in the First World War, and the other, Lieutenant Kent DSC, RNR, a submarine officer, was lost at sea in 1917 when the troopship *Otranto* sank in a gale off Islay on the west coast of Scotland.

I knew that he would rarely, if ever, leave his Operations Room if our group was under any form of threat whatsoever and if he did, he would only leave it if his most experienced Warfare Officer remained down there, firmly in charge in his place. I had spoken to him earlier that morning, and it was his opinion that the Argentinians would attack from the air, with Exocet, on this day. I couldn't disagree although it was just one option amongst several. But it was a view he took the trouble to record in his diary that very morning '... we can expect an all-out retaliatory attack today. The most worrying from our point of view and the most attractive from theirs is a Super Etendard with Exocet'. Paul, with typical care, wrote afterwards: 'The above words were written before dawn on 4 May 1982 at 1055Z.' He had already banned the daytime use of his satellite communications system (SCOT) which could block out his detection of the Etendard radar.

All three of those picket commanders knew the risks they had to take. They knew that if the incoming enemy aircraft 'popped up' and got a contact, the chances were that the Argentinian pilots would release their missiles at the first blip they caught on their radar screen. *Coventry*, *Glasgow* and *Sheffield* had been carefully placed, and left to trust in their missile and self-defence systems almost alone. The only comfort in such a situation is to keep telling yourself that the chaff will work or, if not, that there are two other ships in the same position, and to hope fervently that it will be one of them that catches it.

But they *knew*, all three of them, Hart-Dyke, Hoddinott and Salt, that their situation was very exposed. It remained to be seen how effective the Type 42 destroyer would prove in this situation. Stay alert; that's all they could do and all I could ask.

Some eighteen miles to the east of the pickets lay my second line of defence; the frigates *Arrow*, *Yarmouth* and *Alacrity* and the big, but older, destroyer *Glamorgan*. Behind them, were three Royal Fleet Auxiliary ships, *Olmeda*, *Resource* and *Fort Austin* – placed as a further confusion factor for any enemy radar. Only beyond them could the Etendards hope to find their proper targets, the carriers *Hermes* and *Invincible*, each with her own 'Goalkeeper' in the form of a Type 22 frigate. *Invincible* had, close beside, *Brilliant*, commanded by the dynamic and voluble Captain John Coward; *Hermes* had *Broadsword*, with Captain Bill Canning, an old and trusted friend, in command. These two 4400-ton warships, primarily designed for anti-submarine work, had the remarkable anti-missile system Sea Wolf fitted. This was new in service and its reputation was high. It had, in trials, actually *hit* the high-velocity 4.5-inch shell being used as the target. It was a short-range system, but with this performance we hoped it would find the bigger and slower Exocet relatively easy to deal with.

All that may seem a complicated, carefully thought-out line of battle for a carrier group under threat. And so it was (culled from accepted practice in the Royal Navy and now modified to meet the particular requirements of the occasion in the South Atlantic). It was a classic anti-air attack formation, which any good staff officer could lay out in five minutes on a bar chit. But this one had a couple of refinements that I hoped would set it apart and do something to compensate for the lack of Airborne Early Warning. The big difference now was that this was for real. All eyes were open. Every item of sensory equipment throughout the Group was watching, waiting, for the strike most of us believed inevitable, today, tomorrow, whenever.

The two Argentinian Etendards were about 150 miles west of us when I left the Flag Operations Room on board *Hermes* for a quick lunch. Bedacarratz and Mayora were just entering the clear air that surrounded us, and finding it not quite so difficult to fly right down at wave-top height. A few hundred feet above them, the sweeping beams of the British long-range radars were apparently blind to the Etendards' high-speed approach.

The Argentinians' own search-radar fitted to the Etendards was French-made, like the planes, and was code-named by us 'Handbrake'. If we were quick enough we could locate and recognize it. We could also deal with the subsequent missiles. *If* we were quick enough.

The Etendards had now left the old Neptune far behind, but their final course had been decided. They knew that if they took a chance and 'popped up' to 120 feet, one hundred miles from now, their own radar would almost certainly paint a large contact signifying a big ship within Exocet range. They could also be reasonably sure that it would be a British ship. But there would be no time for any positive identification before they released their missiles, if they were to survive themselves.

By 1350, I was back in my Ops Room. Over in *Glasgow*, still the foremost of our pickets, Captain Hoddinott was sitting in his high swivel seat at the centre of his. Like all his team, he was wearing his yellowish cotton anti-flash hood and gloves, to prevent serious flash burns to the face, head and hands, should a missile get through and explode. The Battle Group, at this time, was on 'Air Raid Warning White' – which was effectively the 'All Clear' of the Second World War days. We had no positive evidence that a raid was on its way. The next warning up is 'Air Raid Warning Yellow' which means that we do have indications of a raid developing. 'Red' means 'Action Stations now. It's happening'.

The Ops Room of a modern warship, with everyone at their computers and controls is, to any visiting stranger, one of the weirdest places on earth. No sun ever shines in there. Actually there are very few lights at all, just the curious surreal amber glow of the screens, the red points of the many indicators and keyboards, and the occasional yellow back-lighting of information boards. The room somehow begs silence and respect, giving an atmosphere of intense concentration, rather like a library; but every figure is hooded with only the eyes showing, expressionless and shaded. Each man has a communications headset on like a civilian airline pilot's, with a slim, space-age microphone in front of his hidden lips. Each operator is connected somewhere, the quiet murmur of his reports going perhaps to the navigation area, or to his fellows in the team on board, or via radio to other ships and their Ops Rooms.

On the internal nets, the Captain can switch in to the Principal Warfare Officer talking to the Sonar Controller, or the Link Operator briefing the Surface Picture Compiler, or the Missile/Gun Director talking to the Surface Detector; perhaps the Yeoman of Signals talking to his young signalman on the bridge. He may hear the Officer of the Watch on the bridge, voice rising, call, 'Aircraft, Red nine-zero, low, unidentified.' It never stops in the strange nether world of the Ops Room. The communications networks are a sort of 'underground' tower of Babel, a mass of words and headsets, microphones and strange jargon-language. The room itself is a kaleidoscope of illuminated information, a scatter of fingers tapping on keys and buttons: a place of 'moon men' in hoods, where you see no lips move, but where disembodied voices seem never to rest.

And near the centre of it all stands the Advanced (or Air) Warfare Officer, assisted by the Principal Warfare Officer. In the Captain's absence from the Ops Room, it is their job to co-ordinate all the information and act appropriately on it. To decide whether to let a set of circumstances drive a call to 'Action Stations', which has a complete life of its own, with a succession of people all automatically taking carefully rehearsed steps. Each of which can only be stopped by a sharp command from the Captain.

It is now 1356. The two Etendards pop up to 120 feet above the sea. They level out and Bedacarratz glances down to see a blip on his radar screen. His gloved hand moves less than a foot to the Exocet activate button. Mayora does the same.

Glasgow's Ops Room, like any other in the force, is packed with people sweating beneath their hoods. It is 1356 and 30 seconds. The air is hot, and the darkness seems to add to it. The Battle Group is still only on 'White Alert' when young Able Seaman Rose blows his whistle and calls the words which, Paul Hoddinott later said, 'caused the hair on the back of my neck to stand on end.'

'Agave radar!' snaps Rose.

Glasgow's AWO, Lieutenant-Commander Nick Hawkyard reacts instantly: 'CONFIDENCE level?'

'CERTAIN!' says Rose. 'I have three sweeps, followed by a short Lock On. Bearing . . . two-three-eight. Search mode.'

Hoddinott swings round to stare at the big UAA 1 console.

Both he and Hawkyard can see that the bearing line on Rose's screen correlates with two Long Range Air Warning radar contacts forty-five miles out on the AWO's display.

'Transmission ceased,' reports Rose.

Hawkyard calls into the Command Open Line: 'AWO to Officer of the Watch – go to Action Stations, *right now!*'

And up on the Bridge, Lieutenant David Goddard hits the intercom button broadcasting 'ACTION STATIONS!' throughout the ship.

Hawkyard, staring at the picture on his big, flat table screen, switches to the UHF radio announcing to all ships: '*Flash!* This is *Glasgow*, Agave . . . bearing two three eight . . . correlates track one two three four . . . bearing two three eight . . . range four zero . . . *Invincible*, over.'

Invincible: 'Roger, out.'

Then Rose calls again: 'Agave regained – bearing two three eight.'

His Electronic Warfare Supervisor, sitting next to him, confirms the second detection. The ship's radar operators, watching their air and surface warning radar screens, also confirm contact: 'Two bogeys. Bearing two three eight. Range three eight miles. Tracking zero seven zero. Four-fifty knots.'

Hawkyard to Hoddinott: 'That's two Super Es. Just popped up for sure. May be about to launch missiles.' And now *Glasgow*'s Ops Room really comes alive. They are one hundred per cent prepared for just this event. It was, after all, precisely what they were there for.

'CHAFF!' calls Hawkyard, and across the room the hooded figure of Chief Petty Officer Jan Ames bangs his closed fists into the big, easy-to-hit-in-a-hurry chaff fire buttons.

Hawkyard again broadcasts on the radio circuit to the whole Battle Group: 'This is *Glasgow* . . .' As he starts to speak he suddenly remembers he ought to have been saying 'Hand-brake', our codeword for Agave radar. Hawkyard now corrects himself, hurriedly. 'HANDBRAKE!' he exclaims, 'BEARING TWO THREE EIGHT.'

Simultaneously the fingers of the Air Picture Supervisor, Leading Seaman Nevin, are clattering away trying to release the full picture of the incoming raid, tracks 1234 and 1235 on the inter-ship computer circuit, Link 10. Then, turning to see his relief standing at his shoulder ready for the watch change, the Electronic Warfare Supervisor, Leading Seaman Hewitt, quickly hands over and fairly flies up the steep steps to the upper deck to help with the re-loading of the chaff rocket launchers. 'I had never,' he admitted later, 'moved at that speed in my entire life.'

As the Leading Seaman goes, Hawkyard switches back to UHF and tries to convince the Force Anti-Air Warfare Commander in *Invincible* that this is real. But he is not succeeding. Hoddinott hears with alarm Hawkyard's voice rising in frustration, desperately trying to convince the FAAWC that this is deadly serious and not just another nervous 'ghost'.

Again he calls: 'This is *Glasgow*. Track 1234 – bearing two three five – range three five – strength two – closing fast. Track 1234 correlates *handbrake* bearing. *Invincible*, over.'

FAAWC, who has dealt with three or four such 'panics' that very morning, wants more evidence. As far as he is concerned, the cry 'Handbrake' has been heard more often than 'Good morning' today, and he isn't going to commit the entire Group to expenditure of our rapidly diminishing chaff stock without solid reason.

Invincible acknowledges: 'Roger, out.'

But at least he must know that *Glasgow* was sure of her own warning. Anyone listening on the Air Warfare net can hear

Glasgow's chaff rockets launch with that 'Whoosh' which is to become uncomfortably familiar to all of us.

Down at *Glasgow*'s EW Console, Rose calls again: 'Handbrake in lock-on mode.'

Bedacarratz is on the point of releasing his missile and Paul Hoddinott feels the chill dread that hits you when you have incontrovertible evidence that a big missile is on its way towards you. For the next few minutes, the technique is for *Glasgow* to place herself carefully among the four clouds of chaff which are blooming around her, and which should decoy the missile off course to miss the ship. But chaff drifts with the wind. And you must stay in the pattern. Speed and position must be very quickly corrected.

Captain to Officer of the Watch on the Bridge: 'Come hard left to zero two five. Adjust speed for zero relative wind.'

At 1402, the pilots release their missiles and bank left. The Exocets fall away, locked on to their targets. Neither pilot has the least idea what ship he has aimed at, nor are they going to hang around to find out. They know only that a radar contact has appeared on their screens in roughly the right bit of ocean. And they get out fast, diving back down, close to the water, beneath our radar beams, heading West.

We never detected them again.

Almost simultaneously, two amber dots, so small they can only be seen intermittently, appear on the radar of *Glasgow*, tracking their way fast across the screen.

'ZIPPO ONE! BRUISERS! Incoming. Bearing two three zero. Range twelve miles.'

Hoddinott orders his Sea Dart surface to air missile system into action to shoot them down.

Hawkyard calls again to Chief Ames, his Missile Gun Director: 'Take Track 1234 and 1235 with Sea Dart.' But it does not work. Unsuccessfully – nightmarishly – the fire control radar can not lock on to the small fleeting targets at that range. They keep trying, but the dots keep disappearing. Frustration mounts and the Captain fumes. Hawkyard again calls *Invincible* advising them to clear two Sea Harriers from the line of fire. But the Ops Room in the carrier answers that they believe the raid is spurious.

Glasgow's AWO now desperate, almost shouts on the radio circuit: 'NEGATIVE! THE FORCE IS UNDER ATTACK! RAID 1234 AND 1235 BEARING AND RANGE CORRELATES WITH HANDBRAKE.'

Invincible still does not agree.

Chief Ames, still furiously trying to engage the Exocet with Sea Dart, cannot help wondering how long the missile will take to hit, fearing it would strike *Glasgow* amidships where the Ops Room is. Like many others he begins to resign himself to his fate.

It is Captain Hoddinott himself who first realizes, with enormous relief, that *Glasgow* is safe. One of the missiles is heading towards *Sheffield*, and the other is going well clear.

Sheffield, with Captain Salt not in the Ops Room, has, for whatever reason, not got her chaff up yet. Hoddinott later recalled saying to Hawkyard, worriedly: 'What the hell's happening in *Sheffield*?' The only response he received was from his own operators who said they could get no answer.

Twenty miles away, things were moving to a tragic conclusion in the small destroyer named after Britain's city of stainless steel. Problem number one was that she had been transmitting on her SCOT satellite communications system at the critical time when the Etendards' radars were used. This blotted them out in *Sheffield*.

The absence of the Captain, incidentally, in his cabin directly after lunch, was bad luck, not bad management. He was perfectly entitled to be in his cabin. The Captain must not try to stay alert and on watch indefinitely if he is to remain effective. He has to pace himself carefully and learn to rely on his watch-keepers.

The second problem was that the significance of the reports from *Glasgow* was not appreciated in *Sheffield* any more than they had been in *Invincible*. There was some kind of a gap in her Ops Room and no action was taken. It is tempting to conclude that if the *Glasgow*'s warning of the Etendard radar had been accepted in *Sheffield*'s Ops Room, chaff would have been fired and might have proved effective; or that *Sheffield*'s own radars might have detected both the Etendards and the incoming missiles. They were, after all, some four miles closer, albeit presenting a much smaller radar target to *Sheffield* than to *Glasgow*. And *Sheffield* had shown herself to be first class at this procedure only a few weeks previously in live missile-firing exercises off Gibraltar. Now, at war, how could their performance be less?

For whatever reason, at 1403 *Sheffield*'s chaff was not launched. Up on her bridge, Lieutenant Peter Walpole and Lieutenant Brian Layshon, looking out over the starboard bow, spotted a trail of smoke six feet above the sea, about a mile away and coming straight for the ship. There were only seconds left. One of them grabbed the broadcast microphone and shouted: 'MISSILE ATTACK! HIT THE DECK!'

The Exocet struck them at 1404. Amidships. Starboard side. A few feet above the waterline. There was some doubt that the warhead went off but several men were killed instantly. A large fire was started, releasing great quantities of heat, smoke and fumes which were to cause others to die, many of them in heroic circumstances. *Sheffield* was the first Royal Navy ship to be hit by an enemy missile since the Second World War. Almost forty years on.

The hole in *Sheffield*'s side measured four feet by about fifteen feet across – from the Auxiliary Machinery Space to the Forward Engine Room. Damage from the blast had gone up as far as the lower structure of the bridge, and the centre of the ship was filling with thick, suffocating black smoke. The fires were feeding on leaking fuel and the firemain water pressure had dropped to zero. Steering was lost, but the big Olympus gas turbines were still, miraculously running.

More than twenty miles away in the Force Ops Room in *Hermes*, we are still in Air Raid Warning White – FAAWC in *Invincible* was still insufficiently convinced to have changed it. I am hearing none of the drama. Actually I am standing in the Ops Room having a conversation with a staff officer about tonight's plan. When, a few minutes after *Sheffield* is hit, we receive our first report, it lacks both detail and immediate impact.

'*Sheffield* has suffered an explosion.' Nothing more definite or descriptive than that. I take note, but permit business to continue as usual, everything moving ahead. It's 1407z.

Explosion? It could still be anything from where I stand – a fire starting, a gas bottle exploding, a weapon malfunctioning on test. The possibilities are endless. Could be a torpedo, but unlikely to be a mine in this depth of water. Could even be a missile. The thoughts speed through my mind. But where were the warnings we should have received in the Flagship?

I wait patiently, saying only: 'Are we still in communication with *Sheffield*?'

Someone replies: 'Yes, sir.' That at least is a good sign. With nothing however coming from her, I'm listening and watching carefully for the reactions of the ships and aircraft nearest to the scene.

Arrow and *Yarmouth* start to move forward towards *Sheffield*. Seems sensible to me: let them run. And there is a message from *Glasgow*. He is leaving his picket station making all speed towards *Sheffield*. Now we know something has happened. Still not exactly what. But something serious.

We can see the helicopters shifting across to help. The picture is becoming clearer – and the one thing in my mind is that if it was a missile, the next one can happen again at any moment now. I get off a signal to *Glasgow*: 'Do not go to *Sheffield*'s assistance. Leave that to the others. Adjust your position to cover for *Sheffield*.' It is probably unnecessary for me to tell him. I get off another to *Arrow*: 'Take charge at the scene of action. You have *Yarmouth* and helicopters to assist.'

I had no intention of taking charge in detail. And I must cast aside any temptation to do so unless things are plainly going awry. After a few more minutes, we finally receive a message from the stricken destroyer that she has indeed been hit by an enemy missile. And now, from *Invincible*, comes the message to everyone else: 'We have had an Etendard attack. Confirm, an Etendard attack. Probably using Exocet.'

The information continues to filter through slowly and methodically. Nothing of the 'Hold the front page' variety. And although I can see that *Arrow* and *Yarmouth* and the helicopters are close to *Sheffield*, there is a rising tension in *Hermes*'s Flag Ops Room. Everyone can feel it, as if we were somehow helpless and that we ought to be doing more. One of my staff blurts out: 'Admiral, you must *do* something!' Which is precisely what I should not be doing, I reckon.

I reply gently enough: 'No . . . leave it be.'

* * *

For I had no intention of issuing a stream of detailed orders, twenty miles from a fierce fire which must be threatening, if it reached the Sea Dart magazine, to blow up the entire destroyer and her people and any other ship or aircraft close by. First of all, I still did not know precisely what was happening, secondly, I did not wish to clutter up the radio communications, and thirdly, my policy was to let the information come in, to let the highly trained men on the spot run the operation and call for what they needed, with us in *Hermes* only making sure they get it. What they did not need was a stream of ill-informed questions and second-guessing from the Flag. Besides, I trusted them. All of them, to do the right thing, near enough.

Having survived the first emerging sign of panic in my own Ops Room, I proceeded to divorce myself from the details of the rescue and salvage work. Like any military man, I am *not* allowed to throw an attack of the 'wobblies' on these sorts of occasion. Never to panic if at all possible. And I was working hard to convey to my staff an atmosphere which I hoped was one of calm and confidence. It's amazing what you can get away with sometimes.

I told myself rather sternly: 'Now here we have a problem. We've probably lost a destroyer from our picket line on Day Four of the war. Well, I have been expecting such a loss for some time now, and I also expect there will be more of the same. I do not feel any real sense of shock, at least not immediately, and nor can I allow anything emotionally primitive, like a desire for revenge, to cloud my judgement. I am just going to deal with this, as I have been trained. We now have a "hole" in our missile screen, two ships from the inner line have moved out. There are three of them milling about in the left field and my problem is how best to deploy the rest.'

Perhaps more than most, I was all too aware that a well co-ordinated enemy could, and should, strike us again as soon as possible, while we are still off balance. At the time, I believed we were on the very outer perimeter of the Etendard attack range. So I issued instructions that would take the Battle Group, in no hurry, to the east, just while we attended to the wounded and sorted out the future of the burning *Sheffield*.

The fire appears to be getting out of control, Captain Salt's men are struggling for water and they need pumps, which we fly over to them. The Computer Room staff stayed too long at their posts trying to keep the ship's defence systems working. They all died. Chief Petty Officer Briggs kept going back into the Forward Damage Control Section Base to drag equipment out. Finally, overcome by fumes, he too died.

The Sea Kings lowered the gas-turbine water pumps on to the decks, together with special fire-fighting and breathing apparatus. *Yarmouth* sprayed *Sheffield*'s starboard side, and *Arrow* the port side with all the fire hoses they could. More hoses were passed over. But it was an awful, losing battle, and the heat crept inexorably forward, towards the Sea Dart magazine.

Then *Yarmouth* thought they heard a torpedo in the water and broke off to try and find the submarine that had fired it. Then it happened again. And again. Altogether they thought they had detected nine torpedoes that afternoon. Some time later we deduced that the propeller noises they kept hearing on their sonar had to be from the outboard motor on the small inflatable dinghy which was buzzing round *Sheffield*, helping to fight the blaze. *Yarmouth*'s Captain, Commander Tony Morton, could not believe this at the time; probably still doesn't!

In the middle of the afternoon, with the increasing danger

of a major explosion, Captain Salt gave the order to abandon ship, and the remainder of the crew was taken off, by helicopter and across to the frigates.

Sam Salt arrived on board *Hermes* soon afterwards. I could see by the way he swallowed that he was close to tears, but he was no less brave for that, on this most terrible day. We did our best to speak in a matter-of-fact tone, to keep a hold on the situation, but I fear that in my worry, I was less than sympathetic. (Years later Sam told me I said, flatly: 'I suspect someone's been bloody careless.') What I remember is being aware that I could not afford to let this situation get out of hand, any more than he could.

The man who shouted 'Admiral, you must *do* something', the nine torpedoes, Sam Salt's tension, my own too, were all symptoms of the trauma of battle. Of men who, in their different ways, were learning to cope with their heightened emotions. Quite apart from those directly involved, that day was, on reflection, a bit of a struggle for all of us. Panic, worry and tension are all extremely infectious. But the loss of this destroyer must not be allowed to dominate my life.

The key to crisis management is control. In my immediate case it was the continued control of the Battle Group and within that, the control of the *Sheffield* situation, the saving of life, the avoidance of unnecessary further risk to life and, above all, self-control, putting down incipient panic, in all of its forms, as harshly or gently as was appropriate. I had to accept that *Sheffield* was no longer a front-line unit. And I didn't want to see a whole team of firefighters on board her when the magazine could go up at any time. Neither could I just leave her for the enemy to find, nor yet did I much want to try towing her out, in case she blew up and maybe damaged another ship with her.

It was, in a sense, the Argentinians themselves who solved the immediate *Sheffield* problem for me. We came across signs that the Argentinian submarine might be moving into the area close by *Sheffield* to attack and destroy ships coming to the rescue. I did not much care for that kind of behaviour. So I arranged to have a hot reception committee awaiting should he turn up. *Sheffield* suddenly ceased to be an embarrassment; her new role was to act as a rather unusual 'tethered goat', floating and made of hot metal. Waste not, want not.

Now more bad news was coming in. One hour after *Sheffield* was hit, three Sea Harriers had taken off from *Hermes* to carry out an attack on the airstrip at Goose Green, hoping to catch some of their aircraft on the ground. Only two returned, the third having been hit by anti-aircraft fire as it flew in at low level over the water. It crashed in flames in the shallow surf and ripped its way up the beach and through the dune grass in front of the strip. The other aviators were sure the Fleet Air Arm pilot Lieutenant Nick Taylor was killed by the shells, since he did not eject, but there was nonetheless great sadness in the Group over his death and I must confess that I felt very 'down' by the end of the afternoon.

I also decided I should not risk any more of our precious Harriers by allowing them to go out on these high-speed, low-level, cluster-bomb attacks against heavily defended Argentine positions. Quite simply, I could not afford to lose my strictly limited force of air defence aircraft – only about thirty-four in the whole country – on this not-very-effective sort of task. It made better sense to wait for the RAF to provide some Harrier GR3s, not much use at air defence and optimized for ground attack. I resolved that from now on, if they were to bomb at all, it would only be against specific high-value targets or from high level – less accurate, I knew, but less expensive in Sea Harriers.

Meanwhile *Sheffield* continued to burn, her deck plates now getting very hot and her paint blistering in large patches over extensive areas. The fire was slowly gutting her, but still not getting to the magazine. Sam Salt wanted to go back and assess the chances of saving her. This was put off until the next day as I did not want to risk losing a helicopter full of good men when we all knew perfectly well she could go up at any moment. Furthermore, poor *Sheffield*, supposing she could be saved, was now so badly damaged as to be of no military value, and not even much as scrap.

At the time, I had too much on my mind to feel sadness. In fact I was too busy to indulge in any psychological luxuries at all, emotions such as sentimentality, shock or awkward feelings about a ship which had once been my 'home'. She was now, as far as I was concerned, just a statistic. I did of course realize that her loss would have far-reaching effects on those directly involved, and also on how the rest of us would conduct our anti-aircraft warfare in the future.

Deep down I feared it should not have happened and, harshly perhaps, told Sam Salt so. We were going to have to get seriously sharper if we were to survive. *Sheffield* had already taught us some hard lessons, and we had better start absorbing them in short order. Sudden death in these cold, wind-swept southern seas was unappealing to say the least, wherever one's duty lay, particularly given the years and years of training we had undergone to avoid such an unpleasant eventuality.

And so I worked quietly, alone in my little steel cell in *Hermes*'s 'Island', supported by a first-class team of staff officers, but nevertheless alone. I drew up my lists of what we must all learn from the Exocet attack. This would form the basis of an immediate operational analysis of the event. What actually happened? Where did the Etendards come from? How did they get here? Can we get at them sooner? What happened to *Sheffield*'s chaff? Can we catch them after an attack? Is our formation correct? Are our procedures slick enough? Plenty of questions – not too many answers yet, but all of them urgently needed.

That evening, with *Sheffield* still ablaze, we returned to some semblance of routine. The recce insertion went ahead as planned, the Special Forces men landing on schedule, all helicopters returning on time. All of the mundane business of running the Battle Group continued – everyone more alert now to the possibility of another Exocet attack. I could start to plan ahead, not least because I was satisfied that the Battle Group was back in balance and that the *Sheffield* situation was being properly managed.

So ended that extraordinary day in the front line. What was happening in London is better known to others, and for this information one tends to hear the most from one's own family. As it happened mine was gathered in some strength at the Cavalry Club in London, where my brother-in-law had taken my sister and wife, Charlotte, to dine. It was apparently a rather joyous occasion. News from the battle front was good, and as far as they could see I would be home quite soon. However, halfway through dinner my wife noticed the waiter moving quietly from table to table imparting what appeared to be quite serious news. When he finally arrived at their table he just said: 'I am very sorry to tell you that HMS *Sheffield* has been sunk off the Falkland Islands.' It was nothing short of an enormous shock, and it brought home to everyone in that dining room – many of them with strong military connections –

that the Argentinians were indeed real, and well equipped to hurt us. 'As from that moment,' declared Char, 'I rather stopped regarding the Argentinian Navy as something out of Gilbert and Sullivan.'

So much then for the extremes of up-front and back-home. I stood somewhere in the middle. My strange position in all this is best revealed by viewing these two accounts alongside the entry in my diary for that day. It reads as follows: 'A dull fore-noon with little happening, until 1415 when an Exocet from an Etendard blew my old ship *Sheffield* away. As I write ten hours later she's still burning out there and I'm hoping to entice the Args to go and have a look, and then chop them when they do.'

That, actually, was all I wrote that night. Almost. There were, however, before I ended, a further five lines, on the over-excited behaviour of *Yarmouth* and her nine torpedoes; a most improbable sequence of events. 'Nothing hit anyone,' I wrote. 'Had to send a very ratty signal . . . I hope he's learning.' The three lines I have left out were letting off steam, which made me feel quite a lot better at the time, but have no rel-evance today.

After midnight now and I walked out on to my little open bridge on the Island above the flight deck for a breath of cold air. I looked into the night sky to the south-west, the direction from which the Etendards had come that afternoon. Far beyond it lay their home base, on the great barren island of Tierra del Fuego, the most southerly point of all the Americas, where the rocky mountains of the Andes finally peter out into the roughest ocean waters of the world, the cemetery of sea-men, landmarked by the haunted face of Cape Horn. A little over 430 miles from where I was standing.

I was, I felt, ready for this battle. My job as the on-scene commander was clear-cut. I must stand back and observe; measure the odds, the gains, the losses and how to make them move in our favour. I must not get too close to the detail, and I certainly must not be pushed into hasty decisions based on inadequate evidence. I believed there might be an element, perhaps among the younger officers, that would wish to hit back at the Argentinians straight away, somehow, with anything we had. But I was not in that game. Under the main directive of 'Operation Corporate' I had to achieve three objectives – to neutralize the enemy navy and air force, to put our landing force ashore safely, and then to give all the support I could – air, gunfire, and logistic supplies – in order to give our land forces the best chance of forcing an unconditional surrender of all Argentinian forces in the islands. This to be achieved by mid to late June, with minimum loss to ourselves, of course. That all done, I would still have the long-term defence of the islands to cover.

I reminded myself of the principles of war, in particular the one called 'Maintaining the Initiative'. This decrees, very broadly, that if you can inflict happenings upon your opponent which cause him to take a series of decisions he has not planned for, with insufficient time to think them through properly, the probability is that he will get a good half of them wrong. If you only force decisions on him for which he is already prepared, the chances are that he will get most of them right; push him, worry him, harry him, and hurry him.

Equally, in defensive mode, if he hits you, as he had just hit *Sheffield*, you must not allow yourself to be thrown by it. His initiative must not be allowed to affect you. Write off *Sheffield*, yes, but don't write off two more ships because you have jumped in the wrong direction as a gut-reaction to a sudden setback.

And now I must try to sleep, which may be difficult, even tired as I am, since our next moves must be planned with care. The key word is control: control of our attacks; control of our defence; and control of ourselves in the face of disaster.

Whichever way you look at it, I had been training for this or something like it for most of my life, albeit in hopes it would never happen. This day, however, was elbowing its way into military and naval folklore. British warship hit by enemy missile. First major attack on the White Ensign for decades. I kept asking myself how I came to be in the middle of all this. I had never asked for a place in anyone's history book. Neither had the Ship's Company of *Sheffield*. And twenty of them were dead.

NAVAL COLLEGE
DARTMOUTH.

2

The Submariner

Ambition has never been a particularly strong suit in the Woodward family. My late father, Tom, the son of a Naval Ordnance Lieutenant, certainly had little. He ended his modest banking career happily enough, as Head Cashier in the Launceston Branch of Barclays Bank. As far as I was ever able to make out, this was his own personal preference perhaps not unconnected with a love for the West Country. My mother was prepared to go along with that.

Maybe my father's three years in the trenches of the First World War had something to do with it. But in all the (only vaguely) traceable history of my family, there is but one personage of any real substance – one of the eighteenth-century allies of Bonnie Prince Charlie, a General Forster, whose surname I bear between the 'John' and the 'Woodward'. That relationship comes via my father's mother, and is, I have to admit, fairly tenuous, not least because the General never married!

I am relatively sure that the General was of no great military stature – certainly he never won a battle. He was just one of those largely cosmetic warriors fashionable in early Georgian England, and his main talent was to have been hovering in the opportune spot at exactly the time Prince Charlie decided he needed a Protestant military figure on his team. And though it did neither of them much good at the merciless defeat of the Jacobites at the battle of Culloden, I am in no position to scoff at the career of any officer who happened to find himself in the right place at the right time.

I too was born with the reluctance of the Woodwards to push forward, and indeed, right up until my appointment as a rear admiral in 1981 I was essentially just another naval officer, and, like so many Cornishmen before me, perfectly content to be so. I never really thought beyond my next pro-motion, by which I mean that as a lieutenant I thought it would be sensible to become a lieutenant-commander, and as a commander, I hoped to become a captain. But I never once, in all my career, spent one moment plotting or planning the best way of being appointed to the Board of the Admiralty. Which was just as well, since I never made it.

How then, you might wonder – and I'm sure most of my peers did wonder – did I, Sandy Woodward, of the Royal Borough of Kingston, come to be standing on that fateful night, on the bridge of HMS *Hermes*, in the South Atlantic, in command of billions of pounds worth of naval hardware and several thousand sailors, with the entire nation looking over my shoulder? At the time, I never gave it a great deal of thought. And since then I've put it down to luck, really. Pres-sure of circumstances, and several rather unlikely events falling into place. Unfortunate for some. Fortuitous for me. Which, you may think, is an odd way to run a navy.

Nonetheless, the truth rests at least in that vicinity; with one important factor standing alongside it – the traditions, the training, the technical grounding, and the principles of leadership which have been taught and refined by the Royal Navy for centuries. The general policy of having a 'pool' of well-trained senior officers, any of whom could assume command of a British Naval Task Group at very short notice, has been a requirement of Admiralty since the time of Drake. There were, for instance, two other sea-going admirals who could certainly have commanded the Falkland Task Groups as well, probably better, than I. There were also several higher ranking admirals who were more experienced and knew at least as much as any of us. But when Her Majesty's Navy is told to move, it does so remarkably quickly, and I, conducting at the time a fleet exercise off Gibraltar, was simply and solely the closest of the sea-going commanders to the South Atlantic.

The process by which the Senior Service transforms a schoolboy in short trousers into a commander capable, in its judgement, of leading the biggest battle fleet to sail from Britain since the Second World War is, as such processes go, found by most people to be fairly rigorous. Of course, when the management at home decided to send me south, they were not dealing with a total stranger. I had been among them in various capacities for thirty-six years. Indeed, I was one of a dying breed of officers who had effectively been in dark blue uniform since leaving preparatory school at the age of thirteen. In my case, since 1946.

For me it was, as usual, a bit of an accident. My parents had privately educated my tough, independent elder brother Jim and equally tough and, in her own way, independent sister

Liz, but they were running out of cash as a result. They had only just managed to send me to Stubbington House, a prep school with a strong reputation as a naval 'crammer', having produced several admirals and a couple of vcs down the years. I finished there in reasonably auspicious circumstances as Head Boy, albeit a very moderate one, having also developed an abiding enjoyment of fairly basic mathematics, thanks to the patience and inspiration of my quite exceptional maths master, Mr Wood.

So it was agreed that the best way of being privately educated at little cost, was to win a scholarship to the Royal Naval College, Dartmouth, known as HMS *Britannia*, which stood in Edwardian splendour some forty-five south-easterly miles across Dartmoor, on the south Devon coast. In those days, they offered about thirty scholarship places a year, requiring a pass mark of eighty per cent in the Public Schools Common Entrance examination. I just made it, I think to the last place available, and was invited to attend the Navy's further require-ments for a medical examination and a greatly dreaded inter-view. That dread was in no way alleviated by the appearance of a huge 'potato' in the heel of my sock on the way there, to the Old Admiralty Building in Whitehall.

I sat before the stone-faced group of officers, very nearly paralysed with worry over my state of undress. No doubt the Interview Board were doing their best to be friendly but I was barely able to give a sensible answer to anything. When finally I took my leave, I took care to back out of the room in order to hide the bare heel. It seemed a mile and a half to the door to me, and probably appropriately servile to them. I long thought that the interviewers must have nodded knowingly to each other, saying, 'Now there's a nice well-mannered boy . . . knows his place . . . didn't want to turn his back on his elders

and betters . . . could do with a few more like that these days
. . . we'll have him.'

So, in the very first days of the New Year of 1946, I took
my place as a 'first-termer' at the Britannia Royal Naval College. In this great institution are the very roots of Britain's
Royal Navy of the twentieth century. Even the name 'Britannia' has an imperial ring to it, though the college is in fact
named after the big old three-decker ship of the line of the
same name that served for half a century as the Navy's principal
training ship, moored in the estuary of the River Dart. In
1905, King Edward VII conducted the opening of the college,
a huge red brick and white stone building designed by Sir
Aston Webb, creator of the façade of Buckingham Palace. On
the lawn was placed the mighty, painted, wooden figure-head
of the old HMS *Britannia*, and the chimes from the clock
tower sounded not the hours of the day but the bells of the
watch, never more than eight except on New Year's Eve at
midnight.

The college bespoke all the highest traditions of the Navy,
in war and in peace. Each one of the cadets was expected to
absorb the broad spectrum of naval history as well as a general
learning in geography, maths, the sciences, English literature,
foreign languages and so on. They also taught us seamanship,
basic craft skills in engineering, how to march and do rifle
drill, how to sail and drive motor-boats, to swim and to shoot,
to read signals by lamp and semaphore and the myriad things
a young officer is going to find useful. 'Oily Qs' was the
expression for Officer-like Qualities, not taught as a subject,
but fundamental to all else that went on, and acquired by a
sort of osmotic process. Or not, as in my case.

It was built not only as a place of learning and training, but
also as a symbol of British sea power. Its position was carefully

chosen, high on a bluff, looming over the estuary of the river, beyond which are the waters of the English Channel – the waters of Jervis and Hood, of Hawke and Rodney, of Howe and Nelson, of Fisher and Jellicoe, of Pound and Cunningham. We were not taught, perhaps as were our peers in the other world of public schools and grammar schools, that such men should be treated as heroes. Our instruction was more on the lines of: 'These are the kinds of men who have *always* commanded the Fleets of the Royal Navy, and the kind of men you should try to emulate.'

I do not recall being over-excited by any of this but, nonetheless, odd bits stuck in the memory. That Admiral Lord Howe roundly defeated the French in the Atlantic on the 'Glorious First of June' in 1794; that Admiral Codrington, Captain of HMS *Orion* at Trafalgar, had given the Turks a bad time; that Admiral John Jervis, the mentor of Nelson and the man who promoted him to commodore, was created the first Earl St Vincent after his famous victory over the Spanish in the Atlantic off the south-western tip of Portugal in 1797. I was also taught some of the folklore of the RN – of the words of Admiral Lord Hawke before the Battle of Quiberon Bay, when he was warned by one of his officers of the extreme danger of the stormy shallow waters which protected the French fleet: 'I thank you for doing your duty in warning me of the danger. And now face me towards the enemy.' I knew of the exploits of Admiral Viscount Hood in the West Indies, of Admiral Sir George Rodney's great victory off Dominica in 1782. I knew of the savage stalemate that Admirals Jellicoe and Beatty had fought against the German High Seas Fleet at the Battle of Jutland in the First World War. And I knew of the amazing exploits of Admiral Cunningham at Matapan and Taranto during the Second World War. The death of Admiral Nelson, and his parting words – 'Thank God I have done my duty' – were impressed upon us. But I was always rather taken with the letter Nelson sent to his former boss, Admiral Jervis, before his final battle: 'Without you, I am nothing,' he wrote. And so it is, for all of us.

While attentive to all the fine traditions, I remember well having, from the very first, a rather personal viewpoint – this was that the very first thing you should do when you see a tradition is to ask what relevance it may have today, to query it, to ask why, to wonder whether the good reasons of two centuries ago still apply now. This bad habit, for it was not viewed with favour, also extended to the edicts of the last week as well as the last century. However, I kept my own counsel just sufficiently to get by – and it remains my way of looking at the world today.

As well as holding to tradition, much of the way of life in the Services is conducted on the basis that 'This is how we have always done things, and we have usually been correct'. To stray from this party line is also frowned upon. I call it the 'Nanny wouldn't like it' syndrome. Nevertheless Nanny too must be questioned, because although she is probably right, she might not be on a particular occasion. I dislike assertions of infallibility, even from myself, and like many psychiatrists, believe that a total absence of self-doubt is the first sign of insanity. Those have always been my instincts, and in later years my considered opinions. Something cannot be copper-bottomed, guaranteed one hundred per cent right just because 'Nanny says so'. And I object most strongly to that assumption. I find it intellectually idle. Whenever we talked about history and tradition in my years at Dartmouth, I was often the cadet to ask the slightly awkward question, to demand to know why this particular tradition was still applicable and, if it wasn't, why we were bothering to discuss it. That is, I would have been if I had had the courage of my youthful convictions: as it was I just tended to mutter a bit.

I have no doubt that both my friends and my detractors found this questioning aspect of my mind not to their liking. But I can recall, all these years later, that in matters of engineering, and indeed of naval philosophy, I had to pick things apart to find out exactly how they worked and why, until I had acquired the kind of personal peace of mind which comes with understanding. I was, in a word, curious. In one sense, until the gaps were filled, I suppose I had endless patience. On the other hand, I had little time for those who fobbed me off with platitudes.

Nonetheless, Dartmouth, over the years, largely won the battle for conformity. My instructors' early advice, usually in the form of 'Shut up, Woodward', slowly mellowed into 'Try to accept that we have been here rather longer than you have' and 'There really are more ways of killing a cat . . .' and 'But wouldn't it sound more reasonable expressed this way?' Thus they kicked that slightly indignant edge off me, teaching me to disagree rather more tactfully. This was the first stage of the Navy's long-term, deep, inductive training, which teaches a man to fit in, which indoctrinates him, brainwashes him some would say, into the ways of the Senior Service, with lessons that will last a lifetime.

As a matter of formality, I should perhaps record that I joined the Navy on 5 January 1946 along with the rest of my term, bar two. One was delayed three weeks by the need for an operation and never really caught up. The other was my old friend George Vallings, who, being extremely 'keen', had arrived the day before the rest of us. Actually his grandmother had packed him off early by mistake, but it sounded good, and it certainly didn't do him any harm as he ended up a vice admiral and a knight. I should also record that it wasn't at Dartmouth that I joined, but at Eaton Hall, the great family seat of the dukes of Westminster, near Chester. The estate had been transformed into a vast camp, with even its own airstrip, to act as the home for the Royal Naval College, which had been evacuated from Dartmouth after a bomb hit in the early months of the war. A part of the main building of Eaton Hall was allocated for the accommodation of the new, thirteen-year-old cadets reporting to Drake house for their first two terms of instruction.

I travelled to Cheshire, all the way from the West Country, by train, a journey which required three changes, and each train, it seemed to me, was more crowded than the last. I had to find a space in the corridor, sitting by myself, perched on my green naval suitcase, self-conscious in my new uniform. Eaton Hall was like nothing I had ever seen. Though I didn't know it, it was like nothing most people had ever seen. It was a gigantic private house, designed by Alfred Waterhouse, on very much the same scale of reckless grandeur as his other Gothic edifice, the Natural History Museum in South Kensington, only worse. It was, in truth, a massive palace, described by one of His Grace's biographers as 'looking like a cross between the Fleet Street Law Courts and St Pancras Station.'

Anyway, it was my home until the end of the summer term, and if I think hard and shut my eyes I can still hear the astounding music of the great campanile, approximately the size of Big Ben, which towered over the colossal mansion of England's richest man. It also towered over me on my first morning on parade when I tripped and fell, while running on the gravel, around a frozen ornamental fountain with my term mates, trying to keep warm. I ripped the knee out of my brand new Number One uniform trousers, bled fairly gratifyingly and was taken away to be cleaned up and issued, four days before any of my fellows, with a pair of short trousers instead. This rendered me unique in the subsequent parades that week, causing me great embarrassment. I think it was the only time I did anything outstanding in my whole four years at the Naval College.

I was soon also at my lifetime peak of fitness. The place was such a never-ending sprawl. To get from class to class, books under arm, you needed the stamina of a middle-distance runner. I would find myself running, possibly in pouring rain, from my English Lit class in 'D' camp – Nissen huts half a mile down the road – all the way back to the main building, surrounded by a hundred acres of formal gardens, approached by five different drives, each two miles long. My maths class was held five floors up in some nasty garret, and was not at all easy to make from 'D' camp in the five minutes allotted. I had to cope with the added problem of not wanting to miss a moment of English literature, because my teacher was none other than the wryly humorous C. N. Parkinson (Parkinson's Law and all that), who taught us very little about English Lit, but was fascinating on the subject of heraldry. And I was quite keen to get to maths which I still enjoyed. Fortunately, maths can still be done while breathing heavily for extended periods, I discovered.

It was, as you may imagine, an awful place in which to get lost. An absolute warren of corridors and staircases – none seeming to have any signposts. The Navy soon taught me a horror of being late, and Eaton Hall was where I started to learn it. One of my recurring nightmares for years was not about some sinking ship, or some maddened captain, but about being lost in an enormous, labyrinthine building, knowing I am getting later and later and *later*.

I duly left, in the summer, to face ten more terms at Dartmouth. I was moved to St Vincent House, one of the five senior houses, named of course in honour of Admiral Jervis. Nothing of great moment happened: the academic work gave no serious cause for alarm; the summers were spent building, then sailing my own dinghy; the winters were spent avoiding violent exercise, particularly rugby.

After completing my four years, I passed out at the end of 1949, eighth in my term of forty-four, three of whom would become admirals. I failed to win anything in that whole time – no academic prizes, no sporting colours, not even my house colours, normally awarded for being public-spirited in one's last term. Zero. It all ranked as a truly exemplary piece of non-achievement, permitting me to keep wholly intact my formidable record of never having earned any prize whatsoever, for anything, between an award for Scripture (unlikely subject) at the age of seven, and a knighthood at the age of fifty.

At the conclusion of this cheerful, reasonably happy, and usually interesting time, my House Officer and Tutor were agreed on my performance. The report contained the phrases: '. . . he will never do himself full justice until he eradicates a certain intellectual laziness . . . his outlook is very parochial; too taken up with his own pursuits and for a boy of his intelligence, very ignorant of the world about him . . . inclined to be irresponsible; at present lacks drive, determination and team spirit . . .' I don't argue with any of that, indeed I have always thought it rather kinder than I deserved, but considering I was in the first twenty per cent of my term, I have occasionally wondered what they must have said about some of the chaps in the last twenty per cent.

Anyway, as a cadet under training, I was sent, in the opening week of the New Year, 1950, to join the 10,000-ton, three-funnelled training cruiser HMS *Devonshire*. The plan there was for cadets to spend one half of their time working the ship, mainly as not-very-able-seamen, scrubbing, washing, polishing, scraping, chipping and painting, all to the accompaniment of four letter words. And the other half was spent in a professional training programme, learning from direct experience on board all we could about how a ship worked. It wasn't a very good time to be an able seaman, because the weather was freezing that January, and before breakfast every morning we had to scrub the wooden upper decks, in bare feet, with the water turning to shards of ice in the scuppers – made the toes tingle a bit, before all feeling faded. Still, learning your trade from the bottom up gets my vote, if there's time, and it played a very important part in the make-up of a future officer. Remember that it was quite within an officer's authority to tell a seaman to take off his boots and scrub the decks, whatever the weather. But once you have done it yourself a few times in mid-winter, you do think twice about telling anyone else to do it.

We sailed away from post-war Britain, still with its rationing and shortages of just about everything, in the middle of January, bound for the West Indies. We steamed south across the Bay of Biscay, then south-west down the trade winds to Trinidad. We slept in hammocks and worked in all the jobs in the ship – in the Boiler Room, the Engine Room, with the Navigating Officer, with the Officer of the Watch on the Bridge. We worked with the Boatswain's Mate, running the basic routine of the ship; or with the Quartermaster, steering it; we acted as the Commander's Runner or 'Doggie', tailing him all day. We manned seaboats, lowered them and hoisted them, practised on and fired the four-inch guns, made signals, stored ship, hurried back and forth, filling each day and most nights it seemed. It was not a bad life and a very considerable change from school. I can remember kneeling beside a large brass staghorn, a sort of cleat for very big ropes, polishing away happily enough in the yellow morning light in Kingston Bay, Jamaica, the sting of Brasso and salt water in my nose and looking forward to a breakfast with lots of fresh fruit, on a scale we hadn't seen in six years.

We called at Barbados, Grenada and the Virgin Islands as well – and the only blot on my horizon was a near total inability to grasp the full significance of the Watch and Quarter Bill. This caused me several problems, because the Navy can seem to run almost entirely on notice boards and notices. I have always considered this to be so because it can take months – in my case years – before you start to understand the garbled noises that came out of the public address system, whistles, called 'Pipes', bugle calls, each telling you to do something different ... distorted, spoken words all in nautical jargon, possibly further disguised in that north-eastern English ver-nacular known as 'Geordie'. If you fail to comprehend the Watch and Quarter Bill, you have failed to find even the entrance to this nautical maze. Life is then apt to become confusing and uncomfortable as the management decides you will have to be taught to try harder.

The Watch and Quarter Bill tells everyone where and when they do everything. Well, just about everything. And there are even times set aside for that, though not specifically mentioned as such. It tells them where they eat, sleep and work, details what watches they are to keep, with whom and what they are to do on watch. It tells them their Harbour Duties, their Sea Duties, their Action Station, and even where, if not when, to

Abandon Ship. Your whole life is laid out on that Bill. I don't think I cared about it at the age of seventeen and a half, which was perhaps as well because I could not find it for some days. When I did find it, I really didn't understand much of what it said; nor did I realize that the reading of the 'Daily Orders' was an essential prerequisite to such understanding. Otherwise I might have looked more carefully at Daily Orders too.

Thus for several weeks, the whole system was a complete mystery to me. We were, of course, working Tropical Routine, a change made about a week after we joined and which entirely escaped me until about the time we returned to home waters and reverted to Daily Winter Routine, which merely completed my confusion. Somehow, I muddled through, as much by the help of my friends as by the help of my Divisional Officer. I was, by any standards, utterly disorganized, a total grasshopper. It was fun though, of a sort.

We were given two weeks' Easter leave before setting off for northern waters, round Jan Meyen Island, into Narvik, and Scapa Flow – what names for a budding naval officer to conjure with – and finally back to Devonport. By the end of that second cruise, I had discovered not just the workings of the ship, its people and its Watch and Quarter Bill, but also how to idle, look busy, avoid the dirty jobs, live safely and quite well: which I think was at least part of what we were sent there for. I passed out of the training cruiser without disgrace and knowing a lot more than I realized. In my report I was commended for my enthusiasm if not for my appearance or timeliness.

Thus I became a midshipman at the age of eighteen, having been in the Royal Navy for nearly five years. At least, I have always assumed that I had been in the Service for this long because I could not get out, should I have wished, without my father paying back the four years' school fees, which wasn't likely. We did not have to 'sign on', no contract was drawn up, nor were we required to take an oath of allegiance, as one must in the Army. I have always been told this was because the Army once mutinied and has never been entirely trusted since! Hence 'Royal Navy', but 'British Army'.

Two white patches were sewn to my collar and I was '. . . directed to take up my appointment . . .' in the submarine depot ship HMS *Maidstone*, then in refit at Portsmouth. The fact that I had been sent not to a cruiser, or a battleship, or an aircraft carrier, but to a depot ship, was a fairly clear indication that I was regarded as anything but a high-flyer. Submariners themselves were not quite the thing – smelt a bit, behaved not too well, drank too much. They were regarded as a sort of dirty habit in tins, and their depot ships were something even less professionally reputable. But *Maidstone* was impressive and big. She was a 10,000-ton accommodation, engineering support and maintenance ship, headquarters to a squadron of some eight submarines. She was nothing less than a floating head office, store, workshop and hotel to the boats that secured alongside her. She had workshops for everything: engine refits, torpedo maintenance and preparation, electrical and hydraulic repair, the list is almost endless. She was purpose-built for the job, and there were a dozen of us midshipmen learning the business of running a large ship and beginning to find ourselves in charge of real sailors for the first time.

After ten months, I was reappointed to HMS *Sheffield*, an 8000-ton cruiser, just coming out of refit and modernization. She was a fast, good design with nine six-inch guns, eight four-inch guns and clusters of 40mm Bofors almost everywhere. We took her out of Chatham Dockyard and up to the Moray Firth for her work-up in a sparkling northern spring and summer, by the end of which I had become Senior Mid-shipman. My pay was £10 a month, of which I saved £5, mostly for lack of opportunity to spend it. This was the old Royal Navy, where they worked you hard and expected you to count your blessings that they were bothering to teach you your trade.

There were also problems. The war, which by definition rendered life in a fighting ship nasty, brutish and short, had not been over for very long, and there were quite a few men around who were suffering from that very old affliction with the modern name of 'stress'. 'Shell-shock', 'twitch', 'lack of moral fibre' were its other, less sympathetic titles. The truly ignorant even described it from time to time as 'cowardice', in a clear throw-back to the bad old days when there was so much courage surrounded by a quite astonishing level of stupidity on the subject of 'stress' in Britain's armed forces. It is as well to remember that stress, with all the horrors it can inflict upon a well-meaning, brave man, was just as real then as it is today. In the immediate post-war Navy, the erratic behaviour of such men manifested itself in many ways, mostly in drastic personality changes. The quiet studious man who became aggressively argumentative. The hell-raiser who became introverted. Some never got over it, and most never let on that they were anything other than perfectly normal. There were also many who found life boring after the excitement of war. Their motivation dropped away and standards of personal and professional behaviour fell with it. In those days it was not impossible to find that the leadership given to young officers under training was nothing like as good as it needed to be, and many promising careers must consequently have been wrecked.

Thus it was always a matter of luck, for a young midshipman, to find himself in a ship with really high-quality officers. I, for example, was invariably allocated more than my share of good fortune. I worked under a succession of truly outstanding naval officers, all of whom went on to prove themselves capable of high command. They coached me, taught me, encouraged me, and occasionally booted me. I could never have got where I did without them and, at that time, things could so easily have gone the other way, particularly with a young officer as naturally unconfident and uncommitted as I then was.

In the autumn of 1951 I went from the *Sheffield* to HMS *Zodiac*, a lovely War Emergency Class destroyer, with four 4.7-inch guns, eight torpedo tubes and still able to do thirty-two knots flat out. She was based at Portland, with the Training Squadron down there. I was nineteen now, but still pretty much a schoolboy. Everybody remarked how immature I was, and I can recall when I went on board that the chief petty officers looked as old as God, and the lieutenant-commander in command slightly older. He must have been about thirty-seven. His name was Geoff Wardle, a wonderful man who had already been uncomfortably close to death many times: his submarine had been sunk very early on in the war and he had been consigned to a POW camp for almost the entire duration – except that he escaped four times, was recaptured four times, and ended up in Colditz. He emerged from there entirely unbowed, but with a new trade under his belt – he had become an expert lock-picker. He could get through any door in a matter of seconds and no one in *Zodiac* ever had to worry about losing a key.

His second-in-command was a twenty-six-year-old lieutenant, Richard Clayton, who rarely went ashore and took his job, and his two glasses of Dry Sack sherry before dinner, very seriously. I enjoyed his sherry if not him, though he always had my respect. He was the son of a rear admiral, and a bit of a Tartar as regards work. And he really put me through it, making me work in every department of the ship and *learn*, really learn.

By the time I received my first gold stripe to become an acting sub-lieutenant, four months on, I was making serious progress. Well before the end of my time, I was allowed to keep watch on the bridge at sea, on my own. I remember the thrill to this day, racing through the night, sometimes feeling the sea thump against the hull, knowing that the safety of the ship and her company rested temporarily upon my shoulders alone. I know now that the Captain must have kept himself at about three seconds' notice to take over if I got it wrong. But I felt myself to be in sole command of this destroyer. It was a very heady experience – I was not yet twenty.

On other occasions, I was allowed to stand in for the Navigation Officer. This was something I enjoyed very much – still do – and the resident Navigator, twenty-four-year-old Lieutenant Paul Greening, himself the son of a remarkably brave Second World War destroyer captain, was a good friend and tutor. I was never surprised at their subsequent careers, Clayton ending up as Admiral Sir Richard Clayton and Commander-in-Chief, Naval Home Command, and Greening as Rear Admiral, Flag Officer Royal Yacht, and eventually Rear Admiral Sir Paul Greening, Master of the Royal Household.

I was sorry to leave *Zodiac* and go ashore, it turned out for nearly two years in all. But the training plan now required me to go to the Royal Naval College, Greenwich, to take the Junior Officers War Course. This combined some rather more advanced teaching in the sciences with an introduction to the amazing regimen of Service thinking and writing. We were taught how to organize our logic processes on military subjects and put them down on paper. I see books appearing in the United States these days, hailed as the greatest break-throughs in management thinking since Sun-Tzu, which simply paraphrase the Navy's Staff Handbook of that time.

We were also invited to take up one voluntary subject – I chose to learn the piano, confident that I was quite incapable of making any useful progress in the time available, and accordingly could take the allotted hours off. Actually 'hours-off' became my voluntary subject, but I couldn't very well have put that down as my choice. Nor did I feel it worth mentioning that I was also learning quite a lot about greyhound racing at the Stadium at New Cross. That wasn't strictly on the curriculum either, although we were expected to broaden our minds and dog racing is no less healthy than the night clubs of the West End.

The studious atmosphere created among the beautiful Palladian buildings of the College at Greenwich (some were designed by Inigo Jones and others by Sir Christopher Wren) was of course an inspiration to us all, confirming a belief among us that we were indeed a vastly more civilized, educated and organized group than officers of the Army could ever be. However, the deep peace which comes with superior intellect and a love of learning was not quite sufficient for us, and we felt obliged to stage a carefully planned and executed raid on our military counterparts at the Royal Military Academy, Sandhurst. This was, by any standards, a successful operation.

We got past the security, drove our cars all over the gravel parade ground, carving deep ruts, whitewashed a few statues of generals, trailed lavatory rolls and behaved like ... sublieutenants on a mess night. We were not caught before we made our retreat, which was probably just as well. The young gentlemen of Sandhurst would not have seen it our way; and the Commandant of the Academy suffered a comprehensive sense of humour failure, which he transmitted, at some length, to the Captain of our college.

Now, our Captain was that redoubtable sportsman and tough-minded submarine commander who was eventually to become Rear Admiral Sir Anthony Miers VC KBE CB DSO and bar, known throughout the Navy as 'Crap' Miers. Concerned, not only about reprisals by the Army students, but also about the likely presentation of a large bill for the damage done, he paraded us all before him and issued a major blast, ranting on about immaturity, stupidity and irresponsibility, with never a thought for our very real achievement. Not everyone could break through the defences of the British Army and humiliate them like that.

Crap, however, had not entirely lost his sense of proportion and he finished his lecture with the flourish you might expect from a man who had not only won a VC in a most daring submarine raid into the harbour of Corfu, but had also contributed considerably to an attack on General Rommel's headquarters in North Africa. 'It was *thoroughly* disgraceful behaviour,' he growled. 'WELL DONE!'

I left Greenwich with an 'alpha' for the Staff Course part and an accurate 'gamma minus' for the academic side. The whole term then went off to Portsmouth for 'Technical Courses', which represented another eight-month slog round the 'Schools', working away at subjects as diverse as Aviation, Navigation, Torpedo and Anti-Submarine warfare (TAS), Gunnery, Electrics, Combined Operations, Administration and the like. There were, however, two strange omissions, propulsion engineering and submarines. Both presumably thought somehow beneath our notice. Two or three subjects went quite well for me and the rest moderate-to-average.

Resignation to perpetual exams was by now taking its toll. They set them: I pass them: seem to have been doing this all my life: what's next?

I am now twenty-one, and their Lordships wanted to know whether I'd like to sub-specialize as a young lieutenant in the Executive branch of the Navy. Come along, Woodward. Gunnery, perhaps? TAS? Navigation? Communications? Aviation? Even that unknown quantity, submarines?

'I don't know, really,' was my incisive reply, so typical of my career to date. The next thing I did know, however, was that I received a letter telling me to report to HMS *Dolphin*, the alma mater of the dreaded submariners – I had been 'volunteered' for submarine training. They did add that if I really hated it, I could apply to get out in eighteen months' time, and would be allowed to leave within three and a half years. This seemed reasonable and anyway some seven or eight of my term were in the same boat, so to speak, so we would be companions in adversity should it come to that.

So started, inauspiciously, Woodward's submarine career. It ended thirty-two years later, when I was still, in my own mind, a 'pressed' man. But grateful for it, and upon reflection, all these years later, it emerges as nothing short of an inspired appointment for me – albeit probably done with a pin by the appointers – because in a submarine, you are required to become a responsible citizen from Day One. You have to grow up, quickly. The Submarine Service is nothing like being on board surface ships, which by and large tend not to sink, and anyway, if they do, are inclined to do so rather slowly, providing a very sporting chance to its company of surviving the event. In submarines, which are apt to sink rather suddenly, you are expected to understand and to be able to work every bit of equipment on board. I was thus required to become not only a semi-engineer, but also to learn in turn to be the Gunnery Officer, the Navigation Officer, the Communications Officer, the Electrical Officer, the Torpedo Officer, the Sonar Officer, before I could hope for a front-line command in about six years' time. Suddenly I was to be permitted, in a position of responsibility, to undertake the very kind of work I had always liked most. It was exactly right for me – though I did not of course know it at the time.

As training proceeded, I found the requirements entirely to my taste. We were made to understand the maze of pipes, cables, hydraulic systems, air systems, water systems, sewage systems, ship control systems, torpedo firing systems, engines, batteries, electrical systems, motors, pumps, valves, cocks, gauges, masts, periscopes and switches. It was another endless list. At the end, we were supposed to be able to find any item of equipment quickly and to be able to work quite a few in complete darkness.

This last required discipline was put to the test by my Training Officer, Lieutenant (later Vice Admiral) 'Tubby' Squires, another instructor who was kinder to me than I could possibly have deserved. He met me at the forward entrance hatch of the submarine which was to be my examination room. It was open and plainly pitch dark inside. 'Go below and restore all electrics,' he said.

Hesitantly I went below, a small voice in the back of my mind saying that the answer had to be found in the Motor Room, well aft. In addition I vaguely remembered that a thing called the 'Reducer' was quite likely to solve the problem. Nothing very difficult: find it, make the switches (Navy jargon for turn them on), electrics restored. I was not, however, that confident as I descended into the darkness, and in tentatively 'making' the vital switch I caused it to start arcing and jumped back from it – a dangerous and stupid thing to do. Tubby leant over and blew out the arc quickly before things started to melt. And waited, expectantly. So I tried again, and shoved the switch over, if anything more tentatively, which caused more arcing and another patient but quick puff from Tubby. There was another expectant pause. Finally, he banged the switch home for me and was good enough to say as all the lights came on, 'Well, I'll pass you for knowing which switch to go to, even if you didn't know how to work it when you got there.'

So four months' training ashore ended and I was sent off to my first submarine, the 800-ton HMS *Sanguine*, for two years in the Mediterranean, based on Malta. I started as the Torpedo Officer and after about six months switched to Navigation Officer. This was real responsibility, allowed me by my competent, genial and very likeable Captain, Brian Baynham – six feet five inches tall and weighing some eighteen stone, he could stand upright only when he was immediately under the tower to the bridge.

We sailed from end to end of the Med. Beirut, where one of our number, now an admiral, on enquiring of the head waiter at a very up-market night club how much the belly dancer cost, was told, in the most perfect Oxford accent: 'A good many more camels than you can afford, young man.' Gibraltar, of so many memories down the years. Trieste, Venice, Naples, La Spezia, Palermo, Algiers, Bone. All with their special events and astonishing times. Living was cheap, a run-ashore in Catania cost two bob, I'm sorry, ten pence, for a bottle of red wine and a large bowl of fish stew. A really outstanding run-ashore might take a ten-shilling note.

I started off living in a fairy-tale castle called Fort St Angelo, built on a rock bluff, overlooking Grand Harbour, 120 feet below. The Knights of Malta had done themselves proud, and I remember it all so well: the steep ramps down to the dock-yard, the 'yells, bells and smells' for which Malta is famous; the many churches with the clock faces showing different times to confuse the Devil; the bar where the Coxswain had set up his office; and the submarine, smelling of hot oil and new paint.

After a year's operational running in HMS *Sanguine*, my second Captain joined; and this proved to be yet another of my lucky breaks. He was a brilliant and delightful officer, whose sometimes suave manner complemented his nice, staccato humour, and disguised the patience and understanding which made him such an effective tutor to a young officer. Unsurprisingly, in my view, he went on to become Admiral Sir Gordon Tait, and Second Sea Lord.

They sent me to Barrow-in-Furness in late 1956 to help supervise the building of a new class of submarine, and to stand by as the crew of the first to complete, HMS *Porpoise*. She was a 2300 tonner, enormous by comparison with little *Sanguine*. After two years in the building yard, we got to sea with another marvellous Captain, Brian Hutchings, who would undoubtedly have become an admiral had he not retired early for personal reasons. As it was, he went on to rise close to the top of the John Lewis Partnership, which was just as good, really. I served him for about a year and a half, as his first lieutenant, before Tubby Squires took over for my last few months.

It was now 1960, and I was twenty-eight. There hadn't been much opportunity to think seriously about girls or marriage, and Brian Hutchings vaguely disapproved of his 'young officers' getting married anyway. Nor did I have much cash to spend on girls at all, especially after I'd bought a superb

Sunbeam Mark III, 2.25-litre rally saloon which would do 100 mph with little bother. In fact the running of this luxurious sports car just about cleared my pay each month, and it proved only a mixed blessing in the serious pursuit of Miss Charlotte McMurtrie. While she thought the car nice enough, it plainly wasn't very practical, and this naturally cast doubts on my suitability.

I solved both problems in one fell swoop by giving the greatly beloved machine to her as a wedding present. I reasoned, firstly, that it would be very nearly impossible anyway to find the money to give her something else. And when the 'transaction' was finally completed, the responsibility for practicality was placed firmly on her shoulders, a burden I am afraid she has been obliged to carry for most of the past thirty years. Mrs 'Charlie' Woodward exchanged the dashing Mark III for a Mini the week after we got back from the honeymoon.

We settled happily into a small Georgian terraced house in Gosport, which cost rather less than the Sunbeam had. Here I dealt with the second major financial transaction of my new marriage, by enlisting the help of my new mother-in-law to beat down the house agent all the way from £1200 to £600. I had chosen my negotiator well. And, aware of my general ignorance in commercial matters after the rather protected life of a serving officer since a very young age, I actually felt rather pleased with myself. However, the grim realities of hard civilian commercialism were quickly driven home. 'Pretty good price, don't you think?' I asked one of the workmen who was doing it up for us.

'Six hundred quid for this, Gov?' he replied, incredulously. 'You was robbed.'

I was now going on to the toughest test for the submariner,

the Commanding Officers Qualifying Course – the old Periscope Course – known universally as the 'Perisher' (as in 'he failed his Perisher' or 'that Perisher doesn't look up to much'). It used to be conducted half in the south in a simulator at HMS *Dolphin*, and half at sea in a submarine, up north. The Perisher was a career-breaker in those days: between twenty and twenty-five per cent of the students failed, and by the time I arrived, not one of them had ever been promoted beyond lieutenant-commander. The cruel but necessary process of the Perisher was enough to 'break' some of the young officers. Indeed, I seriously doubt that *any* of us would have passed had we been able to see, physically, the tiny safety margins allowed – a few feet, and split-seconds only, to separate the hulls of the oncoming frigates and the submarine.

Fortunately for me, our commanding officer was Hutchings again, and it was his responsibility, in his truly eminent position as 'Teacher' of future commanding officers, to put us through the most rigorous test of our careers to date. He had to find out, once and for all, which of us could be counted on absolutely to carry in our minds a picture of what is happening on the surface above, and subsequently conduct the submarine in a safe, aggressive and effective manner. Towards the end of the Perisher, that mental picture, fleeting and ephemeral for some, sharp and clear for others, would not only include the usual fishing boats, ferries, islands, yachts and the like, but would also contain the major confusion factor of five Royal Navy frigates tearing about at full speed, deliberately trying to ruin our day. Brian was not always the easiest man to work for – if you made a minor mistake, he'd tend to rant and rave, which, if you were unused to this sort of thing, could be quite upsetting. However, if you made a really serious mistake, he'd quietly do his absolute utmost to help you out of it. But he was tough-minded and you couldn't pull the wool over his eyes. He generally referred to us collectively as his 'useless officers' and felt entirely free to do so before the ship's company and/or complete strangers. The thing to remember was that he didn't really mean it, did he?

Fundamentally the course was intended to test your ability to stand the stresses and strains of pushing your luck and skill to the limit in very odd conditions. I had personally been well prepared and found it not too difficult. But my performance in the Perisher was entirely due to having been the blessed recipient of the personal, priceless attention of four future admirals. I had also been individually schooled for over two years in *Porpoise* by Brian Hutchings himself. He it was who taught me hard self-confidence; to be rather less concerned for the feelings of others whenever I saw clearly the way forward. This of course does have the effect of converting one into a 'pushy b*****d'. But that's a risk you take.

The key to a submariner's success or failure is partly this, plus the ability to hold a mental picture of the surface scene. It's not a very good analogy, but imagine sticking your head out of a manhole in Piccadilly Circus, taking one quick swivelling look round, ducking back down into the sewer and then trying to remember all that you have seen. The idea is to generate sufficiently accurate recall and timing to avoid a double-decker bus running over your head next time you pop up through the manhole. Near-misses in the Perisher are a natural, frequent and deliberate part of the game. The biggest single worry is of course that to get it wrong is inclined to be expensive in people and equipment. Career-wise, a major foul-up would be personally terminal. It is this formidable strain on the wretched Perisher that usually causes his failure.

I got through it, along with four others and was duly seen

by Teacher on return to the Depot Ship that evening. 'Young Woodward,' he said – a sure sign that what was to follow was not precisely what he meant – 'contrary to all my expectations, you have managed to pass.' After nearly three years of him, I knew better than to react. Finally, he went on: 'Actually, you've done quite well. So I'm giving you first choice of the available appointments in Command. Where would you like to go?'

I told him, deadpan, 'I'd rather like to drive *Dreadnought*.' This was Britain's first nuclear-powered submarine, the 3500-ton Pride of the Submarine Flotilla, not even launched yet, and several light years away from the grasp of young lieutenants such as myself. This gross impertinence did have the merit of providing my Teacher with a good story to tell the Admiral's Staff when he returned south. Meanwhile he arranged for me to be sent, forthwith, to command HMS *Tireless*, as from the 19 December 1960. She was not exactly *Dreadnought*, but to me she was the most glorious submarine afloat; the first day of your first command, is, without fail, the biggest day of any Royal Naval officer's life.

Tireless was an ex-wartime 'T' Class submarine – streamlined and modernized, she was known as a 'Streamlined T-Boat' or sometimes a 'Slippery T' to differentiate her from others of the 'T' Class which were lengthened and which went much faster underwater, called 'T-Conversions' and sometimes 'T-Confusions'. I took my leading role with the Chaplain when we commissioned her on 25 April 1961. I addressed the Ship's Company, seeking His blessing 'upon this ship and all who sail in her'. We spoke the words of Psalm 107 for 'they that go down to the sea in ships; and occupy their business in great waters'. And then I called on the company to pray, from the Gaelic blessing of 1589 . . .

Whom do ye fear, seeing that God the Father is with you?

We fear nothing.

Whom do ye fear, seeing that God the Son is with you?

We fear nothing.

Whom do ye fear, seeing that God the Holy Spirit is with you?

We fear nothing.

The Chaplain recited the prayer of Sir Francis Drake which contains the words he spoke before he sailed to meet the Armada: 'Preserve us from the dangers of the sea, and from the violence of the enemy; that we may be a safeguard unto our most gracious Sovereign Lady, Queen Elizabeth and her Dominions.' And then we all sang 'Eternal Father, strong to save', the sailor's hymn, and I formally took my place as Commanding Officer of a front-line submarine, with a ship's company of sixty odd, six days before my twenty-ninth birthday as a lieutenant of six years' seniority. It was obviously a proud day for me and, looking back, a long way to have travelled already for that small unknown 'warrior' who once had sat on his suitcase in a packed railway train trying to find his way to Eaton Hall in 1946. But the Navy does that – keeps pushing you, on and up, until you fall off the ladder somewhere.

My year in Home Waters in command of *Tireless* contained many good times in delightful company. There was one highlight, though, as we returned from the long and difficult day of my 'Work-Up' Inspection. My Squadron Commander stood on the bridge looking fairly hatchet-faced and saying not very much, while I wondered, pessimistically, how we had done. The final approach to the Depot Ship moored in Rothesay

Bay for Clyde Week is often littered with yachts nearing their finishing line, no doubt full of important local figures more concerned to chop up their opponents than make way for the working classes. In order to get alongside in good time, I had to barge my way through the infuriated Dragon Class helmsmen and, in the end, I had to 'tack' between the leaders and drive across the finishing line with them. I glanced round nervously – to see my Squadron Commander smiling quietly. A dedicated fisherman, he considered all yachtsmen a bloody nuisance, and coming third, in a submarine, in the Clyde Week Dragons Race had really made his day. I had passed Inspection.

I left *Tireless* in early 1962, spent six fascinating months in HMS *Falmouth*, an anti-submarine frigate based at Londonderry, and then returned to the Naval College at Greenwich for a whole year, to take the Nuclear Reactor Course. This was a highly specialized subject, intended primarily for postgraduate engineer officers. I was now a lieutenant-commander with two and a half stripes and faced the hardest work I had ever done. Nor was the work helped by the worst winter recorded in some years. We had the last of the great smogs in November – it took thirty minutes walking to work or forty-five by car. In February, with the snow lying on the ground for six weeks, I was able to ski in Greenwich Park and we had to put all the electric fires in our house in the attic to stop the water system freezing. All this was celebrated by the birth of our daughter Tessa, at home, in the middle of the cold spell.

The mathematics started just beyond where I had left off more than ten years before, as did all the other subjects required to begin to understand the theory behind nuclear reactors and their engineering. There were two hours of homework most nights, and we coped with everything from water chemistry to Einstein's theory of relativity in three-dimensional differential algebra. On top of that, there was a project in the third and last term – design your own reactor. I handed my work in with a huge sigh of relief three weeks before the end of term, only to be asked a few days later whether I'd now be good enough to answer the second half of the question.

However, they allowed me to pass and I went off to do an Anti-Submarine course for another five months before being given command of HMS *Grampus* as a fill-in job while I waited for HMS *Valiant* to complete at Barrow-in-Furness. I was to be second-in-command to Commander Peter Herbert, yet another outstanding man, who ended up Admiral Sir Peter Herbert KCB OBE.

Valiant, 3500 tons and the first all-British nuclear attack submarine known as a Fleet Submarine, or SSN, was powered by a pressurized water reactor which could give her a speed I had never before experienced underwater. She was 282 feet long, slightly bigger than *Dreadnought*, thirty-two feet wide, with three decks below the conning tower, and handled something like a very slow jumbo-jet without windows, carrying a crew of 100. She was based on the Clyde.

We worked her up to join the Fleet and set about the whole series of equipment trials which are always required of a 'First-of-Class' ship. The last of these, before I left, was to go underwater from Scotland to Singapore. My time in *Valiant* ended in 1967 with promotion to Commander. This always seems a most important step, because it is the very first to be made by selection rather than by just passing examinations or serving your time. You also get some gold braid on the peak of your cap and become thereby a 'brass-hat', plainly, for all too see.

At the same time, I was given the job most coveted by all

submariners, that of 'Teacher' to the Perishers. My preparation was one week with the then present incumbent, Commander Sam Fry. It was the last and most difficult week of the previous Perisher. We were having a quick lunch one day, at periscope depth, while the frigates opened out for the next run, when Sam said, quietly, without even looking up, 'They've turned.'

'How do you know?' I asked, in the full knowledge that all five frigates were now at least six miles away. I did not have the first idea how he could possibly have known whether they had turned back towards us or not. The really worrying thing was that neither did he! I questioned him carefully but to no avail. He had no idea how he knew. He just *did*. This was seriously depressing for me. How do you take over from a bloke who operates on a sixth sense? How could I possibly learn from a mystic, in a dark blue suit?

And the frigate trick was not all. Sam could also tell the precise passage of a minute, to the nearest second, without looking at a stop-watch. He didn't even stop talking as he ticked. I began to wonder why the job of Teacher was so coveted. As a student, though you worked very hard not to show it, you always had Teacher there to save you if things went wrong. Because he always held the ultimate responsibility. Now, if things were to go wrong, the responsibility would be entirely mine.

The first few months were very nervous indeed. I lost a stone and a half during the first course, while I re-taught myself all the things I had learned as a Perisher. That done, I was able to concentrate on teaching properly. I taught them the principles of mathematical timing and the stern rules of submarine safety. I emphasized mental agility and accuracy of observation. For example, it takes a whole minute for a submarine to get down from periscope depth to safety, clear underneath the hull of an approaching surface ship, and the Perishers were required to accomplish this with just ten seconds to spare. You will appreciate that this only left about five seconds for Teacher to catch the errant Perisher, if he'd got it wrong – all in the face of the 'enemy' as the frigates thundered past, overhead.

Sometimes, I'd almost hold my breath, watching the depth gauge, counting the seconds, listening to the mounting roar of the approaching propellers, worrying about the wing frigates on either side and whether there'd be time to pop up for a quick look at the target ship behind the escorts, before any of them could run us over. 'Flood Q. Group up, full ahead together. Eighty feet ... Blow Q ... Q blown, Q Kingston shut ... Vent Q inboard' – the roar of escaping compressed air – 'Q vented, Q vent shut ...' The sequence runs, the commands and responses rattle back and forth, while the mind races against the clock to hold the surface picture clear. For a very few, this is heaven under water. For most, it is the severest test they may ever face. For some, it is the ultimate nightmare. To be really good, you have to love it.

And finally, after months of pointed curiosity, I discovered what made Sam Fry say, instinctively, 'They've turned.' Having sat, for ages, in exactly the same place as he had, hoping for divine inspiration, I hit upon the vital clue. It turned out to be a change in the note of the frigates' sonar transmissions, as heard over a loudspeaker in the submarine's Control Room. This is known as the 'Doppler effect' – a common acoustic phenomenon, heard every day in the changing pitch of an ambulance's siren as it goes by. And once I had identified this as the source of Sam's sixth sense, I was able to apply some fairly ordinary mathematics, which, with some simple electronic equipment to do most of the work, produced all sorts of amazing information previously unavailable to us.

It is just one example of the submariner's way of life. You use all of your senses to monitor very carefully all that goes on about you, inside and outside the submarine. The noise of a pump stopping, the click of an indicator, the thump of a valve, the hiss of compressed air, the feel of a fracturing pipe. Sensitivity to every clue buys those critical extra seconds to deal with the unexpected, or the potentially disastrous. Outside is the noise of the sea, a very busy place where the men wandering, in or on it, often wish to hide. And sensibly they seek to mix with its natural inhabitants, who can be a rackety lot. We have our jargon names for many of the strange noises: 'frying fish', 'baby cry', 'snapping shrimps', 'military fish' and many others, anything from the cheerful whistles of the porpoises to the mating cry of the killer whale. Amidst this cacophony, you are listening for your enemy, ship, submarine, even aircraft. Each one has its 'tune'. Every one is a potential 'enemy' until identified otherwise.

Kill or be killed – this is no place for the careless. Even the propeller of an innocent ship tells a tale. How many shafts the ship has. How many propeller blades on each shaft. How fast they are rotating. This is often enough to tell you the type of ship, where it is likely to be going and how quickly. Find only the range, and you have the 'Firing Solution' for the destruction of an enemy.

Like my predecessors, I found I had to fail about one in five of my Perishers. I hated having to do this and I was invariably astonished when, on imparting the dreadful news, they usually smiled. They were, momentarily anyway, glad to be out of it, having knowingly passed the point where they were able to take on any additional information or teaching of any sort. Not only were they increasingly unable to cope during the last few days, but they also had suffered the first symptoms of real, permanent stress, and it was axiomatic that I let no such officers through the net to Command.

By that time there were three Fleet Submarines – SSNs – in operational service, *Dreadnought*, *Valiant* and *Warspite*. I was appointed, after two years as Teacher and six months improving my golf handicap on the Joint Services Staff Course, to command *Warspite*. She was named after the famous battleship of the First and Second World Wars, which served as Admiral Cunningham's Flagship at Matapan, and which met her end aground in Prussia Cove near Land's End on her way to the scrap yard.

I joined the new *Warspite* in early December 1969. It was a good time for me, because by then I was used to command. No one seemed to accuse me of immaturity any more. I was very much Commander Woodward, who'd been through the mill and was as well qualified as anyone in the business to do the job.

My first week was traumatic, for just about everyone on board. On the Monday, at lunchtime, I had arranged to go down to the Chief and Petty Officers Mess to meet them informally over a half pint of beer. Before I left the Control Room, I told the First Lieutenant, James Laybourne: 'When you've finished taking the wireless routine at periscope depth, go on to fifteen knots, ten degrees bow down to 400 feet, and hurry on to our next exercise appointment.'

Down in the Mess, glass in hand a few minutes later, everyone chattering away, it was no surprise to me when the bow down angle came on. But all around me, conversation completely halted. I realised I was looking at an extremely worried group. We levelled off a minute later and the conversation very, very slowly restarted. To my horror, I was watching the most reliable, the most experienced men on board go into a total decline over what should have been a routine change of depth. These men, I saw, must have been going through the submariner's unspoken, universal dread, with voices inside their heads saying, 'The hull of this boat will crush at about 1500 feet. If you start diving at ten degrees bow down and fifteen knots, and do nothing about it, six minutes from now the lights will go out – permanently.'

Plainly these men, the backbone of my crew, have let these tiresome thoughts cross their minds once too often. Angles of up to thirty degrees should be 'normal' enough. So should higher speeds, if this boat is to be fit for war. My new submarine was non-operational. And I was very unhappy.

I quietly finished my glass and returned to the Control Room to tell the First Lieutenant what I had seen.

'Oh,' he said. 'Didn't you know?'

'Didn't I know *what?*,' I said.

And out it all came. *Warspite* had been in collision with an iceberg twelve months before, rolled over to horrendous angles, twice, badly damaging her bridge structure (the 'fin'). She returned home safely enough, but many of the crew never got over it. Some twenty-four members of the crew left the Submarine Service for good as a consequence. Apparently, since that day, she had never routinely been manoeuvred vigorously, in order to spare the rest.

I took the opposite view from her previous Commanding Officer, and I decided to throw the boat about, an exercise known locally as 'Angles and Dangles'. I warned everyone what to expect and when. As soon as they were used to this, I threw her about without warning. Day and night, for the rest of the week. I have to say, I did not much enjoy it myself. On the Friday, I again arranged to have a glass of beer with the Senior

Rates in their Mess. As I left the Control Room, James and I set our stop-watches, and I said to him carefully: 'In exactly seven and one quarter of a minute's time, go on to twenty knots, put on thirty bow down, and make lots of noise as if you're having problems in the Control Room.' Seven and one quarter minutes later, *no one* took a blind bit of notice. No one even spilt their beer.

On such psychological tightropes are battles won, or lost. Sadly, the net cost was one more member of the crew who asked to leave, that weekend. But he was one more for the benefit of the remaining ninety-seven. Actually yet another 'surfaced' years later. I discovered, entirely by chance, that a man I had known quite well as a quiet, rather introverted chap, used to be no such person. He had once been a cheerful, noisy extrovert. I wondered, privately, how many years of his career had he spent in silent terror. Sadly he had not been noticed amidst *Warspite*'s busy life, which was full of incident and excitement around the North Atlantic and the Med. By chance I met him again a few months after the first publication of this book, looking a good deal more cheerful than I expected. He told me, quite simply, that since the day he had read this account, his nightmares had suddenly stopped. After twenty-three years. Over the following eighteen months I learned another whole bookful of extraordinary things in the company of excellent people and enjoyed myself almost as much as I had as Teacher.

When it ended, I was recalled ashore and, with very mixed feelings, I proceeded to the Royal College of Defence Studies at Belgrave Square in 1972. I commuted each day from our newly bought house in Surbiton to Victoria and walked to the College, where, in company with four other similar grade officers, we did much of the administration and also attended lectures as unofficial students. I took a very poor view of the job I now found myself in – which seemed to entail all the most menial tasks, barring actually sweeping the floors. I was also expected to be civil to brigadiers, who were not being very civil to me, and see to the minor needs of any student who thought he might have a problem – basically act as a combined 'Mr Fix-it' and 'Cook's Tour Guide'. I even gave a conducted tour of the River Thames from Westminster to Greenwich in a boat to a senior foreign student, and his wife, in my fractured French.

This was not what I had joined the Navy for. Nor did I take kindly to being taken down several pegs at a go. My wife put me straight by firmly stating it as her opinion that a few months of humility would be good for my soul, since I had become far too pleased with myself. That was small comfort too, for at this stage of my career, as recent Commanding Officer of Britain's latest nuclear-powered front-line submarine, I was unused to being argued with or criticized. As a matter of fact, I was unused even to being interrupted! So I wasn't all that grateful to Char either.

Such a pity, because there was a myriad of good things to do at that time and I was too busy sulking to take full advantage of the opportunities. But it lasted only one year instead of the two forecast, because, out of the blue, I was informed I was on the promotion list to captain and that unless I did something absolutely unforgivable I'd have a fourth stripe in six months' time.

I took a rather more positive view of the College after that and started to think about what I might hope to do as a captain during the eight or nine years I would be on the 'Captains' List'. This is an historic phrase, dating back to well before Nelson's time. You work your way up the list as time passes, eventually to reach the top and either be made an admiral or retired. I was forty by that time, as young as any captain for those days, and it seemed as though I might really have a foot on the top management ladder, slippery though the rungs would be. My boss made several kind remarks about me in his final report at the end of my time at the College, but the sting was in the tail: he described me as having '. . . very great strength of character', by which I'm sure he meant that I argued the toss on everything and made it plain that I disliked the job as much as he did.

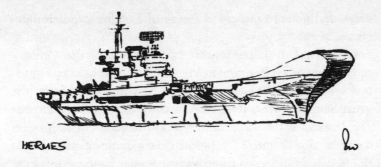

HERMES

3

Argentina Invades

Of all the titles in the armed services, I suppose that of Captain is the most romantic, the one most likely to evoke images of swashbucklers and daredevils of the high seas. For it is a rank which has inspired maritime folklore to blur irreparably the line between fact and fiction, between buccaneers and king's officers, pirates and plain adventurers. The very mention of a few names – Bligh, Cook, Ahab, Kidd, Morgan and Hornblower – there's legend for you.

In the summer of 1972, I stepped forward, if I might be allowed several thousand yards of literary licence, to join them. Captain J. F. Woodward Royal Navy, and proud of it too. However, I did not immediately take my place on the bridge of some mighty warship and start issuing commands. Rather I bought myself a new brolly, and a brand-new briefcase, checked the daily running of the 7.40 Surbiton – to – Waterloo local, and joined the massed forces of London's four million commuters.

Each day I made my way to the fifth floor of the Ministry of Defence Main Building in Whitehall. Gone were the glorious vistas of the seascapes I had lived with for so long, the great Scottish lochs, the Western Isles, the open sea and the sky. Instead, if I looked out of my office window, I could gaze straight down into the spectacular granite cleavage of the massive Goddess of Fertility who guards one side of the North Door of the building. A strange symbol to have at the door of the Ministry of Defence but it had been too expensive to dismantle when the Board of Trade moved out, to let us in.

Achieving the rank of Captain in the modern Royal Navy normally requires a fairly stringent piece of career assessment. The general rule is that you will be offered four, perhaps five jobs during the next eight or nine years, after which they will either make you a rear admiral or thank you perfunctorily for all that you have done and dispense with your services. It's known as 'Falling off the top of the Captains' List' and represents bad news for most. Immediately upon promotion you are required to confer with the officer who masterminds all the captains' appointments, and you are asked whether you'd like to specialize in Policy, or Operations, or Equipment Procurement, or Personnel, or perhaps volunteer to become an Attaché. Or even, in one case I heard, whether you'd like to retire early as they'd promoted more than they'd intended.

My own policy was relatively simple. I would do one job in the submarine business, to pay back some of what I owed; one in command of a surface warship; and I'd aim for two jobs in the Ministry, preferably in Policy, the first to find out how the Headquarters worked and the second to apply what I had learned. Maybe. Almost any other combination would limit my options for further progress in the Navy.

My first job was in Whitehall in the Directorate of Naval Plans. I was appointed Assistant Director (Warfare), a position which would have much to do with Navy Board policy. I approached this new life with some trepidation, imagining myself soon to be engulfed in several cubic yards of red tape and galloping bureaucratic rubbish, which would prove to be total anathema to the serving officer more accustomed to driving nuclear submarines than pushing a pen. I also feared there would be none of the cheerful camaraderie of mess life which I had enjoyed for all of my career so far; none of the imposed self-discipline which was a way of life to me and my kind; and no real social life. I envisaged dull and sleazy offices, with the inhabitants speaking in some kind of lunatic and foreign jargon. I would be, for the first time in a long while, an outsider, captain or no captain.

As I walked out of the building, at the end of my first mesmeric day, I had by no means found my feet. I was in the company of an RAF group captain, but when I wished him 'Good evening' and prepared to walk across the footway on Hungerford Bridge back to Waterloo Station, he seemed quite taken aback.

'Not Hungerford Bridge, old chap,' he said. 'That's known as Other Ranks' Bridge. Officers – we use Westminster Bridge.'

Misjudging the social order of the bridges was not, however, my only mistake in that first week in the Ministry. Contrary to all my preconceived ideas about civil servants, mostly based on Parkinson's Laws which I had learnt so early, I found the people in the department to be extraordinarily knowledgeable, companionable and keen to help me settle to a new career.

The subjects we had to tackle were nothing short of riveting. They ranged from briefing the First Sea Lord on contentious inter-Service issues to preparing staff papers for the Navy Board on almost anything, from the nature of amphibious warfare to the need for a new type of fighter aircraft at the forthcoming turn of the century. Strategy, operations and procurement of naval systems and ships; manpower, training, World and Alliance trends. What kind of a Fleet will Britain require in the year 2010? How long will the next war be? Who may we be fighting? Just what is British Maritime Policy?

My new duties encompassed the entire spectrum of Royal Navy Defence Policy: one of my first assignments was issued to me by the Assistant Chief of Naval Staff, then Rear Admiral Henry Leach, later to become First Sea Lord. 'Let me have, on one side of a piece of foolscap, *all* of the tasks and roles of the Royal Navy – by next Wednesday.' This has been the subject of entire books written over years by the likes of Mahan, Barnett and Cable; but it was a good three-day exercise for the narrow-minded submariner fresh to the strange ways and wider horizons of the Ministry of Defence.

Another task which befell us was to produce the Royal Navy's considered opinion on whether Britain could reasonably defend a remote, ill-charted colony in the South Atlantic known as the Falkland Islands. This was in 1973 and we were dealing, as always, with the possibility that the Argentine government might suddenly carry out its constant threat to take by armed force what they described as their 'Malvinas'. And it seemed to us that Her Majesty's government would be largely powerless to do anything whatsoever to stop them. We couldn't afford to station a force large enough in the islands themselves; nor could we get a reinforcement force out there in the time which would probably be available to us. Careful consideration inevitably pointed to the only conclusion: *impossible*. Strangely, the question of what, if anything, we might do to get the Argentinians out again once they had occupied the islands was never raised.

In addition to such specific problems, I had to learn from scratch the jargon. Without which you cannot survive in the MOD. I had to learn the 'buzz phrases', which mean everything to a naval staff director, but little to a non-initiate: 'size and shape', 'wedge', 'graduated response', 'military years', 'bidding minute', 'cuts exercise', 'force goals', 'Rotherham fleet', 'nuclear sufficiency', and a thousand others. They were all portmanteau phrases to cover the large concepts and techniques by which the MOD conducted its business and it took me about a year to catch on. But without this unearthly vocabulary, your chances of attaining serious High Command are negligible.

As 1973 drew to a close, our department became aware of a likely new development which would keep us all extremely busy. The winter of the coal miners' strike led to the embattled Edward Heath – in accordance with most bookmakers' predictions – losing power to the Labour Party in the General Election of February 1974. For us this meant a Defence Review, with massive cuts being proposed to the MOD's budget, our own intensive efforts being known as 'Pain and Grief' – that is, trying to avoid falling into line financially with the government's intentions, by exaggerating the dark and dire consequences of the cash cuts proposed.

Happily for us, however, the new Prime Minister Harold Wilson did not choose to return Denis Healey to the Ministry of Defence which he had ruled from 1964 to 1970. Instead he appointed him Chancellor, which we all found very helpful. Healey was determined to cut Defence spending but, with his vast experience in the intricacies of the Services and as an intellect of high standing, he was always prepared to listen and adjust his views in the face of hard evidence. Very like Mrs Thatcher, though I doubt either will be entirely at ease with the comparison.

When Healey argued, he argued from knowledge – knowledge he cheerfully agreed he had acquired from making just about every mistake in the book during his previous tenures of office. The experience now served him well and, unlike Mr Nott in 1981, he realized that his cuts could not be achieved overnight and made no attempt to do so. Polaris was the obvious problem, with its relatively high profile, political and financial, but Healey knew all about that and was clear in his own mind that it ought to be kept. By contrast, Harold Wilson adopted his customary role as magician, all things to all men. I remember listening to him talk about Polaris during the run-up to the General Election and deciding that he had said he'd keep Polaris, definitely. Discussing the programme later with an anti-Polaris acquaintance, it seemed to him that Wilson had made it crystal clear that Polaris was to go. This was, of course, something altogether less than bedrock upon which to base a Naval Staff paper, whether it had to argue for, or against.

Did we or did we not have Polaris? I don't think any of us knew, certainly not I. The only thing I knew for certain was that Mr Wilson was a master at not letting anyone know what was happening in his mind. But personally, I am sure he knew precisely what he was doing. While being quite certain Polaris had to go ahead, the trickiest task was to keep the Campaign for Nuclear Disarmament people voting Labour. No one can dispute that both he and his successor James Callaghan achieved both objectives.

During that Defence Review, immediately after Wilson took office, my task was to brief the First Sea Lord, Admiral Sir Michael Pollock, on how work was progressing and particularly on the latest efforts of the other two Services to avoid the cuts at the Navy's expense. Sir Michael's Number Two, the Vice Chief of Naval Staff, then Vice Admiral Sir Terence Lewin, monitored most of my work on its way up. Eight years from then both of them would be taking a much keener interest in what I had to say – Sir Michael because his son was the Senior Pilot of 846 Squadron, the 'Junglies' who nightly flew the big Sea King 4 helicopters from *Hermes* into the Falkland Islands to 'insert' the Special Forces; and Sir Terence because by 1982 he was the Chief of Defence Staff and the man on whose professional military advice the Cabinet depended.

In the summer of 1974, I returned to the Submarine Service, journeying north with Char and the family once more to Faslane, on the Clyde. I was now Captain, Submarine Sea Training, with a staff of about 100 to help me train all submarines coming forward from 'refit' or 'new build' for service with the Fleet.

Put like that, it sounds simple enough. But the process of preparing a submarine, and her crew, for service in the front line is exhaustive, and usually exhausting, for crew and trainers alike. My job was, first, to set the standards of safety, behaviour and operational performance required, then to train the people to meet those standards and, finally, to examine them to ensure they had. I thus became both hatchet-faced inspector and smiling, helpful adviser who encouraged rather than drove. It was a completely new, demanding organization and I did not get many thanks from my 'clients'. Perhaps I smiled not enough and 'hatcheted' too much. The right balance is always difficult to strike and, if pressed, I tend to hatchet first and only get round to smiling if there's time later.

When I left in 1976, it was to take command of my first surface ship, the 4000-ton Type 42 guided-missile destroyer HMS *Sheffield* and she proved to be no great pleasure to me. Indeed she was a long saga of defects, difficulties and disappointments. She was in fact the first of a new class of anti-aircraft destroyers, quite a comfortable little ship, as such matters go. She was scheduled to finish her extensive programme of early trials within six months of my arrival. Then I would take her through Work-Up to join the Fleet as an operational unit in late 1977.

But it didn't happen like that. Her complicated new weapons computer program, delivered the week I joined, insisted on 'crashing' about every four minutes. It was as well we were not at war because although we could work the guns, or the anti-aircraft missile system – Sea Dart – or even the sonar separately, they could not be persuaded to work all at the same time. The new computer program was so bad I decided to go back to the old version, which had been discarded, and attempt to refine it. 'Sorry, sir, we didn't keep a copy, I'm afraid.' Not for the last time in *Sheffield* was I to groan with exasperation.

We went into dry dock for eight weeks, but new problems extended this to four months, and included a complete sand-blasting and repainting of the underhull. On top of this, *Sheffield* had been chosen to lead the Royal Yacht out to the Fleet Review at Spithead off Portsmouth, an extremely rare ceremonial occasion being staged as part of Her Majesty's Silver Jubilee celebrations. This was a considerable honour for the ship and her company of 250 men, and I was faced with a difficult decision. She would be ready only just in time, *if* all went well from about two months beforehand. But with her recent record I had a horrendous vision of breaking down in full view of the world at the Review. So, with the greatest reluctance, I asked that *Sheffield* be withdrawn. She was. And later, just out of cussedness, she proceeded to prove me wrong by twenty-four hours ... showing up from her refit bang on time, in good running order.

Our autumn trials, however, were fraught with further troubles. The rudders and the stabilizers were too noisy, and during the Naval Gunfire Support trials off Cape Wrath, we had a series of equipment breakages which left me with absolutely no confidence that the gun would work at all when it was needed. This was of course not an especially happy situation, should our very survival one day depend on being able to shoot it. We had to change both sets of gearing primary wheels in the engines, which was a mammoth job. The domestic boilers wouldn't boil. The evaporators wouldn't evaporate. The diesel generators preferred holidays. The sewage treatment plants wouldn't 'treat'. Even the white paint on the bulkheads went yellow, almost as you looked at it. Of my 406 days in command of *Sheffield*, I managed only ninety-six at sea, none of them operational.

I did my best with her, to bring her up to the condition needed to start her Work-Up, and I very much enjoyed the excellent people who formed her company. Nonetheless she was a grave disappointment in so many ways. However, she was decent enough to confirm one thing for me – that despite the massive investment in modern, partially automated systems (indeed because of them), in the end it is people that still count. Skill and experience remain at as great a premium as ever, as does good leadership and its natural reward, goodwill.

By January 1978, *Sheffield* was finally ready for her next phase of life, but it made best sense for me to hand over to a new captain who could take her on for the next eighteen months. I had run out of time and once more returned to join the London commuters. This time as the Director of Naval Plans, head of my old department at the MOD, directly above the granite breasts. Actually, it nearly didn't happen. Rear Admiral John Fieldhouse, who was Flag Officer, Submarines, wanted me to be his Chief of Staff and was very sure that this was a rare honour which could scarcely be refused.

When he asked me, I told him, 'I'd rather not, sir.'

'Why not?' As in 'Why on earth not – there can be no better job than this, working for him?'

'I'm not a volunteer for submarines. I never have been and I'm not now,' I said, thinking he'd know about the Plans job and would see the humour in such a remark from a man who had spent the best part of fifteen years in the submarine service. However, it soon became obvious that he didn't know about the Plans job and thought my comment most *un*funny. And he said so in no uncertain terms, starting a professional relationship which was never comfortable, but which, now that I look back, didn't seem to do either of us any great harm.

Anyway, I took my place as head of the Naval Staff's most fascinating Directorate. In broad terms I oversaw the work of the Assistant Director (Warfare), the AD (NATO) who dealt with all our Alliance business, the AD (Naval Future Policy) who looked thirty years ahead, the AD (Polaris) who dealt with all matters naval and nuclear, and the AD (Ships) who masterminded all the calculations of the cost, size, scope and capability that go to make a Fleet. I found myself laying out the entire range of policies and strategies for the Navy in the coming years – for the Navy Board to scrutinize, amend and eventually approve. The job of Director Plans had considerable prestige – one fourth of the directors make First Sea Lord. As such, it was an eagerly sought-after post among the high-flyers of the Navy, and I was very privileged to be retained in the position for three whole years, longer than any other man in the preceding half century.

My first boss was Admiral Sir Terence Lewin, who served as First Sea Lord from 1977 to 1979. I joined in the early summer of 1978 and together we observed the dying months of the Labour government. After less than one year they were gone and we waited quite eagerly to see whom Mrs Thatcher would name as her Defence Secretary, an appointment which would determine the intensity of our forthcoming period of self-examination. In the event, she named the old Etonian Francis Pym, a fresh-faced consummate politician who had served with distinction as a cavalry officer in the war and who proved perhaps too good a friend of the military, occupying the position until the Cabinet reshuffle.

However, during 1979 Sir Terence completed his tenure as First Sea Lord and turned over to the rather more austere Admiral Sir Henry Leach, who, at the age of twenty, had manned one of the guns on the battleship HMS *Duke of York* during the savage Boxing Night action off Norway's North Cape in 1943, during which they had finally battered and sunk the 31,000-ton German battle cruiser *Scharnhorst*. Sir Henry, himself the son of a Royal Navy captain, had married the daughter of the renowned Second World War commander, Admiral Sir Henry McCall. Admiral Leach was a gunnery officer who had commanded frigates and destroyers before achieving the top job by way of the Plans Directorate and command of the Fleet. His creed was simple: what's right for the Navy is right for Great Britain. He was a tremendous man to work for, and one of the best First Sea Lords this country has ever had. If he lacked a bit of guile in dealing with politicians, that would be no criticism; but he fought the Navy's corner tenaciously, and possessed the advantages of great charm and calm in adversity.

Without question, the most serious issue which faced all of the Service Chiefs during this period was Trident, the new strategic weapons system which made Polaris look like an up-market firework and which caused passions to run high in the House of Commons whenever opportunity offered. Trident was not cheap, but then no major project is. The question, as ever, was whether it represented value for money in comparison with other systems, conventional and nuclear. It was, and is, a staggeringly effective system, a deterrent to the strongest enemy in the world. Deployed in a submarine, it is invulnerable to any pre-emptive strike and carries up to 128 independently targeted warheads.

In 1979, the political battle lines had been clearly drawn. Michael Foot, the anti-nuclear pacifist leader of the Labour Party, wanted the entire thing to be put aside, as did most of his colleagues. Now Mrs Thatcher and her new Defence Secretary, the bespectacled banker and barrister Mr John Nott, supported the project from deep conviction. The real trouble for us, I guessed, would be the issue of money – from whose budget would the money come to pay for Trident? 'Not ours!' the Army Chiefs would cry. 'Certainly not ours!' the Air Force would yelp. And that would leave the Navy, the Service that would own it, to pay. Unless special arrangements were made to finance Trident separately from the rest of the Defence budget.

My own view was clear enough, not that they would ask a mere Director of the Naval Staff such as myself. But if I *had* been asked by the politicians whether or not I was for or against Trident, I would have sat on my hands and tried to look vague . . . a useful and under-rated talent in the Ministry. I realized that the Navy's vested interest would be obvious to all, but I would have contended that the Trident system, like Polaris, was a political lever and not a military weapons system. So my line would have been: the whole project is of no real interest to the Royal Navy *per se*. Trident is a national defence system, not a single Service requirement. Faced then with all *three* Services united against the awful prospect of having to pay for this system out of existing budgets, the Defence Secretary would be forced either to spread the costs evenly or to provide additional funds for the project. That would have been my drift. But such devious, even dishonest, tactics were not to be entertained and the 1981 Defence Review went very badly for the Royal Navy . . . Trident was taken into the Navy's budget and our cuts were twice those of the Army, seven times those of the RAF.

It was an emotional time in many ways and during the frequently acrimonious arguments, the Navy Minister Keith Speed lost his post, as had Christopher Mayhew back in 1966, over the decision to phase out the Navy's big aircraft carriers. The formal Defence debate, which was to last for two days in the Commons, opened on 19 May 1981. Mr Speed was quickly on his feet voicing his fears that decisions might be taken 'to impair seriously the effectiveness of the Royal Navy'. He expressed his profound unease that the Review might have 'damaging and lasting' effects upon the surface fleet. In the end, the Opposition's motion, that there should be defence cuts *and* that Trident should be scrapped, was defeated by 313 to 232.

But five weeks later John Nott stood before the House and read out his Statement on Defence which outlined his plans to lose the aircraft carriers *Hermes* and possibly *Invincible*; to phase out the amphibious force; to get rid of nine destroyers and frigates; to cut back between 8000 and 10,000 men, some 15 per cent of the work force; to close the Naval Dockyard at Chatham, home of our largest nuclear submarine refitting complex; to cut back 'severely' the work at Portsmouth Dockyard; and all this alongside further reductions in naval shore bases and establishments, stores and fuel depots.

I had in fact completed my time as Director of Plans a few days before the Parliamentary debate, but nonetheless I shared very much the alarm and distrust felt in naval circles at the time. These were huge changes, to be made in precipitously short order, and they added up to the sale of the carriers, *Hermes* to India and *Invincible* to Australia; it meant the early withdrawal from service of the 12,000-ton amphibious assault ships *Fearless* and *Intrepid*; and the end of two landing ships (Logistic), such as *Sir Galahad* or *Sir Tristram*. The additional reductions in frigates, destroyers and supporting personnel and facilities meant that the Royal Navy would be at its lowest ebb in a very long while. I am quite unable to describe how sad and upset we all were.

We had argued our best, but our arguments had not been listened to, because, however sound they may have been, they were certainly not convenient. John Nott possessed the cold heart of the career banker, and this was not offset by the cool brain of a military historian, much less any knowledge of things maritime. His military experience was confined to that of a lieutenant in the Gurkha Rifles in his twenties, some twenty-five years previously. It showed. The only admirals who would have supported him were Almirante Jorge Anaya and his colleagues. But they were not consulted.

With my departure from the Ministry I received a formal letter which read as follows: 'I am directed to inform you that

Her Majesty the Queen has been graciously pleased to approve your promotion to Rear Admiral, to date 7 July 1981 and your appointment to be Flag Officer, Submarines . . .' I was to relieve my old mentor Tubby Squires, but this was emphatically *not* the time to remind anyone else that I was still not a volunteer for submarines.

In the very best traditions of the Service, or perhaps for good reasons not revealed to me, my assignment was changed within weeks and I was re-appointed to be Flag Officer, First Flotilla, one of only three sea-going admirals in the Royal Navy. I was forty-nine.

My new headquarters were in Portsmouth Dockyard, in a beautiful Georgian terrace. My offices were on the ground floor, and I was also given a pleasant two-bedroomed flat on the floors above. I commuted back to Surbiton on most Friday nights.

One of three surface Flotillas in the Navy, mine was made up of twenty-two destroyers and frigates. For my Flagship, I had the choice of two 8000-ton guided missile destroyers of the 'County' Class, *Antrim* or *Glamorgan*, and I settled for the latter. She was heavily armed with both Seaslug and Seacat missile systems, a twin 4.5-inch gun and four Exocet launchers. Her Captain was an old friend of mine, Mike Barrow, who had joined the Navy on the same day as I and had become one of the two chief cadet captains (sort of joint head boys) at Dartmouth. He was from Hampshire, a veteran Royal Navy captain and an accomplished yachtsman. His father had been a captain too.

My new job required me to oversee the ships in my Flotilla, to ensure that each of them was being maintained at front-line standard in every respect. This entailed much travelling, from ship to ship, wherever they might be, handing out some stick, and some praise, as I deemed necessary. I was also required to prepare myself to act as the commander of a task group, whose composition might vary from two frigates and a tanker to the full panoply of an aircraft carrier with its large supporting cast. Our tasks could range from Arabian Sea patrol to a Third World War and being sent more or less anywhere on the globe. It was a very exciting prospect.

I went back to sea in the late summer, just for a short spell, but I was not scheduled to spend more than a few days at sea at a time until November when I was to join *Glamorgan* in the Mediterranean for one month. This would entail exercises with various navies – Greek, French, American, Omani – as we made our way out to the Persian Gulf to join what was called the Armilla Patrol.

My Staff and I flew to Italy, to the historic dockyard of Naples, and moved into *Glamorgan*. We sailed south, then east to Egypt and through the Suez Canal, for my first time. Another first for me was seeing the famous 'Gully-gully man' who produced dozens of day-old chicks from his copious clothing, but never a 'cheep' from any of them until they appeared in his hand or out of your ear – he charged the ship's company £80 for his performance, and kept the chicks.

We turned east up the Gulf of Aqaba for a short official visit to Jordan, and then sailed down the Red Sea, exercising with the French off Djibouti. Thereafter we proceeded to our rendezvous with the US carrier battle group out in the Arabian Sea, with the long hot coastline of Oman away to the west and the port of Karachi in Pakistan a few hundred miles to the north-east. The heart of the US battle group was their strike carrier USS *Coral Sea*. She carried some eighty aircraft, about double the capacity of a ship the size of *Hermes*. She was in fact a floating air force in her own right, under the command of Rear Admiral Tom Brown and, I'm obliged to say, his business in the area was of rather more consequence than mine.

The situation in the Gulf was very volatile at the time, with American hostages still being detained in the Middle East and Iran fighting a truly terrible war with neighbouring Iraq. Admiral Brown's eye was very much on the real world and its problems, and he was prepared for trouble in any form or to whatever degree it might occur. However, he had agreed to work with us for two or three days and was kind enough to let me plan and run the last two twenty-four-hour exercises.

I was clear in my mind what I wanted to practise: the US battle group, with all its escorts and aircraft, was to take up position well out to sea. Their job was to stop my force from getting through their guard to 'sink' their carrier before they 'sank' us. Admiral Brown was happy enough with that – if you had been in his position, you would have been too. He could spot an enemy surface ship more than two hundred miles away, track it at his leisure, and strike it at a comfortable range from himself with any six of his missile-launching attack aircraft. And that was only the first layer of his defence. By any modern military standards, he was well-nigh impregnable.

I had *Glamorgan* and three frigates, plus three Royal Fleet Auxiliary ships, two of which were tankers and the third, a stores ship. The frigates were all anti-submarine ships and not capable of doing serious harm to an aircraft carrier, short of ramming it. Only *Glamorgan*, with her four Exocets and effective range of twenty miles, could inflict real damage on the *Coral Sea*, and Admiral Brown knew this. Thus my flagship was the only threat to him; his only real target.

We were due to start not a moment before 12 noon and

not a mile less than two hundred from the American carrier. She sat in the middle of this vast stretch of clear blue water, under clear blue skies – effective visibility: two hundred and fifty miles. Admiral Brown was, so to speak, at the centre of a well-defended exclusion zone and I did not even have the benefit of a cloud bank, let alone fog or rain or heavy seas. No cover. No hiding place. No air support of my own either.

I ordered my ships to split up and take position all around the two-hundred-mile perimeter by 1200 and then to hurry in as best they could – a sort of maritime Charge of the Light Brigade from all directions. Three-quarters of an hour before we were due to start, bless my soul if a US fighter didn't appear, spot us, identify us and hurry off home to tell the boss what he had found, where it was and where it was going. We couldn't 'shoot it down' – the exercise had not yet begun! But we may just have lost this one before the starting gates were open. Stand by for a decisive American air strike against *Glamorgan*, just as soon as they can lay it on.

However, you have to keep on trying and we had nothing left to do but give it our best shot. This basically involved reversing course eastwards and racing around the two-hundred-mile circle, the other way, as fast as we could go. Three hours later, we heard the US strike aircraft go in about a hundred miles to the west of us. They found nothing and went home. Nevertheless, as the day wore on, they picked off my ships steadily. Except for one: they failed to find *Glamorgan* again, the only ship they really *had* to stop, the only one who could sink the carrier. We were on the loose, and they could not find us.

Finally the Americans 'struck' my last frigate and, as the sun set over the Arabian Sea and night began to stream in, *Glamorgan* turned into the two-hundred-mile zone. The dusk faded to darkness and I ordered every light in the ship to be switched on, plus as many extras as we could find. I intended that from any distance we would look exactly like a cruise liner – from the bridge we looked like a floating Christmas tree.

We barrelled on through the tense night, in towards the USS *Coral Sea*, listening all the time to the International Voice radio frequencies. Sure enough, eventually one of the American destroyer captains came on to the line, asking us to identify ourselves. My in-house Peter Sellers imitator, already primed for the job, replied in his very best Anglo-Indian: 'This is the liner *Rawalpindi*, bound from Bombay to the port of Dubai. Good Night, and jolly good luck!' He sounded like the head waiter from the Surbiton tandoori. But it was good enough. The Americans, who were conducting a 'limited war', were rather obliged to believe us and let us through while they thought about it. Vital minutes slipped by until we were exactly eleven miles from the carrier, with our Exocet system locked on to her. They still thought our splendid display of lights was the *Rawalpindi* on her innocent business.

Doubt, however, began to enter their minds. And the signs of confusion were revealed when the carrier's escorts got over-excited and two of their big destroyers managed to 'open fire' on each other, over our heads. We could hear the glorious uproar on the radios. Then one of my officers calmly called the carrier to break the appalling news to Tom Brown that we were now in a position to put his ship on the bottom of the Indian Ocean and there was nothing he could do about it. 'We fired four Exocets twenty seconds ago,' he added for good measure, knowing this gave them about forty-five seconds to hit the deck ... about half as much notice as *Sheffield* would receive, six months from now.

The *Coral Sea* was given no time to get her chaff up – and

the American knew as well as we did that he was effectively non-operational. He had lost his 'mission critical' unit and with it his air force.

Understandably, we were all elated, but also a little embarrassed by this at first. We did, however, realize that Tom Brown had a serious and proper preoccupation with the real world, and that our own particular brand of carefree 'cheekiness' was undoubtedly born of the unarguable fact that we knew that we weren't really going to be sunk whatever happened, were we? A debriefing along these lines very soon restored a sense of proportion, and with it a calm assessment of what could usefully be learned. It was nonetheless an important exercise for me because it taught me two vital lessons. The first was to beware of becoming over-engrossed in one area of operations at the risk of ignoring another. The second was that, in a limited war, in perfect weather, under the cover of darkness, one fairly old destroyer or cruiser, or whatever, *is* capable of getting right up to within eleven miles of a modern strike carrier in a full battle group. We had just done so from over two hundred miles away even in the face of Airborne Early Warning Aircraft up over the top and an armada of strike aircraft against us. We had proved that it could be done.

Therefore, reads the moral of this tale, take caution should you ever find yourself as a battle group commander in these circumstances, because it is fairly likely that in *bad* weather, you would lose the battle. This is especially true against a really determined attack in which the enemy is prepared to lose several ships in order to sink your carrier – which he should *always* be, because when the carrier goes your air force and very likely your entire campaign go with it. Six months on, I was going to face a similar sort of situation, this time for real. And, thanks to these few hours with the *Coral Sea*, I would have a clearer idea of how to proceed.

The second of our exercises with the Americans was also fortuitous in its concept. I wrote a scenario for a local, limited war between two relatively minor powers each of which was sponsored by one of the Superpowers, the USSR or the USA. The idea was to demonstrate how neither of the major powers need be drawn in and that the two minor powers could be left to fight it out. Remember this was in the time of the Cold War, with President Reagan just embarking on the process of rebuilding the giant American military arsenal. I ought to state again, my American friends were not playing it quite as seriously as I was, and they rapidly escalated matters to a 'Let's start World War Three' level.

Understandably they wiped out *Glamorgan* at an early stage this time, which was fair enough. No doubt we were still the least of Tom Brown's problems, but for my part I was interested, for some near-providential reason, in examining how to use exclusion zones to the best advantage. This also covered the intricacies of Rules of Engagement during those most difficult times when you may be moving from apparent peace to obvious war. Just about everything I achieved, every lesson I learned in those forty-eight hours, had a direct and critical influence on my actions six months later in the South Atlantic in a war I could not possibly have foreseen. I now had a good idea how to operate in three of the most relevant areas – I had observed some of the difficulties of defending a carrier; I knew the military snags and advantages of exclusion zones; and I was also well aware of how carefully you must study the ramifications of your Rules of Engagement, remembering they have been drawn up jointly by both politicians and the military. This was exactly and precisely the knowledge I would need the following spring.

I have often reflected what an astounding bit of luck this was. When I took those precepts away for myself I never realized I would ever need them. One of them was cast plainly in my mind – that if an enemy is skirting his way around you along the edge of an exclusion zone, there is no way you should allow him to go on doing that. He must not be able to choose where and when he is going to come at you, just because he is a few miles outside the zone.

With the exercises concluded, we then headed inshore towards Oman where Captain Mike Barrow suffered a major piece of misfortune. On leaving the Bay of Bandar Jissah he caught his extremely expensive propellers on a chunk of rock. Generally speaking, this is regarded as rather dull news since in the Royal Navy it can be a Court Martial offence, with a potential charge of negligence, or even gross negligence. And, if the case is proven, it can be a career killer.

In this case, the rock had not been charted, but nonetheless the Board of Enquiry would want to know the full facts of the matter and whether Captain Barrow or his Navigation Officer Lieutenant-Commander Inskip were in any way to blame. Meanwhile I flew home, as planned, feeling rather bad about leaving them in such a state. *Glamorgan*'s divers cropped and filed her propellers to make the blades even and, as there was no dry dock available locally, she was ordered home for proper repairs. Limited to twelve knots to reduce the chance of damage to her gearbox, she made her slow passage home to arrive shortly before Christmas. But the threat of Court Martial was to hang over Mike's head for several months before the Commander in Chief finally decided not to proceed.

While Mike struggled to get my flagship back to Portsmouth, I returned to my office to compile my report on my activities. I noted, with only passing interest, a few days after my return, that General Leopoldo Galtieri had succeeded to the Presidency of Argentina, but the paper I read did not record that he had announced to wild nationalistic applause that 1982 would be 'The Year of the Malvinas'. Neither did it mention that the zealous and slightly sinister Admiral Jorge Anaya had agreed to support the new regime *only* if the General committed himself to the recapture of the islands from the British. They intended to execute this military *coup de main* sometime between July and October of the year, for reasons still unknown to me in detail. It was likely, however, that they had surmised that certain factors would be in their favour by July: Britain's Fleet would be seriously weakened by then; our lone patrol ship down south HMS *Endurance* would have finally gone home, at the onset of winter, to scrap; and anyway, the Royal Navy would be most unlikely to tackle the worst of the winter in the South Atlantic with a force large enough to remove Argentina from her 'rightful' territories. Above all, there was every indication that, by then, we would probably have no operational aircraft carriers, with *Hermes* and *Invincible* both victims of Mr John Nott's Defence cuts. As far as Galtieri and Anaya were concerned the situation was now simple: no British carriers means no air cover, no air cover means no British surface ships, no surface ships means no British landing force, no landing force means 'No Contest'. Their reasoning was perfect. Their timing? That was the make or break factor.

But all of that had nothing to do with me. My operations were conducted at a lower level and as the new year proceeded I was making plans for the major exercise we hold most years, called 'Springtrain'. This is an opportunity towards the end of winter, in March and April, to get a decent number of ships away, and mostly involves destroyers and frigates, though sometimes submarines (the 'loyal opposition') and the occasional aircraft carrier join in. We take them all down to Gibraltar, where the weather is so much better, and we get rid of the ice and gloom of the English and Scottish winter and work them all up once more to full Fleet readiness. Altogether about twenty to twenty-five ships take part in Springtrain and the plan is always to have a week in Gibraltar, play a lot of games between the ships, such as football, stage the Top of the Rock Run and generally have a morale-boosting jolly, culminating in a spectacular concert by the Band of the Royal Marines in the Upper Caves. This is a traditional occasion, and one to which officers and ratings alike greatly look forward.

We set sail in mid-March and exercised our way down to the Med, testing fairly basic abilities in anti-submarine, anti-air and surface-to-surface warfare over a period of ten days. As usual, this woke everybody up and, as the journey progressed, the gunnery became more accurate, the missile systems more efficient, the computer systems better used, the machinery settled and the people worked more smoothly. It was all designed to prepare us for the more advanced Tactical Exercises in the Atlantic after our week 'off'.

For these exercises we carve up the eastern Atlantic into vast boxes and bring large groups of ships together, simulating battle conditions as closely as we can. Every aspect of the mock war has an important role, teaching people to operate as a battle group, training them to work with perhaps ten other ships, with all the complex communications systems which are involved. They must also be trained to work with submarines and aircraft, and it is, by any standards, extremely complicated, requiring a great deal of time and patience. The standards required are high because errors in war are apt to be both unpleasant and expensive, and we prefer to eliminate them by means of exercises.

My Flagship for Springtrain of 1982 was HMS *Antrim*, a sister guided-missile destroyer to *Glamorgan*. This change was required by the forthcoming arrival of the Commander-in-Chief, Fleet, Admiral Sir John Fieldhouse, the ex-submariner who did not always share my personal sense of humour. For his visit to the exercise, he would take *Glamorgan* as his Flagship, while I moved into Captain Brian Young's *Antrim*, from where I would conduct the day-to-day running of the major exercises after we left Gibraltar.

Our last night on the Rock, a Sunday, was quite magical. There in the Upper Caves the pageant scarlet, blue and gold colours of the uniforms, the topical and patriotic music, all combined to produce a traditional and vivid reminder of the old days when Britannia really did rule the waves. I am not much of a one for tradition, but this sort of occasion can be very moving, and perhaps seems unusually so in hindsight, in view of what was so shortly to come. Those few days in Gibraltar seemed to stand for all the good things of naval life in peacetime.

Monday morning dawned bleakly. The Levanter, that nasty, gusty, easterly wind with its sweeping grey rain, was upon us and we sailed out into short choppy seas to begin the exercises to the east and west of the Rock. It is sometimes surprising how isolated you can become in a ship despite the masses of modern communications at your disposal. For instance, as we concentrated on our daily business I had no idea that Argentina was mobilizing her troops for the invasion of the Falklands, or that two of her frigates *Drummond* and *Granville* were heading to South Georgia where Royal Marine Lieutenant Keith Mills was already 'entrenched' with twenty-two men.

Endurance was standing by, preparing to remove the Argentinian scrap metal dealers who had had the temerity to hoist their country's flag on British soil. I did know that the situation in the South Atlantic was not good and that, as had occurred so often before, the Argentinians were threatening to land in the Falklands. Indeed, the Royal Fleet Auxiliary ship *Fort Austin* had been ordered south on 26 March. In hindsight at least, this was Britain's first major move, and the first to affect directly my own command.

We had a busy time that morning getting all the Springtrain ships away to their appointed tasks in good order, and I received a short blast from my Commander-in-Chief for 'allowing dangerous manoeuvring in the Straits', meaning that Admiral Fieldhouse thought that my departure plan was roughly on a par with his assessment of my sense of humour. It seemed important at the time. The submarines *Spartan* and *Oracle* had been withdrawn from Springtrain, but that afternoon were ordered to return to Gibraltar. Warshot torpedoes were loaded from *Oracle* to *Spartan* and the latter made ready to sail. At seven o'clock that evening I flew over to *Glamorgan* for discussions with my C-in-C. He briefed me on the deteriorating situation in the South Atlantic and we agreed on the best way forward for the present exercise. He touched on the possibility of placing a more experienced 'Three Star' vice admiral in command of any task force which might be ordered south. I have since been told, however, that Fieldhouse was quite determined I should stay in command from the very start and his words were merely to keep me on my toes – perhaps to test *my* sense of humour.

I returned to *Antrim* at 2130 and assembled my staff to prepare orders for a Short Notice Operational Readiness Check. This was a standard exercise procedure used by flag officers to test the ability of ships to deal with unusual events, in very short order. I told them we required to prepare five or six ships to go south, fully prepared for war. The cover story was to be that they were headed for the Far East, via the Cape, sailing on 1 April from the Gibraltar areas. The first signal went out at 2300, requiring all Springtrain ships to make a full report of their readiness for war.

At 0630 the following morning, shortly before first light, Admiral Fieldhouse was landed at Gibraltar and flown immediately back to the UK. We got on with our many exercises and HMS *Sheffield*, which had joined us from a three-month tour of duty in the Gulf, was particularly sharp, hitting her missile target with a perfectly executed Sea Dart shot first time.

Reports on the political situation continued to arrive on board *Antrim*, but they did not betray the urgency that was gripping the House of Commons, the Ministry of Defence and indeed the Prime Minister herself. Back in the Falklands, *Endurance* was ordered to leave the Royal Marines on South Georgia and make all speed back to Port Stanley where an invasion by the Argentinians now seemed probable. In Whitehall, the Defence Secretary was being briefed – in fact in his room in the House of Commons. The general thrust was that any defence of the Falklands was 'impossible' for all of the obvious reasons: we could not get down there in time and anyway, once down there, what then? There would be no place for modern jet aircraft to land, nowhere for them to be refuelled or rearmed, to be maintained or repaired – a situation not in any way helped by the fact that the recipient of this information, John Nott, was in the process of selling the only two operational aircraft carriers we possessed.

The official view of the Chiefs of Staff was based on that document last reviewed in 1974, when I was an Assistant

Director in Naval Plans, and recently re-affirmed. All of the above was as true now as it was then – defence against an Argentinian invasion *was* impossible. And retaking the islands was not possible either: the two dozen or so operational, fixed-wing, carrier-borne aircraft we then had were the Sea Harriers – a very limited capability 'fighter', subsonic, single-seat and capable of visual interceptions in daylight only. It was in squadron service with 800 Naval Air Squadron as such and under development by a separate small group called the Intensive Flying Trials Unit (IFTU) under Lieutenant Commander 'Sharkey' Ward. Pitted against a land-based air force of some 200 front-line aircraft, they seemed to stand no chance of achieving an acceptable air situation over a landing force for more than a very short period. So 'live with the accomplished fact' had to be the conclusion and the working hypothesis. But history tends to be dominated by people, not paper. In the MOD in 1982 we had for a First Sea Lord a man with naval warfare in his blood, who would be the first to see that the Navy was not impotent, that while defence was bound to be too late, the islands could be recovered by an amphibious operation which was not just desirable, but essential. His name, of course, was Sir Henry Leach.

Late on that Wednesday evening, in uniform, he entered the foyer of the House of Commons in search of his Defence Secretary. The policeman on duty remained unimpressed and asked him to sit and wait. An official from the Whips' Office finally caught sight of the professional head of the Royal Navy sitting waiting like some tradesman and asked him into his office for a whisky and soda while they sent out to find John Nott. He was eventually found in conference with the Prime Minister.

As soon as Mrs Thatcher knew Sir Henry Leach was

immediately available she had him sent up to her office and there, in a meeting which was to last several hours, the Admiral convinced her that, if necessary, the Royal Navy could mount a large-scale operation to retake the Falkland Islands. He could, he assured her, drive the Argentinian Fleet from the high seas, survive the worst efforts of the two hundred front-line attack aircraft of the Argentinian Air Force, and put a sufficient land force ashore and support it long enough to defeat any Argentinian Army garrison.

Above them, Big Ben had long since struck midnight when Margaret Thatcher said, with an air of finality: 'First Sea Lord – what precisely is it that you want?'

'Prime Minister, I would like your authority to form a Task Force, which would, if you so required, be ready to sail for the South Atlantic at a moment's notice.'

'You have it,' she replied.

John Nott, I am reliably informed, went white as Sir Henry thanked her tersely, took his leave and strode out into the night. I have little doubt that the Secretary of State for Defence realized he had lost more than one battle in that room that night. It must have been all too clear to him that Sir Henry had seized the opportunity to expose the folly of the massive cuts in the strength of the Royal Navy.

But I was far removed from all this. We, off Gibraltar, were hearing little of what was going on. We had no feeling for the possible scale of the operation – and warlike attitudes had not started to develop. We did not even have charts of the Falklands on board the Flagship. Indeed the last comment in the exercise narrative for the 1 April said only '. . . continued unease over South Georgia and Falklands Islands situation'.

In the small hours of Friday 2 April there was, however, a complete change of tempo. The carriers *Hermes* and *Invincible* were ordered to four hours' notice, as was *Fearless* the amphibious assault ship, the frigates *Alacrity* and *Antelope*, and the RFA *Resource*. At 0300 I received the signal ordering Operation 'Corporate', the code name for everything that was to follow, from the Commander-in-Chief. This was the official starting point for us all and I was appointed commnader of all the task groups heading south.

Well before dawn, *Antrim*'s group set course to join up with *Glamorgan*'s. By first light, I had issued a directive on the transfer of stores from the ships that were going home, to those which were now under orders to go south. The home-goers 'topped-up' the south-goers in enthusiastic frenzy, delivering their stores by helicopter, by boat, by jackstay and by hose-line. It was a fantastic job, with high-explosive shells coming across in bags and buckets safely enough, but definitely not in accordance with strict peacetime safety regulations. Everyone was responding with a new sense of urgency. Fleet Staff back in Northwood suddenly found an overdrive no one ever dreamed it possessed: equipment which would otherwise have taken weeks to appear, was now being fired in our direction almost faster than we could find somewhere to park it. By 0935 *Plymouth* had been ordered to close the Rock to pick up the charts of the Falklands which seemed to have arrived by some kind of miracle. The work continued furiously.

At 2130 that evening, we received a signal from the Commander-in-Chief: 'Argentina has invaded the Falkland Islands.' My own mood was equivocal and, though obviously busy, I found time to write in my diary:

> Another day, another place, in April '82. I have been
> a Flag Officer for ten months and am bored with it.
> Too much strutting about, flags flying, ice tinkling,

forks flashing and idle chatter. I hate it all, and thought I'd rather have some real action. So the Argentinians obligingly invade the Falklands, and I wish I'd never had the thought ... Off we go – my good fortune, if good is the word, to be at Gibraltar with the Springtrain forces – the Flag Officer closest to the front line (still some 6000 miles away), so I'm in charge. This could be a loose phrase for 'I'm up front, with everyone else behind in charge'. Not too bad though, and I must say the Fleet Staff have finally come good.

While all this went on, I was more conscious of our need for accurate intelligence concerning Argentinian naval and air strength. What I did know was that they had surface, under-water and air capability and that their fleet was substantial. Quite apart from their aircraft carrier and her strike aircraft, there was the cruiser *General Belgrano*, there were two Type 42 destroyers, six ships fitted with Exocet sea-skimming missiles, and four submarines, two of which were quiet and small enough to be difficult to catch with our sonars. For our part, we had three nuclear-powered submarines on their way south, *Spartan* from Gibraltar, and *Conqueror* and *Splendid* now having cleared Faslane.

As the day wore on, the home-going ships turned north one by one – *Engadine*, *Blue Rover*, *Euryalus*, *Aurora* and *Dido*. As they went, their crews stood on deck, waving and cheering us on our way. I found it very touching and noticed our decks were silent and still for a few moments after they had gone, leaving us, perhaps to fight a war, without them. It was 0200 before the last ship turned north for home, but there was no time to waste and the mad scramble to stow everything away properly began again as we set off down the Atlantic.

We had been told to make passage south covertly, to the tiny island of Ascension, which was to be our forward base for Operation Corporate. So we split up and made our separate, rather furtive ways past Madeira – *Glamorgan* commanded by Captain Mike Barrow, *Antrim* Captain Brian Young, *Brilliant* Captain John Coward, *Glasgow* Captain Paul Hoddinott, *Plymouth* Captain David Pentreath, *Arrow* Commander Paul Bootherstone, and of course the Type 42 guided-missile destroyers of Captain Sam Salt and Captain David Hart-Dyke, *Sheffield* and *Coventry*, neither of which would ever dock in Britain again.

Midshipman Woodward, at 19, Senior Midshipman of the cruiser, the first HMS *Sheffield*, dumbstruck in front of the late Duchess of Kent.

HMS *Sanguine* off Malta in 1954. I ended up as her third hand, the navigator, under the future Admiral Gordon Tait.

Wedding Day, 9 April 1960 – Char and I are married at Wetheral, near Carlisle. Two of my mentors 'Tubby' Squire (*left*) and Brian Hutchings at this end of the wedding arch.

HMS *Warspite* coming into Cardiff docks, 1969. My first nuclear command.

I greet Lord Carrington as he steps aboard *Warspite* at Faslane, Scotland, in 1969.

An old Navy ceremony – the captain leaving his ship for the last time is often rowed ashore by his officers. The picture shows me leaving the submarine *Warspite* in 1970. The oarsman in the bow (*left*) is Chris Wreford-Brown, future Captain of HMS *Conqueror*.

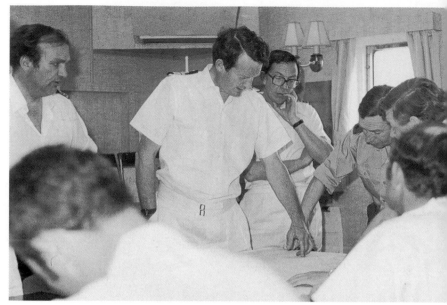

With my staff on HMS *Glamorgan* in the Flag Operations Room, converted from my sitting room, on the way to Ascension. At my right hand is Commander Jeremy Sanders, my Staff Officer Operations.

Ascension Island, our forward base far off the coast of West Africa, was our last sight of land before we set off on our journey to the cold south. That's my Flagship, HMS *Hermes*, at anchor in the foreground.

ASCENSION

4

South to Ascension

We pushed out into the deep waters off the north-west coast of Africa, beyond the Canary Islands. The weather brightened up and the squally clouds gave way to the azure skies which can make the Atlantic seem so deceptively harmless. With the Western Sahara two hundred miles away to port, we kept heading south, all the ships in my little group frantically busy, still sorting out the piles of stores, putting them into some kind of order. Beyond our narrow horizons it was clear from the occasional political reports that the situation between Buenos Aires and London was not improving and that, despite the intense efforts of the world's diplomats, General Galtieri had no immediate plans to evacuate 'his' Malvinas.

The general impression given from Headquarters was that we would gather the entire force at Ascension and then proceed south together as soon as possible to do whatever might seem necessary – a good deal less than specific and simply summed up in the phrase 'Hurry south with everything you've got.' I assumed a firmer plan would emerge as a result of our pending meeting at Ascension. Meanwhile, we should work on this basis as the rough guide and in normal practice, it followed that the combined groups would remain under my tactical command for that stage. None of us had anything much more specific except for the Amphibious Group who would have to prepare themselves for a landing, somewhere, sometime.

My own situation became if anything more isolated as I worked on the formation of what must become a Battle Group, prepared to fight, at short notice but only if necessary, a real war. We began work-up training between pairs of ships, forming Surface Action Groups since it seemed sensible to assume the Argentinians would at some point cause their own fleet to face us in battle on the high seas. I have to say that I found it hard to accept the reality of such a confrontation and I hoped that in preparing carefully for such an eventuality, it would prove unnecessary. However, I was keenly aware that it was almost impossible to predict the nature of such a war, so we went on doing all that we could with the very limited means available at that stage.

On Sunday morning, 4 April, I shifted my Flag back to the more comfortable quarters of *Glamorgan*, familiar surroundings in which we had once hilariously practised our Indian accents to ruin Tom Brown's day. We were involved in more serious business now, and I was sure she would be a better Flagship than *Antrim* for several reasons, one of them being her communications systems.

My staff spent the morning ferrying to and fro with all the cabinets and paperwork. I joined them at midday and we now set about all of the minor preparations for war – painting out bright colours on both ships and aircraft, stripping out soft furnishings and Formica panelling. As in the days of Nelson, a major danger to sailors in battle remains that of flying splinters and they are no less sharp and lethal when made of metal or plastic blown into shards by a missile than when they were made of oak or teak and blasted into the gun-decks by cannon balls. We also recommended, with insufficient conviction for some, that all ships land their silverware and trophies, not because there is any great danger of death by flying soccer cup but because some are irreplaceable and all are uninsurable in war. *Coventry* complied, with one small exception. On board, always prominently displayed, was a mediaeval cross of three large nails, mounted on a wooden plinth. They had been removed from the old Cathedral of Coventry and presented by the city to the ship that bore her name. One young and rather anxious petty officer requested that Captain Hart-Dyke leave the cross in place as it was a symbol of hope and survival for many of the crew. Captain Hart-Dyke correctly agreed it should stay in place. Morale in a front-line picket is paramount.

On Monday 5 April, the carriers *Hermes* and *Invincible* sailed from Portsmouth. I had received a signal from headquarters as to a probable rendezvous somewhere north of Ascension Island. We were all making the best speed we could, intending to use any spare days on arrival at Ascension for maintenance or training. Meanwhile I called a staff meeting and spent the afternoon trying to formulate a plan as to precisely how we should proceed south and what we would do if and when we reached the Falkland Islands. By this I mean the scheduling of such basics as, for instance, what kind of formation do we need for protection of the Amphibious Group in company? From which direction should we approach which part of the

Falklands? What and where are the possible landing sites? Where are the Argentinians least likely to be? Where and how should we deploy our Special Forces for reconnaissance? How can we stop them using their main airfield at Port Stanley? Where are they likely to have stationed their submarines? How many mines could they have laid, and where would be most likely? What kind of approach tactics will their aircraft use, and how do we counter them best? All of these questions may seem very pedestrian – they are certainly obvious and easy enough to ask – but they are not at all comfortable when you have none of the answers. And there were plenty more such questions as well.

Thus our meeting was conducted in an atmosphere of moderate disbelief, combined with a mounting realization of our very considerable ignorance. Our Intelligence had never been targeted on Argentina and, since the Falklands had never been thought a likely battleground, and our knowledge of the seas around was absolutely minimal. I had still not had access to a routine topographical study of the islands. I knew nothing of the weather patterns or underwater acoustic conditions. I had scarcely had time to look at the new charts. We really knew nothing of the detail of the enemy we might be asked to attack, nor of the surroundings in which we might find him. Our knowledge was in fact largely confined to that which was in the public domain. *Jane's Fighting Ships*, the standard reference book on the fleets of the world, was our main source of information on the strength of Admiral Anaya's navy. Jane's companion book on the world's fighting aircraft was our main source of information on their air force, plus, of course, whatever we could find out from various attachés around the world. But right now it was not coming back in any discernible form – it was simply too early for us to make much of an estimate of the opposing 'Order of Battle', too early to establish precisely what we were dealing with and therefore also a good deal too early to be planning with any precision how to deal with it.

From a simple count of opposing air, land and seas forces we doubted whether we could afford to go at him 'head on'. It is rarely much of an idea anyway, but when you are in a big hurry, as we were likely to be in order to beat the onset of winter, it might be the only way. As it was, we still did not know the size of the force General Galtieri had put on the Falkland Islands, how heavily, or how well, it was armed, and how readily it would be prepared at least to defend its own position or, indeed, attack ours when, and if, we landed. The fact was we were nowhere near to completing our own picture of what to do when battle commenced. In general, as the MOD had originally advised John Nott, the prognosis was poor. Apart from the very substantial Argentinian air threat, it also seemed quite possible that we could be outnumbered ashore. And lacking an 'amphibious assault' capability, long since whittled away in serial Defence cuts, a frontal assault, which requires a substantial military advantage, would be a non-starter. The initial reconnaissance was becoming critical to our mission – we simply had to get some Special Forces in there to find out what was going on ashore.

At the conclusion of the meeting I was left with much to think about. The need to become familiar with the vast picture of a whole potential theatre of war was pressing, consciously and unconsciously. But all those years of training were setting off bright little lights in my mind. If we had to fight, I was as ready as could be expected. I had acquired a mind-set that accepted war as a real possibility and now, faced with it, I found no great sense of transformation. I had been trained to believe that one day I might be required to face a live battle and the feeling of reality that was slowly coming upon me was neither new, nor excessively troublesome. Just something that was a part of the job and a job in which I would not be short of all the necessary expert advice, readily to hand. I would have liked the chance to have said goodbye to Char and our grown-up children, Andrew and Tessa, though it would have been both distracting and melodramatic, I guess. But it's too late to worry about that, they are safe enough at home, prey only to the assaults of the media.

I am not alone out here, but soon there will be all about me thousands of men and dozens of ships. The CTF has given me the frontline job of leading them into the fight. He may relieve me with a vice admiral, but meanwhile I am conscious of my present responsibility, conscious too that I must not let them down; conscious finally that I must not allow those concerns to limit my initiative.

On the following day, 6 April, I made my plans to begin my talks to each individual ship's company. The big Admiral's Day Cabin in *Glamorgan* was now converted into the Admiral's Operations Staff Office, and I think that in there, on that day, faced with the increasingly familiar charts, tables, signals, plans and telephones I began my own serious 'transition to war' process. Various ideas and procedures began to come off the staff production line, and that night I wrote in my diary a little reminder, resolving to ask myself more frequently the question: 'What is it today that I will wish tomorrow I had done yesterday?'

The two carriers, carrying as many Sea Harriers and Sea King helicopters as they could get on board, were now making their way south towards us with as much speed as possible – though

Invincible was initially limited to fifteen knots owing to a damaged gear box. On the morning of 7 April I visited *Brilliant* and *Arrow*, and in the afternoon I flew across to *Glasgow* and *Sheffield*. My message to all of them was identical. I told them that we may be going to war, and that they should prepare for it both mentally and physically. I warned them, starkly, that there was a distinct possibility that we would lose ships, and that some of us may be killed in action. I decided that there was absolutely no point in being soft about this, whatever my personal feelings.

'Up until now', I said, 'you have seen fit to take the Queen's shilling. Now you must stand by to front up and earn it the hard way.' I told them there was no possibility of anyone being allowed to opt out now, that this was actually what you joined the Navy for, whether you knew it or not. It's too late to change your mind, so best face up to it. The British sailor has a phrase for it, well known to all: 'You shouldn't have joined if you can't take a joke.'

All contracts were automatically extended, 'for the duration', by the Ministry of Defence, so there was no hope for anyone of avoiding the conflict, and I told them that the best route to survival was to buckle to, learn fast and try harder. The timescale for the forthcoming engagement was, in my view, 'indefinite'. I also outlined our preliminary estimates of the forces we would face, and I went through a routine 'threat reduction' exercise with all of them. 'The Args', I said, 'have nine destroyers and three frigates. We may assume that three of these are out of action, refitting or whatever. Two of them are so old they are probably unseaworthy, and certainly not battleworthy. One of them ran aground in the River Plate a month ago and probably hasn't been mended yet, and that means we will outnumber them in a sea battle by about four to one. And if we cannot handle that then I don't know what any of us have been doing for the last several years.'

Those were the sort of words I used in addressing each of the ships. Their main purpose was to avoid frightening people unnecessarily, and my speeches represented the first step on our psychological build-up to convince everyone that defeat is unlikely provided we all do our utmost. Winners must only dream of victory. We had to go in there sure that we were the best and that we would, in the end, win. At heart, however, the British seaman has been, down the centuries, a pretty straight realist. The only question that was asked in *every* ship I visited was: 'Could you tell us what the rate of Local Overseas Allowance will be, sir?' Or, put another way, 'How much extra are we going to be earning on this little jaunt?'

Shortly after 1330 we received a signal from Northwood ordering one of my fuel tankers, in company with *Antrim* and *Plymouth*, to detach from my group and to proceed south to Ascension Island with all speed. This was the start of the South Georgia operation, important to undertake but adding difficulty for me in trying to bring my ships together for work-up as a coherent group, before the carriers and the amphibians came up to make it all a great deal more complicated. By the end of the afternoon I had completed my talk on board *Sheffield* and returned to *Glamorgan* absolutely whacked. I think my exhausted condition was due largely to the mental strain of coping with personal anxieties at the same time as trying to reassure and strengthen others. I fear I did not do a very good job. Months later, one man from the *Coventry* came up to me and said, 'I remember that day, sir. You knew we were going to be sunk, didn't you?' I must have overdone the realism.

At 2130, shortly after supper, the final message of the day

came through from Fleet Headquarters, Northwood. The United Kingdom had announced an Exclusion Zone around the Falkland Islands, effective from 0400z on 12 April, a little over four days time from now. For me at least, that was something of a bench mark. I think I knew as we headed on across the Sierra Leone Basin, that this war was going to be fought. And exclusion zones were things I had already thought about.

I wrote in my diary that night, and my words betray my own focus on events becoming sharper, perhaps more realistic:

> Of course, there's no way the Falklands are worth a war, whether we win it or not – equally there's no way you should let the Argentinians (or anyone else for that matter) get away with international robbery. It's the 'If not here, then where?' bit all over again. And anyway, they're in no condition to go to war either.
>
> Thus the message to impart (and we must not lose our cool in the process, particularly when the bullets start to fly) is: 'We are entirely prepared to fight over this issue – are you, on balance, prepared to fight us?' If rational, I believe they may well decide they aren't, though they must be thinking the same about us.
>
> Their reply, being in the stronger position on the escalation scale temporarily (possession *is* nine points of the law), has to be: 'Prove it!'

At 0600 the following morning we picked up the BBC World Service which informed us that the Argentinians had responded to the British Exclusion Zone with one of their own – two hundred miles out from the mainland and two hundred miles out from the Falklands coastline. It was impossible now to miss the confrontational nature of the lethal game the two sets of politicians were playing. I realized that, though it was none of my business, none of them were likely to find themselves in the path of an oncoming missile either, as, perhaps, we were.

My diary states that much of the day's activities were involved in complicated, but to those not directly concerned at least, rather mundane, matters such as the immediate future of the (Hong Kong) Chinese laundrymen, the continued employment of civilians in the NAAFI, their South Atlantic pay scales, their legal status, and right to go home, their insurance and indemnities. I mention them in passing because, while they are all dealt with automatically when the Navy officially goes to war, the fact that we never 'declared war' in 1982 left all of these people out on a limb. Their status and terms of employment had to be decided in a hurry. We were also told, formally, that Ascension Island, which is British, yet principally leased to the Americans as a big satellite tracking station, was open for business. The small 1000-yard single runway the Americans had built was now available to the Royal Air Force and the Royal Navy.

We pushed on towards the equator and the weather grew hotter and more humid. We had to think about maintenance and machinery breakdowns over the long term, since an 'indefinite' lack of deep maintenance and continuous sea-time is no way to keep a fleet in being. Problems came and went: *Invincible* was already well into fixing her still-locked shaft, a major job on a massive piece of equipment; *Sheffield* was sent ahead to Ascension to transfer urgent replacements for a computer fault in *Antrim*, and then give herself some badly needed maintenance – she had already been away from the UK for over three months. The helicopters were beginning to show a worrying increase in defect rates, so I ordered them to cut down severely on flying hours, to keep them fit for later.

We also had what I believe was our first human stress case, a man whose mind had been in a silent turmoil over the ordeal we might face, until finally he could take it no longer. We arranged for his immediate return home from Ascension. His illness had nothing to do with 'funking it', it was a genuine breakdown induced through no fault of his own, which rendered him quite unfit to cope with his responsibilities. I felt very sorry for him. He had, I know, not wanted to let anyone down.

As you may imagine, the volume of information now beginning to pour in was very considerable, and I had to form a full-time Staff Intelligence Cell in order to cope with it. On paper, we were now sub-divided into three operational entities, the Battle Group (my own), the Amphibious Group (under Commodore Mike Clapp in *Fearless*) and the eccentrically named 'Paraquet' Group (under Captain Brian Young in *Antrim*) now on its way to South Georgia. I never quite got used to the word 'Paraquet' – it lay somewhere between weed-killer and parrot, and was inappropriate to South Georgia on both counts.

As we all made our various preparations on passage south, we listened carefully for news from beyond our narrow world, with its relatively simple problems. General Alexander Haig was shuttling back and forth from Washington to Buenos Aires, to London, to New York and round again. While I could only applaud his activities, whatever the well-meaning General hoped, wanted, said, thought or promised, there were two facts likely to prove intractable. The first was that Mrs Thatcher was plainly not going to abandon the British people trapped on the occupied Falkland Islands. The second was that the forces of General Galtieri were not about to leave of their own accord. Quite apart from any moral issues, such a course for either government entailed back-down, and subsequent political oblivion.

In any event, General Haig was to me not much short of a disaster in the making. That may seem unappreciative of his great efforts to negotiate peace. But every day he kept everyone chatting was another day's delay to us, so far from base support, and another day for the Argentinians to reinforce their positions in the islands with ever more troops, aircraft, ammunition and food for a prolonged battle on the ground. We simply could not afford to allow them this leeway if we were going to beat them. And by now, 10 April, we were beginning to receive intelligence of a further build-up of Argentine forces in East Falkland. All the indications from Headquarters were therefore that we would proceed straight on down to the Falklands, the whole Task Force in one group, to establish as firm a foothold on the islands as possible before the United Nations could put a stop to our activities and leave us floundering about offshore, awaiting defeat by the forces of time, weather, and international political procrastination. In my diary I observed: 'The future looks moderate to long-haul gloomy.'

My operations staff, aided by our little intelligence cell, was now moving to some tentative conclusions. We had a firm grasp of the speed/time/distance problems involved, huge at first sight, and we had done much thinking about the extra difficulties of the complex movement of ships, aircraft, men, their kit, their weapons and their supplies, 8000 miles from home base. We had devised special defensive formations of ships and aircraft, and debated the intricacies of how to play the two overlapping Exclusion Zones. Being no expert in amphibious matters, though sufficiently well acquainted with their business to realise my own limitations, I knew I could rely on the 'amphibians' to give fearless professional advice on their needs and problems, just as I had to rely on so many other experts – the aviators, the communicators, the air, sea and underwater warfare professionals, the logisticians, the engineers, the doctors, the meteorologists, the photographic interpreters, to name but a few – for theirs.

Of course, the commander brings his own specialist skills, but he must co-ordinate *all* the many forms of expertise available to him if they are to come together and work with any chance of success. I was lucky enough to have direct professional command experience in submarines and surface ships, and in the management of task groups and their tactics. The Navy's training made sure I was well briefed, if not operationally experienced, in all the other special skills – I even knew what the photographic interpreter's main problems were and, at a very basic level I had been the ship's 'doctor' (Heaven help anyone who was seriously ill!) in my first submarine commands.

Under the general instruction to 'Hurry south', the CTF had told me to bear firmly in mind that we might need to set up some kind of 'enclave' in the islands, readily defensible in the long term, in case the UN should impose some kind of 'freeze' on operations shortly after we had landed. This would obviously have to be well clear of the Port Stanley area where we now believed the Argentinians were concentrating. We studied the maps exhaustively, weighing up the pros and cons of a wide range of local sites, where the troops could land, establish a beach-head and cover both the defensive enclave and the offensive repossession options for subsequent action. That beach-head would have to have the potential of scraping an airstrip out of the unfriendly terrain if our few carriers were not to remain at permanent high risk for an extended period, dangerously close to the Argentinian mainland. It would also have to be capable of development to take C130 Hercules transport aircraft and eventually Phantom fighters as well as the lighter Harriers and helicopters if the state of 'enclave' was inflicted upon us by the UN indefinitely.

The selection of the landing site caused perhaps the most argument and discussion. 'Enclave' and 'repossession' were poor bedfellows, quite apart from the often conflicting needs of adequate defence against land, air and sea attacks, and our needing protection from the weather. Reconnaissance was becoming more critical by the day. No final decision on the landing site was possible without it.

Glamorgan sailed into sight of Ascension Island on Easter Sunday, a poetic and possibly providential event, which I have to admit completely passed me by at the time, busy as I was with less spiritual matters. It is, in any case, not a particularly spiritual sort of place – a large, remote, extinct volcano rising out of the mid-Atlantic Ridge in latitude eight degrees south, usually topped by a vast rain-cloud, visible from about eighty miles away. Its eastern side is green, lush, tropical and wet; its western side is an arid collection of multi-coloured cinder heaps with a luxuriant growth of white satellite dishes and radio masts – in short, a moonscape.

The labour force was mostly imported from not-so-nearby St Helena, secured on contracts limited to six months if they are not to lose citizenship. The island represents home to only one indigenous creature, a kind of shrimp, I believe. The island has one golf course, where the greens are 'browns' of oiled cinders, and your ball will scarcely last a single round before it is so badly abraded as to be useless. It has no harbour – ships anchor off the coast and you can only get ashore by boat or helicopter. But it does have the vital airstrip, and good communications.

Early on that Easter Sunday morning, the Fleet padre began his rounds of the ships, by boat, conducting each little service with rather larger congregations than usual. For some of his flock, it would be their last Easter Service. I, in well-established and still useful tradition, called a meeting of the captains and commanders in the company. There is a close camaraderie about such gatherings which is quite difficult to explain, but I think perhaps stems from the unspoken trust that usually exists between the commanders of separate units wholly dependent upon each other's mutual support. In Nelson's day, 'Band of Brothers' was the phrase used – less appropriate today when we spend weeks rather than years at sea – but Band of Brothers we still need to be. Unlike other military commanders, the captain faces battle alongside all of his senior officers, his junior officers, chief petty officers, petty officers and the ship's company (laundrymen and NAAFI canteen manager included). They face the enemy as a fighting unit, with no one much more exposed than anyone else. Those who command ships in the Royal Navy do not *send* anyone anywhere. They all go together.

The captains assembled quietly in the Day Cabin of *Glamorgan* – John Coward, David Hart-Dyke, Sam Salt, Paul Hoddinott, Paul Booterstone and Mike Barrow. We all knew that this would most probably be the last chance of such a meeting, for within a few days we would be heading south again, into more dangerous waters, where communication could no longer be face to face but only by encrypted voice radio-telephone or computer. Most of us had known each other for years, and I suppose in a sense we each knew something of what the others were feeling. For that reason alone there was a slightly forced air of good humour, one to another, but it was tempered by the chill realization that there could only be one valid reason why we should be in this room, in this ship, talking not merely as old friends but as trusted senior commanders, preparing to fight a war. Even then, though, there was a tiny hope, a fantasy, that it might yet all go away.

The meeting was attended by my operations staff among whom was Colonel Richard Preston of the Royal Marines, who had been appointed as Land Force Adviser. Like many naval officers, I have a preconceived concern, based on a cursory knowledge of history, that amphibious operations tend to suffer from two main problems. There is a tendency for political indecision in committing to the actual landing and there is always a subsequent risk of misunderstanding between the land and the sea/air forces. The classic disaster being brought about primarily by political delay being, of course, Gallipoli. More recently there was Suez . . . delay, delay, delay. Its spectre always haunts combined operations, but this time there could be no delay, with winter coming on and the stresses on the ships so far from base support. Fortunately the political management had taken this firmly on board. But nor could we risk misunderstanding between the land and sea/air commanders. The land campaign *had* to complete on time. And I think the Colonel was very aware of my genuine worries on the subject. Early on in our conversations, as he outlined the requirements for seemingly endless reconnaissance, Colonel Richard turned to me and said: 'Remember, Admiral, time spent in reconnaissance is never wasted.'

I looked at him and replied, 'Are you sure?'

'I'm sorry?'

'Surely it should be that time spent in reconnaissance is *seldom* wasted,' I corrected him.

He smiled cheerfully at the revelation that this naval officer knew the old military axiom better than he did and from that moment we became close and harmonious colleagues. His help and advice became absolutely invaluable and with immense skill did he walk the tight-rope of reconciliation between the overall naval and the amphibious force requirements. It is a complex task which requires deep professional knowledge, great tact, endless patience, good humour and a firm grasp of the evolving situation. Colonel Richard made the job seem easy enough. He was there to ensure that relationships with the Amphibious Group never went far astray, and to surmount the real difficulties of our different responsibilities: our geographic separation, poor communications and our conflicting pressures, fears and concerns.

Sadly what he, I, and the amphibious commanders did not realise until years after the end of the war was that we had all been planning to substantially different directives during the first six weeks of the operation. This led to some serious problems for the amphibians, who often felt I was rushing off on some wildcat scheme of my own and had not got their interests truly at heart. But the Task Force Commander appears not to have troubled the amphibious commanders with all the many political 'options' which fell short of full repossession of the islands, or if he did, they were too busy for such matters to seem relevant to their tasks. The CTF may have thought that issues such as an early freeze on operations before landing, an extended period of sea/air blockade, the need for long-term support of a military enclave ashore if a landing was actually to be made, were not yet their concern, and that they should be left to concentrate on their most difficult task – the full repossession of the islands. However, all such options would be my business, should political pressures supervene. I can't say that I liked any of them, but the questions had to be thought through and answered, if only to inform the politicians that such 'options' did not really exist – as practical proposals for a successful operation to recover the islands.

Whatever the problems at the higher command levels, the detailed business had to continue. That afternoon, a fleet of helicopters began transferring more stores, food, ammunition, missiles, spare parts and all the paraphernalia of war from Ascension Island out to the ships. It was a tremendous piece of improvisation in very short order. Ascension had been transformed from a US communications and satellite tracking station into a forward fleet and air base in a matter of days. Everything had been flown out from the UK and stock-piled while we were making our way down from Gibraltar. None of this could have happened without tacit and active support from the Americans, which was not at all easy for them at any stage, much less this early, with political negotiations still very much in process. I met the US Air Force colonel who was in charge of their airstrip, the day after we arrived. He told me he had been instructed 'to give the Brits every possible assistance, but not, under any circumstances, to get caught doing so'. Not an easy task for him, either.

Free use of the facilities on Ascension was critical. But perhaps the single item of equipment most useful to us was America's new AIM 9L Sidewinder air-to-air missile, for which we were but one of a line of anxiously waiting customers. President Reagan's Defence Secretary Casper Weinberger himself moved us to the head of the queue and it is now perfectly clear to me that without those AIM 9L the Sea Harriers would not have been good enough. The 'special relationship' was alive and well.

If the world was watching the political scene, the Russians were watching the military scene, at least locally. Several times we were visited by Soviet 'Bears' (Long Range Maritime Patrol Aircraft). They were free to look, but I hoped they were not talking to the Argentinians. I was in fact a bit surprised to see them at all, because everybody else in the Western world had been warned off by London, being told in clear terms that this was a military group setting off to a theatre of operations. It seemed to me that the implications of that should be plain enough to anyone: British fingers would be light on the trigger against any ship, submarine or aircraft that approached without warning or identification. Sensibly, the Bears did not follow us south; but meanwhile, they had much to watch. A constant stream of advisers and specialists flew out to help. The transfer of supplies seemed to go on night and day, and the ships not at anchor for maintenance were conducting exercises out of sight of Ascension, in gunnery and weapons training. All the time the ships were arriving to take their places in the Task Force.

Shortly after midday on 14 April, *Glamorgan* headed north to rendezvous with the carrier *Hermes* which was now approaching the area. It was time to move my Flag again, to the ship with the most room and the best command facilities. She happened also to be the largest, most capable surface ship in the Task Force. Simultaneously, I had to release the three Type 42 destroyers, *Sheffield*, *Coventry* and *Glasgow* to proceed south 'with all despatch', accompanied by the frigates *Brilliant* and *Arrow*. They were to move off at twenty-five knots, trailed by a tanker, and keep going until they were down to thirty per cent fuel. The rough distance was 1160 miles and the idea was to 'plant' the strongest force as far south as soon as possible, just in case the diplomats negotiated a 'freeze' on any further movements by our forces, pending some other, larger settlement of the dispute.

At the time, the political sense of it was easy enough to see, not least as a mark of our resolution, but nonetheless, I was beginning to get a bit frustrated. It seemed that no sooner did I begin to get some semblance of a battle group together, much less an entire Task Force, than some new need caused it to be split up again. It says much for the Navy's peacetime training that this was possible, without total chaos. We like to think of ourselves as properly drilled, adequately organized, ready to go almost anywhere and have a go at almost anything – provided it's on or near the sea. And I imagine it was pretty much what Sir Henry Leach must have promised the Prime Minister.

Practically the entire morning of 15 April was taken up with preparing for the shift to *Hermes*. As we sailed north in *Glamorgan*, my staff was working flat-out to pack up all the papers, charts, maps and books in wicker-work 'hampers' and move us into the carrier. I boarded a Sea King 4 helicopter and flew the final two hundred miles ahead of my staff, through brilliant blue skies. We landed on the flight deck of *Hermes* to be greeted by the Captain, my old sparring partner from our Ministry of Defence days, Linley Middleton. My tropical whites were covered by the green flying-suit overalls we call 'baby-grows' because the trouser legs stop short to accommodate flying boots. I have always felt fairly daft wearing this kit, which is completely strange to a submariner, and my worst fears were realized when I later saw the picture of my arrival in a national newspaper. That ridiculous figure prancing about on *Hermes*'s flight deck can't be me, can it? 'Afraid so, Woodward.' But it *is* our working rig for flying, practical if not fashionable.

Here then was another big step in my process of going to war. I had finally left the familiar surroundings of *Glamorgan*, and my own Flotilla. Indeed I had left entirely the smaller world of destroyers and frigates, with which I had become well-acquainted. Instead, I was aboard a 29,000-ton aircraft carrier, which was almost completely strange to me – in all my time to date, I had spent only one week at sea in carriers, some ten years before. Just the same as my amphibious background, I knew well enough what carriers and their aircraft could and could not do in strategic and tactical terms. But I did not know the geography, the hierarchy, the people or their habits, the detailed technicalities, not even their language really. They too would have to be relied on to give fearless, expert advice whenever needed. And now I had to change fast. It was a sort of end to innocence. I was leaving the *Glamorgan* days of sunshine, relatively simple exercises, visits and that open, fairly carefree peacetime life, for the narrow confines of a carrier in which everything was going to be very different. For a start, there is surprisingly little open air, unless you work on the Flight Deck, which, of course, I would not. And it is certainly no place for idlers, since everything is concentrated on aviation with all of its complications, mechanical awareness and sudden bursts of activity. Basically we are operating a small air force out of a large tin box – actually a ship built to Second World War standards for battle-robustness – stark, gloomy and functional. It made lovely, shiny, roomy *Glamorgan* seem like a millionaire's yacht.

My personal quarters did absolutely nothing to alleviate the general atmosphere of no-frills travel. It was situated up in the 'Island', well above the Flight Deck, it was a nine-foot-square cabin, with a five-foot-square shower and 'heads' off it. The decor was cream-painted steel-ornamented with electrical cables and exposed pipes, a masterpiece, in its way, of neo-classical, early twentieth century, functionalism. A three-foot-wide desk, a table at which three could eat, one bunk, a wardrobe, some drawers and an upright chair completed the inventory. Barring my own staff, I was also with a completely new team, some of whom I knew, but many I did not.

An aircraft carrier is nothing less than a mobile airfield and I'm not really used to airfields. *Hermes* represented an acutely comprehensive change from peace to war. She felt more war-like, she looked more warlike, and the trappings of peacetime in the Navy were no longer apparent. Upon reflection her Spartan qualities were no bad thing. Concentrated the mind.

My Flag Operations Room was a few steps along a narrow corridor from my cabin. There was an 'Admirals Bridge', a sort of 'Goofers Gallery' one deck below, with a splendid view of the whole Flight Deck. These became the physical confines of my world for the next two and a half months, and their simplicity did much to protect me against any possible distractions from the job I had been charged to complete. But it was a curious existence. For recreation, I would have the choice of occasionally watching the ship's internal television, or reading. The rest of the time would be work, eat, sleep and wait. The waiting time would not be difficult to fill – I would need to use it to think and rethink what we were doing, had done and were about to do. My diary would become a part of that process. I gazed around my new quarters, and I knew there would be times when I would be very lonely up there. But, of course, that would have to be so – the real-time management of battle cannot be done by co-equals in committee.

My staff arrived on board with all their hampers later in the afternoon. It was a major struggle to make the transfer while continuing normal business. Already we were receiving signals that *Arrow*, *Glasgow* and *Coventry* had developed propulsion defects, probably due to their high speed run south. These reports came in as purely routine, regardless of their seriousness. At my twice-daily staff meetings, we always went through the ships' defects, in order to keep a firm and accurate handle on every vessel and her state of health. A frigate with a suspect propeller shaft that we had known about for several days is plainly going to be of no use for high-speed work. But the last thing I want is a ship which only tells me her problems when she is told to go. Too late.

It was an even greater struggle to take in the vastly increased responsibilities of the operational management of an entire Carrier Battle Group with the Amphibious Group about to become an integral part of it for a rapid passage south. Plainly, I needed to talk to the Amphibious Group naval commander, as much as my own staff. And while there was a set form and order to all these meetings, it was easily lost. We were speculating, trying to bring all the myriad pieces of this enormous jigsaw into shape, and at the same time trying to muddle through the mountain of homework. We tried to put together every thought, every piece of information, every possibility, to lay out, eventually, a picture which would contain clarity, direction and purpose. It was no easier for us than it was for all the many other staffs at sea and at home, trying to cover the kaleidoscope of Operation Corporate, from high strategy to the commercial and legal complications of hiring the liner *Queen Elizabeth*. From fitting air-to-air refuelling to the Hercules transport aircraft to bringing forward weapons and equipment still in the earliest development stage. And poor inter-group communications did not help.

The main thrust of our thinking was still towards assembling all information pertinent to the selection of a landing site. Although most of that would have to come from the Amphibians and nothing could be finalized until reconnaissance was complete there were many other critical factors to take into account as well as their highly specialised requirements for the Amphibious Operations Area.

The following day, I flew over to *Fearless* for discussions with the Commodore, Amphibious Warfare, Mike Clapp, known as COMAW, and Brigadier Julian Thompson, Commander of the reinforced 3rd Commando Brigade. Mike Clapp had invited me to come over by signal some days earlier: my reply to say I was coming only reached him about five weeks later – such were our communications difficulties. As a consequence, I arrived all fired-up to discuss how we were to set about proceeding straight on down as an integrated group, with myself in charge of it, 'obeying the last pipe' as it is called, from our CTF – anxious to try to agree the many matters falling out of that, since it appeared to be the very next thing we'd have to do – and just as anxious to get back to *Hermes* and my new and wide range of responsibilities there.

For their part, they had not been expecting me at all, much less to drop out of the sky unannounced. Mike had other matters on his mind and believing we only had to decide what to discuss with our CTF, he felt the meeting would be of little interest to him. It seems he was unconscious of my 'Hurry south' instructions or the questions that were being fired at me about the efficacy of blockade or the consequences of a UN freeze on operations. By contrast, the captain of *Fearless* had told Julian that I knew 'absolutely nothing about amphibiosity' and he decided to brief me thoroughly on their detailed business, rather than pass me the one essential fact I needed – that they were unready to land in any kind of fighting posture before they had restowed their ships. In other words, the orders I was working to were no longer remotely practicable.

With such disparate starting points and no agreed agenda, the meeting was probably doomed. After the usual greeting civilities, and at about ten minutes' notice, their briefing started with a detailed description of the topography of the Falklands by Major Ewen Southby-Tailyour, Royal Marines, very much the force expert on the subject. While immensely valuable to the amphibians, as far as I was concerned this was detailed information on a level with the engineering problems of keeping Sea Harrier radars maintained. It was emphatically not what I needed unless there was ample time for me to do a ten-week refresher course on amphibiosity with particular application to the Falkland Islands. So I interrupted him less than kindly, and tried to go on to matters I felt were relevant to the problems of inter-group interest if we were to go straight on south in the days immediately ahead.

They obliged, reluctantly it later emerged, perhaps because they already had enough worries of their own without my producing some more for them to think about. Mike Clapp had largely stayed clear of the meeting to get on with his own business and had left it to Julian Thompson. Julian was understandably put out by my abrupt refusal to listen to his detailed briefing. For my part, if they had serious amphibious concerns about the overall plan at that stage, I assumed they would have told me about them at this, the first opportunity. And if their problems were matters of detail only, they knew I had a colonel and a major, Royal Marines, on my staff to keep me straight on that sort of thing.

After I had left to go back to *Hermes*, the whole meeting was debriefed to Mike Clapp as interference, arrogance, total lack of sympathy or even 'wish-to-know' from an admiral who plainly thought he was in charge of everything, including them. Hardly surprising, because at that particular moment and for the next day and a half, I believed I *was* in charge and that as they had presented no major problems standing in the way of obeying my C-in-C's orders, there was a range of matters I needed to settle with them, there and then. Hardly surprising also, from their point of view, that suspicion of the Battle Group Commander's reliability developed within the Amphibious Group from command level down from that day. It is best described by Ewen Southby-Tailyour in his book, *Reasons in Writing: A Commando's View of the Falklands War*:

> This meeting and its lack of success was to dominate our thoughts. It certainly hardened opinions. In the days to come whenever signals [known irreverently by the Naval Staff as Windygrams] were received from the Battle Group they were read against the background knowledge that it was likely to be a dictum and would not be seeking advice or confirmation. The meeting did nothing for morale nor our faith in the Admiral's ability to support any amphibious phase with the degree of concern we felt it was due. This may not have been the case in practice but it was our perception, and a most genuine cause for concern in *Fearless* at the time – an unnecessary and added worry. . . We realised that sympathy for, and understanding of, our problems was going to be in very short supply.

It is also hardly surprising either that this misplaced attitude persisted for so long when communications between us continued to be so limited. But at least there was no difficulty agreeing that the landing should only be made where the Argentinians were not. We all knew we had no substantial amphibious *assault* capability. After that, it was not so easy, and while discussion seemed amiable enough to me, several others have reported it quite differently. We were worrying about different things. My immediate concern at that stage remained the major problem of how to look after everyone while we all went together straight on down to the Falklands. Their chief and probably still unconscious, concern was to avoid going straight on down altogether, as they were anything but ready to do so and just beginning to understand the full scale of their own specialist problems. As to the choice of eventual landing place, we plainly still had a wide range of possibilities. Stevelly Bay, out in West Falkland, held particularly good prospects for the early construction of an airstrip it seemed. Low Bay in Lafonia (South-east Falkland) offered clear arcs of fire for our anti-aircraft systems and a good, large, well-protected anchorage. Cow Bay, in the northeast, gave good beaches for landing and a fairly short trek to Port Stanley. San Carlos looked good for several reasons, none obviously outstanding. Teal Inlet was another good possibility, much closer than Carlos. So it went on – all subject to reconnaissance.

But Stevelly was way out to the west and we would still have to cross the Falkland Sound if we were to take Stanley. Similarly, Low Bay meant having to get through the narrow strip of land at Goose Green: fine for a long-term defensive position but not so good if we wanted to advance on Port Stanley. Cow Bay meant little protection from heavy seas. Carlos seemed on the small side and required the entrance to the Falkland Sound to be free of mines. Teal had a narrow entrance, fairly easily blocked by accident or design. All needed examination by Special Forces, just to narrow down the options. None yet stood out as the only sensible choice.

Nor could it ever have been a decisive meeting on this as on many other matters. Most of the big decisions would have to be made by the CTF at Ascension in a few days' time. Then, hopefully, a concrete plan would emerge for the first time, agreed by all the commanders and taking account of all the politico-military factors from home. Some of that plan would still have to wait for more information. All we needed to do at this stage was agree what subjects we might need to raise with him and prepare to present our ideas on how we might set about our joint business in accordance with such vague directives as I presently had. In my haste, I failed to make all this clear – I assumed they had the same instructions.

Years later, I discovered from their own accounts that they concluded I was untrustworthy on a variety of counts, broadly as debriefed to Mike Clapp. For my own part, I left that meeting with the same high confidence in them to do their particular job that I had arrived with. Mike Clapp was an old, if not very close, friend who seemed calm and collected enough in these difficult circumstances. Our career paths had not crossed for many years but the cultures of aviators and sub-mariners are seldom far apart, and all our training demanded that mutual trust should be the starting point. Unconsciously, and imperceptively perhaps, I thought I had it, but their books told me otherwise. I am sad to have added to their problems; they are perhaps sad that they didn't feel able to tell me about them.

By early evening our small fleet was back at Ascension. It comprised now *Hermes*, and *Invincible* (fully repaired), under Captain Jeremy Black, *Glamorgan*, the Type 12 frigate *Yarmouth* under Commander Tony Morton, the Type 21 frigate *Alacrity* under Commander Christopher Craig, the Type 22 frigate *Broadsword* under Captain Bill Canning, and the Fleet Replenishment Ship *Resource* under Captain B. A. Seymour RFA. We returned to *Hermes* by boat to prepare for the arrival in the early hours of the next morning of Admiral Sir John Fieldhouse, the Commander-in-Chief, Fleet. He was to be accompanied by some twenty of his Headquarters Staff including his Land Forces Deputy, Major General Jeremy Moore. They arrived in *Hermes* at 0815 and within the hour we were joined by COMAW and the Brigadier. The programme included a briefing by the C-in-C's staff, another by my own, followed by COMAW's team and then four seminars, dealing with Command and Control, Intelligence, Logistics, and Communications. This was all completed by lunchtime but by the end we felt there was still a lack of form to it all. There seemed to be no hard facts on which to base anything. After lunch, the senior members met in the Admiral's harbour quarters right down aft, to mull things over.

I still remember standing down there, on the starboard side of the cabin, with some cardboard and a pair of scissors, cutting out differently coloured strips, representing various lengths of time. On each I wrote down a date, or an objective, or the name of a ship. Basically, it was necessary to work the campaign out backwards, starting from the chilling thought that the Task Group would be falling apart by mid to late June without proper maintenance and with winter setting in. This did not allow for enemy action, since reinforcements and replacements from the UK should cover that. So we were obliged to make a crucial assumption, there and then – that the land battle would have to be over at least by the end of June, and preferably a good two weeks before that. The retaking of Port Stanley was obviously a 'critical path' for military planning, unless the politicians of the UN said different. On that basis, therefore, if the land forces were to be given reasonable time to do their stuff, we had to put them on the beaches by about 25 May. That would give them about a month to establish the beach-head, break out, march to the likely main positions around Stanley and defeat the Argentinians on the ground. Say by mid-late June. During this time, in addition to our own tasks, expressed simply as 'neutralising the Argentinian Navy and Air Force,' the Battle Group would provide them with all the artillery and air support we could; hopefully enough for their needs. And throughout the operation we had to keep the sea and sky sufficiently clear to allow reasonably safe passage to and from the beach-head, with stores, people, ammunition, food and fuel – by ship and by helicopter. We had to prevent the Argentinian sea or land forces playing a serious part in their essentially land battle. And when that was done, we would still need to keep that air and the sea wars won, indefinitely. There could be no guarantee that success on land would end the air/sea war.

I duly pinned my cardboard dates into place on the overall calendar. It was a mobile 'bar-chart' of the kind dearly loved by all planners. We continued to work backwards: we must be here by X, there by Y, have established an airstrip by Z. In the end, I remember one piece of cardboard proving to be the key to most of our problems. Upon this was written the name '*Intrepid*', the sister ship to *Fearless*. We *had* to have her in the South Atlantic as a stand-by amphibious headquarters ship, just in case *Fearless* should be sunk. The problem was that in late March, *Intrepid* had been 'destored' and put in reserve, as an early step in Mr Nott's singular strategy for reorganizing defence towards concentrating our efforts on Central Germany. To get *Intrepid* south, we *now* had to reverse that complicated process. As far as we could estimate, there was no way she could get down to the Falklands, properly prepared, before 16 May. She would be the last ship to arrive, the last piece in the jigsaw, and so all the timings depended on her.

There were still, of course, unknowns like the weather, enemy action, accidents, political initiatives and settlements.

But here was a hard plan, give or take about ten days. It was a military plan from which there could be no political diversions if we were to fight and win. The 'landing window' extended from 16 May (the first day *Intrepid* could arrive) to 25 May. Inside that time frame we had to have most of the land forces ashore. And, to be in good shape by mid-May, we were going to have to get the Special Forces ashore for reconnaissance very soon. It was now 17 April, and the bar-chart showed us we could enter the Exclusion Zone by 1 May if we pressed on hard. South Georgia should be clear by then, and sixteen days should suffice for the reconnaissance phase.

The amphibians would be able to wait behind, stay in hard training at Ascension, re-stow their equipment in better order, and set off south ten days from now, prepared to go ashore any time after arrival, wherever recce suggested was the best place. This part of the plan had the added merit of allowing the Battle Group the option of entering the Exclusion Zone without the encumbrance of the amphibious ships. The possibility of taking on the Argentinian fleet and air force with a large convoy of amphibians and merchant ships requiring simultaneous protection – all wallowing about at twelve knots – had been a considerable source of worry to me for the last week or so, hence the need for a meeting with COMAW. Now we had the option to fight without one hand tied behind our backs, which was a good idea, really. Rather better than going all that way as escorts to a large convoy.

One way and another it was emerging as a pretty good plan of operations. And somehow, we would manage to keep it, almost to the day. Step One was critical – the entire thing pivoted on our initial departure time, which meant the Battle Group must clear Ascension by tomorrow at midday, no ifs, ands or buts. There were also two refinements we would make.

Firstly, we intended to set off on a course which might just suggest we were approaching Buenos Aires rather than the Falklands. Secondly, we would use chaff to make it appear (to any radar that 'saw' us) as if we had the Amphibious Group in company. The first aim was to encourage the Args to leave some of their navy and air force in the north. The second aim was to make them commit their sea and air forces in defence of the Falklands against an apparent British landing on 1 May.

So Admiral Fieldhouse was able to return to London that night to advise the Chief of the Defence Staff Sir Terence Lewin that the line to take in Cabinet, from the military point of view, would have to be as follows: 'To eject the Argentinians by force, we *must* be on the edge of the Exclusion Zone by 1 May. You thus have until that date to succeed in your political negotiations, because every day you slip past 1 May is one day less for us to complete the land campaign. Don't forget, it is only in the Argentinians' interest to prevaricate. *We* are already right up against the stops.'

It had been a grim day with little light relief but at last we had a good foundation for our actions. We now had a plan which would take us, with reasonable chance of success, through to the end. It also gave plenty of opportunity for political settlement at its various stages. The vital thing was to have identified the military milestones at which options for political solutions had to change. The good thing about milestones is that they give a hard indication of how far you have travelled, how far you have to go, and a check that you are still on the right road.

I trusted Admiral Fieldhouse to make our case in Whitehall trenchantly, because our margins were too small for comfort. Before he went he told me he had been pressed to find an alternative to relieve me. Vice Admiral Derek Reffell was an obvious choice, since he knew *Hermes*, the carriers and amphibious ships were part of his Flotilla and he'd been COMAW some years before. He was senior, better and all round more suitable. And Mr Nott was keen to send someone like Reffell, 'because', as John Fieldhouse with a grim smile reminded me, 'when – not if – it all goes sour, he wants somebody important enough to sack!'

That night I wrote and told Char what he had said, adding:

> Still, at least they'll maybe let me retire gracefully, meanwhile I am busy trying to keep my head above troubled waters, and *think* – 'Think or thwim', as they say in the Tactical School . . .
>
> There is so much to do. None of our plans seems to hold up for much more than twenty-four hours, as Mr Nott footles about, wringing his hands and worrying about his blasted career. And the Ministry men play their intricate and interminable games with an eye to the aftermath ('get in quick if there's credit, be elsewhere if there's not').
>
> I'm not intending to prove I'm an 'ace' or whatever – it's mostly about trying to do whatever I'm charged with doing in the most economical and effective way. Which means getting no more heads blown off than can be helped. Sometimes that will mean sending a friend to his death in order that eight others will survive. I don't look forward to those sort of decisions, you may imagine.
>
> I am sorry to rattle on, but we're far from home, and as I go on the rounds of seeing my people, I greatly fear I may be seeing some of them for the last time. Morbid really, but I suppose realistic too.

And, with that, I signed off, and returned briefly to the Ops Room which was, as ever, extremely busy. Like all of the other Ops Rooms in our little fleet, it would remain so throughout the night, as I and my captains prepared to sail, at midday tomorrow, for the cold south, and the Battle for the Falkland Islands.

5

'Weapons Tight!'

Of all the varied creatures which inhabit the vast lonely stretches of the world's oceans, I think perhaps the sailor is most impressed by the whale. The eye is always pulled to watch the majestic appearance of the earth's largest inhabitant bursting out of the waves in that glorious slow motion he has, blowing his huge jet of water into the empty skies as he clears his enormous lungs. But this giant of the seas has, I am afraid, a major fault in his design. To an active sonar, he looks just like a submarine. Even to the professional eye looking not quite in the right direction, his fleeting white swirl on the water can falsely signal the menace of a periscope.

The morning of 18 April was a prize example of the confusion he can cause. At 0900 our newly arrived tanker *Olmeda* reported the sighting of a 'feather', the wash of a periscope. It did not require a great stretch of the imagination to work out that the Argentinians could easily have put a submarine into the Ascension area in a bold attempt to finish the war before it started.

All ships were ordered to weigh anchor. *Hermes* was underway by 1000 – two hours earlier than planned. Within thirty minutes, all ships had been ordered to form up – and the Battle Group was quickly into formation, with no hitches. Sonar operators worked swiftly to establish the identity of the submarine contact from its behaviour and, inside the hour, as we moved quickly away from Ascension, we believed it not to originate from Argentina. We were more inclined to think it might be a Soviet nuclear boat, because it took fast, evasive action over a extended period. Only two creatures of the deep possess this tremendous power – Red October, and Moby Dick.

Our fears and hopes were not finally settled until a patrolling RAF Nimrod reported sighting a school of whales close by and we formally classified the contact as such. This was to become almost routine for the men who searched the sea for submarines – the sonar operators – as we made our way along the migration routes of the world's largest mammals. The incident had disrupted our logistics transfers a bit, but nothing irrecoverable. It earned COMAW's considerable displeasure, but he had not realised the cause. And when it happened to his own group a week or two later, he also sailed early with the same results. From my personal point of view, the whole event had been a useful work-up as well as a way of getting all ships to sail early. This was by no means the last occasion that whales caused us to get over-excited and I'm afraid that, later on, when the use of anti-submarine weapons had been permitted, we must have killed quite a few. I had plenty of sympathy for whales, but not enough to counterbalance my strong dislike of Argentinian submarines. The whales' design fault was too often fatal.

Anyway, we were away in good order and good time – *Hermes*, *Glamorgan*, the frigates *Broadsword*, *Alacrity* and *Yarmouth*, in company with *Olmeda* and *Resource*. *Invincible* was scheduled to leave later and catch up overnight. We had twelve days to make our way down to the Exclusion Zone. Our plan was to enter from the east, at night, to launch a Sea Harrier strike on Stanley airstrip at dawn with as many aircraft as we could sensibly muster. We would shell the Argentinian shore positions most of the day and send two anti-submarine frigates inshore to search for submarines. After dark, we'd start getting the Special Forces ashore.

Twelve days may seem plenty but there was still a great deal of training to be done, particularly for the aviators. The ships also needed to get used to having so many aircraft about. And some night flying practice was essential, particularly with the dim deck lights required in war. Everyone now had to learn how to operate beyond standard peacetime safety limits: flying faster, lower, and in worse weather, for instance. War requires a complete change of attitude – the emphasis shifts from avoiding the low chance of a silly accident, to dealing with the high chance of destruction by the enemy. But no one had set any wartime safety standards and we had to learn fast that limits were still required. More than once, we found out the hard way.

Meanwhile the preparations were proceeding apace: the *Antrim* group (Operation Paraquet) was hurrying on towards South Georgia; the *Brilliant* group, with *Sheffield*, *Coventry*, *Glasgow* and *Arrow* was well ahead with their tanker *Appleleaf*; General Haig was still shuttling; the amphibians were sorting themselves out at Ascension; and the sonar operators in the Battle Group were finding whales in great numbers. None of this took much of my attention, but there was one consideration which my diary reveals as very much on my mind. London had put me under orders to go towards a two-hundred-mile-radius Exclusion Zone and make aggressive noises, but only when I got there. Presumably they hoped this would frighten the Argentinians into going home. It was certainly worth a try. But it wasn't that simple – exclusion zones seldom are. I wrote down my thoughts about the weaknesses in this strategy in my diary that night:

> Militarily not very sharp, since, should the opposition decide to the contrary, they will be able to carry out a co-ordinated pre-emptive strike on my aircraft carriers and ruin any chances we had of retaking the Falkland Islands. It is not as if the Args had not already proved they were prepared to pre-empt – witness South Thule, South Georgia, and finally the Falklands themselves. Not happy with this state of affairs.

There were, in addition, some other hard truths to face, the first being that we could not, in the face of a two-hundred-strong enemy air force, put forces ashore anywhere on the islands without air superiority. This does not mean providing total immunity from enemy air attack, only that the land forces be given reasonably effective air cover, sufficient to ensure that their operations on the ground are not seriously hampered. Opinion on what constitutes 'sufficient' differ sharply depending on your situation. The Royal Marine watching the approach of an Arg Pucara ground-attack aircraft coming straight for him will certainly see the matter more urgently than the distant Force Anti-Air Warfare Co-ordinator who is desperately trying to juggle his strictly limited numbers of aircraft to do an apparently unlimited number of jobs.

The Argentinian Air Force must not be allowed to dominate the skies – and to stop them we do have a small number of fairly basic, naval interceptor aircraft; not many, just a couple of dozen Sea Harriers so far, with a few more coming down in *Atlantic Conveyor*, before the country's entire Sea Harrier inventory is fully committed. We do have large numbers of RAF interceptors, but they are of no use whatsoever since they require large airfields to operate from. And there is no such airfield where we are going. We have one at Ascension, nearly 4000 miles north of the Falklands, but from there would take eleven Victor tanker aircraft to get one long-range Vulcan bomber over the islands for five minutes, and then bring it back. The only other British airfield in our area is at Port Stanley but that isn't going to be available until mid-June, at the earliest. And it would not be fit for RAF Interceptors [Phantoms] for however long it took to lengthen the runway after that – like some months. This leaves us with two working aircraft carriers: the bigger *Hermes* is nothing like big enough – certainly Admiral Tom Brown wouldn't have thought so, since she carries about half the aircraft he could on his USS *Coral Sea*; the other British carrier *Invincible* has roughly half the capacity of *Hermes*. There is a third, *Illustrious*, but she is presently not due to complete building and workup until the middle of next year. The two we have will need to last until long after any land battle is over. We are going to have to find some way of keeping at least one of our two operational carriers out there for some months after the land battle is over. Lose *Invincible* and the operation is at least severely jeopardized. Lose *Hermes* and the operation is over. One unlucky torpedo, bomb or missile hit, even a simple but major accident on board, could do it.

Right now I only had loose instructions to go into the

Exclusion Zone and keep the Argentinians out of it. We usually call this a 'Show of Force', which is fine if it succeeds in frightening the enemy off without a shot being fired. But what if the Argentinians are *not* frightened? What if they call our bluff? What if they make a really determined effort of, say, fifty aircraft in a major strike? What if they are prepared to lose twenty or thirty aircraft in an all-out attempt to sink one of our carriers? What if they choose to do what I did to the *Coral Sea*? What *are* the Malvinas worth to General Galtieri? This is what I meant by the diary phrase 'Not happy with this state of affairs'. The other aspect that occurred to me was that Mrs Thatcher, like any Prime Minister who agrees to fight a war, is unlikely to get much sympathy if it goes wrong. My diary put it simply enough: 'She might call it "naval incompetence" and gracefully wrap her hand in.' With John Nott's question in mind, I added, 'Nasty thought.'

Thus, on this April night, far off the Atlantic coast of Brazil, I am less than optimistic, too aware that if they hit *Hermes* or *Invincible* the Royal Navy will somehow be publicly disgraced, that I will certainly be court-martialled, whether 'important enough' to take all the blame or not. Worse yet, the British military will become the laughing stock of the world, limping home in defeat. John Bull humbled at last. At sea.

However, moods pass and the daily events helped to drive the darker fears away. I settled down to deal with the inappropriately named John Coward. I do not think the later Vice Admiral Sir John Coward KCB, would think it that much of a slight if I suggested that his basic instinct was to start the war against Argentina all on his own. He made it clear that he was keen to hurry on over to Port Stanley and set about them at the earliest possible moment. As he was still far closer than I was to the Falklands, I rather felt I should discourage this. But

I knew Coward well, his courage and his competence, and I found myself writing thoughtfully: 'He could swing it, I expect. Though I'm not sure what he should do thereafter . . . and it would be splitting the force (against Rule One) . . . but it *would* get the war under way before the Args can pre-empt on the aircraft carriers.'

Ultimately I thought better of such expendability and sent him a sharp signal saying, 'Do nothing of the sort. Wait for me. And stay out of trouble.' He was unconvinced and continued to press. It was, I mused that evening, a classic case of the young bull saying to the old bull, 'You see that field of cows over there, let's rush down this lane, jump over the gate and chat one of them up.' 'No, Captain Coward, let's not. Let's walk steadily down the lane, open the gate and see to the lot of them.'

I rounded off the diary entry by recording:

> Coward is reading more into the Rules of Engagement than is intended, and fancies starting the war all on his own. Can't entirely blame him, but a pesky nuisance all the same . . . Meanwhile I shall have to amplify the ROE so that all the Commanding Officers can know what I'm thinking, rather than apply their own interpretations, which might range from 'Ask them for lunch' to 'Nuke 'em for breakfast'.

Our Rules of Engagement at this time forbade us to attack any ship before we entered the Exclusion Zone, unless of course we ourselves came under attack, in which case we were permitted to defend ourselves using minimum force. Understandably, this was how the Cabinet wished Britain to be seen in the eyes of the world community. In reality, of course, things may turn out rather differently. But that would not be the fault of the British Government. That would be the fault of Admiral . . . ummm . . . whatsisname . . . Woodward, overstepping the mark.

On Wednesday 21 April, some 1500 miles out from Ascension, our understanding of the Rules of Engagement were all put to the test. Around midday, the *Hermes* radar operators picked up a high-altitude unidentified air contact at long range. We immediately sent up a Sea Harrier to intercept – which took longer than I had hoped – but the pilot reported a Boeing 707 in Argentinian Air Force regalia, out to have a look at us. No weapons could be seen on him and, on sighting the Harrier, the pilot altered course to clear the area.

Our pilot took a photograph from alongside, and it was clear enough that the Boeing had been converted into a military reconnaissance aircraft. It also seemed likely that it was using its weather-avoidance radar for surface search to pin-point us, see how many ships we had and where we were going. It was quickly nicknamed the 'Burglar'.

We immediately raised the anti-air warfare readiness of the force, since an air strike can always follow a reconnaissance flight. We also changed the formation of the ships and thereafter kept at least two Harriers on deck alert, ready to take off and intercept any intruders at short notice.

This put an important question in my mind. Am I going to let this 'Burglar' go on reporting our latest position back to Argentinian headquarters, possibly telling their carrier where to send a pre-emptive air strike? Or am I going to 'splash' him, in flagrant defiance of my own Rules of Engagement, perhaps to save ships and lives in my own force? I guess not, but he is a considerable worry. I know all too well what can follow up behind recce aircraft – strike direction is one of their prime tasks.

At 0230 the following morning, another high-altitude contact showed up, a hundred and forty-four miles to the southwest – the direction of the South American mainland. Again we sent a Harrier, up into the night, and he intercepted sixty-five miles out, identifying a Boeing 707 carrying airliner navigation lights. The Harrier drove him out to the north-east of the Battle Group. But then the Boeing broke cover and turned sharply south for home, identifying himself as the Burglar beyond any reasonable doubt.

It seemed to me that this sort of thing could not be allowed to continue, so I 'tweaked' Fleet Headquarters in Northwood to leak information that we now had instructions to shoot the Burglar down in the hope that this might put him off. Actually, I went further than that and I asked for permission *to* shoot him down. And, to my slight surprise, I got it via DSSS (the long-range secure speech radio via satellite); at least I thought so at the time. With a couple of qualifications that – a) he came within a certain specific range limit, and b) we had 'positive identification' that he was, indeed, the Burglar.

At 2000 that night, again in darkness, the Boeing made yet another appearance. By now, everyone was in a high state of agitation. The Force Anti-Air Warfare Commander in *Invincible* sent two Harriers off after him inside two minutes, and a third three minutes later. I considered this well over the top, and my diary records my irritation. 'Ridiculous,' I wrote. 'So gave AAWC a hard time. Not well handled at our end either – helicopters slow to get airborne and Communications Intercept not warned. You wonder how we'll ever get it to go right.'

At 1134 the next morning, the 707 came again. We detected his radar and sent up a combat air patrol. However, we did not manage an intercept and the aircraft vanished, we guessed without detecting us. He was becoming something of a habit, a bad one and unwelcome with it. Just after sunset that evening, up he comes again, this time from the south-east, two hundred miles away, obviously high, heading straight towards us, and with his radar switched on as usual. *Invincible*'s Sea Dart system locks on in good time, giving us accurate course, speed and height, and telling us exactly where the target must be for us to hit it at the maximum range of our missiles. But this is well beyond the specific range permitted by my ROE. So we hold our fire as he comes on in at 350 knots. He is within two minutes of reaching the limit – at which point he is ours.

It crosses my mind at that point that it could just be someone else. I don't *think* it is, because the Burglar has been visiting regularly now for three days. It is time to remove him, firstly because he could be the fore-runner for a strike, and secondly, as they said about the shooting of Admiral Byng – 'to encourage the others'. Nevertheless, I still call for a final check, 'Do we have any record of any scheduled commercial air flights anywhere over the South Atlantic?' The reply is a confident negative. Then that, I thought, is that. If he comes any closer, he'll have to go. One final, final check though. 'Just lay off his course, forward and back from his present position, on a map of the South Atlantic. *Quickly now!*'

We are only a minute from missile launch against the Burglar. Every ten seconds he is getting a mile nearer. The Deck Alert Harrier, launched too late, is not going to get up there until the Burglar is well past. Still no answer from my General Operations Plotter. But with twenty seconds to spare, it comes back. 'He seems to be on a direct line running from Durban to Rio de Janeiro,' came the careful reply.

'*Weapons tight!*' I order, and the GWO immediately broadcasts it, denying all ships permission to fire.

The Harrier is sent to get close in and check visually. Sure enough, he reports back that it is a Brazilian airliner, with all the normal navigational and cabin lights on, bound no doubt from Durban to Rio, and now fast disappearing away to the north-west.

At the time it didn't seem a particularly noteworthy event. My diary simply said, 'Intercepted a Brazilian airliner – international scene?' But if we had made a mistake, it would have meant the kind of world-news furore that so haunted the Soviets after they shot down the Korean 747 on 1 September 1983. We can only have been one minute away from missile launch when the order 'Weapons tight' went out, and once the 'bird' is on its way, it's hard to make yourself abort it.

I have considered that short scenario many times since, searching for the real reason for hesitating at the last moment. I believe I must have been thinking, 'This contact is no immediate threat to me. He is not going to bomb us, the worst he can do is report our position, and do I really need to obliterate him if there is even the tiniest risk of being wrong? Have I really met all the criteria for "positive identification" – height, speed, radar, general behaviour?' *Yes.* But positive identification? Plainly, I tried very hard to find a reason *not* to shoot, without having given much consideration to the consequences of getting it wrong. But in the light of the KAL 007 incident a year later, this was another of my lucky days. *If* we had shot that airliner down, it would have probably left the Americans with no choice but to withdraw their support; the Task Force would have had to be recalled; the Falklands would be the Malvinas; and I would have been court-martialled, doubly damned by the fact that I had *not* actually been given permission – I just thought I had been, by the verbal advice of the Chief of Staff at Northwood, over DSSS but not by formal, hard-copy signal – that essential part of any major decision for which DSSS was no substitute. These would have been the consequences of the international community's rightful horror at the news of a battle group shooting down several hundred civilians by mistake. It's a small word – 'if'. And it dogs the path of the Royal Navy today as it always has done. As General Moore was to remind me gratuitously some months later: 'Only the land forces could win the war, but the Navy could *always* lose it.' I do not agree with this view about the sole prerogative of land forces, but this was one day when the Navy could indeed have lost it.

By now the weather was worsening, and we experienced our first taste of severe winter conditions in the South Atlantic. Gales blew up from the south-east and the seas became big enough to hide the hull of a frigate from the bridge of *Hermes* at half a mile. This sort of swell looks large enough from the *Hermes* but from a frigate it's really impressive. But we headed on down towards the Rio Grande Rise, a stretch of notoriously rough water caused by the ocean floor rising from nearly four miles deep to just 650 metres. This was the first time I had seen spray bursting over the high raised bow of *Hermes*, nearly sixty feet above the waterline.

There was little, if any, good news around. Our progress was slowed by the head sea and down in South Georgia, which Brian Young and the Paraquet group were trying to take back from the Argentinians, the situation sounded ghastly. Two Wessex helicopters, trying to evacuate SAS from appalling weather conditions, had already crashed on the Fortuna Glacier in strong winds, fierce cold and a snowstorm 'white-out'. That night, we too lost a helicopter, one of the new Sea King 4s from *Hermes*, which crashed into the sea a few miles to the south of us. We managed to rescue the pilot, but the crewman was lost, and I ordered *Yarmouth*, *Resource* and *Olmeda* to remain behind and search the area until one hour after dawn, while the rest of us pushed on further south.

Commander Christopher Craig's *Alacrity* trailed behind with engine problems. The Burglar tried again just before dawn but the 'Deck Alert' Harrier got to him at eighty miles – so something went right at last. We were now some fourteen hundred miles east of the southern Brazilian town of Port Allegre, steaming right over the Rio Grande Rise. *Yarmouth*, *Resource* and *Olmeda* are a hundred and twenty miles astern, *Alacrity* somewhere in between, and their positions highlight my concern about the scattering of my Battle Group. I am extremely keen to join *Sheffield*, *Coventry*, *Glasgow* and *Arrow* with their tanker *Appleleaf* waiting for us up ahead, and I'm looking forward to the return of *Antrim*, *Brilliant*, *Plymouth* and *Tidespring* from South Georgia, if that bit of business can be settled quickly.

My diary on the night of 24 April records my worries:

> Tension is heightening, South Georgia op seems bogged down for fear of Arg submarine (conventional, *SANTA FE*). Maritime Radar Recce aircraft incapable of useful surveillance at this range from Ascension sadly. We are slowed down by unforecast low pressure area, giving gale force winds and swell from SE. A taste of things to come, I fear. I'm anxious to catch up with my forward group – not having been allowed to bring them back. So I'm caught with our escort force ahead, and my RFAs astern.

The winds began to die during the night and, shortly after breakfast on Sunday morning, things began to look up. We were through the 'low' and pushing on at better speed. Some kind of miracle had happened in South Georgia, where Brian Young, John Coward and David Pentreath, with more than a little help from Nick Barker in *Endurance*, had somehow managed to put the Arg submarine *Santa Fe* out of action. She was now beached, at Grytviken.

By 1700, most of the *Sheffield* group had rejoined us, and one hour later we received a signal that South Georgia had fallen to us. The message home from *Antrim* was simple enough: 'Be pleased to inform Her Majesty that the White Ensign flies beside the Union Jack in South Georgia. God save the Queen.' Not quite my style, rather too much of an Imperial ring to it – 'Op Paraquet Completed' would have done for me – but then I have little sense of occasion.

That day ended with an uncomfortable shambles when *Yarmouth* got a sonar contact that seemed very submarine-like to him. It would not have mattered too much had *Yarmouth* not just been bringing the two RFAs, *Olmeda* and *Resource*, back to join the Group. Now we had a 'probable submarine' on the loose, in the middle of the Group, in pitch black conditions, with no navigation lights burning, and with ships all over the place as they tried either to track the contact or to take up their new stations in the formation. It was nothing short of a mêlée.

You can tell from my diary of that night what kind of a day it had been and how concerned I was over almost everything. I thus reproduce the passage in full:

25 April – we're through the Low and cracking on. Quiet night. International scene hardening further. I remain very upset that I have still not been allowed to gather the Battle Group together – hence it remains unworked-up, and dangerously vulnerable. During the

day, we picked up nearly all the other members of the Group (bar *Brilliant*) one by one and listened to the South Georgia action. After all the talk about recce and the submarine threat, the Arg Guppy was caught (probably unable to dive anyway) hammered and driven ashore in Grytviken – and the landing and surrender accomplished before the main party of Boots [Royal Marines] [in *Tidespring*] could be brought to bear from outside the two-hundred-mile limit! On this occasion, the time spent in recce was largely spent rounding up the 'brave' Argentinians – one hundred and forty of them. By midnight the Georgia problem appeared to be reduced to wondering what on earth to do with the prisoners.

My main worry was how to control *Appleleaf* and *Yarmouth* as we made the final rendezvous – both were running around like mongrels after a cat having totally lost their cool, apparently. An unseamanlike and dangerous mess.

I later made a further note on this:

The *Yarmouth/Appleleaf* incident in the middle of the rendezvous between the Battle Group and the *Sheffield* group rejoining could well have been the reason that another surface contact was 'found' in among the Group on this occasion. In any language it can be a difficult business bringing such a large number of ships together with no lights in the middle of the night, but when one frigate thinks it has found a submarine in the middle of the whole event, the margin for disaster increases. It was all quite exciting for a while, but order eventually emerged out of chaos.

So it was all part of the learning process and what a lot there was for us all to learn. But I was no happier about the ROE situation. Some of the captains had been looking very carefully at the small print dealing with what we could, and could not, do. At this point, with diplomatic solutions still not forthcoming as far as I could see, there was an unmistakable increase in tension throughout the Group. Men were beginning to face the fact that someone might try to kill them quite soon and under those circumstances they would like to be empowered not only to hit back hard, but also to strike first if the danger seemed obvious.

I had already earned a mild rebuke from Fleet Headquarters for assuming, and apparently saying to the Press, that I regarded the Exclusion Zone as applicable to aircraft as well as surface ships. This focused attention on the meaning of 'Total' at a time when there had been much confusion in my mind as to nomenclature (although I am told it was crystal clear to the people at home in the MOD!). We seemed to have several choices: Selective/Maritime/Total Exclusion Zone/Area, each with their acronyms, TXA, MEZ, TXZ, MXA, SEZ, and so on. My request for guidance on what it was finally to be called resulted in the shortest signal of the whole operation from Fleet Headquarters: 'Tis TEZ.' I suspect that this was dreamed up by my old friend and mentor who was the Chief of Staff there, Vice Admiral Sir David Hallifax KCB, ever a one for the short, precise answer.

But this was the only light-hearted part of it. I knew that some of my commanders were worried. Mike Barrow, for instance, who had the court-martial hanging over his head from Bandar Jissah. I considered, wrongly as it turned out, that Mike was playing it extra safe, nit-picking over his authority, or lack of it. But the truth was, like the rest of us, he was getting a bit upset about those Rules, which on first reading seemed to render us impotent against an enemy who was becoming a little more real every day. I realized that considerable local amplification of the ROE was going to be critical. I was sure they made excellent sense at the political interface in White-hall, but they were sometimes less than crystal clear in the front line, where there was no time for debate as to subtleties implied but not stated. In any case I had two senior commanders, in Barrow and Coward, who were basically reading them entirely differently, and I reckoned they, and no doubt others, needed advice as to how we were expected to behave during those vital first exchanges.

First and above all, I wanted precise control of when and how the 'war' started. So I invented a local procedure called 'Confisticate'. It's not to be found in the dictionary, and I borrowed it from a country parson who didn't like to use ruder words when he fell off his bicycle. Said with accent on the 'fist', it can be quite efficacious. It meant: 'Start the war' and could only be given by me. Until the moment I released that signal, the war, as far as we were concerned, had not started. I had, in effect, taken away some of my commanders' right of self-defence, further restricting the rules from home which allowed them to fire back. But I did not want this war to go off at half-cock, because that would be likely to cause disastrous confusion and loss of control . . . a state of affairs I had witnessed first hand in the Arabian Sea the previous November in exercises.

What was worrying *me* most was that political requirements could result in our entering the TEZ with our hands tied behind our backs. I thought it all too possible that I was going to be told again, 'The enemy *must* fire the first shot.' So, if those rules did prove to be the ones under which we must fight, then the first shot must clearly arrive on board one of my less-valuable frigates. Not too easy to arrange. And not too pleasant for the frigate selected. I wanted to fire the first shot myself and needed to convince my CTF. As far as I was concerned, I said, the first shot was fired on 2 April when they walked into the Falkland Islands. It's already been fired, so let's not muck about.

Our conversation was long and detailed over the DSSS (Long-range secure speech radio via satellite). I went over all the lessons I had learned with the *Coral Sea*, knowing well what the probable political argument against me would be: that Great Britain wished to be seen as the wronged party, the peace-loving victim who had been unfairly attacked and was now being attacked again. That we should accept the first shot, which would become a new *casus belli* and which would then, of course, be 'not our fault'. It was, however, clear to me that if the Argentinians knew what they were doing and hit one of my carriers, we would not need a *casus belli*, a reason to *start* a war. The war would already be over.

Having voiced my fears to Admiral Fieldhouse, and apparently convinced *him* anyway, I could relax on that front while he went to make our case to the Chiefs of Staff at the Ministry of Defence, and the Chief of Defence Staff took the matter to the Cabinet. My job was to ensure that the C-in-C had as much of the 'local colour' as possible before he went in to brief those who would make the final decisions.

So ended another day – but the next, Monday 26 April, started in the early hours when we detected another surface contact a mere fourteen miles away, too close, and very late on our part. It was eventually identified as a neutral merchantman, but once again I could not help thinking of that faraway night in the Arabian Sea and worrying about my near-total lack of capability for surface search around the Battle Group.

Finally we got some sleep, but throughout the morning the weather deteriorated, slowing us down yet again. In the afternoon the temperatures dropped rapidly, with wind speed increasing to a steady, chill south-easterly blow of over thirty knots. The seas got up again, but we nonetheless staged a fairly major Anti-Air Warfare Exercise. This was particularly difficult because, as we approached the Falklands, the exercise 'enemy' could too easily have turned out to be the real one.

On this day I also ran into trouble from an unforeseen, though probably unwitting enemy, the British Press. I should point out that I had never dealt with this phenomenon before, thus I was unsure how to handle them and what to tell them. I had been given, a week or so earlier, a complicated briefing from Headquarters which instructed me, in one line, to give them 'every co-operation'. On the next page and a half I was given all the details of what I was *not* to tell them. This could all be summarized simply enough: 'Co-operation, yes; information, no'. I was faced with providing a general interview for the reporters on board *Hermes*, in addition to the television interview I had done with Brian Hanrahan and Michael Nicholson a few days previously. I was not to know at the time, but apparently they all reached the public at about the same time.

The result was a minor catastrophe in the eyes of the Foreign Office, and on downwards. And upwards for that matter. I was quoted as having said: 'South Georgia was the appetizer, now this is the heavy punch coming up behind. My Battle Group is properly formed and ready to strike. This is the run-up to the Big Match which in my view should be a walkover. I'd give odds of 20 to 1 on, to win.' The headline 'WALKOVER WOODWARD' haunts me yet. But I am reasonably sure that those of you who have stayed with me since I made my way, somewhat hesitantly, to Eaton Hall several thousand words ago, would agree that it does not sound much like me. And the tape I have of the interview does not contain the phrase '... should be a walkover', though I do remember using the word itself in a slightly different sense. I had been asked what I thought the odds were of Britain being successful, and I can remember the thoughts cascading through my mind. 'Who is going to hear my reply? The Argentinians? Members of the British Government? The British public? The Americans? The world ... ? Well, whom do I care about most? Quickly, Woodward, make a decision, at whom will you aim your next words?'

The answer was obvious enough – none of those. I could only speak to the people who were with me, the thousands of anxious young men facing battle for the first time. I must not, cannot allow them, any of them, nor any of their loved ones at home, to think there is any real doubt about the outcome of any battle to come. The odds were uncertain, but I must not be. '20 to 1 on,' I said. Defeat must be cast from their minds as unthinkable. This is my team we are talking about here, and there is no way I can tell them we might be on to a loser, any more than if I were a football manager giving *his* team a last-minute lift before the Cup Final. I am going to tell them the biggest single lie I can sensibly get away with, to encourage everyone. And maybe also to frighten the Argentinians a bit at the same time. I added, safely enough I thought, 'But frankly, I'd really rather be given a walkover.' I meant this strictly in the tennis sense, that is, a walkover when your opponent fails to turn up for the match. I was not to know that subtleties such as that are rarely respected in the newspaper world.

After another very rough night, bashing our way into rolling head seas which reduced our speed-made-good to only seven knots, I was very firmly on the carpet first thing the following morning. This was one of the four or so occasions that Admiral Sir John Fieldhouse in person spoke to me on DSSS. He delivered formal notice of the displeasure of Her Majesty's Government at my remarks. He passed on the message from higher up that I was to do the interview all over again and be: 'Less jingoistic, more sober, peace-loving and quietly determined.'

'*Peace-loving!*' I exclaimed. 'With respect, sir, here I am, commanding a Battle Group, in a howling gale, seven thousand miles from home, preparing to fight a war most likely starting next Sunday, and *they* want *me* to sound *peace-loving*?'

'Yes,' he said, patiently, rather like Florence in that lovely BBC programme for children, 'Magic Roundabout'. He went on to point out that there had been a big splash in the home Press. And although I had no idea what he was on about, I did realize that I had not actually seen how it had been reported. However, the natural arrogance of the man in the front line towards the ones who are not, permitted me the luxury of total non-comprehension. Could they not see at home that a press conference ranks about eighty-third in my list of a hundred priorities? Out here, in the real world of big seas, strong winds, Rules of Engagement, missiles, shells, computers, 'Burglars', 'Spooks', whales and worried people, a few words to the Press ranks with me somewhere near the level of 'Pass the sausage rolls'. And yet here was the Commander-in-Chief himself, the Task Force Commander, lecturing me about those few sentences said, with some care, in front of a TV camera to encourage the men under my command. Never mind the massive problems we faced, never mind that *Alacrity* had just reported a man overboard, never mind that the Group gathering around me would soon number some fifteen war-ships, as many again supporting auxiliaries, with ten thousand men and all the weapons and aircraft. Never mind the distance from home and any base. Never mind the Argentinian Navy and Air Force, waiting to receive us.

Surely, if they didn't like it at home, they could get organized sufficiently well to cut out the offending bits? Surely they could understand the different requirements of the front line from elsewhere? 'Did you, or did you not, Woodward, say it would be a walkover?' Damned if I cared what I had said. The Press, as far as I was concerned, could do something very difficult to itself. But Sir John remained thoughtful. He made it clear that the government wished me to do the press conference again, in audio only, as we were now too far south to get any film back in time. I finally deferred to his wishes – there wasn't any choice – and undertook to be something close to craven in my peace-loving statements.

As it happened, I made the situation considerably worse.

'Er, Admiral . . . do you think this could be a long war?'

'Well, it could last a few months which could seem like a long time' – (pretty clever I thought – after all, I knew that we would be incapable of fighting at all by July – but couldn't *say* that, of course).

'Could a lot of people get killed?'

'Well, there is bloodshed in most wars. I doubt this will be any exception.'

'WOODWARD FORECASTS A LONG AND BLOODY WAR'.

'Oh, Sandy? C-in-C here. The Prime Minister is not terribly pleased with your contradictory remarks – first you say it will be a walkover. Now you forecast it will be a long and bloody war'.

At this point I realized that this was one battle I could not win. I also considered the whole lot of them might be losing their sense of perspective. But I also resolved that the Press and I were going to have to find a way to get along a whole lot better than we had so far. But such conciliatory thought did not long survive. Even then the *Sunday Telegraph*, behind the by-line of one Ivan Rowan whose experience of high command I suspect may be limited, came right out, three days later, and concluded a long article about me with the words: 'Seeing him on television, half sitting, half lying back, hiding his mouth behind his knuckles as he reaches hesitantly for the right words, you see what happened on the *Hermes* (sic) last week. An Admiral got out of his depth.' This did not of course refer to the business of making our plans for battle. That requires thought, study, intellect and most of the time available. It refers only to the way I had spoken to the Press. That was all that mattered. And there was not, apparently, the least vestige of thought as to the effect that beautiful line 'Admiral . . . out of his depth' could have on those directly concerned, the young men who may have to fight and die in the coming days.

The fact was that the Press did not see itself as being on 'our' side at all. It saw itself as a fearless seeker after truth and I believe they found a considerable amount of it. The Argentinian generals and admirals admitted after the war that they gained ninety per cent of all their intelligence about our activities from the British Press. The BBC World Service was particularly helpful. And the trouble was that they wrote down my every word as though I agreed with their attitude and had made a factual, objective, cold assessment of our chances. I had tried to answer their questions as carefully and as cheerfully as I could, but in no sense could I be some kind of extension of the BBC World Service. We were bound to be at loggerheads, at least at first.

Thus far, with a couple of days still to sail before we entered the TEZ, I now rated the Press one of my biggest problems, and one I felt aggrieved that I had to deal with at all. I did not have the time, the experience, the skill and certainly not the inclination. Plus that every time I spoke to them, the Ministry blew a fuse. We simply did not understand each other and the blame lay fairly equally. None of them had ever gone to war in a Battle Group, or even attended a major Fleet exercise. No more had I been prey to the requirements of a Fleet Street editor, with his quite different motivations. They were outsiders, looking on from a position of safety; we were insiders, watching out with our necks on the line. We just operated on completely different mind-sets. Theirs was a mix-ture of 'It doesn't matter much who wins or loses as long as we report it fairly and as, in our judgement, we see it.' There was also, on the editorial side, a bit of 'As long as we can sell it better than our competitors'. My mind-set was: 'Say and do whatever you have to to win.' Which is euphemistically worded these days as 'Be economical with the truth' by civil servants or 'Tell the biggest lie you can get away with' by spin doctors. Hardly surprising then, that we started so far apart. More surprising, perhaps, how quickly we all adjusted in the follow-ing few weeks. Perhaps this sort of attitude is another of those naval traditions we must make some compromises on.

Whatever else may be said about the traditions of the Royal Navy, their appropriateness to today and their value, there is one at least that I hold to be fundamental to all the rest. I call it the 'Jervis Bay Syndrome'. This refers to the armed merchant cruiser HMS *Jervis Bay* which had formerly been a 14,000-ton passenger liner, built in 1922, and called to duty in the Second World War with seven old six-inch guns mounted on her deck. She was assigned to convoy protection work in the North

Atlantic and placed under the command of Captain Edward Fogarty Fegan Royal Navy. In the late afternoon of 5 November 1940, *Jervis Bay* was escorting a convoy of thirty-seven merchant ships in the mid-Atlantic. Suddenly, over the horizon, appeared the German pocket battleship *Admiral Scheer*. Captain Fegan immediately turned towards the *Scheer*, knowing his ship would be sunk and that he would most likely die, out-ranged and out-gunned as he was. *Jervis Bay* fought for half an hour before she was sunk and later, when a ship returned to pick up survivors, the Captain was not among them. Edward Fegan was awarded a posthumous vc. But that half hour bought vital minutes for the convoy to scatter and make the *Scheer*'s job of catching and sinking more than a few of them too difficult. His was the moment we all know we may have to face ourselves.

We are indoctrinated from earliest days in the Navy with stories of great bravery such as this and many others like it, from Sir Richard Grenville of the *Resolution* to Lieutenant-Commander Roope vc of the *Glowworm* who, in desperation, turned and rammed the big German cruiser *Hipper* with his dying destroyer sinking beneath him. We had all been taught the same – each and every one of the captains who sailed with me down the Atlantic towards the Falklands in the late April of 1982 – that we will fight, if necessary to the death, just as our predecessors have traditionally done. And if our luck should run out, and we should be required to face a superior enemy, we will still go forward, fighting until our ship is lost.

CONQUEROR

6

The Final Approach

The weather now held us back badly, with great seas, poor visibility, rain and wind. However you looked at it, the hostile vastness of it all made even the 750-foot-long *Hermes* seem insignificant. For three days we had not seen the sun. The nearest thing to brightness we ever glimpsed was a rare, pearl ray from behind the hurrying clouds, breaking through to paint icy patterns on the blown foam of the wave-tops. It was an altogether forbidding scene even to the eyes of seasoned sailors as we lumbered forward through the long grey swells. It was all very much what we had been led to expect – extremely unpleasant, and very likely to remain so, we thought. I set about negotiating our arrival a day later than originally planned. We must of course hurry, but equally we must not permit these very tough conditions to inflict any more storm damage on our ships than is absolutely necessary. Not at this early stage.

By 27 April, we were less than a thousand miles from the Exclusion Zone. This increasing proximity to real war, plus the foul weather, was beginning to take its toll not only of ships but also of people. Our second stress case surfaced – a young officer had to be relieved of his present duties and given less-worrisome employment. Such personnel adjustments are not difficult to arrange if they are caught early enough. The problem very often comes down to persuading such people to face the facts.

These incidents always made me very sad because I knew that none of those involved were in any way cowards, or even shirkers. It was just that their minds became too pre-occupied with their own worries, entirely against their will. Most psychiatrists accept that a man can operate under immense strain when only half of his mind is pre-occupied with personal fears. However, when that stage is exceeded, the man becomes rapidly less able to respond correctly to external stimuli. He will tend just to go on doing whatever it was he was doing beforehand, as though nothing had changed. It is rarely his fault, and I say this in the face of all the fourth-rate, quasi-medical opinions that have been prevalent in the British Services for a very long while, and which are only now beginning to change in the light of hard evidence.

I have often wondered whether my own father, Tom Woodward, was just such a stress case. He must certainly have had an awful time in the trenches of the First World War, and steadfastly throughout the rest of his life would never utter one word about it. Then, towards the end, when his mental resistance was gone and his powers of coherent speech had left him, I shall never forget seeing him seize a chair, pushing it out in front of him and lunging as if it were a bayonet, his face set. The horrors of 1915–1918 must have been with him for all of those fifty years, and in the end they were the last, and still the most vivid, memories in his mind. But there are still too many military men prepared to dismiss the entire subject of stress, both pre-battle and post-battle, with a shrug and an insult about cowardice. Such a waste.

Within a few days a third case surfaced – an intelligent and responsible young man who was found dressed in his immersion suit and anti-gas respirator curled up in a ball, in the foetal position. He was under a table and he was absolutely unreachable. This was a classic example of complete mental breakdown, under the stress of forthcoming battle. I spoke at length about the subject with the Principal Medical Officer of *Hermes* and told him how I personally had noticed one of the previous cases developing; how I had observed the man unable to accept any more new information; and how he had become slow to react, dangerously unreliable. I explained that I had therefore intended to move him to a less demanding, real-time job to see how he reacted. The PMO confirmed my instincts (I had no real knowledge of the subject), and told me I could expect about a five per cent serious stress case rate during this campaign. He also told me to watch for any sudden, excessive drinking and went on at some length, in the manner of most professionals absorbed in their work. Eventually, getting bored and yawning a little, I asked him what other early symptoms to look for.

'That's one, for a start!'

'Eh?'

'Yawning, sir.'

I found that a bit of a jolt. Especially as I thought, secretly, that he was absolutely right. I was myself exhibiting several symptoms of stress at the time and have continued to do so in varying degrees and in varying circumstances ever since.

The timely warning of the PMO, edged with a touch of his own embarrassment, was a very good warning to me – to watch and take care of my own mental state, as well as remaining alert for observing the symptoms of others. Knowledge in this much-avoided subject is a tremendous help in dealing with it, and a fundamental qualification for modern management. Above all, it need not be crippling, as I hope this book shows.

Looking back on those days of mounting tension, I can now discern more clearly the subtleties of our gradual transition from a peacetime group of ships brought together for an exercise, to a battle group which was actually going to have to fight, to wage war, and thus accept damage, loss of ships, and loss of lives. Commands throughout the force became more terse at all levels. They say the first casualty of war is always truth. In our case, I believe it was politeness: '*Get that done right now!*' '*Don't just stand there, do it!*' Men were more on edge; tasks that once had seemed insignificant now appeared critical. The full range of Navy reasoning and habit which so often in peacetime had appeared petty, pedantic and even churlish, no longer seemed so. Reasons which had once seemed obscure came into sharp focus. It is quite remarkable how the prospect of a possible early demise can bring out the best in everyone.

There was of course a human toll in all of this – not just the stress cases, but also among the men who found it difficult to raise their game. But mostly I would say that everyone suppressed their worries and rose to the task, much as we had thoughtlessly expected, in the unquestioning traditions of the Services. There were the usual macabre jokes as wills were made out and last letters home were written. The men stayed cheerful, determined and, I noticed, slightly righteous about the entire operation, as if the action of the Argentinian High

Command was some kind of a personal affront to each and every one of them, entitling them all to an extra display of that rather reassuring (from my point of view) British bloody-mindedness.

The increases in efficiency and activity also had, in a sense, a hidden advantage in that everyone was kept much busier than normal, which left little time to fret and worry about the less attractive aspects of our journey. Quite simply, everyone was trying a lot harder. This brought further complications to my attention and there were constant temptations to embroil myself in the details of various operations, a luxury that was not only hopelessly inefficient but actually downright dangerous. You cannot command any operation effectively if you involve yourself with any form of trivia whatsoever. You need every moment to think and to assimilate the broadest possible picture, in the effort to out-manoeuvre your opponent.

Our chain of command was thus going to need some very serious honing, because in battle it would need to ensure maximum back-up for all decisions, maximum compliance with all commands, and yet an intensive attention to every detail, permitting nothing to fall between the cracks. Throughout it all I also had to try to maintain that essential flexibility to deal with the unexpected. In addition, the chain of command must work autonomously, keeping me informed but also permitting me the time to step back and take stock of any given or developing situation. Calling me every ten minutes all through the night for decisions would, in the end, prove counter-productive. The operation must run routinely, whether or not I am awake. I was thus extremely careful with the staff officers I appointed to occupy the executive positions closest to my own.

I also decided, exceptionally, to provide myself with two deputies, called Group Warfare Officers, to manage the real-time decisions of the whole Battle Group on my behalf. Two were needed so that one could always be on watch. And both would have to be captains. I should mention that it would have been the standard practice to have appointed two or even three relatively junior officers to act as GWOs – a commander perhaps, and two lieutenant-commanders – but this would not have given me the level of authority I wanted in the job. Any man who has reached the rank of captain has already gone through a stringent and individual selection process twice since the time when he was a lieutenant-commander. He has already demonstrated clear qualities of high intellect and confident leadership. If I was to trust the GWO on watch in this Battle Group, I had to have such men. If my commanding officers in the other ships were also to trust the decisions being made from the Flag Ops Room, on my behalf, they too had to have such men.

I do not think it would be betraying too great a sign of human fallibility to admit that I selected an old and trusted friend for my first GWO. He was Captain Andy Buchanan, aged at the time forty-six, a fellow submariner, and former Commander of HMS *Devonshire*, a 'County' Class guided-missile destroyer, like *Glamorgan*. He had in fact been sent down to join me in case we needed to control, from *Hermes*, the submarines which were on station with us. In the event, this did not occur, despite my wishes, which left Andy with a new and demanding role in the forthcoming campaign. He was tailor-made for the GWO job. This tall, sandy-haired, freckle-faced Hampshireman had also commanded Britain's fifth SSN, HMS *Courageous*, and indeed had served with me years before in HMS *Porpoise*. Aside from the fact that he knew me so well, and understood precisely what I would expect of him, I had total confidence in his professional background and competence. Also, should tempers ever grow ragged, I knew he would know more or less how to make the boss laugh, a talent which ought not to be underestimated in any walk of life.

My second, but in no sense lesser GWO was Captain Peter Woodhead, a slim, rather angular man in both personality and physique. He was of very high intelligence, having worked as Assistant Director (Naval Future Policy Staff) when I was his Director. I recalled that he had consistently impressed me greatly as our resident 'Mr Guess-the-Future'. I had no knowledge of his 'front-line' competence, but what I knew of him, professionally and personally, gave me every cause for confidence. In addition, Peter was a naval aviator and would act as my air adviser, a position fraught with difficulty, dealing on a daily basis with the prima donna attitudes of the many different specialists in aviation matters. I suppose the very nature of their job, with its uncomfortably high rates of crash, death and injury, inevitably creates a certain type of person. In my experience, naval aviators can agree among themselves on only two things as beyond dispute: a) that anyone who is not a naval aviator is a troglodyte; b) that this particularly applies to the Royal Air Force. Within naval aviation, Sea Harrier pilots consider themselves to be men apart, arrows in the sky. Anti-submarine Sea King pilots consider Sea Harriers to be flashy and irresponsible. And the 'Junglies' – the pilots of the Commandos' Sea King 4s – are despised by both the first two as airborne truck-drivers.

For the record, Peter Woodhead had been a 'Jungly', actually one of a number of quite amazing fliers who perform a unique task under the most hazardous conditions, and who generally reckon that they are the only ones who have any real need for flying skills. Fortunately, Peter was too much of an intellect to subscribe to any of this childish repartee – which must be one reason why he is now an admiral, and Flag Officer, Second Flotilla. In addition he proved to be a most balanced and reliable air adviser, which was particularly important in view of the lack of any such service provided by the Royal Air Force. Not that they hadn't offered – but the naval aviators at home, I have always assumed, had said they could manage without.

If I might digress for a few lines, I would like to explain the function of our Junglies. They are specialists, their principal task now being to insert, in secret, under the cover of darkness, the recce forces of SAS and SBS who would report back to us the lie of the land, and where we ought *not* to be in the face of heavy Argentine defences. If you read that last sentence quickly, it does not sound too bad. In practice, the pilots would soon be required to fly in bad weather, in complete or near-complete darkness, over enemy-held territory, very low indeed. They would not know, until it became all too apparent, where the enemy actually *was*. Sitting behind them, in the helicopters, would be the teams of Special Forces, ready to go as soon as the pilots, peering down through their passive night goggles, were able to find the right spot. Those goggles they wear do enable them to see quite well in starlight, or better in moonlight. However, any lighted bulb, either in the cockpit or even a distant street light, will blind the pilot until he can get it out of the field of vision. One way and another, the Junglies are a very special breed and understandably they have a very special pride in what they do. Peter Woodhead was one of them, and he understood all the other aviators as well – their prejudices, their problems, their requirements and their attitudes, which made him, one way and another, just about invaluable on an aircraft carrier going to war.

If I were asked to compare Peter and Andy, I would be tempted to say that Peter would have been well suited to the Army's 'Regiment of the Intelligentsia', the Green Jackets; while Andy would have been more comfortable in a good armoured regiment or, in an earlier century, the cavalry.

Now, as we approached the final days of our journey to the south, we instituted a system of six hours on, six off, for these two key people. During their watch, they took overall charge of the minute-to-minute stuff, filtering and directing the information, ordering and controlling every activity of the Group to ensure that the plan for each day and event was sensibly carried forward. Both Captain Buchanan and Captain Woodhead answered of course only, and directly, to me. The cry 'Admiral to the Ops Room!' always available to them in moments of near-panic or major surprise, was never used throughout our long weeks in the Falklands area – not because I was always in the Ops Room, but because they were always prepared, and had prepared me, for the rapidly unfolding events.

Working alongside them, in an equal but very different capacity, was my Staff Officer, Operations, Commander Jeremy Sanders, a communications specialist who had already commanded his own frigate very successfully. Indeed, had I not instituted the GWO system of two watch-keeping captains, he would have been the senior GWO. As it was, he looked after the bigger picture on a longer-term basis. For example, I would receive more than five hundred signals a day, coming in from Headquarters in Northwood, the Ministry of Defence in London, Ascension Island, other ships in the Group, wherever, and Jeremy saw every single one of them, filtering them by assigning action on each signal to appropriate staff officers, and ensuring that I only saw those signals that I absolutely *had* to. This relieved me of a vast quantity of unnecessary detail and hassle-factor. No commander in the field can operate without such a person. Great trust is placed in him, but few thanks are given.

No matter how great the harassment factor, Jeremy would somehow handle it. Every couple of minutes of the day he dealt with sudden needs, obscure commands, implicit suggestions, conversations on Cackle, translating my wishes into clear and precise written instructions for the rest of the Battle Group. And his duties did not stop there. For he was also in charge of what American corporations describe as 'compliance', in other words, having issued the orders (for example, that *Coventry* should take up position off Port Stanley airstrip with *Brilliant* tomorrow morning), he was the man to check that this did indeed happen and that all who needed to know (COMAW, FAAWC, Warfare Officers, the ships concerned, nearby aircraft, and so on) did in fact know, precisely, and in good time.

I am very conscious that it would have been totally impossible to have run such an operation without a man such as this. And, as an added asset, Jeremy Sanders possessed the rare gift of tact, always highly valued in the Senior Service, and a commodity which I am often accused of lacking.

The operations staff planners, a group of commanders and lieutenant-commanders, answered directly to Jeremy Sanders. These were the officers who covered the detail in each major specialist skill – surface, air, submarine, land forces, Special Forces, communications, electronic warfare, supply and logistics, engineering, medical – anything that had to be co-ordinated with other activities.

That was the senior line-up in my Operations Room in *Hermes* from where I commanded our naval business against the Argentinians. One deck above me was the Ops Room of the Captain of *Hermes*, Linley Middleton, another naval aviator, whose function was to run this floating airfield. His responsibility was to drive the ship, get us in the required place, make sure the airfield and its aircraft were operational at all times and to provide a home for the Flag. His responsibilities were entirely separate from mine, and though we were by definition required to work together, as were all of my captains, we followed essentially different paths of responsibility on board this ship.

By Wednesday 28 April we in the South Atlantic no longer discussed the possibility of war – it was too close for us to think or plan otherwise. From time to time we received reports from London that General Haig was having one final throw at achieving peace, but it was an irrelevance now to us. Our job was simply to be prepared to defend ourselves, to be prepared to attack at the best opportunity and to set about landing a force of perhaps ten thousand British troops on the Falklands. And that is precisely what we were doing.

Though we didn't know it, back home this would certainly have been approved of by the editors of the national newspapers who were apparently baying for an old-fashioned sea battle, writing editorials calling for an end to futile negotiations. One can in a sense understand their point. Sea battles probably look quite fascinating, even vaguely romantic, from Orpington, if not quite so entertaining from the front line.

That day, by signal, we heard that the Junta had rejected Haig's final attempt at peace. And Mrs Thatcher was, in my opinion, no more likely to back down. She had said we would fight if we had to, she knew the military deadlines as laid down on my bar-chart back at Ascension, and that was an end to it.

But whatever went on at those high levels, I had other problems. One in particular was the question of who was to control the three nuclear submarines we now had in place in the South Atlantic. There was HMS *Conqueror*, an improved Valiant Class boat of 4000 tons commanded by Commander Christopher Wreford-Brown; HMS *Spartan*, of the slightly bigger Swiftsure Class, commanded by Commander Jim Taylor; and HMS *Splendid*, sister ship to *Spartan* and commanded by Commander Roger Lane-Nott. All the submarines and their commanding officers were well known to me.

It was my opinion that I should take control of them myself, rather than have them run directly from Northwood by the Flag Officer, Submarines. I felt there were several good reasons for this:

a) I had Captain Buchanan on my staff, and one of the main reasons he was with me at all was to act as the local Submarine Force Coordinator.

b) It made more sense, to me at least, that the submarines should be under my command locally in case it became necessary to deal with a quickly changing set of circumstances which required very early action.

c) It might be alleged that I knew something about the subject of submarine warfare in my own right since I had been appointed, admittedly only for a week or two, to command the Submarine Flotilla in 1981.

d) *Hermes* was fully equipped with all the necessary
   submarine communications channels to do the
   job.

Above all, I wanted to change the operating methods – make
them better suited to the conditions prevailing in the south.
Up in the North Atlantic, where in the NATO context the
main task is anti-submarine warfare, there are very large
numbers of ships, aircraft and submarines operating in quite
close proximity to similarly large numbers of the enemy. We
thus divide the ocean up into areas. We then allocate them to
submarines, so that each one has, so to speak, his own 'patch'.
To minimize the chances of a 'Blue on Blue' (attacking each
other), they are not allowed to trespass into each other's
patches, neither are our ships or aircraft allowed to attack
submarine contacts in such areas, unless they have been positively identified as enemy. Such identification is not an easy
thing to do at the best of times, least of all when you need to
shoot first in the selfish interest of personal survival. Our policy
in war is therefore relatively simple: keep your submarines in
their patches; that way, should the occupant of the patch detect
another submarine, it *must* be the enemy and you can shoot
'from the hip', confident that you are not about to sink one
of your own. Keep them separate – keep them safe.

Except that these conditions did not apply in the South
Atlantic, where our likely enemy, Argentina, actually only
owned four submarines, one of which, the nearly forty-year-old
Santa Fe was already wrecked at Grytviken. Her sister ship,
Santiago del Estero, which was nearly as old, was, we believed,
laid up, non-operational. That left them with a couple of small,
hardly ocean-going, German-built Type 209s, *Salta* and *San
Luis*. Best suited to inshore, fairly static operations, I believed

that these two, if indeed both were available at the same time, would be given patrol areas fairly close to Port Stanley. This, after all, was the single most likely place for them to find British ships, eventually. Certainly these two little submarines were not likely targets for, or threats to, our own SSNs, which were there primarily to stop the movement of Argentinian surface ships.

Therefore, I concluded it was no longer necessary to confine our SSNs to separate areas, provided they were forbidden to engage submerged contacts. By releasing the SSNs from the constraints of separate areas, I could attach any of them (or they could attach themselves as the chance offered) to any group of Argentinian surface ships, ready to attack the moment they got final clearance from London.

However, Northwood, probably for mainly political reasons, did not wish to alter the patch system at this late stage and did not transfer control of the submarines to me. With the Flag Officer, Submarines, *and* the C-in-C both senior to me and *both* submarine specialists to boot, I was in no position to continue arguing. So I retired from the debate with as much grace as I could summon, which, as I recall, was not all that much.

By 28 April the offshore areas around the Falklands had been divided broadly into four quadrants – *Conqueror* had the south-west and south-east, *Spartan* the north-west and *Splendid* the north-east, with the two northerly SSNs being changed around quite frequently. None was allowed to trespass into the areas of the others. This was to have major consequences a few days later, and I am proud to confirm I have never once, to any of them, in all of the intervening years, uttered, or even implied, the phrase 'I told you so'. Well, not very often, anyway.

Meanwhile, the days passed and, despite the bad weather and some delay, we made adequate progress south. The whole Battle Group was finally assembled, we achieved a good full-scale air defence exercise on that Wednesday afternoon, which put everyone in a slightly more optimistic mood, and we caught and drove away the 'Burglar' a hundred and thirty miles out when he turned up at sunset.

That evening I completed a letter home to Char which began:

The days go by surprisingly fast with no real political change. You cannot help feeling – now here's an extra-ordinary business. Can we *really* be going to war? Is it me that's in charge of fifteen thousand men and the biggest fleet we've put together in thirty-five years? I never asked for a place in anyone's history book, and I don't view the prospect with any enthusiasm. Par-ticularly if it involves sending old friends up front . . . the picture is gloomy and politicians are probably going to tie my hands behind my back . . . and then be angry when I fail to pull their beastly irons out of the fire for them . . .

As the day goes on, most of the plans for the first few days of battle are set. They are necessarily very flexible, but I've done my thinking about it and conse-quently feel easier in my mind. Of course, in the final hours/days, options do reduce, so decisions are a bit easier. Even the thought of death has to be faced up to as a not-very-likely outcome, and taken for what it is – like, unavoidable if it happens. But do your best, and maybe it won't. Generally though, I feel much easier in my mind: our business end is about wrapped

up for a few days – it will be a busy time, and it is as
well to stop worrying, and 'rest up' to be ready.

From those words you can feel that the possible realities of
war were beginning to affect me. My diary written that night
just before midnight reads as follows: 'Weather went down so
we got the refuelling done in the lull before the next storm.
Final preps for the run-in are mostly complete now – just hope
the politicos can pull back in time, otherwise a lot of people
are going to stay out here.'

Thursday 29 April, approximately five hundred miles from
the TEZ, we spent much of the day refuelling and replenishing
supplies on the assumption that all too soon it might not be
so easy. *Brilliant* and *Plymouth* rejoined us from South Georgia.
Captain Coward flew over to debrief me on the action there,
and also to report on a sad incident on board the *Santa Fe*.

Apparently, once the *Santa Fe* had been captured, some
Royal Marines had been put on board as guards for the several
members of the Argentinian crew who were operating the
ship's systems under our orders. Down below in the Control
Room, a Marine had told an Argentinian engineer to stop
doing whatever it was he was doing – fiddling with some control mechanism, it seemed. The engineer had continued working to control the submarine's buoyancy and the Marine,
fearful that the man might be attempting to scuttle the boat,
issued him one last warning. When this too was ignored, he
shot and killed him.

I think Captain Coward decided that this course of action
might be regarded in official quarters as being over-hasty at
best, and contrary to the Geneva Convention at worst. Just as
well that I should hear it first from him, as he was in charge
of the *Santa Fe* when it happened and anyway he was perhaps

instinctively aware that I would sympathize with the Royal Marine, war being war. Sad but unsurprising; misunderstandings and accidents will always happen when people find themselves in strange situations and confronted with apparently menacing behaviour by an incomprehensible enemy.

That night a real late-autumn fog drew in – like England in November – and enveloped the Battle Group in a swirling grey shroud of cold and damp. The wind dropped and, though the sea dropped too, we cancelled all flying because of the hopeless visibility. After dinner, I spent some time in conference with my captains, and by midnight we all knew there had been no further political progress. Sitting alone in my cabin, I wrote home: 'The time available has just about run out. I shall have to go in and make aggressive noises off Port Stanley, and start losing lives. Not quite the way we all thought I'd be spending my half-century birthday, in the late Autumn!'

A quiet night – fog does have its good points – was followed by another busy day of topping up fuel ready for the final run-in. In the late afternoon one of the Harriers on combat air patrol found a fishing vessel which was identified as a Canadian research ship by the name of *Narwal*. I thought nothing of it at the time.

Now two hundred and fifty miles out from the TEZ, our new Rules of Engagement came in from London. I had permission to open fire on any combat ship or aircraft in that Zone identified as Argentinian, when we got inside it.

As we shaped up for our final approach, President Reagan imposed military and economic sanctions on Argentina. Apparently very much to the Junta's surprise. Plainly they had not known anything about Caspar Weinberger's orders, by which we had been supplied with air-to-air missiles, ammunition, fuel, the facilities in Ascension, certain critically important satellite communications channels and other less public help. Indeed for several weeks now, little had been spared in the way of help short of AEW aircraft and the big attack carrier required to operate them from. But this would have meant American men directly involved in the front line, and that was much more than we could have reasonably hoped for. Britain was always going to have to fight her enemy alone, if it came to that.

Very soon after I had read and digested our new ROE, a call came in from the C-in-C on the satellite link informing me that it was now 'Go'. I was formally given leave to proceed inside the TEZ and start the process of recapturing the Falkland Islands.

The tactical picture was now becoming clearer as to the whereabouts of the Argentinian fleet. Up to the north-west was their carrier *Veintecinco de Mayo*, with her two escorting destroyers. On her deck would be some ten A4 fighter bombers – possibly also some Exocet-armed Super Etendards – all well-trained and qualified to attack surface ships. Down to the south-west was the heavily armed cruiser *General Belgrano* and her two escorting destroyers, each carrying eight Exocet.

It looked to me as though I would be facing a pincer movement by these two groups as I made my way west in towards the Port Stanley area for my landing deception. My hope was to keep *Conqueror* in close touch with the *Belgrano* group to the south, to shadow the carrier and her escorts to the north with one of the 'S' Boats up there. Upon the word from London, I would expect to make our presence felt, preferably by removing their carrier and, almost as important, the aircraft she carried from the Argentinian Order of Battle. Uppermost in my mind was the need to avoid any major inter-surface group battle and the risk of anything like the *Glamorgan/Coral Sea* fiasco: I wanted the SSNs to deal with their surface ships; they were my front line.

Alas, the first development was not good. Though *Spartan* was closest to our best estimate of the *Veintecinco de Mayo*'s position, she had already been diverted twice by her masters in Northwood from what I viewed as her prime task (which was finding the *25 de Mayo*) – to go and look for other, less important or threatening targets. Now, she was too close to the edge of her patch. She was forbidden to cross the unseen line beyond which we believed the *25 de Mayo* was steaming.

At this point the North Atlantic rules were still operative, and they were very clear – unless in 'hot pursuit' of an enemy ship, the SSN must stop short. *Spartan*'s Captain felt he could go no further, that he should not trespass in *Splendid*'s patch. But he had no idea *Splendid* was too far away, since Commander Jim Taylor had spent the day responding as best he could to confusing intelligence reports. Now it was too late. To my complete frustration, I had to face the fact that neither of the two SSNs could reach the only target we really wanted. Thus, my SSN shield to the north failed to mark (naval jargon for 'locate and shadow') the Argentinian carrier. And Anaya's Naval Air Force lived to fight another day, sadly to inflict great damage upon our ships.

On the profit side, we re-identified the *Narwal* as an Argentinian trawler, maintaining rough station on us at a respectful distance. I thought she might be shadowing us and so *Alacrity* was sent out to warn her off, which he did. *Narwal* duly disappeared, and not a moment too soon, as the last thing I wanted was an Argentinian shadow during the final approach telling his beastly friends precisely where I was. 'What's more, you horrible man, if you put another foot wrong, you've had your last warning, whether I'm officially allowed to shoot at fishing vessels or not,' I thought.

My day ended with a little more to Char:

> We're off then. Tomorrow is called 'C' Day (my invention, to avoid confusion with 'D' Day, and because navalese for 'C' is Charlie), so the auguries are good at least, whatever actually happens. Naturally rather nervous, but actually no more so than on the racing start line, or just before starting a speech. Maybe worse tomorrow, once it starts in earnest, and we are finally committed.

I did not go to bed after my short note, however, because we were about to sail into a kind of no man's land ... the *Argentinian* Exclusion Zone, which was about sixty miles further out from the Islands than our own. Whether or not we, the British, recognized it, we did have to face the possibility that they might well feel free to attack us as soon as we entered it. The problem was that I could only defend myself if attacked. I was not free to shoot first unless I found the enemy inside *our own* Exclusion Zone, some sixty miles further inshore ... a dangerous, unmilitary and unsatisfactory state of affairs. I could only hope the Argentinians would not take advantage of our vulnerable situation, as we hurried across. Anyone who was not nervous on this night, did not understand the realities.

Meanwhile the Battle Group maintained its course to the south-west in anti-air formation, with the Type 42s, *Glasgow*, *Sheffield* and *Coventry*, out to the west, their long-range air warning radars alert for approaching aircraft. Down in the Ops Rooms, three decks below the bridge, there existed a state of war, unmistakable in its urgency, hard in its purpose. The quiet watchkeepers, in their anti-flash gear, continuing their babel of business, terse comments into microphones, in the strange half light, to the accompaniment of clattering keyboards. The Principal Warfare Officers usually standing, the better to monitor the overall conduct of the Ops Room; the supervisors moving softly behind the young operators in front of their screens, concentrating now perhaps as they had never done before. And every time the ship hit a big wave, the sudden dull thump of it against the hull, once just routine, now ping-ed your fears.

There was a natural tendency for people to gravitate towards the Ops Room. Anyone who could find a reasonable excuse to look in, would do so. And be told to bugger off for fear he would get in the way. It was as if somehow the closeness, the singleness of purpose, and the extra concern of the officers, made them all less vulnerable. As I mentioned earlier, in the Royal Navy, we do not *send* anyone anywhere. We all go together.

Those of us in *Hermes* were well aware of what was going on. Lin Middleton was on the bridge, I was in the Flag Ops Room with Andy Buchanan, and no one was saying much as we steamed across the unseen line that marked the Argentine Exclusion Zone at 0130 that black Atlantic morning. 1 May. The war starts today. It's my fiftieth birthday.

SEA HARRIER

7

1 May – The War Begins

Sir Walter Scott's epic two-hundred-page war poem *Marmion*
– a tale of Flodden Field – contains the words that every child
learns in kindergarten, either the best advice, or perhaps the
sternest warning, on the subject of telling lies:

> O, what a tangled web we weave,
> When first we practise to deceive!

The tone of the learned nineteenth-century Scottish writer
and historian is both wise and disapproving. Which does, in
a sense, highlight one of the major shifts in military behaviour
since King James fell to the English in that brutal but nonetheless straightforward battle at Flodden in 1513. By 1982, almost
470 years after Sir Walter's Lord Marmion died heroically for
England, it had become standard practice in modern warfare
to surround your opponent with Scott's 'tangled web'. Lies,

disinformation and a string of elaborate deceptions are deliberately employed to lead the enemy into misunderstanding your actual intentions. Only in this way can a weaker force prevail over a better-placed but less devious opponent, or a stronger force minimize its casualties.

In any event, in the South Atlantic we certainly 'practised to deceive', but the web we wove for the benefit of our opposite numbers, on land and on sea, was not going to get tangled if we could possibly help it. I do not suppose the author of *Ivanhoe* would have thought much of it, but basically I had been in the deception game for several thousand miles now. Indeed, as far back as the 8th parallel, we had started that long feint towards the South American mainland, just to let General Galtieri know that it was not impossible that we might strike straight at Buenos Aires. Also all the way south we had tried to deceive the Argentinians into believing that the amphibians were with us. This was achieved by the use of 'chaff', small fragments of radar reflective material, cut to specific sizes to deceive specific radar frequencies. We deploy it in rockets and shells, and from aircraft, in packets. It is used principally to baffle incoming missiles: we send it up from the ships, in giant fireworks called chaff rockets, and when they explode the millions of chaff particles 'bloom', forming a cloud, larger than the ship, which we hope will cause the radar-guided missile to change its mind about us and take a swing to the bigger and more inviting radar contact of the chaff. Clearly you do not want to send the cloud up, straight in front of the ship, or else the missile will fly straight through it and hit the ship anyway. There is considerable skill involved in getting the chaff up; in the right place, at the right time, and keeping it there. The men who are trained to do it are a vital link in the defensive chain.

The other useful function of chaff concerns the deception of reconnaissance planes watching your group with cloud-avoidance radar from a distance of say two hundred miles. The moment we caught a glimpse of that Argentinian Boeing (the Burglar) on our radar, we would send up about a dozen 'chaff stations' which from that distance would look exactly like ships on his screen. Thus the enemy could be made to believe we were a battle fleet of, say, twenty-five ships instead of only fifteen.

Actually, at this juncture, the words of Sir Walter had to be heeded. This web of deception which we had now woven needed to be carefully tended: for instance, we had to replenish the chaff as it faded, in order to perpetuate our fabrications to the Argentinian Air Force. So helicopters had to clatter off tirelessly into the sky with packets of chaff which the pilots 'sowed' into the old chaff clouds, re-seeding them, until the Burglar went away. The overall effect of this particular deception was, I hoped, that the occupiers of the Falkland Islands would believe we were accompanied, in our front line, by the Amphibious Group, which we were not. In this way I suspected, rightly, they would believe, wrongly, that we were on our way to Port Stanley for a full-frontal assault, straight in, with the Royal Marines and the Paras landing and charging up the middle of the High Street, so to speak. This, we thought, should cause the Argentinian land forces to stay concentrated in that area, while we actually looked elsewhere, because it was the doctrine the Args had been taught by the US Marines, whose instinct in the field of amphibious assault has usually been to go straight through the front door, kicking it down whether or not it happens to be locked.

Thus I felt sure I could second-guess the Argentinian military mind. They would assume that we would act as the

Americans – their mentors, and our traditional allies – would act under the present circumstances. In fairness to the warriors who have fought beneath the Stars and Stripes, they have achieved a great deal by charging through the front door, and indeed have won many a remarkable victory with such tactics, for they are unfailingly bold, and usually brilliantly equipped.

We, on the other hand, down here in the lonely windswept wastes of the South Atlantic could afford no such John Wayne manoeuvres. We shall win this battle, I often thought to myself, but it's going to take an element of stealth and slyness, which would perhaps have seemed pretty ungentlemanly to the creator of Young Lochinvar. Not to mention the English knights who fought at Flodden Field. But times have changed, and we had to fight our battle in the Age of Deceit. So we encouraged them in every way possible to believe that dawn on 1 May, or possibly the 2 May, was 'D-Day'.

Our plans were now simple enough. We would strike hard at Port Stanley Airfield with the Vulcan raid from Ascension first and then, at dawn, use the Sea Harriers against Port Stanley Airfield again at the same time as we hit the strip at Goose Green. Whether or not these raids proved successful in disabling these airfields, they would benefit us in other ways: firstly, they would keep the Argentinians convinced for at least another twenty-four hours that we planned a straightforward landing at Port Stanley; and secondly, the dawn strike would take the Argentinian heat away from our really serious purpose of the day/night – to land the Special Forces reconnaissance troops on to the darkened islands to begin the perilous business of assessing the enemy defensive positions. But the real spin-off from the opening attacks was that we would be forcing the Argentinians to reveal their defences to us in a way which no intelligence can, on its own, match. I hoped to draw their air force into action in some form or another, for a day or two. I hoped to use the Carrier Battle Group to draw their navy out for the SSNs to deal with, without the amphibious ships in company to slow me down. And I hoped, with the aid of a major naval bombardment from the sea, to be able to concentrate the minds of their land troops on an assault mission which was *not* about to happen.

The profit side for us, on this the opening day of the war, was in my opinion very good. The downside – losing a dozen Sea Harriers or several ships – was unthinkable. The opening attacks in any war are inclined to be a risky business at best and an essential 'feeler' for later operations. But, as they say, you won't win the lottery if you don't buy a ticket.

Meanwhile the 'brains trust' which surrounded me at this particular stage of the proceedings was having its own steel tested down in the Ops Room where it had been concentrated throughout this night. In deadly secret, high above us and far from us, one of the most difficult long-distance bombing raids ever attempted was unfolding in a tenuous, complicated manoeuvre which will probably be talked about long into the twenty-first century. At least in Royal Air Force circles it will be. They were attempting to fly a Vulcan bomber on an 7860-mile round trip from Ascension and back with one specific purpose – to blast a bloody great hole in the middle of the runway of Port Stanley airfield. We all knew it would take a very large bomb dropped from a very great height to penetrate and break up the tarmac sufficiently to stop its further use by fast jet aircraft, and hopefully for others as well. But by any standards this was an air-raid of heroic proportions, and one which many of my officers doubted could ever be done. In fact when it was first mentioned to us, some aviators – not entirely unsurprisingly – thought it sheer folly to attempt, since it was unlikely to succeed and anyway, would bring all other air activity at Ascension almost to a standstill.

My own view was more succinct: 'The mission has my unqualified support.' This is not meant to demonstrate special knowledge on my part, merely to confirm that anything anyone can do to help prevent the Args fighter/attack aircraft getting off the ground from Port Stanley to bomb my ships has my automatic 'unqualified support'. I did not have to give the matter more than about three seconds' thought, and for every mile they flew they carried my heartfelt good wishes.

I did not of course know, but the mission ran into trouble almost from the start. One of the eleven re-fuelling tankers, the Victors, developed a fault, still within sight of Ascension and had to turn back. Then the Vulcan bomber itself developed a problem in its pressurization system, and *that* had to turn back. But the immaculate planning of the Royal Air Force had taken care of both these upsets before they occurred. They had a spare Victor with its tanks full already up there and they knew they only needed ten re-fuellings anyway. And of course they had sent up a reserve, fully laden Vulcan bomber with an equally competent crew. The mission proceeded as planned.

Flight-Lieutenant Martin Withers of 101 Squadron was now at the controls of the lead Vulcan, with twenty-one thousand-pound bombs aboard. It was going to take *five* air-to-air refuelling rendezvous with the tankers just to get the Vulcan to the target. Martin Withers was a brave and determined man, as were all of those who flew with him. The operation was code-named 'Black Buck'. It had been agreed that no conversation would pass between the Battle Group and the Vulcan, save for one word, to announce that he had dropped his bombs in roughly the right place. The word was to be: 'Superfuse'. Then, once more in silence, they would begin the long four-thousand-mile fuel-starved, nerve-wracking journey back up the Atlantic to Ascension.

And now we could only sit and wait for the codeword. The seconds ticked by until we estimated they were about fifty miles from the target, and by that time Withers would be pulling the big Vulcan into a steep climb to reach ten thousand feet, the attack altitude necessary to give his bombs sufficient velocity to penetrate the runway, disrupt it and thereby render it unusable by fast jet aircraft. This was the most dangerous part in terms of being spotted, although there was not a whole lot the Args could do about it in the short time left before Withers would deliver his attack.

He came in over the airfield in the pitch dark at four hundred mph, heading south-west – textbook RAF bombing procedure. The twenty-one bombs were spaced fifty yards apart, and they were released from the aircraft five seconds apart, two miles short of the runway to allow for the throw-forward effect of an aircraft travelling at this speed.

No one knew it yet, but the first bomb had hit close to the centre of the runway, the rest caused considerable damage around the airfield and also woke up the entire town. However, the Vulcan was round and heading for home, fourteen miles away and climbing before the bombs arrived and the Args guns opened up. Too late. This war had started, and they had lost Round One. 'Superfuse!' said Withers's radio operator, quietly. It was reported somewhere that clenched fists had punched the air in the Ops Rooms of the British Battle Group, but I never saw them.

While the arrival of the bombs announced formally that Margaret Thatcher's government was not best pleased with the antics of Galtieri's forces, we steamed into the Total Exclusion

Zone – roughly a hundred and forty miles from the coastline of East Falkland, on an east-north-easterly bearing from Port Stanley.

There were twelve warships in my Group, and we did not yet need to be concerned for the safety of the far-distant amphibious ships. Right now we were here on our own, and every one of us was here to fight. I trusted that the events of the past few minutes had sent a message to the Argentinian troops that we were irrevocably committed to their removal. Nonetheless on that dark morning the general mood in the Battle Group remained grim. We were about to launch our own opening attack and *Hermes* was to become the single busiest spot in the South Atlantic. Our plan had been refined to the last detail, and now we were going to test our ability to carry it out.

We made fourteen Sea Harriers available from *Hermes*, two of which were 'spares' in case of unserviceability. The plan was to send in twelve of them, splitting into three groups as they headed into range of the shore defence batteries. Speed and surprise were the keys to this, of that we were certain. The first wave against Port Stanley airfield was designed to make the Argentinian anti-aircraft defences keep their heads down. The second wave was to damage the runway. Simultaneously, the third raid would hit the airfield at Goose Green where we guessed there would be considerable back-up aircraft and personnel.

I watched from the safety of my bridge the preparations for the raid going on, almost in silence, far below. The Harriers were lined up along the starboard side of the Flight Deck, ready to move aft in turn and take off with the good run at the 'ski jump' needed for their heavy bomb loads. The Flight Deck parties moved swiftly around in the dark making their last-minute checks, while the white-gloved pilots climbed into their cockpits before they too went through the essential disciplines of their own last-minute checks.

It was still completely dark on the deck when one of the line of Harriers reported it was unserviceable, disrupting the ritual dance which forms the pattern for the full launch as the aircraft move aft and take off along the port side. I remember standing up there, watching the others swerve out to go round the broken-down Harrier as if partaking in some lunatic game of musical chairs.

The Commander of 800 Squadron, Lieutenant-Commander Andy Auld opened his throttle, driving the Sea Harrier forward, up and out into the night. I waited as always for that heart-stopping moment when the Harrier dips down towards the waves before recovering and climbing away ahead of the ship to the west. I counted them out, twelve of them in all, and they headed off to the west-south-west towards the Falkland Islands. Once more we could do little else but wait.

The sun was beginning to climb out of the Atlantic to our east and on East Falkland it was shortly before 0800 (1100z for us), when the British attack force screamed in low over Macbride Head. They were twenty-one miles north of Port Stanley when they split up, with Lieutenant-Commander Tony Ogilvie leading four toss bombers to the south-west for the defence-suppression run. Andy Auld and his men took one quick orbit to give Tony Ogilvie some room, and then flew south straight for Port Stanley airfield.

Ogilvie's group struck first, their half-ton toss bombs detonating in mid-air and pouring down millions of hot sharp metal splinters on the Argentinian anti-aircraft gun positions on Mary and Canopus hills, set diagonally to the north and south

of the airfield. With the Args' defence now temporarily pre-
occupied Andy Auld's group of five lay-down bombers came
in and bombed the airfield, dropping the dreaded six-hundred-
pound cluster bombs on parked aircraft and stores, setting fire
to buildings and destroying one aircraft. The last of them,
Flight-Lieutenant Dave Morgan, flew low into the middle of
the general uproar going on below with bombs, shells and
missiles exploding everywhere, and was hit by a 20mm shell
in his tail fin. It punched a hole the size a tea-cup through the
metal and gave him a nasty jolt. As the aircraft began to shudder, Morgan dropped his bombs, ducked and dived out of the
way of a radar-lock from a guided-missile system, and headed
back to *Hermes* with his colleagues.

Meanwhile the other three Harriers had raced down Falkland Sound at wave-top height, passing below Fanning Head
and Chancho Point which guard San Carlos Water. They then
angled inshore, lifting over the Lafonia coastline and, taking
a line on the airfield at Goose Green, they came in very low to
launch their attack, taking the defences completely by surprise.
They blew up an Argentinian Pucara as it was taxiing to take
off, killing the pilot and several ground crew.

We saw them coming back in over the horizon in ones and
twos, and I did not leave the bridge until I had seen all twelve
of them thump down on the deck of *Hermes*. I well remember
Brian Hanrahan, standing beside me, sensibly asking if he
might report how many aircraft were used in the raid. I said
that I'd prefer he didn't mention any numbers but that he *could*
say he'd seen as many come back as went out. 'I counted them
all out and I counted them all back' was the result of *that*
conversation and it showed how easy it could be for press and
military management to get it right.

I was thinking, as they rushed Dave Morgan's aircraft down

below into the hangar for repairs, it had been a relatively good day. We had struck at the enemy several times, with some apparent success. And we still had all the Harriers. However, above us there were still six more of them from *Invincible* on duty, guarding the skies above us while we cleared up the general confusion that breaks out on a carrier deck when twelve aircraft arrive back on board at once. It highlighted for me once more the absolute necessity of a 'second deck', because without the combat air patrol which now flew above us we would be very vulnerable to attack. As it was we had a few minutes' grace to refuel the aircraft, make running repairs and get ourselves into order, because I simply could not see the Argentinians staying passive for much longer.

While all of this was going on we had detached *Glamorgan*, *Arrow* and *Alacrity* to bombard Stanley airfield from the sea. As always, I was terribly aware of the acute danger we faced if the Args ever managed to repair that runway sufficiently to get fighter/attack aircraft off the ground, with the British Task Force patrolling only seventy to a hundred miles to the east. My own opinion was that frequent bombardment of that strip of tarmac from the sea would permanently discourage them from ever using it as a take-off or landing area for fast jets. I fully expected them to bodge it up with cement and rubble and packed earth sufficiently to run in the old Hercules freighters with supplies or even acting as ambulance planes to remove the wounded, but I did not care too much about that. I cared about fast jet fighter-bombers striking at the British carriers and my general policy was to make life a misery for anyone planning to operate them against us from Port Stanley. High-speed combat aircraft need a very smooth and long surface to get off the ground, or even to land, and we intended to make sure that was an impossibility.

Glamorgan's little group was expected to arrive on station some three miles off the Falklands capital at 1600Z, and they were under instructions to keep up the bombardment long into the evening. This plan of attack did not meet with the approval of Northwood who were greatly exercised about the possible loss of a guided-missile destroyer. They did, however, object too late and with some reluctance accepted that the ships were well on their way and it would be absurd to bring them back.

Bearing in mind that we knew they had laid a minefield in the eastern approaches to Port Stanley, since one of our submarines had watched them do it, my old submariner's instincts told me the underwater threat from the Args would be found clear to the north and/or south of the minefield. So I also sent *Brilliant* and *Yarmouth* to the area off the north-east corner of the islands above Berkeley Head to conduct an anti-submarine offensive, on the off-chance. They too could contribute to the completely false idea that we might be about to land in that vicinity. *Brilliant* and *Yarmouth* would be joined by Sea Kings from *Hermes* in a prolonged hunt intended to exhaust the batteries of the Argentinian submarine. This would force him to come up to recharge them, and in the process offer us a good chance of catching him.

Fifteen minutes after the ships had left, the main Task Force came under attack for the first time, from the air. Two French-built Dassault Mirage IIIs were homing in on us from a hundred and thirty miles out to the west. We had two Harriers at fifteen thousand feet over Port Stanley, but the incoming raiders were higher and they dived towards the two British naval pilots, firing one radar-homing Matra missile from four miles away, and another from two.

The Harrier pilots, at a serious disadvantage, took evasive

action and the missiles passed close by. The two pilots were also treated to a first-hand view of just how swiftly the Argentinian Mirage pilots could make their getaway, flying at supersonic speed. This particular fracas had, in addition, a side issue which was somewhat tiresome, in that one of the pilots reported that the second Mirage was an Etendard, and that when it fired off a missile, which was immediately reported to be an Exocet, it caused some amazingly fast action by the British ships, swinging their sterns to the threat and firing off chaff in abundance. A simple enough error, but with expensive consequences.

Nonetheless that had been the very first 'dog fight' of the war, and although it had ended indecisively, the incident had apparently shown us the general tactic the Mirage pilots intended to use against the Harriers. It looked as though they planned to patrol at high altitude in order to conserve fuel, using their height and superior speed to choose their moment to attack and subsequently get away. They continued to fly all afternoon, always retaining their advantage of height, but apparently reluctant actually to attack.

Four hours went by before the air forces of Argentina finally made a move – and it was against *Brilliant* and *Yarmouth* as they worked away to the north-east on their anti-submarine sweep. Irritatingly, after all of our efforts, four propeller-driven Turbo-Mentor attack aircraft laden with bombs somehow got off the ground from Port Stanley and headed out towards the two frigates. Two Harrier pilots, Lieutenant-Commander Nigel Ward and Lieutenant Mike Watson, hurried over to drive them off and the sudden appearance of the Harriers caused the Args to jettison their bombs and scuttle back to Port Stanley. The afternoon was, however, not over for these two particular Harriers and they had to survive a high-speed pass from two further Mirages both of which fired their missiles, happily inaccurately.

Meanwhile Captain Mike Barrow in the destroyer *Glamorgan*, in company with *Alacrity* and *Arrow*, was now bombarding the Argentinian positions around Stanley from his three-ship gun-line some four thousand yards off-shore.

At around 1830z, I was to learn much later, with the sun still fairly high over the horizon (1530 local time), the High Command of the Argentinian Air Force elected to launch a full-blooded attack on the British Battle Group, much as we had originally hoped they would. That, after all, was what the deception plan had been all about. They launched a fleet of some forty aircraft against us – a flight of Canberra bombers, with Daggers, Skyhawk fighter-bombers and Mirages in support. But very few of these aircraft were ever detected by the Battle Group: *Hermes* and *Invincible* were able to provide the combat air patrols to cover the inshore groups on a busy rotating basis all day from well offshore to the east of Port Stanley.

Two Harriers from 801 Squadron, piloted by Flight-Lieutenant Paul Barton and Lieutenant Steve Thomas under the control of *Glamorgan*, were directed on to two Mirages at around twelve thousand feet over the north coast of the islands. The first dual-missile dog fight of the war thus took place high above the clouds and, thankfully, the Argentinians missed again. Paul Barton's American-built Sidewinder, however, blew one of the Mirages in half and he watched the two sections burst into flames. The pilot ejected to safety, but it represented our first air success. Lieutenant Thomas just missed with his Sidewinder, but it detonated so close to the other Mirage as to cause severe damage. Captain Garcia Cuerva nursed his aircraft back towards Port Stanley, only to be mistakenly shot down and killed by his own possibly over-excited troops. So the first 'Blue on Blue' went to the Argentinians; bad luck, really, but one less for us to deal with.

A few minutes later the main Argentinian assault from the air was upon us. Two, possibly three formations of the Israeli-built Daggers (a straight copy of the Mirage) were sighted and one of them, a tight group of three, swept round the headland at more than four hundred mph, right above the waves, and made straight for *Glamorgan*, *Alacrity* and *Arrow*. Mike Barrow's Ops Room was swiftly into action and, in the precious few seconds they had, *Glamorgan* fired a Seacat missile, which missed its target only narrowly.

Arrow, in desperation, opened fire with its only 20mm gun off the port beam, and *Alacrity* had time to loose off a few rounds from a machine gun up on the Bridge. But the Daggers were in and ready first. One of them opened fire on *Arrow* where Able Seaman Ian Britnell was hit and wounded by splinters, thus becoming our first casualty. One of the Daggers also raked *Glamorgan*'s decks with 30mm cannon fire. And before streaking away over the horizon, at a speed of seven miles per minute, they had time to release two one-thousand-pound parachute-retarded bombs which exploded on either side of *Glamorgan*; and two more astern of *Alacrity*. But no significant damage was done.

Right behind them, at a far higher altitude, two further Daggers providing cover turned to face the Sea Harriers of Lieutenant Martin Hale and Flight-Lieutenant Tony Penfold, closing some fifteen thousand feet below them. The Argentinians committed themselves first, once more falling into their standard high-speed high-pass formation. Five miles out they fired their missiles. Martin Hale jinked away heading down for the clouds until the missile ran out of fuel. The Args, however, had not seen Penfold who suddenly pitched up two miles astern of the Daggers and fired his Sidewinder straight at the exhaust of one of them. Martin Hale, turning back to join the fight, saw the Dagger explode out over Pebble Island. The pilot never had a chance. He was Primer Teniente Jose Ardiles, a first cousin of the Tottenham Hotspur midfielder, who I trust was enjoying a somewhat less hazardous Saturday afternoon in London.

Some of the Harriers now began to return to base for refuelling, and the deck crews on both *Hermes* and *Invincible* were working at full stretch, the hours of drilling and training finally paying off. The pilots, some of them quite shaken by the ferocity of the combat, turned their aircraft over to the maintenance crews and hurried below for urgent debriefing, so that their newly learned lessons could be passed on to the pilots on the next combat air patrol.

Shortly after 2000 the Harriers were busy yet again. A close-knit formation of six Canberra bombers was heading east over the islands on a course which suggested they were looking for the British carriers. *Invincible* locked on to them some one hundred and ten miles out, flying at a low level, and Lieutenant-Commander Mike Broadwater, in company with Lieutenant Al Curtis, was guided in towards their target. Al Curtis fired his Sidewinder straight at the Canberra of the left-hand wingman, watching it explode in a fireball. He thought that a second Canberra might have been slightly damaged, and the third one turned away. The other three vanished from our screens.

So far, slightly to our surprise, everyone was still alive, and the Harriers were more or less intact. Even Dave Morgan's tail fin was patched up and the aircraft was fully operational again. I hate counting my chickens, but at this moment I would have to say the war is unarguably under way, and we are clearly winning it. I was grateful for whatever bits of luck had gone our way, and hoped that we could continue to perform to the maximum of our ability. We had removed from the Args' air inventory one Pucara (at Goose Green), one Mirage, one Dagger, and one Canberra, with another damaged Mirage shot down by the Args themselves.

The action in the late part of that afternoon had lasted for just a little over half an hour, and there is clearly a very long way to go before we can make a serious dent in their over-powering numerical superiority in the air. But I am not here to gripe and moan about the odds. I am here to ensure that we keep battering away at them until they give up. Battles of attrition are usually slow and painstaking, and this one was going to be no different.

Up on the north-east side of the island there had also been an action-packed day when the *Brilliant* group detected what they believed to be a submarine. The helicopters and the frigates blasted the local waters with depth-charges, and they did in fact sight what may have been an oil slick, 'half a mile long', though nothing was ever confirmed. In time, however, there would be a report that *San Luis* announced she had attacked a British ship with a torpedo on that day. Even now, I remain fairly sceptical about the ability of the Argentine submariners, and I would be mildly surprised to this day if it ever came to light that either of their submarines had ever been very close to a British warship above or below the surface. I am still surprised that they seem never to have made a positive sighting, or a definite classification, of any of our ships despite the many occasions that we passed along the coast. Perhaps my submariner's instincts were completely wrong and *San Luis* was neither where I thought they should have placed her, nor where she said she was later. Certainly, if the *San Luis*'s account is true, then her commanding officer would not have passed a *British* Perisher.

Taking stock of the first day of the war, we had to draw the conclusion that it had been a busy and useful start to hostilities. The Sea Harriers seemed to be working well. We had shot down several aircraft, Argentinian pilots had been killed, we had damaged two airfields and killed ground crews. In turn they had fired upon two British warships, dropped bombs very close to a big destroyer and a frigate, launched several fighter sweeps towards us, fired missiles, and attempted a strike at our anti-submarine ships and indeed at the carriers, both of which we had forced away. And now, late in the evening, as I attempted to write my diary, the ships of the Royal Navy were still bombarding Argentinian positions off the dark coast of East Falkland.

I do not believe that, back home in the UK, people had any idea how viciously this war had begun. Nor indeed that there were major consequences, several of which were yet to be fully understood, from the day's actions on both sides. Unknown to us at this stage, of course, the Argentinian fighter aircraft would never again, throughout the conflict, attempt to engage us in dog fights, or indeed any air-to-air combat. We had forced their air force to show its hand, as we had planned to do, and they had not much liked what they had seen, mainly that the British pilots were superior and that the American AIM-9L Sidewinder was a better air-to-air missile than anything they had.

It had been a day in which we had been feeling our way forward, not knowing how our enemy was going to behave, and basically starting off with no real concept of their attack plan. That was now largely changed. Their Fleet was deploying, though we were not yet entirely sure just how far or where they had gone. Their air force had tried its best – though we didn't know it – and failed. I could not have asked for a better response to the deception plan. The trick was to make the most of it.

Plainly we still had a great deal to learn about Argentinian intentions, but in turn they were suffering from one serious piece of ignorance: they were not at all sure where we were. The pattern and looseness of their raids, especially as we pushed to the north-west during the late afternoon, revealed this lack of hard information on their part.

Today had been, I felt, a day of success and hope, and, I regret to say, we were feeling rather pleased with ourselves. This war had started, and we were doing well. No one had died on our side and we were a lot wiser than we had been fourteen hours ago when the first bomb had gone off on Port Stanley runway. My diary provides a personal view of the events of 1 May 1982:

> Fifty today, and first day of the war. Vulcan went in as planned and did his business, as confirmed by Sea Harrier strike on Port Stanley (three other Harriers to Goose Green). Many alarms and excursions about Arg mainland air strike [a major strike by aircraft from the Argentinian mainland against the Battle Group] but I think not somehow.
>
> Mirages bobbing about over the Falklands, but not coming in strongly, suggests Port Stanley Combat Air Patrol and Arg strike held in reserve until they get a handle on us. Cat and mouse. Meanwhile Naval Gunfire Support [bombardment] and Anti-Submarine Warfare inshore groups going in, and Fleet telling me not to risk the NGS.

But I think I have to do so: firstly they are nearly there, like halfway! (by the time Fleet recommend no), secondly we have to loosen the Args. It should make them keep a submarine there in future if there's not one there already. Thirdly the Args will hate it. It may be risky but I believe we have to take some.

Everyone (me included, I guess) very jumpy, periscopes, torpedo HE [propeller noise], Exocet release, columns of smoke – but actually very little other than the strike of ours has come to anything yet.

2100 – and the day wore on in very good weather, thank Heavens. I wouldn't have cared to fly at these rates and notice in typical bad weather. So far we've been lucky. The NGS Group were bounced by four Mirages. The covering DLG (*Glamorgan*) was too close in (in the gun-line, I think) to cover properly and *Glamorgan* and *Arrow* received minor damage having completed the first barrage.

CAP splashed a Mirage in front of *Alacrity* but others bombed and went away. Three Canberras went past *Brilliant* off the N. coast, and disappeared low in our direction, but never made it. *Invincible* CAP splashed one other, two went home, one badly, one lightly damaged.

The Canberra attack tells me that:

a) They are out of AAR [Aircraft-to-Aircraft Refuelling].

b) They want to hit us.

c) They probably can't.

So far so good – but I don't really see how it can last. They clearly had very little idea where we were – the Canberras were groping a bit. *Glamorgan* and team then resumed NGS after a tiny bit of needle. But only a straight suggestion which I think they would have eventually made for themselves. *Brilliant* continuing with *Yarmouth* overnight in their little area bashing the living daylights out of some wretched sardine!

Come the morning, after a talk with David Hallifax [Chief of Staff to C-in-C Fleet] we intend going off-shore to E for a quiet day leaving it to the Args to react.

Late that evening I ordered the *Brilliant* group and the *Glamorgan* trio (or the Three Musketeers, as they were now calling themselves) to return to the main Battle Group before dawn. It had been a long and eventful day, and we had achieved much of what we had planned – mainly that we had got this war under way in no uncertain manner. Back in the middle of April at the big staff meeting on board *Hermes*, my chart had specified that we *must* begin the campaign on 1 May, on the basis that every day we missed at the beginning of May was just another day we might have to fight in the middle of June – with the South Atlantic winter closing in on us, and the inevitable attrition and general break-downs of the ships which occur when you have been too long out of the garage.

At least we have started on time, I thought, which may prove a critical factor when we approach the other end of the war. But there was another critical factor which I was sure would encroach upon my sleep this night. It involved the Argentinian Navy and its general whereabouts. Remember we had still not found their carrier, the 20,000-ton *Veintecinco de Mayo*, with her two escorting destroyers and her deckful of aircraft. We are also uncertain where three other Argentinian frigates have disappeared to, up in those north-western waters. It was an awful blow to me when neither *Spartan* nor *Splendid* could find them. At that time I knew the whereabouts only of the heavily gunned cruiser *General Belgrano*, with her Exocet-armed escorts, and their behaviour so far suggests that they are waiting, they may think safely, out in the wastes of the Antarctic for the order to close in on us. They were about two hundred miles away from *Hermes*, uncomfortably close, to my mind. I was not sure how good they were, but six months ago I had crept up on the Americans in the Arabian Gulf, in circumstances very nearly identical to these.

I walked slowly along to my utilitarian little cabin, with mixed feelings of relief at what was just past and anxiety about the immediate future. I sipped a small glass of whisky to round the day off, wondering whether I should perhaps have issued one last instruction to the GWO in the Ops Room: 'If the local Tandoori phones, don't hesitate to sink them.'

BELGRANO

8

The Bells of Hell

We established, I believe, several thousand miles back, that while truth is generally recognized to be the first casualty of war, the second is almost certainly politeness. After just one day in battle, I now know the third. Sleep. A commodity rapidly becoming as rare as the first two. I replaced it, largely, with adrenalin. Having retired to bed in the small hours of 2 May – the first night of my second half-century on this earth – I was awakened about one hour later at 0320 with the message: 'Possible Arg Tracker (recce aircraft) to the north. Harrier despatched to investigate.'

I got up, went to the Ops Room, asked a few questions and returned to bed, pre-occupied with the careful advance of their surface fleet, and wondering how to deal with it. Sleep was just about impossible and anyway, within the hour, they called me again, when one of our probing Harriers reported several surface contacts on his radar out to the north-west, range two hundred miles. My feet hit the floor before they had finished telling me.

As I walked quickly along the short corridor to the Ops Room it was becoming all too clear what we were up against. The contacts were just about where we expected them to be – north-west of the Battle Group and north of the islands. They represented, almost certainly, the Argentinian Carrier Battle Group: the 20,000-ton *Veintecinco de Mayo*, pride of Admiral Anaya's Fleet, and her escort of perhaps five ships. Two of them, I suspected, might be the Type 42 anti-aircraft destroyers *Santissima Trinidad* and *Hercules*, sister ships to *Coventry*, *Glasgow* and *Sheffield*.

The moment I entered the Ops Room this was confirmed in my mind. The Harrier pilot's report said he had been 'illuminated' by a Type 909 Sea Dart tracking radar – and that had to be from one of the Args' Type 42s. It took only a very short meeting with my staff to assess the situation and to conclude that they were about to attempt a dawn strike, launched against us from the deck of the carrier. Since she could carry ten A-4Q Skyhawks, each armed with three five-hundred-pound bombs, we could expect a swift thirty-bomb attack on *Hermes* and *Invincible* at first light – around 1100Z for us. She might also have Exocet-armed Super Etendards to add to our problems.

And in the middle of that rather sombre night, out near the edge of the British Total Exclusion Zone, we perforce prepared to 'form Line of Battle' for the first major set piece action of the war. The Royal Navy versus the naval and air forces of Argentina, quite the last kind of action I wanted and incidentally anything but a 'Line of Battle'. Modern tactics require formations which look completely haphazard at first sight, and anything but a 'set piece'. The commander who so indulges himself makes it altogether too easy for his opponent.

I elected to finalize my arrangements two hours from that staff meeting, at around 0700, when the *Glamorgan* and *Brilliant* groups returned. For the moment we had a great deal more thinking to do, because *Veintecinco de Mayo* represented only one half of our problem. The other was situated two hundred miles to the south-west of me and to the south of the islands – the *General Belgrano* and her two destroyers. In addition to all of the above Argentinian ships, there were three frigates in the area, plus their only tanker.

Rear Admiral Gualter Allara, their Commander at Sea, was in the carrier, and it all looked to me very like a classic pincer movement attack on the British Battle Group. To take the worst possible case, *Belgrano* and her escorts could now set off towards us and, steaming through the dark, launch an Exocet attack on us from one direction just as we were preparing to receive a missile and bomb strike from the other. Our choices of action were varied, but limited. We could of course take immediate evasive action and head away from our position to the south-east, making it more difficult for the bombers to find us, and possibly placing ourselves beyond their effective range, for lack of fuel or useful weapon load. We had worked specifically towards bringing their fleet to action with the SSNs, and I did not want to be squeezed out of our own Total Exclusion Zone like a pip from an orange. That would have given added complications to the ROE, it would scarcely have been in the traditions of the Royal Navy, however sensible, and anyway I had work to do inshore tomorrow night too. No, I could not allow that. But equally I could not just stay there and do nothing. I had to make a move, and since we were in contact with the *Belgrano* group, but no longer so with the carrier group, my thoughts began to centre on the cruiser.

The *Belgrano*, on her own, was not that big a threat, but neither was she likely to be a push-over. A cruiser of 13,500 tons, and over six hundred feet long, she carried fifteen six-inch guns, and eight five-inch guns – all bigger than any guns in my entire Force. She was old, built in the United States in the mid-1930s as the 'Brooklyn' Class light cruiser *Phoenix* and had seen active service in the Pacific during the Second World War, having survived the Japanese attack on Pearl Harbor in December 1941. In the American naval archives there is a picture of her coming out of the Harbor under her own steam, past the enormous wreck of the *Arizona*. A year later she became the flagship of General MacArthur's navy commander Admiral Thomas C. Kinkaid, and for extended periods MacArthur himself was on board, conducting the Pacific campaign. *Phoenix* saw service in exalted company for many months as MacArthur and Kinkaid drove the Japanese back, all through the southern islands. She was purchased by the Argentine Navy in 1951 and, five years later, re-named the *General Belgrano*, immediately after the overthrow of President Peron.

Now she was ranged against us and, in a sense, against America, whose total support we now had. Commanded in this war by Captain Hector Bonzo, she was an historic ship with a thousand tales to tell. But I was rather afraid this venerable armoured veteran was approaching the end of her journey. I simply could not risk her group launching an attack on us with ship-to-ship guided missiles – the same Exocets with which we in *Glamorgan* could so very easily have eliminated the USS *Coral Sea* six months ago. And should it come to the point where I considered ourselves in danger of attack, when it may be us or them, my choice was simple enough – *them*.

So now I and my team, gathered high in the 'Island' of

Hermes, had to 'Appreciate the Situation', that rather grand military colloquialism for 'thinking it through', in short order. Both of the Argentinian surface groups could now be less than two hundred miles away, north and south of the Falklands, outside the TEZ. The aircraft of the one, and the Exocet-carrying destroyers of the other, could both get in close to us very quickly in the present calm weather. The long southern nights gave them fifteen hours of darkness, and between now and first light there was still six hours, during which either *Belgrano* or *Veintecinco de Mayo*, or both, could have moved comfortably within range for a decisive battle which would give them, tactically, all the advantages. We assessed that we could probably shoot down five or six of the incoming Sky-hawks – but that it would be very bad news if sixteen Exocets arrived from the south-east at more or less the same time. Also we wished fervently we knew a little more about the strength of the Argentinian warships in the inshore waters around East Falkland, which might have been waiting their chance to slip out and join in with the other attacks.

It was clear enough that unless we were extraordinarily lucky we could find ourselves in major trouble here, attacked from different directions, by different weapons requiring different responses, all in the half-light of a dawn which would be sil-houetting us. At the very least, it was going to be a two-pronged strike, a straightforward pincer movement on us, from the south-west and the north-west. *Coral Sea* had failed to deal with a much lesser threat, with a far greater capability.

There was but one fast solution. I had to take out one claw of the pincer in order to free up my movements. It could not be the carrier, because our SSNs *Spartan* and *Superb* up there were still not in contact with her. So it would have to be the *Belgrano* and her destroyers. I am obliged to say that if *Spartan* had still been in touch with *Veintecinco de Mayo* I would have recommended in the strongest possible terms to the C-in-C that we take them both out this night. But as things were I had no right hand, just a left, and the best I could do would be to use it with as much force as I could manage.

The situation in the south-west was fairly clear. *Conqueror*, commanded by Commander Christopher Wreford-Brown, had been tracking *Belgrano* throughout the night, having picked up her tanker more or less by accident late on Friday afternoon, and had stayed close until *Belgrano* turned up to refuel. Christopher, a thirty-six-year-old former pupil of Rugby School, was married with three children and had served as my correspondence officer in *Warspite*. I knew him quite well and took some pride in the fact that I may have influenced his career in one or two minor ways during our time together. In manner he was rather shy and very restrained even in his delivery of important information. But he was very steady in controlling a situation, thoughtful, and correct. There was, I always thought, rather more to him than his obvious intelligence and courteous, rather droll manner. I could be sure enough that in battle, should it ever come to that, he would be coolly effective, even though he had only taken command of *Conqueror* a few weeks ago.

On this night, as we conferred in *Hermes*, he had come to precisely the same conclusions as we had. Remarkable, you may think, given our vastly different perspectives. But remember, we both had the same picture of what was going on, we both had the same training, and we both had the same operational doctrine. So it's hardly surprising that Commander Wreford-Brown was accurately tuned in to the mind of his old boss. I may be an ex-submariner but in spirit I am always a member of that strange brotherhood which fights its battles from underwater. Having already put in an enormous amount of work in finding and tracking *Belgrano* this far, Christopher privately considered it would be a bit of a waste to do absolutely nothing. Thus he was hoping for a signal changing his Rules of Engagement, giving him permission to attack, *outside* the Total Exclusion Zone but inside the general warning area announced back in April, giving him permission to attack *any* Argentinian warship, giving him permission to sink the *General Belgrano* and her Exocet-carrying destroyers.

He also had to ponder the intricacies of torpedoes. He had two types, the first being the old Mark 8** of Second World War vintage, with a fairly accurate and very reliable close-range capability, plus a sizeable warhead, amply powerful to penetrate the hull of the big Argentinian cruiser and do great damage. This is a pretty basic torpedo which travels at a pre-set depth and on a pre-set course with no 'ears' or 'eyes' in the front. Basically, it is dead stupid and runs straight until it either hits something or runs out of fuel. It is nothing more intelligent or subtle than a large, motorized lump of TNT, which will do about forty knots in whatever direction you fire it. It is called a 'salvo' weapon because we usually fire at least two and possibly as many as six at a go. This is done because, although it is necessary to aim as correctly as possible, all sorts of errors can creep in to ruin your 'solution' to the torpedo attack problem: you may have misjudged the target's course or speed or range marginally; the target may alter course or speed after the torpedoes have left the submarine; the torpedoes themselves may not run entirely accurately. The 'salvo' is also used because you may want *more* than one torpedo to hit the target, particularly if you are trying to sink a large warship, and submariners do not relish having to go back for a second attempt against heavily armed and now alert opponents. *Conqueror* also carried the wire-guided Tigerfish torpedo, a 'single-shot' weapon with a longer range and the ability to be guided from the submarine all the way to the target, but which had become a cause for concern due to its rather doubtful reliability at the time. To use the Mark 8** Christopher was going to have to get in close, to less than a mile. If the attention of the two destroyers and their depth charges should be too great, he would have to give it a shot with the Tigerfish from further out. The trick was to stay undetected, as I had taught so many of my 'Perishers'.

Back in *Hermes* my own view of the situation was more simple: the relatively heavy armour plating on the cruiser was such that I had only two weapons that could put her out of action – thousand-pound bombs, which would be nearly impossible to deliver, or Christopher's torpedoes. The decision was obvious. However, we had to face the added problem of the Burdwood Bank, a large area of fairly shallow water which sits on the edge of the South American continental shelf. It runs over two hundred miles from east to west, passing some hundred miles to the south of East Falkland, at which point it is about sixty miles across, north to south. Further south, the Atlantic is more than two miles deep, but around the Falkland Islands and inshore to the continent, the sea-bed slopes up to the continental shelf, giving a general depth of about three hundred feet. On the Bank, however, the bottom rises to shallows just one hundred and fifty feet below the surface. These shoals are quite well charted, but they can be a lethal place for a submerged submarine trying to stay with a cruiser making more than twenty-five knots through the water. To do that speed in a nuclear-powered submarine, it is necessary to run at a minimum depth of two hundred feet to avoid leaving a clear wake of disturbed water on the surface.

At one hundred feet, which is where they would have to be as they crossed the shoals, they would leave a marked wake which would be fairly obvious to the hurrying surface ships.

There is then of course the additional problem of tracking an enemy: at high speed you cannot hear or see because the sonar is drowned out by the noise of the water rushing past your hull, which means you have to slow right down to listen, or come up to periscope depth to look every so often, to check your quarry has not altered course. It's a sort of Grandmother's Footsteps, with lethal consequences if you're caught. The additional problem here is time: the moment you head to the surface and your periscope breaks clear of the water, like a big broomstick, you are immediately vulnerable to detection, either by the look-outs who are trained to spot a submarine or by the enemy's radar. Thus you put a periscope up for the shortest possible time, for a very quick look, and a few seconds' gulp of information. The man who looks through the periscope needs a photographic memory, and he needs to use every bit of his training in the Perisher. Each time the submarine conducts this time-pressured manoeuvre it loses precious speed and distance. Thus the submariner's rule of thumb is that you need a thirty per cent speed advantage to trail an enemy successfully, because you have to keep stopping. Under calm-surface conditions *Belgrano* could probably outrun a submerged *Conqueror* without working up too much of a sweat. In a race across the Bank I was afraid the Argentinian would be a heavy favourite.

If the three Argentinian captains were clever they might decide to split up and rendezvous later, closer to the Falkland Islands, in which case we would have little chance of locating them accurately. Perhaps more likely was the possibility of all three of them making a dash for it, across the Bank, deep into the TEZ, knowing the near-impossibility of a submarine tracking them among the shoals. (And remember, when we caught the USS *Coral Sea* in *Glamorgan*, we achieved it by means of a high-speed run, at night, from outside *her* TEZ – even if we were wearing turbans.)

My conclusion: I cannot let that cruiser even stay where she is, regardless of her present course or speed. Whether she is inside or outside the TEZ is irrelevant. She will have to go.

Even now, in the hours before dawn, both the *General Belgrano* and her escorts are heading eastwards at about thirteen knots, which may not sound very much, but it is a speed which would give her a lead of well over a mile on any of the upwind legs in the old America's Cup races for twelve-metre yachts. She is staying about twenty or thirty miles outside the TEZ, moving, apparently, around the perimeter, towards us. Even at her present low speed, she and her escorts could turn up right behind us, at a range of about fifty miles, some fifteen hours from now. And under my present Rules of Engagement I can do nothing about it. As they say in New York, thanks, but no thanks.

However, deep down, I believe she would continue to creep along the back of the Bank, and then when she is informed that the carrier is ready to launch her air strike, she will angle in, on a north-easterly course, and make straight for us, the Exocets on her destroyers trained on us as soon as they are within striking range. I badly need *Conqueror* to sink her before she turns away from her present course, because if we wait for her to enter the Zone, we may well lose her, very quickly.

As we all sat in the Ops Room of *Hermes* that morning, I knew I had to find a way of getting the Rules of Engagement changed in order to allow Christopher Wreford-Brown to attack the *Belgrano* group as soon as possible. This, actually, was a bit of problem because the proper procedures were inclined to be rather slow and, in theory, *Belgrano* could already have changed course without my yet knowing, and five hours from now, still just before dawn, she would be in a position to attack us. The correct, formal process for any commander to alter his ROE is as follows: sit down and draft a written signal, in hard copy, which says, at length, 'Here is my tactical and strategic situation. I wish to do this and that, and I am faced with this, that and the other. My conclusion is that I need a change in my Rules of Engagement, namely permission to attack *Belgrano* group before she enters the Exclusion Zone. That is, as soon as possible. Like, now.' And preferably an hour ago. Actually three hours ago by the time you get this. And eighteen hours ago by the time *Conqueror* gets your answer.

Of course, it all takes time: time to write, carefully and lucidly, and then, because it would be rather better if no one else heard it, the signal must go in encrypted code on to the satellite to Northwood. It will then be read by the duty officer on this quiet Sunday morning in the western suburbs of London. He will then inform the Chief of Staff, who will take it to the C-in-C, who will ring up the Ministry, and they will brief the Chief of Defence Staff, Admiral of the Fleet Sir Terence Lewin. When they have all read it, all understood it, and are all quite clear why Woodward wants to proceed with this major change in the plan, Sir Terence will then take it to the War Cabinet, for Mrs Thatcher's final approval. Only then can the process of sending the reply start. And that can take just as long again. And *then* it might not be the reply I wanted and needed. All of which was largely hopeless from my point of view, since it could not take much less than the best part of twelve hours, by which time (unless I blatantly exceeded my ROE), we could all be swimming around in the South Atlantic, getting a bit cold, and wondering where the hell those sixteen Exocets just came from.

I thus clearly have no time to hang about writing a formal assessment. Nor yet can I risk getting the 'wrong' answer. As far as I know, *Belgrano* and her escorts may already be on their way to us and, if they are, *Conqueror* is going to be so busy trying to chase her over the Bank, there is never going to be time for him to slow down, come to periscope depth, whistle up the satellite and start exchanging formal messages to Northwood. The general drift of such a signal would have to be something like this: '*Belgrano* has changed course to the north-east. Am attempting to maintain contact. Does the change of course affect my ROE? Am I permitted to attack? Urgent advice needed.' All of which would have been quite hopeless. With such a delay *Conqueror* would probably lose the cruiser altogether, just while sending the signal. Therefore the question is: how can I startle everyone at home into the required and early action? I have to get those ROEs changed exceedingly fast and to do so I instituted the formal process by getting Jeremy Sanders to get on to DSSS and spell out to the Duty Officer at Northwood precisely what my feelings were. Meanwhile I immediately put on to the satellite my permission to *Conqueror* to attack immediately. The signal read: 'From CTG [Commander Task Group] 317.8, to *Conqueror*, text priority *flash* – attack *Belgrano* group'.

Now, I knew that the captain of *Conqueror* would know that I was not empowered to give him that order – you will recall that the submarines were being run from London (against my advice). Thus I could expect a very definite set of circumstances to break out upon receipt of my signal. For a start Northwood would read it. Having then seen what I had done, the Flag Officer Submarines, Admiral Sir Peter Herbert, my old boss in *Valiant*, would know, beyond any shadow of a doubt that I must be deadly serious. It would serve as the strongest possible reinforcement of the formal request being prepared now by Jeremy Sanders in readiness for his phone call home. What is more, my signal will be in London in the next twenty minutes, which should provide them all with an interesting jolt at six o'clock in the morning.

As it happened Peter Herbert's staff read my signal and immediately took it off the satellite, in order that *Conqueror* should not receive it, which indeed she didn't. I had quite clearly exceeded my authority by altering the ROE of a British submarine to allow it to attack an Argentinian ship well *outside* the TEZ. Such a breach of Naval discipline can imply only two things – either Woodward has gone off his head, or Woodward knows exactly what he is doing and is in a very great hurry. I rather hoped they would trust my sanity, particularly because there is always another aspect to such a set of circumstances – that is, should the politicians consider it impossible for the international community to approve the sinking of a big cruiser, with possible subsequent great loss of life, I had given them the opportunity to let it run and then blame me, should that prove convenient. I quite understood it might be extremely difficult for them to give what some were bound to see as a ruthless order. Indeed I am keenly aware that there are some things politicians simply cannot do, no matter what the extenuating circumstances may be. But now they could do it. And if it went wrong, I was there to be blamed. But if it went right, they could take the credit.

Actually I had intended the signal to get as far as the Commander-in-Chief, Sir John Fieldhouse, and I had rather expected he would personally recommend that it should be left to run, given the urgency of my message, while he negotiated with the MOD and the Cabinet. FOSM had pre-empted me a bit, by pulling the order off the satellite. Nonetheless I imagined they immediately went to the C-in-C and said: 'Look what Woodward's done.' This, I felt quite sure, would have gingered him up, and caused him to go to Admiral Lewin and tell him, 'Look, Woodward means this. They need a change in the Rules of Engagement out there. Fast.'

Whatever the true process back home actually turned out to be, this was how I saw it happening from my little perch, high up on *Hermes*' bridge. Actually, my CTF and fellow CTG – FOSM – had already started the ROE change process without telling me. Suffice it to say, by the time the War Cabinet met at ten o'clock in the morning at Chequers everyone was apprised of the situation. After quick but careful consideration of the military advice, the Prime Minister and the War Cabinet authorized changes to the ROE which would permit *Conqueror* to attack the *Belgrano* group. I do not suppose it occurred to Mrs Thatcher for one moment, certainly it did not occur to me, that in a very few months from then a certain section of the House of Commons would endeavour to prove that this was a decision which could only have been perpetrated by a callous warmonger, or at least a group of callous warmongers, of which I was very much one. But political thinking and military thinking are often diverse, even when both sets of executives are on the same side, with overwhelming public support. And, by necessity, the military commander under the threat of missile attack is required to be more crisp than someone thinking the matter over some weeks later in front of the fire in a country house in the south of Scotland.

My own case is simply stated, because it comes from the

same folklore as that followed by Admiral Nelson, Admiral Jervis, Admiral Hood, Admiral Jellicoe and Admiral Cunningham. The speed and direction of an enemy ship can be irrelevant, because both can *change* quickly. What counts is his position, his capability and what I believe to be his intention.

At 0745Z on 2 May my signal had gone and Jeremy Sanders had talked very succinctly to the duty officer at Northwood. There was little more to be done about the *Belgrano* except await the outcome. By now the anti-submarine group were back, as were *Glamorgan* and her group. I felt we were a bit less exposed, but I was still irked by the fact that the other submarines – not *Conqueror* – were somehow unable to find the Argentinian carrier.

We were positioned some eighty miles east of Port Stanley and as prepared as we could be to receive a dawn strike by the aircraft from the deck of the *Veintecinco de Mayo*. I deployed the three Type 42s *Sheffield*, *Coventry* and *Glasgow* some thirty miles up-threat as our front-line defence, the picket line. Much, I thought, would depend on the speed of the reactions of their Ops Rooms. The bigger 'County' Class destroyer *Glamorgan*, her guns only just cooled from the night bombardment, was positioned in an inner anti-aircraft screen – and if necessary, an anti-submarine screen – with the frigates *Yarmouth*, *Alacrity* and *Arrow*. They would form the second line of defence in front of the two Royal Fleet Auxiliaries *Olmeda* and *Resource*, which would take up a position near *Hermes* and *Invincible*. Each of the carriers would operate in company with a 'goalkeeper', one of the Type 22 frigates. Ours would be Captain Bill Canning's *Broadsword*, while *Invincible* would operate with John Coward's *Brilliant*. The latter combination packed enormous punch, because Coward was likely to be extremely quick off the mark with his Sea Wolf missile system, and *Invincible* carried a Sea Dart system. We did not have any airborne early warning radars to assist the pickets, which meant our maximum radar range against low-fliers, from the Type 42s, was about forty-five miles out from *Hermes*. We would of course fly constant combat air patrols from the decks of both carriers, but with the Skyhawks coming in very fast, at wave-top height, I thought we might have our work cut out to down all ten of them.

And so we waited, all of us very much alert for a co-ordinated air and sea attack from almost any direction. But, to our surprise and relief, it never materialized. Sea Harrier probes to the north-west found nothing.

Out here in the notoriously windswept South Atlantic, what we had not even considered had happened: with winter approaching, the air was absolutely still. And the Args could not get their fully laden aircraft off the deck without at least some natural wind, regardless of their own speed through the water into the breeze. With daylight approaching, the constant threat of our SSNs finally catching up with them and the slowly growing realization that we were not in fact about to put the Royal Marines on the beach at Port Stanley, their carrier wisely turned for home and safety, though of course, we did not know it.

By 1130, however, we were fairly sure the carrier group had in some way withdrawn, simply because no air attack had arrived. We regrouped after a quick lunch to decide what time we should once more head west towards the islands for our second night of recce insertion, and at that time the scene switched very decisively to *Conqueror*. I should mention here that I knew nothing more about the subsequent activities of the submarine for many hours. In the ensuing months and years since the war, I have pieced together from the people most closely concerned what happened on that chill but wind-less Sunday afternoon. I cannot, as a submariner myself, resist providing some detail of one of the more riveting days in the history of the submarine service.

We now know that at 0810z *Belgrano* and her escorts reversed course, and were in fact on their way home. But they headed back to the west on a gentle zig-zag, not apparently in any great hurry or with any obvious purpose. When I became aware of their westerly course that afternoon, I still had no reliable evidence as to their intentions. For all I knew they might have received a signal telling them to return to base; but perhaps they had only been told to wait and come back tonight; perhaps they hadn't been told anything. But if I had been told to return to base, I wouldn't hang about, that was for sure. I'd get on with it, PDQ. Either way, *Conqueror* trailed her all morning. At 1330z she accessed the satellite and received the signal from Northwood changing her Rules of Engagement. Commander Wreford-Brown had, apart from self-defence, thus far been permitted to attack the Argentinian aircraft carrier and, within the TEZ only, other Argentine combat ships. The change said quite clearly he may now attack the *Belgrano*, outside the TEZ.

Actually the significance of this change was clear to all the British ships *except* poor old *Conqueror*, the only one that really needed to know it. They had, unfortunately, a very dicky radio mast that kept going wrong, and they could not make sense of the signal. Neither could they hang around indefinitely, at slow speed with masts up, trying to re-access the satellite. The danger of losing the *Belgrano* was too great. Commander Wreford-Brown went deep and fast again to continue the pur-suit and all afternoon they tried to fix the mast, as they trailed the Argentinians, furtively, through the depths of those grey seas, south of the Burdwood Bank. At 1730 *Conqueror* came up again, accessed the satellite once more to get a re-run of their signal, and this time they could read it.

The Captain took a careful look at the *Belgrano* and the two destroyers before going deep to try to catch them up from his position some seven miles astern of the cruiser and her escorts. The Argentinians were steaming in a V-formation, *Belgrano* to the south, with one destroyer positioned about half a mile off her starboard bow, the other one a mile off her starboard beam. As an anti-submarine formation the British captain considered it 'pretty pathetic, especially as the ships were largely obsolete, and the crews were displaying a fairly minimal amount of skill'. They did not, in fact, even have their sonars switched on.

In retrospect I am inclined to go along with Christopher's assessment: had I been the captain of the *General Belgrano*, I would have been doing many things differently at this time. For a start I would have put my ships on a high level of damage control readiness, I would have had my two escorts positioned on my port and starboard quarters using intermittent active sonar, rather than have them both, passively, to my north. Also I would never have been dawdling along at thirteen knots for hours on end, if my fuel state remotely allowed it. Rather I would have been zig-zagging determinedly and varying my speed quite dramatically, occasionally speeding up to twenty-five or more knots, making it much more difficult for a shadowing submarine to stay with me. At other times I would have slowed right down, making it equally hard for a shadowing submarine to hear me, but allowing me perhaps to hear *him* charging along in the rear making a noise like an express train. Finally, I would have edged up towards the Burdwood Bank, thereby making it less likely that an SSN would approach from that direction and enabling me to put my escorts in a better place.

Captain Hector Bonzo was doing none of this. He was no submariner, nor had he any experience of what SSNs could or could not do. He was mentally not yet at war, and all the while, right on his stern, there was *Conqueror*, following in a standard sprint-and-drift pursuit – running deep at eighteen knots for fifteen or twenty minutes, then coming up for a few minutes to get another visual set-up to update the operations plot for the Fire Control Officer. Every time they came up, they reduced speed to five knots or so, which of course lost them ground as they 'drifted', but they made it up again in the eighteen-knot 'sprint'.

It was approaching 1830 when the British submarine captain judged they were close enough for the final approach, at a range of just over two miles. He went deep at high speed to take a long swing so as to come up on the port side of the Argentinian cruiser. He wanted to fire his torpedoes from a position just forward of her beam, at a range of about two thousand yards. Having had plenty of time for solid thought, Christopher had decided to use the Mark 8** direct, straight-running torpedoes. The tubes were loaded with three of them, but he had also taken the precaution of loading three Tigerfish just in case it should prove impossible to get in close enough.

By 1857, *Conqueror*'s captain estimated he could turn in for the firing position, and come to periscope depth for the final fire control set-up. Up forward, in the torpedo space, they were making ready to fire three Mark 8** torpedoes in the standard fan formation, with each of them aimed off, ahead of the *Belgrano* sufficiently to ensure that torpedo and ship would meet in the identical patch of water.

The tension throughout the submarine was high, as the

sonar operators listened carefully to the continuing steady beat of *Belgrano*'s three-bladed propellers . . . '*Chuff*-chuff-chuff . . . *chuff*-chuff-chuff' . . . rising and falling in the long Atlantic swells, slightly fainter as the stern ploughed deeper. In the control room, Commander Wreford-Brown ordered *Conqueror* to periscope depth – and, as the 'eyes' of the submarine came up out of the floor with that familiar 'Whoosh!', his hands grabbed for the handles before they reached knee level, ducking down to use every precious second of sight. (Remember the manhole in Piccadilly Circus I told you about during the Perisher Course? Commander Wreford Brown was now in it.) Time was running out for the big, grey, American-built veteran of Pearl Harbor.

He called out bearing, then the range – 'Three-three-five . . . Thirteen-eighty yards' – then under his breath he said, 'Damn. Too close.' But there was no time to correct that. He hesitated for a few more seconds, as *Conqueror* slid forward, now on a perfect ninety-degree angle to the Argentinian ship. Then he called out the final order to his Fire Controller: 'Shoot.'

The sonar recorded the double-thump as the first torpedo was discharged from its tube and then the high-pitched whine as the torpedo's engine started up and it accelerated away at forty knots. *Conqueror* shuddered. Seven seconds later there was another, then another. As the whine of the third torpedo died away there was again silence, save for the '*Chuff*-chuff-chuff . . . *chuff*-chuff-chuff' which had been with the British sonar operators for so long.

The seconds ticked by, and the big cruiser steamed on, still at thirteen knots, moving ever closer to the fatal patch of water the British captain had selected. Fifty-five seconds after the first launch, number one Mark 8** smashed into the port bow of the *General Belgrano*, aft of the anchor but forward of her first gun turret. Very nearly blew the entire bow of the ship off. Through the periscope, Christopher Wreford-Brown was astonished to see a big flash light up the sky.

Conqueror's sonar operator matter-of-factly reported in the same tone of voice you might count sheep, 'Explosion...' Then came, '... Second explosion...' Three more reverberating explosions combined the sound of the 'echoes' with the two torpedoes which struck home, the second one hitting below the after superstructure. The last of the explosions sounded different, more distant, more metallic, lighter. One of the escorts, the destroyer *Bouchard*, said later that she had been hit a glancing blow by a torpedo which had not gone off.

It had been, by any standards, a text-book operation by Christopher Wreford-Brown and his team, which is probably why it all sounds so simple, almost as if anyone could have done it. The best military actions always do. As the young Commander said rather drily some months later, 'The Royal Navy spent thirteen years preparing me for such an occasion. It would have been regarded as extremely dreary if I had fouled it up.'

Back in *Conqueror* they all heard the unforgettable impact of the strike and knew their torpedoes had hit something. Then, as the noise subsided, for the first time for twenty-four hours the '*Chuff*-chuff-chuff' of the enemy's propellers had gone. There was only silence, save for an eerie tinkling sound on the sonar, like breaking glass or metal, echoing back through the water, like the far-lost chiming of the bells of hell. So sounds the noise of a big ship breaking apart on a modern sonar perhaps.

Every Argentinian account since has reported a 'fire-ball' rushing through the ship, in which three hundred and twenty-one men were lost. Which suggests the cruiser was ill-prepared for war. If the blast did travel so quickly in this way it must have been because too many bulkhead doors and hatches had been left open, rather than kept tight shut, with their clips on, in readiness to hold back both fire and water. Keeping hatches and doors properly shut is domestically inconvenient because it can then take about fifteen minutes to get from one end of the ship to the other, unlocking, unclipping every door to get through, then clipping up behind you. Captain Hector Bonzo learned to his cost that if you are in the process of invading another country's islands, and they are, in turn, not pleased with you, it is probably best to remain in a fairly efficient defensive position. But he was acting in a way which suggested he believed he was in no real danger, despite receiving a warning a few days before, from the British government, that Argentinian ships posing any threat to the business of the British Fleet would be sunk, provided only that they chose to go outside the mainland twelve-mile limit. Here, perhaps, was a man who had not yet quite accepted the reality of the situation we were now all in, and of course he was not alone in his attitude.

On board *Belgrano* the flames, the heat and the damage were merciless, beyond control, and totally ill-contained. Sea water flooding in quickly shut down all power, a combination of fire and water shut down the auxiliary generators, which in sequence shut down the anti-flooding pumps and the fire-fighting emergency equipment. All the lights failed, and the communications systems crashed simultaneously. The captain and eight hundred and seventy-nine of his company managed to abandon the now darkened ship, and it took half an hour for them all to find their way into the inflatable life rafts. A quarter of an hour after Captain Bonzo left the deck, the

General Belgrano rolled over on her port side and her stern rose high into the air as she pitched forward and sank. Packed into the surrounding life rafts, almost nine hundred of her crew, some of whom would not survive this freezing night, sang the Argentinian National Anthem as she went. I am always startled by the emotions the Malvinas can stir in the breast of an Argentinian. For us this campaign was a tough and demanding job on behalf of our government. For them it was something close to a holy war.

Commander Wreford-Brown, whose nearest experience to such an event had been on exercises from Faslane, was almost overcome by an immediate instinct to wipe the sweat from his brow, pack up and have a cup of tea, before setting about collecting all the copious records required to establish whether his 'attack' had been successful or not. But that lasted for all of a split second, as reality returned. There were a few urgent tasks to accomplish: first, avoid the destroyers, get clear – fast. That means deep, too. Rudder hard over, down they went and away to the south-east, away from the chaos that always surrounds a stricken warship, away from the retribution the surviving ships will hope to exact.

Within a few minutes the sonar operators heard three explosions which the captain assessed to be depth-charges from the Argentinian destroyers. They sounded fairly close. Your first one always does. But this was no time to be curious, so he ran on, still deep, for four or five more miles until the Argentinians faded astern. He wondered, perhaps warming to his new task, whether to go back and have another shot, perhaps sink the other two. However, discretion proved the better part of valour and he elected to ensure that *Conqueror* stayed in one piece rather than engage in further heroics on this particular day. In the intervening years he has refined that view yet further. 'In retrospect,' he told me recently, 'I do not suppose Mrs Thatcher would have thanked me all that much if I had reloaded and hit the other two ships.' An opinion I would have assessed as more or less faultless because, as far as I knew, he only had permission to fire at the *Belgrano* anyway. I have to add that Christopher is equally sure that he had received permission to attack *any* Argentinian warship any-where up to the twelve-mile limit of her shores. I am always amazed at how two trained observers can harbour totally opposed views on a 'simple fact'! And even more so if it turns out that I am the one who is wrong.

Indeed Commander Wreford-Brown did return on the fol-lowing day and saw the two destroyers, quite a way south-east by now, because of the wind and current, helping with the search and rescue of the many Argentinian survivors. But they were engaged on a mission of mercy now, not war, and Chris-topher Wreford-Brown turned *Conqueror* away, and left them to their unenviable task.

From my own perspective, it was rather a disjointed sort of day. Of course we were unaware of the activities of *Conqueror*, just as they knew nothing of our pre-occupation with the poss-ible attack from the Argentinian carrier. In turn neither of us knew, at that time, what was in the minds of the Argentinian High Command. In fact, by 0900 Argentinian time it was clear to them that the wind would not return in the next few hours and the dawn strike against us, which was very definitely planned, was called off. *Veintecinco de Mayo* and her escorts were ordered back to the mainland. At more or less the same time, the *General Belgrano* was ordered (we learned much later) to proceed to a waiting position. She was already steaming west and she merely needed to keep on going. Admiral Anaya, faced with the non-functioning of one of his 'pincers', quite reasonably decided to cancel the whole operation, get his carrier home and maintain an option for a later strike by his southern group if opportunity offered.

We of course knew nothing of this. Thus, as that Sunday morning wore on, we continued to search to the north and north-west for signs of an incoming attack, trusting that *Conqueror* would deal with the threat from the south. I kept the Group in a high state of anti-air warfare readiness, at least until the afternoon when we began to head west in preparation for the recce insertion that night. At 2200 I once more detached *Glamorgan* and her group to bombard the Argentinian positions around Port Stanley, with the intention of maintaining their belief that we were about to land in the Port Stanley area and still in hopes of defeating their Fleet, now on the following day.

It was not until 2245 that we received a signal from Northwood to tell us that HMS *Conqueror* had sunk the *General Belgrano*. We received the news without excitement. There was only temporary relief that the threat from the south-west had, for the moment, diminished. I did, however, realize that this news would make all kinds of headlines back home and that it would be immensely good for morale. Not wishing to rain on this particular parade, Northwood recommended that I recall *Glamorgan* and the two frigates, in case one of them should be lost. I agreed. Probably just as well too. On the face of it, it had been another moderately successful day for us: we were still more or less intact, and we had reduced the sea threat to the Battle Group by one cruiser. We were not to know for weeks that the effects of *Belgrano*'s sinking would be so all-embracing. Even as we planned our next activities, late that night, the entire Argentinian fleet was on the move. The two destroyers in the south were on their way back to Porto Belgrano, the carrier and her Type 42s were heading back towards the River Plate, and the three other frigates had also made an about-turn and were heading west for home.

What no one knew then was that Christopher Wreford-Brown's old Mark 8** torpedoes, appropriately as old in design as the *Belgrano* herself, had sent the navy of Argentina home for good. Unwittingly we had achieved at least half of what we had set out to do from those days at Ascension: we had made the Argentinians send out their fleet and a single sinking by a British SSN had then defeated it. We would never see any of their big warships again.

25 de MAYO

9

The Silence of HMS *Sheffield*

With the *General Belgrano* now gone, and no identifiable threat from the south-west to worry us for the moment, I could readily discard the sinking of the enemy cruiser from my mind, and press on with thinking about future business. However, unknown to me, eight thousand miles to the north, there were forces in action dedicated to placing the demise of the Argentinian warship equally firmly *into* the minds of anyone with even a passing interest in the current proceedings in the South Atlantic.

Fleet Street, the old traditional headquarters of London's national newspapers, was in the process of going, rather noisily, berserk. Editors were reaching for what I believe is known in the trade as 'End-of-the-World' type. Enormous headlines were being set to proclaim, with lunatic nationalistic pride, that the Royal Navy had struck a massive blow for Margaret,

England and St George against the evil forces of General Galtieri. 'GOTCHA,' bellowed the *Sun*, rather unchivalrously, in the biggest typeface ever seen on its front page. And many of the others were equally unrestrained, announcing the sinking in terms which could only be described as celebratory, even gleeful, or to use the correct Fleet Street sub-editors' cliché, 'jubilant'.

I, of course, knew nothing of all this excitement being foisted upon a shocked world, which was just as well because it was not part of my job to be shocked. Nonetheless I was pretty surprised when it was all over and I was able to look at some of those front pages and see for myself how the news from the war had been treated. Rarely has the huge difference in perspective between the front line and the front page been better illustrated, although I am obliged to admit that the *Sun*'s 'GOTCHA' came perhaps the closest to echoing initial general feeling in the Battle Group. For greater accuracy, it would have required the addition of the phrase 'YOU BLEEDER'. But in the typeface favoured by that particular tabloid it might not have fitted. There is also the question of nuance, and I trust that the *Sun*'s perceptive headline writers were tuned in to the subtlety of 'salvation' as opposed to 'jubilation'. Our metaphoric cry of 'Gotcha, you bleeder!' was strictly that of the former, of someone who has finally removed an angry wasp from inside his trouser leg without getting stung.

Nonetheless, deep in the Total Exclusion Zone on that night, we were not giving thoughts of the *Belgrano* one single moment of our time, whether a nationwide party was happening at home or not. The fact was, her removal posed for us a completely new set of problems: from where would the Argentinians strike back in order to take their revenge for such a humiliating loss on the high seas? Where now were the *25 de*

Mayo and her escorts? What was the plan for the two Exocet-armed destroyers which had been with the *Belgrano*? Would the Argentinian commanders elect to come back at us from the sea, perhaps using a variation on the pincer movement they had been planning for Sunday? Or would they change direction completely, afraid now of the British submarines, and come at us from the air? No one knew the answers, and all I could do was make my best estimations, beginning with what I would do if I had been in their shoes and had just lost the second largest warship in my fleet. Admiral Anaya, I thought, the Malvinas hawk of the Argentinian Junta, must surely try from the sea again, and unless he wanted to risk something nastily close to ridicule at home, he had better be quick about it.

These were the thoughts that preoccupied me in the immediate hours following the accurate firing of Christopher Wreford-Brown's torpedoes. My diary records fairly faithfully and succinctly in just three paragraphs the course of events for me on Sunday 2 May 1982:

By 0400 already apparent Args reaction. Their carrier is hurrying through the SSNs to strike at us. *Belgrano* going south-about at the same time. However, all my chickens will be home to roost by 0800 and we can retire to maintain reasonable arm's length until dawn. Not much of a 'day off', but indeed this *could* be decisive one way or another. I fear that the SSNs have missed their chances. Of course they should get another go as the Args return to base.

By midday, still no news and no strike, we all began to relax. *Conx* [*Conqueror*] at 1400 finally reporting that *Belgrano* Group had turned back at 0800 having nearly reached the E end of Burdwood Bank. Nothing from the SSNs up north who should have intercepted *25 de Mayo* and her team. All in all it seems the Args must have decided that we weren't the landing force [they were expecting] after all, and that the sally wasn't worth the risk.

Quite correct. But in the process I have had a free rehearsal of their plan, my response, and greatly improved Rules of Engagement because everyone got a fright when I released (against top orders) *Conx* to attack. I am no doubt in trouble, but providing I'm not relieved immediately I expect it will be forgotten!

As always, the diary reads very businesslike with a dash of the cavalier thrown in. Perhaps I thought I was writing for posterity, mindful that one day my words might be read post-humously, should the Argentine navy or air forces somehow break through our defences and ruin my day. I suppose any commander would wish in the final reckoning to be re-membered for bravery under attack and coolness in assessing the danger, and I do not claim to be any less susceptible to these subconscious vanities than anyone else. In reality, we had been facing the strong likelihood of a full-scale surface fleet action that morning, with all the major units of each country involved, and to this day I have not the least idea how it might have turned out – nor, to my knowledge, has anyone done an analysis of it. The chanciest of circumstances – an unlikely lack of wind near the *25 de Mayo* – decreed the battle would not happen that day. The sinking of the *Belgrano* decreed it would not happen at all.

I was by then becoming accustomed to nights of broken sleep, not to mention dreams, and the one in the aftermath of

Belgrano was of course no exception. Shortly before 0130, a Sea King helicopter investigating a well-lit but unidentifiable surface contact was suddenly fired upon with a machine gun. The chopper did an about turn and tracked the vessel from a safe distance, reporting the incident to the *Hermes* Ops Room. I was summoned from bed just as the 'Junglies' made it back from the recce insertions of the night, and we immediately ordered *Coventry* and *Glasgow* to despatch their Lynx helicopters up to the north-west to check on this aggressive contact. And its attitude had not changed, because the unidentified boat instantly opened fire on their approach, which prompted *Coventry*'s Lynx to blow it away with a well-aimed Sea Skua missile. All this was fairly routine except that it seemed the missile had caused a bigger explosion than anyone had expected, suggesting to us that it could have been a bigger ship, perhaps an A-69 corvette and that the British missile had in fact hit an Exocet canister. We never did find out what that target was.

Glasgow's Lynx, in which they had been trying to repair a faulty radio, finally got airborne and, twenty miles from her base ship shortly after 0500, detected a second surface contact. This one was unlit and it too suddenly opened fire. The Lynx replied promptly enough with two Sea Skuas, one of which hit the bridge, killing the captain and seven ratings, and reduced the ship to a hulk. She was, it turned out, the 700-ton Argentinian patrol boat *Alferez Sobral*, a former US Navy ocean-going tug.

Back in *Hermes*, we transmitted a message on the international distress frequency to tell the Argentinians to get out and look for survivors. We, of course, could not stay. It was far too close to the mainland for my taste, and we would have ended up with the Argentinian air force around us like flies on a cow pat. I did despatch one carefully briefed Sea King to do a last surface search in the area, and in the middle of this we had yet another drama. *Yarmouth* (in my diary I actually wrote 'bloody *Yarmouth* again') started a panic by reporting that he heard a voice on HF saying: '*Emergency, emergency, emergency!*'

'Christ!' we all thought. 'The Sea King has fallen out of the sky.' What broke out next was the kind of swift, efficient, all-bases-covered, search-and-rescue operation which always accompanies the news that we may have lost one of our own. In hindsight, however, I would have to describe it as an over-reaction, because at the conclusion of the sortie, the Sea King turned up very cheerfully having suffered no problems whatsoever.

With that, I elected to head to the south-east, from which direction the weather was visibly now worsening. Banks of low cloud and sea mist were rolling in on an increasingly gusting breeze. The sea was getting up and the barometer was falling rapidly. At best visibility was about a mile, and it was bitterly cold. I thought we would be better to remain in the 'clag' because I expected a determined Argentinian attack at any moment. We had foiled them yesterday and indeed had sent them into retreat. That was not, however, any guarantee that they would not return to the attack this afternoon, or this evening, or first thing in the morning. We held a south-easterly course through rough seas with the Type 42s *Glasgow*, *Coventry* and *Sheffield* still to the west of us. I wondered where the Argentinian carrier could be: it had not been located by us since we'd had that sniff of her from the Harrier two nights ago, and the SSNs were still depressingly silent on the subject.

As the evening drew in the weather worsened, the sea mist

turning into unmistakable fog, and in these miserable conditions we received a hurried call for help from one of the recce parties ashore in the Berkeley Sound area, a big bay due north of Port Stanley. Four Special Forces men were apparently being pinned down by some Argentinian ground patrols. Now they were requesting assistance from the air, possibly a ground-support sortie by a couple of Harriers. I considered the matter carefully and naturally my normal reaction would have been to help immediately, to do whatever was necessary to get them out alive. However, these were not normal circumstances and fate had jammed my Battle Commander's hat down very firmly upon my head.

I refused their request, on the basis that the probable loss of two Sea Harriers, possibly with their pilots, unable to land back on deck in the fog, represented another big chunk out of my limited air force. How did this weigh in the balance with four members of the SAS? Out of the question. The risks to the four soldiers and the two pilots were, arguably, the same – but the Harriers were irreplaceable. There was only one conclusion open to me. My diary summed it up in seven words: 'Nasty decision. Getting inured to them. That's awful.'

That night I wrote home to Char in a way that perhaps reveals how I was having to suppress many ordinary human feelings. 'The scene is greatly changed,' I said. 'We are fully at war, and I am having to harden my heart and alter my ways.' I explained that there were a couple of personality conflicts which were not helping me much, and I continued, 'This does little, with a war on my hands and an entire fleet to manage, to help me get through the day ... sometimes I have to put on my stone face with the people on board too. I did not enjoy consigning some Argentinians to their graves last night; but it has to be done. No more do I fancy sending

SSNs to sink cruisers. However, it has to be faced up to. The Argentinians will do the same to me given the small half of a chance.'

The night for once passed without any incident, given that we were nestled in the deep dark fog and that the Argentinians had shown little inclination, thus far, to conduct any operations after sunset. The morning too passed peacefully enough, until shortly after lunch when they blew *Sheffield* away, the incident I have described in some detail in the first chapter of this book. When we left that depressing scenario, you will perhaps recall that my old ship was burning fiercely some twenty miles away and the crew were being evacuated. With Captain Sam Salt now safely on board *Hermes* I shall try to illustrate the effect of the first major missile strike on the British Fleet in forty years.

With twenty men dead and a further twenty-four wounded it would be folly to claim that we, as a team, were not profoundly shocked, although I would consider myself a great deal less shocked than some. I had been expecting this, or something very like it, for several weeks now, and I thought I was quite prepared mentally to face the loss of life and ships. Also I was in no doubt there would be more to come. However, I was not of course inside the cauldron that *Sheffield* had become and I had not witnessed that unique, numbing trauma that can grip the people on board when a warship takes a major hit. History is clear enough that there is nothing quite like it – the roaring fires below decks, the blistering heat, the billowing, choking smoke, the cries and whispers of the injured, and the awful sight of dead friends. In addition there are terribly interlocked feelings of anger and fear, outrage and helplessness, and the near-manic heroism which invades the minds of some survivors. Beyond it all is the unspoken dread that another such missile may be on its way in.

It is this, all of this, upon which I cannot afford to spend one moment of my time, save to satisfy myself that everything possible is being done for the wounded, and that the rescue operation is now complete. *Sheffield* herself must burn alone for a while until I am entirely satisfied that her Sea Dart magazine is not about to explode. My new task is to conduct a careful analysis of the events, not to apportion blame, but to find out precisely what happened and to ensure that somehow we all learn from the experience; that somehow tomorrow we will be better, more alert and less vulnerable to that fairly basic French missile we had thought we knew all about, but failed to cope with on this day, 4 May. We do after all operate behind millions of pounds of the most highly sophisticated equipment of war. But this had not sufficed to prevent the Argentinian missile from hitting *Sheffield*. My logic tells me there were only two possible causes: a) our equipment did not work; b) someone, somewhere, somehow, had failed to operate it correctly. I know much about the equipment, and am thus inclined to option b. And I had, apparently, blurted out this fear to Sam Salt. Nonetheless, as commander of this group, I *had* to know. My own guess wasn't good enough. Was there a component that was letting us down, electronically? Or had there just been a human error in our complicated defensive chain?

It would be many months before any of this could be finally settled. As in all sinkings of our ships, a Board of Enquiry would be duly convened for each which would seek to find the causes. It would also recommend whether there was a prima facie case against any person or persons involved. Upon those latter recommendations, the Commander-in-Chief would decide whether to proceed with a court martial or not – the decision lay with him and him only. He eventually decided to hold no courts martial, regardless of the Board of Enquiry findings, to avoid, he told me, the more doubtful cases creating the wrong atmosphere in the Press and souring the general euphoria. He added that he did not expect me to agree with his decision and left it at that.

But this would all take place in the distant future. There ought, however, to be lessons from the incident to be learned here and now. I sent out an immediate signal to all ships requesting them to shed whatever light they could upon it and to send their observations in soonest. They had no time to draw conclusions from each other and, when their reports reached my Ops Room, the bare bones were roughly to this effect – *Glasgow*: 'Detected Handbrake. Saw the missiles on radar. Fired chaff. Told everyone. Tried to shoot the missiles down. Couldn't.' *Sheffield*: 'Saw and heard nothing until seconds before impact.' *Coventry*: 'Heard Handbrake. Fired chaff. No other contact.' *Invincible*: 'Heard *Glasgow*'s warnings. And many others before. No contacts. Unconvinced.' *Yarmouth*, fourteen miles away: 'Missile sighted, passing close by. Orange fins.' Some further detail was added, but not in all cases.

Now I had a fairly simple set of opinions, deductions and facts to draw on. The Argentinians must surely have conducted their attack very much as we would have done in their place. Their Etendards had taken off from their home base at Rio Grande, climbed out, refuelled en route, and then let down to wave-top height to get under the beams of our radars. These, because of the curvature of the earth, miss completely the air down near the water from about twenty miles out. Forty or fifty miles out they had 'popped up' to about a hundred and twenty feet, switched on their radars to try to locate us. In those few seconds, their transmission pulses were detected in the Ops Room of *Glasgow*. Then the pilots switched their radars off and dived below our own radars again. *Glasgow* alerted the Battle Group. No one believed her. At least the Ops Room in *Invincible* didn't. Twenty miles later the Argentinian raiders 'popped up' again. *Glasgow* again detected their radar pulses. The Argentinians activated their missiles' homing systems and released them at the first target they saw, then went low again to turn away and head for home. *Glasgow*, looking directly down the correct bearing, spotted the missiles on her own radar and began to yell, metaphorically, at all the British ships, especially *Invincible*, which continued to dismiss the attack as yet another false alarm. *Glasgow* and Coventry we now know, were the only British ships to get their chaff up in good time to deflect any missiles aimed at them. But they were safe. The Argentinians had aimed them further to the south, towards *Sheffield*, which was hit by one of them, shortly after 1400. The second missile was sighted by one or two lookouts, in particular by the every-ready *Yarmouth*.

As a matter of fact I thought the damage, judging by the French films I had seen – produced by the manufacturer of the Exocet – would be far worse. But the missile had not, apparently, exploded. It had merely ploughed around the engine room flinging fuel all over the place, which then ignited. Basically, I suppose we all knew what had happened, and indeed how it had happened. The question was, what could we now do to stop it from happening again tomorrow? I chose to start my analysis from a point which was at least well defined, definite and likely to be constant: from the moment the incoming Etendards 'popped up' for a radar sweep of the sea in front of them. That, I concluded, is the one un-variable aspect of an enemy missile attack. It will be the ensuing series of events from the Ops Rooms which will decide the fate of the targeted British ships.

As far as we could then tell, *Glasgow*'s Ops Room acted in exemplary manner. They detected the Etendards' radars at the very first opportunity. They spotted and reported the incoming missiles in the very short time span available. Their AWO and their captain moved with commendable speed and efficiency to keep the Battle Group properly informed. My assessment was that they had the picture on the screens for all ships to see within a minute.

So what had happened in *Sheffield*, I wondered? Very little, it appeared. They had not detected the raid, they did not fire chaff, the first thing they seemed to know was sighting the missile about five seconds before impact. There was plainly no real sense of threat in her Ops Room at the vital moment. For whatever reason, they did not fire their chaff. (They did not even alert their Captain in his cabin, I found out later). At this early stage, it was impossible for me to establish why, but the clear fact was emerging that *Sheffield* did not react at all to *Glasgow*'s report. There should have been a link picture coming in, the means whereby *Glasgow*'s tactical picture is radioed across to other ships in the force, but they did not react to that either. I could not tell whether this was an electronic fault, or whether some of their people were mentally or physically just not 'on the job'. Either way, it was a most disturbing set of circumstances – one picket down, two to go and replacements still a long way away.

Our tried and tested drills for a possible air-launched Exocet attack were crystal clear. When the information appears on your screen or over the radio net – either first hand, or second hand from another ship – there are vital seconds only in which to act. The AWO must immediately say and do the things which deal with the worst possible interpretation of the limited facts. This buys time and safety while he sorts out what else to do, like track and maybe destroy the aircraft, and/or their missiles, and report the events in detail for others to take similar defensive measures. Plainly, that did not happen in *Sheffield*. For whatever reason, *Glasgow*'s message was not acted upon. We had one further clue in that we knew that *Sheffield* was using her SCOT terminals – the satellite communications – which interfered with her own ESM, rendering her deaf to any first-hand warning of the Etendards' radars such as *Glasgow* had received. But *Sheffield* might have been able to pick up the aircraft on her own radar – even though *Glasgow* was calling the bearing from *her* detection of the Etendards radar pulses. *Glasgow*'s consistent cry of 'Two-three-eight' would have been about 'Three-zero-zero' degrees from *Sheffield* – and that may have caused her to miss those small fleeting blips on her screens. Remember that *Glasgow*'s radar operators were looking straight down the bearing given them by Able Seaman Rose and his supervisor Leading Seaman Hewitt from their ESM. So they knew exactly where to look, unlike the operators in *Sheffield*. Of course, I do not know exactly how long it took to get the link picture in *Sheffield* either. It should have been quick, and it should have been quick enough. *Glasgow* appeared to have done all that was necessary as swiftly as anyone else could have accomplished.

Our overall conclusion was that the Argentinians had not only done exactly what we would have expected, but that they also knew all about Sea Dart and intended, when attacking, to stay as low to the water as possible from a very long way out. What could we do about that? Without Airborne Early Warning (AEW), not a lot. The Etendards, unless they bore on in towards the carriers and past the pickets, would only be within Sea Dart range for less than a minute – not long enough for the missile to get out there before the Etendards disappear again. And Sea Dart was unlikely to be very effective against the Exocet missile itself. That leaves us with chaff alone, until the incoming missiles fly closer to the carriers. Then the Type 22 frigates, right beside us, should be able to bring their Sea Wolf systems into action effectively. To keep the Etendards at arm's length from the carriers we had no option but to keep the Type 42 pickets, with their long-range radars, out in front. And if chaff were to prove ineffective, I might have to regard them as expendable, however reluctantly. The problem was my carriers were *not* expendable, and there was nothing I could do about that either.

The analysis thus confirmed much of what we already knew. The real difficulty was two-fold. How long will morale in the Type 42s hold up? And what do we do when we run out of Type 42s? The Royal Navy had eight of them, five at home, two down here still on duty and one out on the horizon on fire. Replacements were going to be needed. Soon. Preferably tomorrow. And plainly more than one. At the same time, Lin Middleton, *Hermes*'s captain, is pressing me to consider *his* top problem. He believes that the continuous pressure on the Sea Harrier pilots, flying sorties day and night, means that we will have to use one of the carriers up front for a five-day stint, with the other one held far back, a hundred miles to the east, in order to rest up the aircrew. Standard operating practice, he informs me.

Lin was himself a 'fixed wing' aviator who had *twice* gone over the edge of a carrier and into the sea while at the controls of fighter aircraft. On one occasion – in order to avoid coming up into the ship's propellers – he had gone right underneath the length of the carrier before getting out of the cockpit, perhaps as much as a hundred feet down. As such he was understandably sympathetic to the stresses and strains on the fliers, who, at this time, were on call twenty-four hours a day.

My own view was less so. For a start Sea Harriers fly for only about two hours at a stretch; and, even if a pilot has to do three sorties a day, that is still only six hours actual flying. There is, of course, about six hours of preparation and debriefing to be done as well. But they are all young, tough and fit. And this is war. And it has to be over in less than eight weeks from now. Also I need two decks up front and I only *have* two decks, just *Hermes* and *Invincible*. Finally there are surely going to be days down here when we can't fly anyway and those will have to suffice for 'rest' days. Sorry, Lin, can't agree.

So the submariner over-ruled the aviator, not without misgivings, and told him to find a way to run it regardless of the difficulties. This did not make for the easiest of relations between us, and was a less than desirable way of starting our partnership in the front line. But circumstances worked in our favour, we slowly discovered. For we did not know, at this stage, of one fundamental factor which was going to dominate the thinking of the Argentinian aviators. This was their high regard for the effectiveness of the British Medium-Range Surface-to-Air Missile System, Sea Dart. And it caused them to decide against using the middle and upper air, to get below Sea Dart at all costs. This left them with only very low-level flying. And that meant air attack at sea would come only during daylight and in clear visibility. Without very special equipment, no pilot can fly that low, that fast, for very long, if he can't see. It would have been nice to know all this in advance. As it was, it took some while for us to find out. Therefore, even if we did require the pilots to fly three combat air patrols in a day, most of them would usually have a good night's sleep, and that should keep them sharp. The 'family discussion' between Lin and me, before we tuned in to the 'no night-flying syndrome', caused some friction for a while. Which was a pity, because we were both doing our best. War, with all of its tensions and ultimate menace, often strains personal relationships.

The general analysis of the *Sheffield* calamity concentrated our minds on a number of these peripheral points as well as on the main event of trying to stop a six-hundred-knot missile coming inboard. We did not, as a result, make any drastic changes to our *modus operandi*, but there were many minor details which were swiftly refined. Nonetheless, I was personally left with the nagging worry that I just could not quite understand how the disaster had happened. And to me it fell to ensure that it did not happen again. My personal irritation factor was, of course, high, because the absence of straight, irrefutable logic in such matters tends to prey on my particular sort of mind. And, at that time, I still did not know *precisely* how that missile had got through. I couldn't *afford* Admiral Beatty's famous Jutland pronouncement – uttered as his battle-cruisers blew up, one by one – 'There's something wrong with our ships today.' I kept wondering. Have I missed something? Am I too close to see? But I could get no further, and had to accept the given evidence as fact, with the single reservation that I would 'watch this space' closely for the future.

Meanwhile we put together our analysis and passed it out to all commanding officers. It was in no sense a rallying cry, much more a plaintive message: 'Now come along, chaps, we must all do better' – what else can you say when you don't quite know what went wrong? But we did have a close look

Captain Mike Barrow (*left*) of the guided-missile destroyer HMS *Glamorgan*. An outstandingly brave commander, Mike took his ship into the dangerous front line of the inshore bombardments night after night – until they were finally hit by an Exocet.

Captain Paul Hoddinott (*below left*) of HMS *Glasgow*, a real sea dog, from a Royal Navy family going back for generations. He firmly believed the Argentinians would try to avenge *Belgrano* with an Exocet attack against us on 4 May. He was right.

Captain David Pentreath (*below*) of the ancient Type 12 frigate HMS *Plymouth*, which scored the first hit of the battle in Carlos Water – blew the aircraft on the far right of the trio out of the sky with a Seacat missile.

Captain Sam Salt (*above left*) of the ill-fated guided-missile destroyer HMS *Sheffield*. I could see by the way he swallowed that Sam was close to tears when he came aboard *Hermes*, but he was no less brave for that, on that terrible day.

Captain Kit Layman (*above*) the stern-mannered, highly efficient Captain of the embattled frigate HMS *Argonaut*. They opened fire with everything they had, but ten thousand-pound Argentinian bombs came in, eight exploding in the water around her, two more crashing into the ship.

Captain David Hart-Dyke (*left*) of HMS *Coventry*. Members of his distinguished family had fought many an action on the high seas, and he recognized the dangers. He faced them all with perhaps the highest form of courage there is.

June, *Hermes* again – you can see the sea stains along the hull and my Flag at the masthead. There are seventeen Harriers on deck and one Sea King, which is beside the After Lift from the Hangar Deck below.

Captain Lin Middleton (*inset, right*) of HMS *Hermes*, a former fixed-wing aviator who had once ditched on launch from his carrier in a fighter aircraft. The ship went on right over his sinking aircraft. Lin was apt to be sympathetic to the stresses on our Harrier pilots.

Captain Brian Young (*above*) of the destroyer *Antrim*, one of the two leading ships which steamed silently into Carlos Water on the morning of the landing, 21 May – at 0350 Brian ordered the guns of HMS *Antrim* to open fire on the Args' stronghold high on Fanning Head.

Commander Alan West (*above right*), Captain of HMS *Ardent*. With one-third of his ship's company killed or wounded, and with terrible fires blazing below deck, Alan ordered them to prepare the 4.5-inch gun and face the enemy once more.

Captain Jeremy Black of our 'second deck' (the little airfield) HMS *Invincible*. He managed the Battle Group's air defence for me.

Captain Mike Harris of the Type 42 guided-missile destroyer HMS *Cardiff*. '. . . At 0400 *Cardiff*'s Ops Room was suddenly jolted into action . . . an unidentified air contact moving slowly east . . . Mike Harris made the only decision open to him: "Take it – with Sea Dart." '

Commander Christopher Wreford-Brown, Captain of the nuclear-powered submarine HMS *Conqueror*, ordered her to periscope depth, called out the range and bearing . . . Time was running out for the big, grey veteran of Pearl Harbor, now named the *General Belgrano*.

Commander Tony Morton, Captain of the Type 12 frigate HMS *Yarmouth*. It was his first command and, as one of seven British warships which escorted the troopships to the landing beaches, he was often in the thick of the fighting. Tony brought *Yarmouth* through unscathed.

at our decoys, our jammers and chaff patterns to see what improvements could be made, and there were some that looked useful. More significantly, though, we decided to fire chaff regardless of the warning we had received – which meant that we would too often respond to a cry of 'Wolf' in order never to miss the real thing. This put us almost immediately into a state of chronic chaff shortage, a situation saved only by the prompt action of a certain Ian Fairfield, the chairman of Chemring, chaff-makers of Hampshire. He moved heaven and earth, opened a new factory in weeks, and increased his output eightfold, all more or less on spec. He was, of course, paid for it all in the end, but the CBE he was awarded for his efforts carried with it the grateful thanks of a good few thousand British sailors.

We also finally understood what the signal 'AIR RAID WARNING – WHITE' actually meant. Not – 'There are no enemy aircraft coming our way' – a sort of 'All clear' from the Second World War days. It indicated only that we have not detected any *yet*. There is a big difference – there is no guarantee in the White warning. There may be an Etendard detected in the next three seconds, with a missile three minutes behind. Nor, after *Sheffield*, was there any further need to exhort people to wear their anti-flash gear – the light, yellowish, cotton head-masks and gloves which will protect our skin from instant burns in the sudden flash-fire explosion of a bomb, shell or missile. Sailors and officers alike had been prone to wear them round their necks below their chins rather than suffer the inconvenience of covering all the face except the eyes. The speed and heat of the hit on *Sheffield* ensured that only those with a particularly contrary turn of mind would ever again walk around without the full protection of their anti-flash gear instantly available.

Sheffield had told us that you can get badly hurt out here. Very quickly. Some did not have to be told but it was now obvious to all – and immediately the differences began to show. People started to sleep above the waterline. There were many camp beds and mattresses ranged along the passages. People just stopped going down to the mess decks below, preferring to sleep 'upstairs'. This sort of self-protection was really only applicable in the Second World War when a torpedo could come in below the waterline, but it made people feel safer, sleep better, in the South Atlantic, and both the captain and his master-at-arms smiled benevolently upon this new breed of gypsy sailors who littered the passageways. Another difference, and perhaps the most positive spin-off we had from the incident, was in general attitudes. There were those who never thought they would start pressing triggers or buttons and actually killing people. After *Sheffield*, that was no longer so; life became more precious, more earnest and getting the job exactly right became a great deal more important. I concluded my own analysis with the thought that today, on Day Five of the war, I fully expected us to be sharper, quicker and altogether more effective under attack than we had been yesterday. At least if we planned to stay alive, we had better be.

Out beyond the horizon, *Sheffield* went on burning. The fires which had begun in the engine room, and in the galley, spread forward and aft and were never brought under control, despite all the efforts of *Sheffield*'s crew and the help of *Arrow* and *Yarmouth* close by. Abandoned now, she burned alone out there, with little we could do except watch and wait. And see if the Argentinians came to have a look – with their little submarine perhaps. While the Battle Group retired to the south-east, I considered the possibility of sinking her by gunfire, or with a torpedo. But on reflection, I decided to wait, for two reasons. Firstly we still suspected that the Argentinians did indeed intend to send their submarine to the spot, with orders to sink any ships that came to help *Sheffield*. Not calculated to make us feel more kindly towards our enemy. And secondly, if she didn't blow up, we might just be able to tow her to South Georgia and make some kind of a fist at salvage. This meant waiting for the fires to die down, and for the hull to cool. Of course it might never happen, in which case she'd sink and cease to be a problem anyway.

I managed to get a letter off to Char, a part of which read: 'Just had your letter of the 15th April today when a steamer came in from wherever it was; and glad of it, though you all seem very, very far away, indeed in a totally different world. I saw the bit of shrapnel that went through our first casualty yesterday (a young able seaman in the *Arrow*). He's OK – it was only a piece of 20mm shell the size of my little fingernail, but it went right across his chest and into his liver. That's nice. I do not think I shall ever be quite the same again, and I am not very happy about it – it's getting to be very lonely, but Andy B continues to be a real blessing.'

The sixth day of May was a lousy day for about four hundred and twenty-eight reasons, the main one being the loss of two of our precious Sea Harriers, and two good pilots in them. Lieutenant-Commander Eyton-Jones and Lieutenant Curtis – the same Curtis who had shot down an Argentinian Canberra five days before. They took off from *Invincible* on a routine combat air patrol, in not very good visibility with patchy low and middle-level cloud. There was a possible low altitude aircraft radar contact south of the Battle Group and the two Harriers dived towards it.

But they were never seen again. At 1125 *Invincible* reported she had lost contact with them. Within minutes we had set up a search centre to investigate but we found nothing. Professional opinion was that they had collided in cloud on their way down to investigate the radar contact, and gone straight into the sea. Apart from the awful personal tragedies, I felt it had been so unnecessary and could find no comfort in the thought that accidents *will* happen. They bloody well should not and we bloody well could not afford them. Ten per cent of my present Harrier force gone at a stroke.

If that wasn't enough, the weather remained murky all day, and it highlighted my mounting frustration with several aspects of my life at the time. I will not try to reconstruct it all, but rather will quote from my diary which, written that evening, conveys more than I ever could, writing eight years later.

An *Invincible* helicopter, by getting his navigation thirty miles out, managed to keep me and three Lynx helicopters up for two hours chasing a rock off Port Stanley!

It's morning. And while the weather is good enough for Sea King helicopters, it's too variably thick for Sea Harriers. This sort of thing makes air planning nearly hopeless and crew fatigue a pressing problem.

The Junglies seem to have mislaid a couple of blokes. And the rest of the day went no better. The [covert] search [for a submarine] around *Sheffield* failed to produce 'trade', and neither did the Dippers [anti-submarine helicopters using active sonar] behind them.

Two Harriers fell out of the sky for no apparent reason, chasing a report of a 'contact tracking 250, fast'. This was patently a surface/helicopter contact and probably spurious – not one for the Combat Air Patrol – all so bloody unnecessary.

Then, as it became clear that there was no aircraft contact about, people started seeing surface contacts, and getting fire control radars locked on to them. And so on. And so on. Very nervous lot here! And so we move on through another very frustrating day.

I'm getting very upset about the stalemate position I have been strapped in. I can only fiddle about in the Total Exclusion Zone, which is now topping up with fishermen, and the whole thing is getting totally out of hand. I can't hit anyone outside the TEZ. I can't take risks. The Harriers can't fly for the weather and, if I'm not careful, I shall be picked apart. Feeling very hassled and suspicious of Cabinet. If we're not allowed to take any risks, and not allowed to go to war in any but the most limited area, if we have to live in an area into which the enemy can strike from safe havens, the strength we came with will be whittled away. I might as well leave the area.

Made a long signal to Commander-in-Chief giving a list of the riskier possibilities for the next week or so, but really pointing to the need for me to know whether the Cabinet will actually decide to *land*, on the day. If not, then it's silly to get our people's heads blown off now (though I can see why it may be thought a good idea). If they do intend to land, then there are several things we *ought* to do to test the water and impose some attrition on the Arg forces beforehand.

To cap it all, the submarines have been stopped from doing anything nasty in the area of the main Arg surface force. It looks very much as though *Hercules* [an Arg Type 42 destroyer] is to be let go for the second time. It's unbelievable: you just can't expect to be given two bites, much less three, at the cherry. The SSN force is becoming a laughing stock: joining the rest of us!

Months later, I reread my entry for that day, 6 May, and shuddered a bit. I wrote below it the following words: 'In this day's log it is quite obvious that the general nervousness was shared by the Task Group Commander [me]. These moods come and go – and keeping the log did much to help me through them. It was, by any standards, a bad time for everyone. Sailors hate fog. *Sheffield* had been hit. We had lost two Sea Harriers. The Arg carrier was still an unknown factor. And my surface and air surveillance around the Battle Group was anything but leak-proof.'

The tiresome aspect of 7 May was that it was very much like 6 May. We sat out on the eastern edge of the TEZ in the fog; 'prosecuted' (as we call it), a submarine contact with enthusiasm until it proved to be another whale, persecuted rather than prosecuted; visited *Sheffield*, still burning, blistering but upright and not settling noticeably in the water. The evening almost saw us lose two more Sea Harriers. In the dense but patchy fog, we had declined to launch our routine CAPs on the basis that if we couldn't see anything, neither could the enemy. But at 1807 we received convincing indications of an air raid. Whether by Canberras, Mirages, Skyhawks, Etendards – we knew not. Neither could we figure out how they could attack us in this fog.

Invincible orders two Harriers up immediately, through a chance clear hole in the fog, and tells them to head out to the north-west. Half an hour later, the Anti-Air Warfare Commander (AAWC) in *Invincible* reassesses the raid as a false alarm, just as the hole in the fog (known as a 'sucker hole' to the wiser aviators), closed, plunging the two carriers back into dense fog again.

Wonderful. Now I have two Harriers trapped up there, unable to see the carriers' decks below. Indeed, they are unable to see any ships at all. We can only look for another hole, and hope the Harriers don't run out of fuel before we find one. At least we know where they are and should be able to save the pilots if they finally have to eject. But *another* two Harriers lost unnecessarily? Like yesterday? This is definitely not my day. But then, suddenly another 'sucker hole' appeared in the gloom and the visibility improved just long enough to allow *Invincible* to recover them, very quickly indeed. Which was just as well, because, moments later, she ghosted back into the murk.

An uneasy peace then broke out over the Group as we slipped along under our thick grey blanket. Until suppertime, that is, when *Broadsword* came perilously close to being rammed by *Hermes*, still in fog. This was a really close one. Though we never saw the frigate herself, I shan't forget seeing her wake right under our bows, still swirling, green and fresh and frothy. There can only have been a matter of tens of feet in it.

Then, three hours later, as *Yarmouth* brought a small group of RFAs back into the force, the surface plot got into a fearsome muddle, with unidentified contacts coming up on the screens like measles and everyone getting in each other's way as they tried to sort it out before a real 'hostile' could get in among us. I actually went to bed just after midnight as usual, after talking to Northwood on DSSS, reading the day's signals and taking a quiet glass of whisky 'to settle the tum'.

For a day in which absolutely nothing of importance had actually happened, it had been amazingly busy.

The fog cleared on 8 May and with it, my mind. I decided we were getting absolutely nowhere with aviation and that I was going to have to get on with my war largely without it for a while, the best way I knew how. At the staff meeting that morning, I made plans to harass and attack the Argentinian positions on the Falkland Islands. I think I was influenced, perhaps needled, into a new sense of urgency by the latest reports coming in early that morning on the state of some of the ships. For a start, *Hermes* herself had locked her port shaft while seeing to a lub oil problem. *Invincible* reported trouble with the leading edges of 820 Squadron's helicopter rotor blades. *Glamorgan* reported a 992 radar problem, which we certainly did not need. Then *Glasgow* checked in with a 965 radar problem with short-pulse and target-indication difficulties. This is just terrific, I thought. We're on half power in the flagship, the helicopters are falling apart, *Glamorgan* can't see straight, and *Glasgow* can't shoot straight. Come on, Woodward, let's get going before we are all dead in the water.

Brilliant was to go to Falkland Sound north end to terrorize anything that moved, or anything that seemed likely to move. This was just the sort of free-range directive that Captain John Coward liked best. Commander Christopher Craig's *Alacrity* was to be sent to the 'gun line' off Port Stanley to bombard Arg positions. This was firstly to keep them awake ashore, and secondly to help maintain the fiction that we would eventually land in the Port Stanley area. *Yarmouth* was to tow *Sheffield* out that night, and we formed a plan to send in *Broadsword* and *Coventry* in the small hours of the morning to shoot at *any* aircraft trying to land or take off from Port Stanley airstrip.

I would say now, though I didn't know it at the time, that this day was another turning point for me personally. *Sheffield* had been, undoubtedly, a shock for all of us, including me. Perhaps I was lucky that the weather had allowed me this recovery period, a bit of time to steady up. I remember well enough, though, telling myself not to be shocked. Trying to convince myself that *Sheffield* was nothing more than a statistic. Inconvenient, yes; worrying, yes; but not shocking. But I wasn't very good at it. A ship was broken. My old ship. Men had died. My men. People on board had been burnt, some very badly. My people. Down in *Hermes*'s sickbay, the surgeons were facing reality on a scale not met before. And in the quiet retreat of my cabin I had to tell myself to put it all away, that this could not be allowed to dominate my actions.

Three days later, it seems I was able to get back into the game, quicker than some. But all around me there was no shortage of nervous cries of 'Wolf'; too many Ops Rooms were over-reacting to a flock of seagulls. But that's entirely understandable. We will get better, I said to myself. And hopefully we will turn *Sheffield*'s disaster to our advantage in the end – by improving our performance when we come under threat next time and learning from the unfortunate mistakes inevitable in any human enterprise.

NARWAL

10

The End of the Trail for *Narwal*

All through the small hours of Sunday 9 May, while I slept, *Alacrity* pumped 4.5-inch shells from the gun line off Port Stanley into the Argentinian entrenched positions around the local racecourse. They fired over ninety rounds, each shell whistling in from nowhere and making sure that our general policy was fully implemented: 'While we don't expect to do much damage, we want to keep the buggers awake all night, keep them worried and keep them busy.'

In turn I intended to have a more peaceful, cerebral morning in a full staff meeting immediately after breakfast. We would attempt to clarify our plans for putting the land forces safely ashore somewhere suitable to their business, and providing air, sea and logistic support for such time as might be needed for the prosecution of any land battle – whatever form that might take. While obviously critical to the whole operation to recover the Falklands, it was still only one of my prime tasks as the off-shore commander. I was also required to neutralise the Argentine navy and air force, preferably, but not necessarily, beforehand and to keep them neutralised indefinitely, long after any land battle might be successfully concluded.

I need to bring you more fully into the military process which decides matters such as working out the best place to put five thousand British soldiers and all of their supplies, ammunition and equipment, without getting wiped out by the enemy either during the sea approach or while the actual landing is taking place. Any army faced with crossing a beach – either arriving or departing, as most famously at Normandy or Dunkirk respectively – is in a situation which A. A. Milne might have described as *not* what 'Tiggers like best'. Especially if the enemy has a reasonably effective air force still in operation. Even more so, should the enemy have substantial land forces in the area too.

We, in the South Atlantic, with our original air force of twenty-odd Sea Harriers, and perhaps another eight on the way, were up against a two hundred-odd strong Argentinian air force, most of it land-based. We were obviously going to have to be even more careful than the historical norm. The landing force was going to be, for a short while at least, immensely vulnerable, and it was up to us to ensure that this danger was reduced to the absolute minimum.

On this Sunday morning we were still feeling our way, because our General Directive, issued when we left Ascension Island in mid-April, was, still less than crystal clear. Its wording was thus: '. . . to land . . . with a view to repossessing the Falkland Islands'. Delightfully vague, were the subject not so serious. To me it seemed to mean: 'Get into position, be ready to land and then be ready to go forward only when, and if, we say so.' The key words were 'with a view to repossessing'. They did not mean '*do it*' – and we might, conceivably, have to wait indefinitely. We had quickly cast aside any possibility of a fully effective blockade because: a) we were not a big enough force to seal the Falklands off; and b) we could not stay out at sea long enough to enforce a starve-them-out programme, even if such a scheme could be made to avoid, somehow, starving out the islanders at the same time.

We would have to land where we could establish a forward-operating base, from which we could attack the Argentinians if we were ordered to do so. But at this stage, the choice of landing site was greatly complicated by a further political requirement from home, passed on DSSS, forcefully to me but not to COMAW, as I eventually discovered. Back in the UK, there was still serious fear of a United Nations resolution ordering an immediate 'freeze' on military operations by both sides. If this occurred before we could defeat the Argentinian land forces and regain the use of Port Stanley airstrip, we would have a major problem. We of course, would still have our forward operating base but it would then have to become a long-term, defensively-sustainable military base, sited well clear of Port Stanley, but from which we could nevertheless attack should circumstances change again. And so our landing objectives, in those early seemingly far-off days of only three weeks ago, were becoming a bit clearer, if still well short of settled. We would need to create not a only a beachhead from which to mount our attacks – we would also need an air-head. For some readers, this should not be taken to cast aspersions on the quality of local commanders. It means merely a place ashore from which our fighter and supply aircraft can both take-off and land. That is, we needed to build an airstrip, as soon as possible. The envisaged airstrip needed to be perhaps only eight hundred yards long at first, because the big Hercules C-130 transports have a fairly short take-off, and while Harriers of course *can* go straight up in a vertical take-off, they can carry far more fuel and weapon load if they have a short run and/or a ski jump. But both types of aircraft are vital for an enclave: the Harriers to defend both troops and airstrip; the transports to bring urgent supplies (men and *matériel*) without, as at present, having to drop them in the sea for the ships to pick up! But, if we were 'frozen' in the enclave for any substantial period we would have to extend it for use by the RAF Phantoms before we ran out of Sea Harriers. This would be a much more difficult and time-consuming job.

An enclave also requires a harbour, deep enough to bring in almost all of our ships at various times for resupplying and repairs and maintenance. Like the airstrip, this too must be carefully chosen, and very defendable against attack from Argentinian land, sea and air forces. Of course the classic way to defend against a land force counter-attack is to select a place as far away from the Args as might be reasonably possible – preferably forcing them to cross water to come at us – but always bearing in mind that we, in turn, may wish to get at *them* in due course. There were thus various options open to us, the first being West Falkland (possibly the Steveley Bay area) which might just be far enough away for us to build an airstrip without coming under attack from land forces, though it would be closer to Argentinian mainland airfields and further away from the support of the Battle Group. But it would also mean, should we eventually be told to repossess the islands, a second, dangerous landing in East Falkland. The more favoured selection in my mind was Lafonia, the vast inhospitable southern part of East Falkland, with its indented coastline and huge bays with adequate depth of water. The most suitable here was Low Bay, some forty miles directly along the seaboard running due south-west of Port Stanley. This sheltered inlet washes into the much deeper fifteen-mile-long Adventure Bay, both protected from the Atlantic by the flat, almost featureless, boomerang-shaped Bleaker Island, deserted at the time, but now home to one man, one woman and two thousand three hundred sheep. No piece of land upon this planet was ever more accurately named.

Low Bay and the area around looked promising, because it had some major advantages:

a) it was very nearly impregnable from the sea:

b) its waters were deep and clear and adequately surveyed, so that it would probably offer us a navigationally safe harbour, reasonably protected against weather;

c) the surrounding land was at least flat, which would facilitate the building of an airstrip, though its firmness was an unknown factor;

d) it was one of the furthest easterly 'safe' areas of the Falklands and almost as far away from their mainland air force as it is possible to get without getting your feet wet;

e) while Low Bay had no surrounding hills, no cover behind which either men or ships could hide from enemy aircraft, this also had its 'up' side – in that it would make life a great deal easier for operators of the British anti-aircraft guided missile system Rapier, which was, if given half a chance, an extremely accurate weapon, well capable of knocking either fighter-planes or

bombers out of the sky, but possibly less effective
if hemmed in by cliffs or hills;

f) it would surely provide a very long and difficult
overland journey for the Argentinian ground
forces if they attempted to counter-attack us, for
they would have to fight their way over the low
ground on the narrow strip of land which forms
the 'bridge' joining Darwin to the Goose Green
settlement. But that same strip of land would be
equally difficult for us to advance over, should
that become the requirement, instead 'Be prepared to wait, indefinitely'. Provided it offered
reasonable beaches, it was possibly the right
place for an enclave, but not for any advance to
re-possess.

We also gave some thought to Cow Bay, which sits in the
extreme north-east, in a rather exposed position, to the north
of Berkeley Sound. Its forty square miles of deep water would
have separated us from the guns of Port Stanley, but our artillery experts assured us that an enclave in Cow Bay might very
well put us within range of the Argentinian's 155mm shells,
which we considered more trouble than the proposed site was
worth and we dismissed it without great difficulty.

Another consideration was Teal Inlet, a deep penetrating
bay with a narrow entrance off the straight northern coastline
from MacBride Head, leading into a huge inland sea 'lake'. We
assessed we would be completely safe in there from submarine
attack, but hopelessly vulnerable if the Args decided to block
the narrow entrance and bottle us up for days, maybe weeks.
Teal Inlet: bad news.

The other site we considered was of course Carlos Water,

well protected as it was by hills, but very moderate as a place to build a major airstrip, and potentially vulnerable to an overland counter-attack by the Argentinian army. As a place to establish an enclave it was, in my view, not the prime choice. But as a place from which to advance and repossess, it had plain advantages for the land forces over just about anywhere else.

All of these areas were considered and discussed. I was very much in favour of building the airstrip, because it would take the pressure off my carriers. In the longer run, it would even allow the carriers to go home – which they eventually *must* do – when we set up the long-term defence of the islands. Two carriers are not enough to keep one permanently on station, 8,000 miles from their base and the accelerated building programme for *Illustrious* was still highly dubious. Generally speaking I would say the Battle Group at this stage would have voted first for Lafonia for a defensive policy, Carlos for an offensive policy and for West Falkland as a poor third.

But in the early days of May, it was beginning to seem likely that our Directive from the C-in-C would be altered to one which would order us to land a force 'to repossess the Falkland Islands' . . . deleting the words 'with a view to' and with them any requirement for us to establish an enclave and build a sizeable airstrip within it. At that point we would be free to go on in and take theirs, the old British one they had borrowed from us on 2 April, the one at Port Stanley. We all knew that Admiral Fieldhouse was not in favour of the 'with a view to' wording and had himself always considered we should just land and repossess the islands and have done with it. The Ministry of Defence and the politicians had, up till now, always favoured the more cautious approach, but now they were losing the argument in London. My own land force adviser on board *Hermes* in succession to Colonel Richard Preston was the Royal

Marine Colonel John Fisher and he was fairly sure we would see our Directive changed in the next few days.

Colonel John was a highly intelligent Marine, whose keen, acerbic wit was not entirely beyond a few quiet jests from time to time at the expense of his own Regiment – an idiosyncrasy fellow Marine officers for some reason are apt to consider a form of low treason. But Colonel John, who suited me perfectly, unfailingly had his ear to the ground, and his opinion was that the mobilization of the Army's Fifth Infantry Brigade and the requisitioning of the *Queen Elizabeth II* to bring them to the South Atlantic clearly and undeniably inferred the creation of a much bigger land force. 'Five Brigade' now contained troops from the Scots Guards, the Welsh Guards, the Gurkha Rifles and the Royal Artillery. Their addition could really only mean one thing: the enclave theory had the skids under it, and Northwood was already planning a straight landing, advance and repossession strategy. Which was fine by me. 'Enclave' had never looked too cheerful and I would be glad to be off that 'hook'.

This was the reason why now, on the morning of 9 May, the minds of my staff, plus those of the Commander Amphibious Warfare Mike Clapp, Brigadier Julian Thompson and the other senior land force commanders far away up the Atlantic, and indeed those at Northwood, were converging on a single solution. However, at that time I still only had the original Official Directive from my C-in-C, and my training had taught me that I probably ought not to dump it in the waste-paper basket too hastily. I therefore continued to consider all of the problems in the widest sense, but to concentrate, too, on the likely conclusion that if the Directive did indeed change, we would unanimously go for a landing in Carlos Bay.

From our short list of West Falkland, Lafonia and Carlos,

we would obviously have to discard the first one because it was much too far away and it involved a second landing, with all its attendant risks. And, for the same reasons that the narrow neck of land at Darwin made Lafonia a good place to defend against an Argentinian counter-attack, it was a poor place for us to attack *them* from. That left Carlos Water very clearly at the top of the heap. All of the planners now favoured that area, tucked behind the great jutting mound of Fanning Head, the eastern sentinel commanding the northern approach into the Falkland Sound. Its advantages were several:

a) its beaches were partially protected against air attack, both by the hills which run south-east from Fanning Head and by the Sussex Mountains to the south;

b) the Navy were happy with the depth of the water and with the quality of the 'holding ground' for our anchors, so it was navigationally 'safe' though a bit tight for space;

c) it had two main entrances from open ocean because you could run through Falkland Sound easily enough from the north *or* from the south, and both these entrances were wide enough to make the use of blockships ineffective (unlike Teal Inlet) and the existence of two entrances made it doubly hard for the Argentinians to cover them both with submarines and/or mines;

d) it gave good shelter against wind and bad weather.

So we continued in the Ops Room of *Hermes*, around the General Operations Plot, to go over the intricacies of the total problem. But it was not for me to calculate the details of the tide's rise and fall, the effects of wind, sea and swell, or note the best landing points from the ships. Not for me to search for the thick black mud any naval captain will prefer for his anchor holding ground. Nor did I fuss about where we might find sand, weed, clay, shingle and shells, or about the beach gradient and how this would be affected by a swiftly falling tide – discussing, for example, whether the beach would allow the landing craft to get in close enough or whether it would go shallow so gently that the troops would find themselves saddled with huge packs of equipment and ammunition, wading through freezing water perhaps four or five hundred yards from the actual beach, making the distance too far, too tiring, too hazardous. These were the tasks of the dozens of Royal Navy and Royal Marine experts to whom these problems are not much short of a way of life. No mistakes, Woodward, I told myself. This thing has to be done dead right, first time. But I must continue to rely on the experts.

So, at a higher level, we asked ourselves: is this prospective beachhead defensible against a determined land force attack? And, is it defensible, in the short and long term, against air attacks with bombs or missiles? Can we defend it against attack from the sea? From the surface or from a submarine? How can we know it has not been mined? At which point does the sea bed slope upwards to a depth of less than about sixty feet, the minimum water a small submarine requires to approach submerged? Can we get the ships in fairly tightly against those hills to shelter from incoming air attacks? Can we minimize the Argentinian *off*ensive capability, and maximize our *def*ensive capability? This was a difficult one – the hills were a very much a mixed blessing, because they ensured we had no clear arcs to see our enemy approaching early, in time to get our weapons locked on to him. Two hundred miles offshore we had maximized our capability of seeing him early, but in turn our position had maximized *his* capability of hitting us with 'stand-off' missiles, like Exocet. Inshore, beneath those hills, we minimized his capability to strike us, but also minimized our own chances of catching him. I think it was the late John Paul Getty who said that for every plus there is somewhere, somehow, a minus. The tight-fisted old oil billionaire was right.

Of course, the skill lies in getting the *balance* right. And this *we* eventually did, whether by luck or good management. What sometimes still surprises me is that the Argentinians didn't come to similar conclusions. But at this stage, no final decision could be taken and so our staffwork continued. By now *Alacrity* had returned from the gun line, *Brilliant* was back from North Falkland, and *Yarmouth* had placed a tow on board the stricken hulk of *Sheffield*. *Coventry* and *Broadsword* were on their way to try to impose the 'air blockade' of Stanley, and, for a change, life seemed relatively peaceful here in *Hermes*. Not, however, for long.

At 1150 two of our Harriers, armed with 1000-pound bombs, under the control of Captain David Hart-Dyke's *Coventry*, detected a surface contact fifty miles south-south-east of Port Stanley which they were now investigating. This would normally have caused an instant broadcast '*Admiral to the Ops room!*' Unnecessary this time because I was already in there.

Thoughts raced through my mind. It couldn't be the Argentinian carrier: they had no need to place it so far forward, and anyway it surely wouldn't be on its own. Indeed, I did not think it could have been *any* of the Argentinian warships since they all appeared to have gone home. And yet . . . in the eastern side of the TEZ, I did not at all want to get within Exocet range of an Argentinian warship – and there had to be a five per cent chance that Anaya's fleet could make a comeback.

From across the room, my General Warfare Officer Captain Peter Woodhead said, 'It's that bloody fishing trawler again, sir. They just identified it. The *Narwal*, the same one we warned off ten days ago, the night before we arrived in the Zone.'

My emotions said, 'Damn it. The last thing I need is that little toad reporting our *exact* position, night and day, back to his bloody air force.' But my logic, grinding smaller, was saying: 'Careful, Woodward. This is the same kind of situation as the Brazilian airliner. This boat is full of fishermen – civilians. Be sure of your ground before you blot them out. There'll be hell to pay if they're innocent.' The fact was I was still not allowed to attack any fishing boat, Argentinian or not. My Rules of Engagement expressly forbade it. I was only empowered to hit warships. 'The Harriers might be able to get her to stop with some 30mm cannon shots across her bows,' I thought, 'but there are only minutes before the Harriers must leave the *Narwal* for lack of fuel – then she is free to proceed and disappear again. There's no way I can get anyone else there in time to look more closely, so she may get away to continue her business – whatever it may be. Where has she been these last few days? Why haven't we tripped over her before this? What is she up to?' My thoughts kept racing with the question, 'Is this the same as the Brazilian airliner? Do I now face identical circumstances?' I pulled back at that. After further thought I tried to buy myself some time, asking out loud, 'Are we quite sure of her identity?'

'Yes, sir,' came the steady reply. 'The pilot flew in low – the name *Narwal* is on her stern.'

In the next few seconds I was happy at least that this was not at all the same situation as before. When the Burglar/ Brazilian Boeing had come lumbering into our air-space three weeks ago, I was not absolutely certain of her identity. Neither were we at war, declared or not. Nor was the Battle Group within easy reach of the land-based Argentinian air force. Nor were we in the TEZ. But now we were at war. That was for certain: ships had been hit and sunk, planes shot down, and men killed and burned. This was not the same. Besides, I *knew* the identity of the trawler. We had seen her twice before, and on the last occasion I had personally told *Alacrity* to warn her off, just hours before we entered the TEZ. Now she was here again, not in international waters (or airspace as the Brazilian airliner had been), but right here in our internationally declared Total Exclusion Zone. Was she an innocent fishing vessel? I suspected not – not unless they were very stupid indeed. Was she shadowing my Battle Group? It seemed quite likely. Otherwise what on earth was she doing here, in this very public theatre of war, having been told in no uncertain terms by a Royal Navy commander to get the hell out of the area?

Right now the personal risks were fairly high. If I had hit the airliner and been wrong, the whole operation might well have had to be cancelled and I would have carried most of the responsibility, public and private, quite properly. Now here I was with another high-pressure decision, with no time to take advice from above. I told myself this was what high command was all about – that I had been hired to break the rules if necessary, just so long as I was right. So, what were the probabilities? Fishermen are, on the whole, not stupid. This is not the most sensible place to be fishing this week. If they hadn't heard it on the radio, they had heard it direct from *Alacrity*. So she is probably *not* fishing. If she is not fishing, then surely she is trailing us. There isn't anything else to keep people at sea around here. If she is to trail us properly, she will need professionals. So there would have to be Argentinian navy personnel on board, for overall command and for reporting communications as well. While I was fairly sure there would be civilians on board the *Narwal*, this makes her a war vessel in *my* book, and in more or less anyone else's except my book of ROE. She may not be able to damage us herself, but she can tell the opposition precisely where we are, with unacceptable consequences very close behind. Though I knew I did not have permission to attack any fishing vessel, I was fairly sure this was *not* a fisherman. Also I was personally very much at war. I had been fighting for nine days now and that had hardened my heart. I was standing for no bloody nonsense. From anyone.

I ordered the two British planes to try and stop her, immobilize her, that is. Not at all easy under minimum force rules when you only have 30mm cannon and thousand-pound bombs available for a matter of minutes before the Harriers have to break off for lack of fuel. So they started with the cannon; *Narwal* pressed on, hoisting the Argentinian national flag as she did so. Finally the pilots asked if they could put a bomb into her – for fusing reasons as likely to blow the Harrier out of the sky as *Narwal* out of the water, and probably both. I did not need her to be sunk, but I did very much want her rendered totally ineffective. There was no chance I was going to let her get loose again and I gave permission to proceed with the bombing.

Fortunately for everyone concerned, the one thousand pounder was fused for dropping from high level, and so from this low altitude it failed to go off on impact. It did hit the *Narwal*, killing one wretched crewman instantly and making a large hole in the ship in the process. The second aircraft peppered *Narwal* with cannon-fire. *Narwal* eventually stopped, wallowing, crippled in the swell.

At 1220, I decided we should board her as soon as possible – by helicopter, using SBS or SAS. I had no wish to kill fishermen by sinking her out of hand if I could help it, but also I needed evidence, one way or the other, as to her employment. *Invincible* was told to set this up. So far, so good.

Written later, my diary covered the next few hours of the *Narwal* story succinctly enough. 'Then the saga begins: if you try to do anything unplanned in aviation or with Special Forces, it all takes sixty-two times as long. Ships improvise, everyone rehearses, checks and delays. Result is hours of bogging about, the near loss (for lack of fuel) of a Sea King Mk 4, and much confusion. No doubt it will sort itself out by breakfast tomorrow.' At the time, I merely instructed the Ops Room to alert me when they heard the contents of the Argentinian trawler and later we reconvened the staff meeting which was planning the landings, an extremely complicated business.

By 1400Z *Coventry* was reporting unknown air contacts a hundred and sixty-five miles to the west which turned out to be an Argentinian C-130 Hercules transport, escorted by two or three Mirage fighter aircraft, trying to get into Port Stanley. *Coventry* opened fire immediately, locking on at the far end of her range and firing two Sea Dart guided missiles at the little air convoy. The missiles all missed, apparently because the Argentinian pilots turned away to the west. When Captain Hart-Dyke informed me that Sea Dart had not been successful, I guessed it was almost certainly a range problem and told him, 'Steady, David. Don't fire till you see the whites of their eyes.'

Eventually, at 1600, the Special Forces team got aboard *Narwal* from the Sea King helicopters, finding thirteen men on board, including one dead. They also found Lieutenant-

Commander Gonzales Llanos of the Argentinian Navy and with him there was documentation which proved beyond all possible doubt that *Narwal* was no innocent fishing vessel. There were code books, charts, references and special military transmitting and receiving radios. But by then she was shipping water and everyone was taken off, leaving her to sink.

When I look back upon the incident it does not send shivers up my spine quite so briskly as does the memory of the Brazilian airliner. On reflection I think many of my immediate doubts about *Narwal* were probably allayed by my conditioning in the North Atlantic. Russian surveillance trawlers had long been a normal part of the scenery up there. The Soviet ships were very sophisticated – and their electronic interception equipment could readily be seen by even an untrained observer. We used to call them Elint trawlers and I knew exactly what they looked like. The fact that the *Narwal* – which to us was just as deadly a threat – did not conform in appearance to my preconceived idea of what a spy-trawler should look like was probably the main reason for my hesitation. Nonetheless, it should be, and is always, a tough decision to break your laid-down ROEs deliberately – the standard defence, 'Well, on balance, at the time, it seemed right to me,' will not be any use at all if you're proved wrong later, no matter what the 'balance at the time' may have looked like.

My conclusion for the benefit of others has to be: 'Don't do it . . . unless . . .' At least the Argentinians themselves regarded the matter as a 'fair cop', and never complained that the 'filthy British had bombed an innocent fishing trawler'.

Anyway, with that now off my mind, I retired for a cup of tea towards the end of the afternoon, with three problems of varying dimensions pre-occupying me. I needed to think by myself for a while because all of them had serious implications.

The first one was simple. Why had *Coventry*'s three shots with Sea Dart all missed their target? The *Coventry* Ops Room claimed the target was 'feasible', but I know that that is machine language. It is also only a prediction and is entirely dependent on the incoming aircraft maintaining its course and speed towards the firing ship until it obligingly meets the missile at its extreme range. In other words, the target has to be co-operative! As far as we knew, all four of the Argentinian aircraft got away scot-free and I am obliged to say I faced a very similar conundrum as that which I had pondered over during the staff debriefing after *Sheffield* was hit: either the equipment was failing us or someone was using it incorrectly. It had to be one or the other, and by far the worst of the two options was the first. How could we possibly fight the forthcoming sea-to-air war if our main anti-aircraft missile refused to hit where we aimed it? What I fervently hoped was that David Hart-Dyke and his team had launched it too soon, at the far end of the missile's range, with his targets too high. This course of action gives the aircraft time to spot the upcoming threat, and take evasive action in time. By so doing, they plainly have a good chance of making their escape because by then the Sea Dart is fast running out of fuel and soon will drop harmlessly into the sea. The trick is to let the enemy planes keep on coming, let them get nearer, right into the range envelope of Sea Dart, from which there is no escape, no matter how quickly they turn away and run.

At 1900 the problem was solved. A signal came in that *Coventry* had blown an Argentinian Puma helicopter (perhaps searching for *Narwal*?) out of the sky with a correctly aimed Sea Dart missile. Lesson learnt – I hoped – and I could imagine that rather shy smile on the face of Captain Hart-Dyke when his AWO's shout of 'SPLASHED!' was heard in the Ops Room of HMS *Coventry*. He immediately sent me a more cheerful signal which said, 'You will be pleased to learn the Argentinians *do* have whites to their eyes!' (Years later, this entire exchange between David and myself may have been proved redundant. Some Argentinian sources admitted that two of their little air convoy had never got home that day. Had *Coventry*'s captain hit them after all?)

The second problem troubling me was the Argentinian air base on Pebble Island. They couldn't put fast-jet aircraft on the grass airstrip there thankfully, but it was entirely suitable for light ground attack aircraft like the Pucara. Various clues showed us that they had definitely deployed to the airfield and our intelligence estimated a sizeable garrison of men along with the aircraft. One aspect of this concerned me greatly: that those aircraft were awfully close to Carlos Water – only about nineteen miles as the crow flies, which in my opinion was precisely the way they would fly, straight enough, on to the British landing force. If they made around 250mph it would take them just over four minutes from take-off to come in over the Carlos Water beaches – giving virtually no notice.

I sat in my cabin looking at the charts, wondering how quickly the Args' air force could launch a serious attack from that desolate little outpost, right off the north shore of West Falkland. Before I had dinner I called a staff meeting for the following morning with one simple objective: to find the best way to remove all those aircraft on Pebble Island, in relatively short order, like before the earliest date for the landing.

I wrote my diary that night rather grumpily. Looking back I can tell it betrays signs of worry, that I had a lot on my mind. That's when I grow most grumpy. Against the time 0830 I wrote, 'Am obviously worried for the 42/22 combination. But this trial is essential in my book. If it fails we shall all know the landing is off in sufficient time to stop it happening, at great saving of life. A long day groans on.'

These latter references concerned my third problem. I had high hopes for using the Type 22 frigates as 'goalkeepers' for the Type 42 destroyers. Their job would be to catch the Argentinian bombers which managed to get past the Sea Dart and gun defences of the destroyers. The general idea was that when the incoming raiders got too close for Sea Dart, *Brilliant* or *Broadsword* could open fire with their Sea Wolf missile systems. These are specifically designed for close-range defensive work against modern, very fast missiles. We had not actually tried them against aircraft, but we felt they ought to work and, if they did, we would have the essential counter to *any* form of close-in air attack from the Argentinians. But two ships working together often find the whole exercise very difficult, especially when there is a requirement for split-second timing, which, in this case, there most assuredly would be. The two ships would have to operate together as a single unit, giving each other support and advice. Under attack, they should have decided that just *one* of them shall have the final say as to who goes where. Any other arrangement would be likely to lead to chaos, confusion and possibly catastrophe. I *had to* find out if it could be made to work.

The best report would have been one which told me both ships had performed well under attack and that the Type 22s' Sea Wolf had caught all the 'leakers' missed by the Type 42s' Sea Dart. The worst news would have been that Sea Wolf had missed them and that another of my Type 42s was hit. I was actually of the opinion that if the ships could not protect each other, we probably should not land at all. Thus the 'trials' were occupying an increasingly important place in my thoughts. I also wrote down a very hasty account of *Coventry*'s own wayward marksmanship with Sea Dart, adding, a bit spitefully, the unnecessary fact that the three missiles which had apparently missed did so 'at a cost of £750,000 to us'. Even the downing of the Puma did not please me much, since I wrote pessimistically, 'We show a profit, but the Arg Press will no doubt make much of it as a sea – air rescue for the wretched *Narwal*, which turned up 50 miles off Port Stanley, for all the world as though there was no war at all and we hadn't warned her off a week ago.' I made a brief note that it seemed likely that *Yarmouth* would make it out to the tug *Salvageman* 'with the not-so-shiny *Sheff*'. And, with some relief, I recorded that, 'The *Broadsword/Coventry* combination had the desired effect. The Args got nothing into Port Stanley today. I think I'll have to replace them for tomorrow; twenty-four hours inshore must be very tiring.'

Some months later I cringed a bit over the generally truculent tone of my diary for 9 May 1982, and felt obliged to write by way of explanation the following note underneath:

> The 'saga' concerned the boarding of *Narwal*, after she had surrendered to the Harriers, by the Sea King 4: but it was eventually done some four hours later, and the *Narwal* was finally left to sink eight hours later. I was personally very relieved to find the lieutenant-commander on board: the political consequences of shooting up an innocent trawler might have been awkward, and the Sea Harriers had not attacked before I had given my personal permission to do so, albeit with some misgivings. What decided me, of course, was that we had warned her off on 30 April.

Before I finally went to bed I ensured that *Brilliant* and *Glasgow* were under way for the nightly bombardment of Port

Stanley airfield, but we received a signal before midnight that *Coventry*, returning 'home' through thick fog, had a major defect on her main gun and might be out of action for a few days. She and *Broadsword* eventually rejoined us at 0615, and forty-seven minutes later we received a signal from *Yarmouth* that *Sheffield* had sunk while under tow. I made a curt note in the diary: '*Sheffield* has apparently sunk at last, perhaps saving us a lot of bother.' Much hinged on my word 'apparently', which I had used because *Yarmouth* had actually reported *Sheffield* as, 'Sunk. Am searching to confirm.' My diary again gives a clue as to the state of my mind: 'This is not a very confidence-inspiring statement. Like he's not sure whether she *has*, in fact, sunk! Oh dear. The battle for information is never-ending and often largely fruitless.'

The following morning the staff meeting began early and I outlined to everyone my fears regarding the Argentinian air forces on Pebble Island and their potential danger to us during, and indeed after, the landings. I laid out the options, which were after all pretty basic: either we launch a massive bombing raid and completely break up the airstrip or we try to bombard the aircraft to bits with 4.5-inch shells in the middle of the night with 'spotting' from helicopters with flares. Both of these courses of action offended my sense of subtlety, and efficiency, for they were not without risks and involved too high a degree of uncertainty. As I recall, I had just slipped into a facial expression which my wife describes as 'vacant', but which usually signifies I am lost in thought, when a chap materialized, whom I did not even realize was in the Ops Room. As far as I could tell he had either come straight through the wall, which is made of steel, or out of a cupboard, although he was a bit tall for that.

'I wonder if we might be able to help out, Admiral?' he said quietly.

Of course by this time I had identified my resident SAS officer, who always sat in on these meetings, but who somehow never seemed to be there. I've always thought that these people must spend at least half of their time practising the art of vanishing, just disappearing into the woodwork. You never seem able to see them, unless they want to be seen. I suppose that is a key part of their trade, just as moving stealthily through the ocean's depths in a submarine was once a key part of mine. But how he managed his disappearing act in *Hermes* Ops Room I shall never know, dressed as he was in 'jungly' camouflage and six foot four tall with it.

Anyhow, I was very glad this particular officer had spoken up. It was, he said, the type of operation for which his men were ideally suited. Given sufficient time, he felt confident they could get on to the island, make a detailed recce, and then get a force of perhaps a dozen chaps in – when they knew where they were going – and 'take out' all of the Argentinian aircraft. Which all sounded excellent to me, except that I did not have all that much time to give them. We were still working on that 16 to 25 May landing window we had planned back at Ascension and our general view of any attack on Pebble Island was that it must be completed by 15 May – five days from this moment. My fastest mental arithmetic told me that about 0230 on the morning of the fifteenth was what is known in the trade as 'Drop Dead Time' – that is, it's time to bag the whole thing and try some other way.

'How long do you have in mind?' I asked him and for a moment he hesitated, calculating the kind of detail which is life and death to an SAS man.

'Three weeks,' he replied.

'No good.'

'I'm sorry?' he said with a slightly worried frown.

'What about five days?' I cheerfully asked.

He gave me a look of total incredulity, followed by a mumbled phrase which I took to mean 'Jesus Christ!' or 'Doesn't this – ****ing idiot know *anything* about Special Force ops?' or something like that. The thing about the SAS is that they have an image which has nothing whatsoever to do with their reality. To the public they are perceived as a team of daredevils made up entirely of chaps who look and behave like a magnificent mixture of Errol Flynn, 007 and Batman. Everything about them contains a substantial amount of rumour and hidden threat, coupled with sudden, fast, decisive action – their attack on the Iranian embassy in London, their reputation as the scourge of the IRA in Belfast, their apparently simple removal of terrorists in Gibraltar. And it is true that they are Britain's deadliest and most effective armed force. They do not, however, achieve anything by taking lunatic risks and acting in a way which might ever be described as swashbuckling. Their every success has been the result of the most meticulous planning, an almost fanatical attention to detail and the near-total elimination of surprises. When the SAS go in, they *know* the problems, every aspect of every problem. And, in the normal way, for them to destroy a squadron of aircraft on Pebble Island they would want to know the contours of the ground down to the last puddle; they would want to know every blade of grass, every cow pat – stopping short only at the Christian name of the cow that dropped it; they would want to know the position of each sentry, exactly how many men were on the base, the position of the moon, the anticipated brightness of the Big Dipper, the wind-strength, which gate might squeak, and much else. To achieve this preferred level

of intelligence they like to insert perhaps four men in there
for a week, and then another four for another week, and finally
to make their move when the reports have been studied to the
last detail, and conditions are perfect sometime in the following
week after several days rehearsals. It is a method which has
brought them almost superhuman success. No surprises.

Naturally, therefore, a look of utter incredulity flickered
briefly across the face of my SAS adviser when I informed
him that we would have to cut his recce time down from three
weeks to three days, with two more for rehearsals and the
actual operation.

'I'm sorry, Admiral,' he said. 'That may not be possible. We
shall need three weeks to get it right.'

'I am afraid it's got to be five days,' I replied bluntly. 'It's
the 15 May or never.'

What followed was another little 'family discussion'. Both
I and my staff had to agree we did not even know where the
damned Argentinian airstrip was, far less how to get on to it
quickly and wipe out this little section of the Arg air force
without everyone getting killed. 'Hey, Gringo! What you do
here?' was a demand none of us particularly wanted to imagine
in the dead of night. Especially if it involved looking down
the barrel of a machine gun. My job was to get rid of those
aircraft, but it was also to convince the SAS commander that
it was his as well. In five days.

By the end of our meeting he had agreed to give it his best
shot. The first SAS recce party would go in tomorrow night,
landing on the northernmost coast of West Falkland and
making their way across the pitch-dark, usually rough stretch
of water to Pebble Island by inflatable dinghy. The distance
was about one and a half miles, but if they misjudged the
current I had no doubt it would seem like five.

Looking back on the staff meeting I am forced to admit that I behaved in a very stony manner. I realized of course that the SAS officer was trying to do his best for his very expensively trained men, making sure they were not wasted. My problems were different. I knew that those aircraft were capable of wreaking terrible damage on the British landing force, perhaps killing hundreds of men, caught at their most vulnerable moment, during the actual landing. If I had been told in advance, 'You can wipe out the Arg Air Force on Pebble Island, but it will cost the lives of ten SAS men', I am afraid I would have said, without hesitation, 'So be it.' I am not proud of it, but that is how I have been trained to think. Presumably that was why I was there. And the SAS would understand it too, as they did then, really.

My second major task of the day – on top of the three problems plaguing me from last night – was no less worrisome. It concerned yet another unpleasant possibility. Mines. One of our submarines had already watched the Args laying mines to the east of Port Stanley harbour entrance (called Port William, incidentally), which was after all the most obvious place for us to land. So we knew well enough that they were perfectly capable of laying mines across the northern end of Falkland Sound as well. For that matter they might even go for the southern end too, depending on how many they had, how much time they had and whether they thought it necessary. And since it now seemed fairly certain that our General Directive would change in a way which would render Carlos Water our automatic choice for the landings, I wanted to do my best to ensure that we did not lose half a dozen ships and a couple of thousand men four miles short of the landing area. I don't like mines any more than anything else that can sink a ship, but what was making me dislike them very much more than usual was that we had no mine-sweepers down here. Nor would any arrive in time. This left me with a considerable problem: how to find out if there were any mines laid in the Falkland Sound.

Perhaps I should just outline how simple moored mines and mine-sweepers work. For a start, a moored mine is a sizeable floating iron shell containing as much as one thousand pounds of TNT. That, by the way, is just short of a half-ton of high explosive, sufficient to break the back of most ships. If you hit such a mine, even with a glancing bump, it will certainly blast an enormous hole in the ship, killing anyone nearby. By and large, big mines, professionally laid, sink ships quickly and noisily. They float below the surface of the water, perhaps ten to fifteen feet down, just enough to make sure they can never be seen, but close enough that even shallow-draft ships will hit them. They are anchored by a mooring wire to a heavy weight (called the 'sinker') on the sea floor and are usually laid in 'fields' over a carefully selected area of water. In its simplest form, the highly specialized vessel the mine-sweeper trails a cable which is pulled out to one side by an underwater kite. The cable has wire cutters along its length and when it snags a mooring wire, it scrapes down the cable until it stops at a cutter, which then chops it. The mine, no longer moored to the bottom, floats up to the surface, where hopefully it can be seen and dealt with before anyone's ship hits it. There are various methods of getting rid of a free-floating mine – the traditional and most spectacular of which is to detonate it with rifle fire.

If I had been an Argentinian and had suspected even for one moment that the British were coming in to land in Carlos Bay, I would have laid as many mines in the north and south entrances to Falkland Sound as I could. That would have eliminated all worry about the Brits landing *any*where along either side of the Sound. It would have been a considerable weight off my mind. We did not, of course, know whether they had done just that . . . or something very like it.

For my part, however, mine-sweepers and their special equipment I did not have, which meant that I would have to use something else – and the hull of a ship was the only suitable hardware available. The only steel which would go deep enough. Now, plainly I could not use the two indispensable Type 22 frigates *Broadsword* or *Brilliant* with their close-range Sea Wolf systems. I also clearly could not send in my remaining Type 42s *Coventry* and *Glasgow* with their invaluable long-range Sea Dart systems. And equally surely, it really wasn't on to send a merchant ship or RFA. It had to be a ship though – and it would have to be a Royal Navy warship. But it would also have to be something cheap and cheerful which I could replace, like a 3000-ton Type 21 frigate. Like *Alacrity*. Like expendable *Alacrity*.

Now, I did not particularly relish the prospect of ringing up Commander Christopher Craig and saying, 'Tonight I would like you to go and see if you can get yourself sunk by a mine in the Falkland Sound. By the way, I will put *Arrow* up at the northern end to observe events and in case she's needed to pick up survivors.' Nor, when it came to sending the amphibians in, could I possibly follow the instincts of the fabled American Civil War admiral, David Farragut, who roared at the entrance to Mobile Bay in 1869, '*Damn the torpedoes. Full speed ahead!*'

I did neither. Instead I phoned Commander Craig on the voice-encrypted network and said, 'Er . . . Christopher, I would like you to do a circumnavigation of East Falkland tonight. All the way around to the south, then north up Falkland Sound and out past Fanning Head to rendezvous with *Arrow*.' I also told him to come up the Sound very noisily, exploding a few star-shells and generally frightening the life out of the Args. I added, 'If you see anything move, sink it, but be out of there and home by dawn, so you're clear of the land before they can fly.'

He was silent for a few moments and then he said, 'Umm, I expect you would like me to go in and out of the north entrance a few times, Admiral. Do a bit of zig-zagging.'

'Oh,' I said, feigning surprise and feeling about two inches high. 'Why do you ask that?'

'I expect you would like me to find out whether there are any mines there,' he said quietly.

I cannot remember what I said. But I remember how I felt. I think I just mentioned that I thought that would be quite useful.

He replied, with immense dignity, 'Very well, sir.' Then he went off to prepare for the possible loss of his ship and people the best way he could. I shall remember him as one of the bravest men I ever met. This was Victoria Cross material but, strangely, only if it went wrong.

I personally felt awful not to have had the guts to be honest with him and wondered what the devil he was going to tell his ship's company about their task tonight and about my pitiful performance, which, for a sea-going admiral to one of his commanders, beggared description.

BROADSWORD

11

Glasgow's Bomb

You will have little trouble believing that I was unable to sleep that night, my thoughts far away from my little cabin in *Hermes* ... somewhere on the bridge of *Alacrity*, as she turned north into the mist shortly after midnight to begin her dark, dangerous journey up the Sound. And that I kept trying not to think of the people I knew in *Alacrity*'s company, trying not to imagine the ship-killing explosion of a mine against the frail hull and the awful consequences for those on board, and all the while knowing that whatever befell the gallant Commander Craig and his ship, and all those who sailed in her, would be, inevitably, my fault. And that I tried, unsuccessfully, to console myself with the thought that the job did have to be done, since to wait for the arrival of the entire British amphibious force in order to find out if they were sailing through a mine-field, would have been less than clever.

How easy it is to picture myself that night, trying to cast the worry from my mind, lying there unable to sleep, pondering Commander Craig on his sinister journey – essentially, as we all are at times like this, on his own. Did I, at least in my heart, go with him?

I'm afraid not. In fact none of the above is true. I know that it ought to be, that those would have been the reasonable human thoughts of anyone who found themselves in my position. Indeed, in the ensuing years, I have probably described it in precisely this way to others. But when I am coldly honest with myself and relive such moments in the small hours of nights as dark as 11 May 1982, I know it was not so. It could not have been so. Yes, all these thoughts would have occurred to me, but only prior to the decision itself. I took the journey in my own mind *before* I spoke to him – not after. The decision taken and *Alacrity* committed, I crossed them off my list of problems and settled down to await results, good or bad. Such apparent callousness is not fashionable but that was my job, management of the mind, a fundamental element of military training, to be rested and ready to cope with whatever *else* may befall this night.

I certainly did not know, as the clock crept around past one in the morning, that life for Commander Craig had already ceased to be furtive. In fact the situation in *Alacrity*'s section of the Falkland Sound more resembled Guy Fawkes Night. Following our policy of trying to keep the dreary opposition awake at all hours, *Alacrity* had fired star-shell over Fox Bay settlement, illuminating the Argentinian positions in an unearthly, soul-chilling light. Beneath the hanging yellow moon of a star-shell burst I'm sure they must have wondered if this was a prelude to the end of the world – or at least to the arrival of the nearest SAS patrol, which often amounts to the same thing. A few miles further on, *Alacrity* got a radar contact which turned out to be the Argentinian naval transport *Isla de los Estados*. The British frigate's star-shell over her would also have had the effect of putting dread in the hearts of the wretched crew, but for them the end of the world would more likely arrive in the form of high explosive. Which is precisely what happened.

Alacrity hit *Estados* with three 4.5-inch shells, starting a fire which only ended when the 325,000 litres of aviation fuel in the hold of the *Isla de los Estados* exploded in a fireball which should have been seen for miles, but which was actually little more than a dull glow in the thick mist from the bridge of *Alacrity*. Thus occurred the *only* surface action between British and Argentinian ships of the entire 1982 War.

That formality dispensed with, *Alacrity* continued north into the doubtful waters of the entrance off Fanning Head. Darkly now, she made her way forward, checking for mines the hard way. When they finally could see the great jutting promontory of Fanning Head off their starboard quarter, Commander Craig reversed course, heading back to widen the 'cleared channel'. With a last pass to the north again, they finally rendezvoused with *Arrow* just to the east of Cape Dolphin. Thus ended quietly, and no doubt gratefully so, an extraordinary story of courage, which will go, I'm afraid, largely unnoticed in the annals of maritime history. COMAW certainly was completely unimpressed by *Alacrity*'s efforts. But had it ended in tragedy it would have joined the sagas of *Jervis Bay* or *Glowworm* being presented to young naval officers of the future as a supreme example of selflessness and devotion to duty. If they had hit a mine, Commander Craig would have been most strongly recommended for the award of a vc – but, thank goodness, he didn't.

So much for *Alacrity*. The news from our other front, the gun line off Port Stanley, was mixed. Paul Hoddinott's *Glasgow*, with John Coward's *Brilliant* in company, had been bombarding Moody Brook where we believed there might be a sizeable Argentinian position. However, in the process of setting up that bombardment, we found ourselves in a bit of a muddle on this typically busy night. *Coventry* and *Broadsword* had been ordered to head west from the Battle Group to relieve *Glasgow* and *Brilliant*. This seemed simple enough, but we had changed our minds, once, about the task of *Broadsword*, at first considering she should go in and meet *Alacrity*. Somehow or other she had received the signals in the wrong order and when they first set off it seemed that *Coventry* and *Broadsword* had all too good a chance of meeting *Arrow* and *Alacrity* unexpectedly, in fog, at three o'clock in the morning, bang in the middle of the likely Argentinian submarine patrol area. As mix-ups go, that one could have been special. Anyway we sorted it out, and had everyone back on bearing before any harm was done.

The intermittent fog and mist had kept the Argentinian Air Forces out of the sky for the last few days, which was just as well because, even without being attacked, we were absorbing a lot of punishment to the ships and aircraft. Sheer wear and tear was the problem: defects and difficulties came and went in endless succession as time and weather took their toll. *Glasgow* was having trouble with her generators, with one running on a drive shaft they had actually made on board, while another was under repair. As the morning wore on, all of the Harriers on board *Hermes* were grounded for maintenance and by lunchtime we were getting reports that *Coventry*'s 4.5 Mark 8 gun was defective and that *Broadsword*'s precious forward Sea

Wolf system was down for a while. My general relief at the safe return of *Alacrity* was such that I remained optimistic that we could cope with all of this, and the only aspect of the day now proving to be a real bore was the weather forecast which had a serious low-pressure area heading right for us, with gale-force westerly winds, rough seas, broken cloud and improving visibility. All of which was bad news, together with the fact that tonight's insertion of the advance party of SAS going into Pebble Island was probably going to prove something of a trial for everyone.

In the middle of everything *Invincible* complained (my diary used the word 'bleated') that they had been put on the up-threat side of the force without a Type 22 frigate (*Broadsword*) as a 'goalkeeper'. Unfortunately, it was on a circuit that the Captains of all the other warships in the Group could read. I was obliged to remind him that *Hermes* had been in this position on and off for about three days now; that, unlike them, we did not possess the advantage of a Sea Dart system of our own; and that perhaps it was his turn now. He took the point perfectly well.

They may have been unnecessarily harsh words, but I could only do my best during this waiting period and try to cope with the stresses upon ships and aircraft and people – the last category becoming rather more vulnerable as the tense, indecisive days wore on. We were all nervous, some more, some less than others.

Quite a few individuals had by now cracked up. I am sorry to say we lost an aviator for whom the trauma of high-risk flying proved to be the last straw. This was a very telling case because it was clear the poor guy was under stress of an entirely different nature before he even arrived here. Perhaps we should have noticed, but I am afraid no one was looking. We also had a doctor fall apart, and an engineering officer, and there was possibly another on the brink. Symptoms vary greatly, and I made a mental note to examine my own – particularly the one which I had been warned about by the PMO in April when the first stress cases had appeared, the tendency of such cases to want to nod off the whole time. As a matter of fact I *had* found myself spending more time lying on my back than usual, but I was not cracking up, just finding it a bit more difficult to sleep when I was supposed to and a little easier to sleep when I was not supposed to.

It is quite hard to know what to do about men who are obviously suffering from stress. Of course the real cases, where a man is obviously not able to do his job, are easy: they must be sent home by whatever means available. But there are others for whom trauma is not sudden or obvious, men who do not betray the classically obvious symptom of just not absorbing any new information. These are men who just go on doing that for which their brain has been programmed and can, by self-protective means, hide for a very long time the real truth that, in any emergency, they will fail to react in a relevant or effective manner. This is not because they don't want to, or are too lazy, but because their mind has just shut down at a certain point. I have often thought that at least a few medals for gallantry may have been won in this way – by men who were so banged out, they just kept on going, or firing, or defending a position, despite the obvious hopelessness of it, because their minds had nothing else to tell them. The transmission centre of their brains had simply jammed – just shut down because of mental trauma. I resolved to remain watchful and observant for such behaviour in myself, just as I was trying to remain watchful and observant towards the stress cases among the ships.

At our staff meeting, convened specifically to finalize our plans for the landings, everything seemed to be going more smoothly than I had anticipated. We all agreed that the amphibious objective area should be in weather-proof waters and that Carlos Bay was as good as we could hope to find unless the 'enclave' requirement re-surfaced. We agreed that the waiters – that is, the ships waiting to go in to Carlos – should remain to the east of the Battle Group which would stay roughly where it had been for the previous few weeks, well offshore, providing air cover on a long-term, reasonably assured basis. We believed that the Commodore Amphibious Warfare (COMAW) should proceed inshore with an escort including the two Type 22s *Broadsword* and *Brilliant*, the big county class guided-missile destroyer *Antrim*, the two Type 12 frigates *Plymouth* and *Yarmouth*, plus *Argonaut*, and the two Type 21s *Antelope* and *Ardent*. No one disputed that we should send the landing ships in and out, at night, as required, making the sea passage from Battle Group to Carlos Water as small convoys, in the comparative safety of darkness. We also considered that the priorities for the landing force were, beyond question, a secure beach head, the establishment of local defence against air attack (Rapier) to relieve pressure on the escorts, and a smooth build-up for the land-force advance towards Stanley. I had another important need: to get ourselves a small airstrip ashore as a forward base from which to operate Harriers – firstly, to ease the pressure on my carriers and secondly, for the same sort of reasons, in reverse, that I had needed the Argentinian aircraft on Pebble Island removed, permanently.

By 1700 the weather front was closing in on us fast, with the winds and sea building. The eight-man SAS team was ready to go for Pebble Island, but it was clearly going to be a difficult journey. The 'Junglies' took them in, flying over the pitch-black ocean, praying for starlight above the shore line, in order to utilize their passive night goggles. By the time they left they were flying in a forty-knot cross wind out of the north-west.

The sea below was pretty fierce, but the starlight was right, and in the small hours they landed the men and their boats in the hills behind the beach, and made it safely back. The SAS men planned to lie low for the remainder of the morning and prepare to make their crossing to Pebble Island the following night. By the time they had sorted themselves out, *Glasgow* and *Brilliant* were back on the gun line off Port Stanley, the dull thump of *Glasgow*'s shells being whipped away by the now gale-force wind.

It was a routine sort of night, allowing me plenty of rest – enough anyway for me to take the Royal Air Force to task the following morning. Plainly, I'd not had enough rest, you may say, to make my judgement reliable. I went to the Ops Room early and proceeded to draft a rude signal, indeed it set a new benchmark for rudeness, but fortuitously I cannot recall, nor do I have a record of, its exact wording. A failure to keep a perfect log of everything is perhaps as well. My basic annoyance with the Light Blue involved their expeditions down to the war zone in the big RAF Nimrod maritime patrol aircraft with its excellent Searchwater radar. The idea had always been that they would fly over the area at a suitable height and report anything they found to us. This they did with whole heart, tireless effort and great enthusiasm. The trouble was they kept getting it wrong, which may not matter too much in peacetime but can be disastrous in war, because we had to react . . . just in case they were correct. My 'battle for information' was made much more difficult if the information provided was positively misleading, as opposed to merely inadequate.

For instance, in mid-April they signalled that they had located a group of fishing vessels in the precise spot I knew the forward *Brilliant* group was sailing. They reported the ships as fishing vessels, I imagine, because they were fairly close together, milling about on different courses, going nowhere in particular. The trouble with this was that the RAF did not *know* they were fishing vessels by positive identification. It was only their best guess. But they hadn't said it was only a guess. In this case, however, it hadn't mattered much because I had better information than they; but it was hardly confidence inspiring.

So I had ignored that error, but they kept happening. Then more recently they had alerted us urgently to the Argentinian aircraft carrier which they pin-pointed for us, well out to sea. Fortunately, I knew perfectly well that it could not possibly have been the carrier, and in fact it turned out to be a large, harmless container ship, which can look very like a carrier to a Searchwater radar at times. 'But that's not my problem,' I was saying to myself. 'It's theirs. All I am insisting on is that when I am given positive information like, "Argentinian carrier at a certain latitude and longitude," that the information is guaranteed. Otherwise don't give it to me. Or at least, if you insist, preface and conclude the signal with the words, "I am not altogether certain about this, but it could be . . . and this is based on the following limited evidence only." And above all stop trying to interpret. Leave that to us. We are the unfortunates who have to cope with the detailed consequences. Thank goodness,' I thought at the time, 'the Args appear to be doing nothing aggressive at all at the moment.'

Having fired off my signal to Northwood, I waited for a

response, which was not long in coming. Northwood hit the direct satellite line to *Hermes* and informed me coldly that I appeared to have upset the entire High Command of the Royal Air Force. My reply was impolite. I intimated that I did not give a **** how upset they were, they had better start concentrating on accurate factual reporting. I also ventured the opinion that their pettiness in being so upset was childlike in the extreme. I ended my retort with something like, 'They would do a great deal better to listen carefully to what I say, and *learn*.' Then I stumped along to my cabin and made an entry in my diary which it is as well to omit from this book. It was, I suppose, all part of the therapy, along with the original rude signal itself.

Meanwhile, out on the Sedgemoor gun line, off Port Stanley, patrolled *Glasgow* and *Brilliant*, now in broad daylight. This would have to be described as a very high-risk position, because the Argentinians could not just ignore the 42/22 combination situated in such plain view of their positions ashore. To help focus their attention, *Glasgow*'s gun continued to bombard them, using her Lynx helicopter as a further irritant while it clattered around marking the fall of shot. It's worth mentioning here that an army Lieutenant Colonel had gone with Captain Hoddinott to help select targets and manage the bombardment. Various excitements ensued, not least when the Args opened fire on the Lynx. The pilot reported he was under heavy fire and was pulling back.

At this point, the colonel called down the line, in all seriousness: 'Report the calibre of the shells! *Report the calibre!*' It was, I imagine, about the last thing on the minds of the helicopter crew as they dodged away from the ground fire. And the Ops Room crew fell about laughing, as they will on such occasions. There was, of course, no way the air crew could have reported the calibre of the shells – you don't see them that clearly as they pass. Hence the hilarity. But the information was important: the next enemy shells might be from guns big enough to reach *Glasgow*.

This was only a brief moment's levity. They all knew that *Glasgow* and *Brilliant* were involved in the test to see if the 42/22 combination would actually work. They were plainly vulnerable to attack; the question was, how vulnerable. I felt that the long-range Sea Dart system and the short-range Sea Wolf system made a pretty good package and I expected them to more than hold their own. But whatever the outcome, we still had to know before the landing force was sent in. We did not have to wait long to find out.

Shortly after lunch, *Glasgow* and *Brilliant* were just turning back out to sea when a British Harrier, returning unannounced from a bombing run on Port Stanley, suddenly pitched up on the surveillance radar, which pulled their minds back from bombardment and excited helicopters, to the air warfare problem, sharply. Everyone's thoughts began to lock on to the drills for dealing with a very low-level bomb attack. The advice from the aviation experts was divided as to whether it was best to present your ship beam or end on to the approaching bombers – there were good arguments for either, until we started to observe that the Argentinian bombs were tending to bounce when they hit the water. That new fact, unnoticed by COMAW, changed the whole scene. It is, of course, a nearly overwhelming instinct to present your enemy with what you think of as the smallest possible target, like your bow or your stern, if there is time. But you have to remember that bombs from very low aircraft, doing four or five hundred knots, do not 'fall', they 'come in' on a very shallow angle, almost like a missile, and may even bounce on the water if incorrectly delivered and/or fused. The pilot finds it hard enough to line his aircraft up on an evasive ship target; his harder task is to judge the precise split second at which to release his bombs. If the ship target is end-on, he has at least eight times as long to judge it. The additional and critical new factor in favour of presenting the ship beam-on is the fighting chance that the bombs the Argentinians seemed to be using so far would bounce right over the top, perhaps even through a low part of the superstructure. But if you are end-on, it is most unlikely to bounce the full length *and* the full height of the ship.

Furthermore, if you stay beam on, all your defensive systems can be brought to bear – end on, about half of them are not working for you. And finally, if the 'making-it-too-easy-for-line' worriers were still unconvinced, going full astern in these gas-turbine driven escorts would change the crossing rate just as much as a major alteration of course, without being as obvious to the attacking pilot.

Paul Hoddinott and Nick Hawkyard knew the drills backwards, as did John Coward and his AWO, and now they were surprised to see their 'enemy' – the Harrier – correct its mistake and disappear away to the north-east without firing a shot or anything else. Relief again. But then *Brilliant*'s Ops Room spotted them . . . four incoming aircraft, Argentinian A4 Skyhawks they turned out to be, single-seater American-built five-hundred-knot low-altitude bombers, carrying either four five-hundred-pounders, or two thousand-pounders, neither option holding much appeal. *Brilliant*, riding shot-gun, informed *Glasgow* immediately. The trouble was his radar operators could not pull up the picture on either their 965 or their 992 screens. Hoddinott's command computer remained blank.

Hawkyard spoke quickly to *Brilliant*, who transferred their picture, on the link, back to *Glasgow*, and now the AWO could see the four tiny paints hurtling towards them, still coming across the land, some eighteen miles away. Three minutes' distance. Tension in the Ops Room is not yet being recorded on the Richter Scale, but that's the next step.

The Air Picture Compiler calls the track number and Hawkyard knows there is no need to interrogate. These are hostile. 'Get ready!' he snaps. 'Missile Gun Director, *take them with Sea Dart!*'

Chief Petty Officer Jan Ames hits the buttons to get his 909 Fire Control Radar to search for the A4s as they approach the open sea, where the radar should work better.

Hawkyard again calls range and bearing. Chief Ames confirms, 'Roger, gottit on the bearing. Tracking.'

Now Hawkyard and Ames are in a kind of trance, watching the radar, waiting for the indicator on the MGD's tote screen to flash 'VALID TARGET'. Seconds tick by.

'Valid target – fifteen miles,' says Chief Ames.

'*Take it!*' replies Hawkyard.

And the veteran MGD presses the buttons for a Sea Dart salvo, the agreed method of dealing with a close-packed attack of four aircraft, as this most certainly was.

Up on the foredeck the missiles come smoothly up out of the magazine, on to the launcher, which swings round to the firing bearing. But there is no 'Launcher Ready' indication. They didn't know it but the little micro-switch on the launcher has become encrusted with salt and is malfunctioning, as a result of hours out there in a big sea with waves breaking over the bow. Hawkyard nonetheless thinks the missile will still launch. It is in place, but the computer does not recognize this fact. Chief Ames hits the buttons to over-ride the computer – nothing happens. So they hit the 'Launch' button.

'Please work,' mutters Hawkyard. 'Please work.'

But it did not work. Instead the screen flashed the dreaded words, 'Port beam malfunction.'

'It was', recalled Hawkyard later, 'the biggest silence I had ever heard in my life.'

He orders Chief Ames to try the other launcher, but the computer has been told to fire a salvo, not a single missile, and it does not recognize the command.

'JESUS CHRIST!' shouts someone, as the captain, realizing it is now almost too late for Sea Dart anyway, orders the Mark 8 gun into action.

Over in *Brilliant* John Coward's men have Sea Wolf locked on and tracking. The incoming aircraft are now under five miles away. Both ships are turned beam-on: *Glasgow*'s gunnery crew blazing away as best they can with their single Mark 8 gun; at 1644, Captain Coward's AWO orders his missiles away. The first one blows the Argentinian lead bomber out of the sky. The second one blows the second Argentinian bomber out of the sky. The third incoming bomber tries to turn away, misjudges it and hits the sea at four hundred knots still heading towards *Glasgow*.

'Christ, Chief!' exclaims a certain Leading Seaman Duffy Chambers talking to Jan Ames from up on the Gun Direction Platform. 'It's like a ****ing war film up here!'

The fourth bomber gets through and, as he does so, *Glasgow*'s gun jams. The pilot releases his bombs and they appear to tumble through the sky. One of them goes into the water fifty yards short of *Glasgow*, but the other bounces off a big wave and shoots through the sky, passing in an arc about thirty feet above *Glasgow*'s upper deck, just missing the mast. It crashes into the water harmlessly on the far side of the beleaguered Type 42 destroyer.

Everyone breathes again, but within five minutes *Brilliant* detects a second wave of four more incoming bombers and alerts *Glasgow*, whose weapons engineers are working frantically to free up the Sea Dart system and unjam the gun. They fix the gun, but have no time to deal with Sea Dart. Then the entire command computer system crashes and Paul Hoddinott, calm and understated in the face of an Ops Room nightmare, orders the Mark 8 to open fire once more, as soon as the raiders are in range. Then he orders everyone who can fire a gun to the upper decks, to man the machine guns. *Glasgow* might go down, but her captain and his crew will ensure she goes down fighting.

Brilliant carries on tracking and requests *Glasgow* to shut down her Mark 8 because the shells are coming up with tracks on the radar. Now *Glasgow* is almost defenceless, save for her little army of machine gunners on the decks. 'Never', said Chief Ames later, 'had I felt so utterly helpless.' Seven miles out the Args pilots begin to weave and zig-zag to confuse the Sea Wolf system, and they are successful. Captain Coward's men this time cannot 'lock on' with the short-range guided missile which served them so well in the opening raid. Now the Args are through.

Brilliant fires at them with every gun she has, two bombs bounce off the water and sail over her decks, just missing the British frigate. *Glasgow*'s gunners, crouching on the upper decks, unleash a desperate volley of small-calibre fire, pumping bullets into the only A4 still coming at them. But they were too late. The bomb hits *Glasgow* amidships just three feet above the waterline on the starboard side. In the Ops Room they feel their ship shudder and hear the 'WHOOMMFFF' of the bomb as it crashes through the hull and travels clean out of the other side without exploding, causing much damage in the after auxiliary machinery room and the after engine room but, miraculously, injuring no one.

Captain Hoddinott hears someone shout, 'What the bloody hell was that?'

Almost simultaneously his damage-control team is on the line from deep in the ship, reporting two gaping holes into which tons of freezing sea water are pouring. The gale outside has not abated and the ship, with both cruising turbines completely knocked out, is rolling heavily. Each time she heels to port the sea gushes into one hole and, as she rolls back, it gushes in the other. The damage-control parties are already standing waist deep into the extremely cold water stuffing mattresses into the holes, fixing heavy wooden beams, especially provided for this very emergency, into place, slamming them tight with sledgehammers.

Lighting is a problem: *Glasgow* already has one generator out, with another jury-rigged, and now she has another badly damaged. The fire-main has gone, as have the high-pressure air compressors. The diesel fuel supply system is damaged. By any standards, *Glasgow*'s life is hanging by a thread as the men struggle to rig pipes and hoses to suck out the water.

Back in the computer room and up on the missile launcher the weapons engineers work under quite extraordinary pressure to re-arm their stricken warship. Inside thirty minutes they have the gun freed, the Sea Dart working and the computer system back on line. We offer to increase the combat air patrol above them in order to get them back safely, but Captain Coward declined, saying he is now confident his Sea Wolf system will do the job.

Fifteen minutes after this, the Argentinians come in for their third attack. *Brilliant* locates four aircraft circling out to the west but, hearing perhaps what has happened to the first four, they seem to think better of it and withdraw. They may also have observed another sight to make them think twice: the pilot who had pressed home his attack on *Glasgow*, and been hit by the machine gunners on the deck, had been shot down and killed by his own men as he limped in over Goose Green.

And so Captain Paul Hoddinott and his men narrowly cheated disaster on that rough and windy afternoon. I was absolutely delighted of course to learn in the early part of that evening that they had all survived. Their only casualty was in fact one man who went into shock, a reaction for which he could scarcely be blamed. I spoke in some detail to both captains, not only about the damage, but about re-programming the systems to cope with this kind of air attack. The problem with the gun was also trying, but I was used to the fact that the Mark 8 4.5-inch gun had a tendency to shake itself to bits, until it jammed. It had happened all too often when I had been captain of *Sheffield* five years before.

Meanwhile *Glasgow*, in company with *Brilliant*, limped back slowly towards to the Task Force – battered and leaking – and I ordered her to remain sixty miles inshore of us, out of the worst of the big seas, while she effected her repairs. Her fighting spirit was perhaps best illustrated by the words of her captain. 'Don't worry, sir,' said Paul Hoddinott. 'We'll be patched up in a couple of days, and back out there.' He was too.

The verdict on the 42/22 defensive combination? Well, you would have to say that if Sea Dart had not failed, it was likely that *Glasgow* would have splashed at least one, possibly two, of the Argentinian attack aircraft. I am assuming they would have launched two salvos in the short time available. That would have meant, I suppose, that none of the A4s would have made it through to drop their bombs. If they had repeated the process in dealing with the next four, I imagine the third group would have lost their nerve even quicker than they did with just three of their colleagues dead. Thus in principle the 42/22 combo would have to be given the green light, as would the advice to remain beam on. Although the implications of the fact that the one bomb that actually hit *Glasgow* hadn't gone off were not conclusive – it began to look as if their bomb fusing might be seriously wrong. The problem remained Sea Dart and its reliability, and the hiccup on Sea Wolf's homing system. We immediately got talking to the manufacturers' representatives on board *Brilliant* to try to iron out both faults. But I still fear there is a Sod's Law involved here: today it was a salt-encrusted switch; tomorrow it will be something else; and the day afterwards something else again.

I wrote in my diary that night a rather cold assessment of the day's activities.

Weather finally cleared so started high bombing Port Stanley airfield. Probably very inaccurate. By late pm the Args (midday their time) had obviously decided to 'do' *Brilliant* and *Glasgow* with three lots of A4s. First lot, two taken by Sea Wolf, one spun in, one escaped. Second lot, Sea Wolf went to reset just before moment to open fire and so all four came through unharmed, and one bomb went right through *Glasgow*'s after engine room. Third lot were probably deterred by high CAP up-threat by then (previous policy had been to hold them back) or, possibly, by news of the mauling the first four got.

2100. *Glasgow* has got it under control, but I expect she'll have to go home. Fleet Trial [the 42/22 combination] has made progress, but still needs its final test. Meanwhile Sea Dart, as an anti-low-level system, is looking to be fairly useless, because it does not always fly.

Aside from the fact that we also lost a Sea King that day – it ditched in the sea, but the crew were all rescued – it had been a rather bleak few hours really. At this moment I was down to only one immediately available Type 42, *Coventry*, which meant I would be obliged to cut out all daylight bombardment of the Arg positions on the islands.

It may be surprising that I have written all this about *Glasgow*, but I want you to follow the life of the Type 42 destroyers, the pickets, with whom we started this story. And I want to show you, once more, the enormous difference between what the commander has to think about and what the unfortunate in the front line must actually cope with. And now I would have to abandon my 42/22 'Trials' and my air blockade of the Port Stanley strip since I dared not risk losing my only remaining forward long-range radar and long-range anti-aircraft missile ship. Two other Type 42s were on their way to join us, but HMS *Exeter*, under the command of Captain Hugh Balfour, having cleared the port of Belize in the far west of the Caribbean, was still two days north-west of Ascension, while *Cardiff*, commanded by Captain Mike Harris, had cleared Gibraltar only hours previously.

News over on the coast facing Pebble Island was not so good either – the terrible weather and sea conditions meant that the SAS could not make the crossing and had elected to stay hidden for another day on the mainland, in the hope that the weather would improve sufficiently tomorrow to let them get in for the recce.

In fact the only positive thing that happened all day was that we did receive the alteration in our General Directive regarding the basic objective of the Task Force. The dangerously vague words 'with a view to repossessing' were struck out. 'Enclave' had finally dropped off of the political 'worry' list and off my 'worst case' list too, thankfully. West Falkland and Lafonia dropped out with it. The new wording instructed us simply to land and repossess the islands. Only now, on the 12 May, with the northern entrance to the Falkland Sound cleared for mines by *Alacrity* as best she could, and the overall directive itself changed, did Carlos Bay become the definite and commonly-agreed objective for the beach head. No further discussion was required unless new evidence came to light. I found out much later that COMAW had been greatly exercised by my persistent 'going-on' about the advantages of Low Bay as a landing area, but then he hadn't been briefed from home to consider any of the politically-driven, and militarily highly undesirable suggestions short of 'landing to repossess'. Our CTF probably thought COMAW didn't need to be worried by such matters, though it naturally didn't help COMAW to understand my concerns and, in the particular case of 'enclave' much angst could have been avoided between us.

Anyway, I retired for the night and while I slept the gale died away to be replaced by fog, which was excellent for the SAS and for *Glasgow*'s repair crews, a day off for the Harrier pilots, and a bit dull for the rest of us. *Glasgow* spent much of the day racing round in tight circles, literally, trying to keep one side up out of the water while the welders went to work patching the plates. But at the end of all this she was still not fully watertight. She was going to be a dockyard job.

I spent a few minutes writing in my diary in the early afternoon:

> *Glasgow* seems to have it under control, but the thread has to be thin. Bloody lucky the bomb didn't go off or we'd be another 42 down. The essential question is whether to keep her here or send her home. Sent for *Salvageman* [tug] anyway. Meanwhile thick fog again brings the entire war (I hope) to a standstill.
>
> Final analysis of the second raid: really we were both very unlucky and very lucky. *Glasgow*'s Sea Dart went defective right from the start, and her gun jammed on the sixth round; *Brilliant*'s Sea Wolf switched off completely. So defensive fire was two 20mm and two 40mm only.
>
> To have received just one non-exploding bomb out of some eight or twelve is just bloody lucky ... but this is now just the weather we want for the landing.

So far we had received no recce reports from Pebble Island and were not altogether sure whether the SAS had even reached the airstrip. Thus we had something of a timing problem: if we just waited there for them to contact us by radio with the information we would be too late to go.

I pondered the situation, working as ever from one of my personal little bar-charts much as we had needed back at Ascension when we were trying to fix the landing date. For this evening's expedition I again had to work back from the finish line. *Hermes*, the deck from which the SAS Direct Action (DA) force will leave, *must* be well off shore by dawn, if we are to avoid unacceptably increased risk of attack from the air. That means we ought to be on our way 'home' by 0600. The operation of wrecking the Argentinian aircraft should take five hours, in addition we should allow a couple of hours' general foul-up time, like helicopters not starting or having to sink an Arg patrol boat. We should therefore be in position off the coast of Pebble Island by 2300. So we must start by 1800 since it is a five-hour journey. Thus, if we stay out here waiting around for the radio report from the SAS recce crew, we will be starting too late. Therefore we leave on time and keep pushing forward, hoping to hear from the advance party during the journey.

At 1755 *Hermes*, *Broadsword* and *Glamorgan* detached from the main Task Force, at a speed of twenty knots, to insert our DA team into Pebble Island off the north-east coast of West Falkland, with the objective of destroying a significant part of Argentina's local air force on the ground. Broadly our tasks were as follows: the four Sea Kings with the SAS men were in *Hermes* and we would take them in as close as was sensible, about seventy-five miles from the landing zone. *Broadsword* would be *Hermes*'s 'goalkeeper' with her Sea Wolf in case we came under air attack. *Glamorgan* would move inshore and open up a diversionary 4.5-inch gun and Sea Slug missile bombardment to take the Args' eye off the ball while the DA teams went in and did their business.

We headed in for two and a half hours, but we still heard nothing from the recce party and shortly thereafter the SAS commanders called the mission off for the night on the basis of insufficient information. I ordered the ships to come about and return 'home', rather grimly mentioning to anyone prepared to listen that this mission *must* be carried out tomorrow night, no matter what.

We had a brief meeting that night on the way back and retired to bed, beneath the safety blanket of fog, to await, during the night, the recce report. By the following morning we had it. I sent two Harriers in to bomb Port Stanley and the rest of the afternoon was spent in preparation for the Pebble Island raid.

At 1800 sharp we set off. There were four Sea King 4s on board, to land forty-five men of D Squadron SAS, plus a naval gunfire support team (spotters), on Pebble Island. I delegated *Invincible* to assume command of the remainder of the Task Force in my absence. The weather by now was filthy, the fog having been replaced during the late afternoon by a southerly gale. Big frigate though she is, *Broadsword* had to give up the struggle to stay with *Hermes*, and dropped back to a more reasonable pace. *Glamorgan* and *Hermes* were able to push on though. Two hours into the journey I ordered *Glamorgan* to detach and make for Pebble Island on her own: 'Proceed in accordance with previous orders' is the stock phrase.

So now we had *Broadsword* making only twelve knots some fifteen miles behind *Hermes*; *Hermes*, Britain's main airfield in all of the South Atlantic, entirely unescorted, with no air defence to speak of; and *Glamorgan* somewhere up ahead. This was something less than tight control, mutual support and concentration of force – three of the basic rules of warfare. We ended up bringing *Hermes* within forty miles of Pebble Island, since we needed to find a way to reduce the fuel requirements of the Sea Kings on this nearly one-hundred-mile round trip in really awful weather.

This was not our only problem. As we slowed down to launch the helicopters, it rapidly became apparent that there was going to be difficulty getting them away. We had one helicopter on deck, but the wind was so strong they were unable to 'spread' its rotor blades. This is a very critical decision because if you do spread them in too high a wind, and a gust gets underneath them, it will whip the blade up and rip it straight out of its mountings. Finally after half an hour there seemed to be some kind of lull. They moved swiftly, spread the blades and got them safely rotating. The familiar roar of the Sea King 4 could now be heard above the gale and the crews dived for the second chopper. This one could *not* be spread – the lull had passed. So it was decided to get the remaining three back below into the hangar, put them one by one on the elevator, spread their rotors, get them rotating and only then take them up to flight deck level for launch. This is not a recommended process but seemed to be the only way of doing the job.

The elevator transported them down and the crews pushed them all back, started one, then another. But it all took time and by now the first one they had started did not have enough fuel to complete the mission. So that had to be refuelled. I can easily still remember standing on *Hermes*'s bridge that night, wondering if they'd *ever* be ready. Finally, however, it worked and off they went, much later than I had hoped, but still just inside the two hour 'imbuggerance' factor.

The forty-five men were landed on the gale-swept north coast of Pebble Island, a little over three miles from the Argentinian airstrip, and silently they picked their meticulous path across the dark, deserted island and placed their explosives on the eleven assorted aircraft they found there. Several weeks later, when I finally landed personally on the Falkland Islands, I went up to Pebble in a helicopter to take a look for myself at the remnants of the operation. It really was rather spooky, like a surreal landscape. All of the eleven aircraft were still there; at first glance, unharmed, ready for take-off. Then I became aware of a strange noise, an almost ghostly rattling in the wind, and I noticed that close to the cockpit of each aircraft there were just a very few broken bits dangling from electrical wires, which occasionally swung in desultory submission against the fuselage. It was the only sign that these aircraft would never fly again. It was also the only sign that the British SAS can, when the need arises, move very fast indeed.

"SEA KING"

12

Talking Trees and Etendards

The gale never abated all the way back from Pebble Island. It varied in strength from Force Five to Force Nine, but fortunately it shifted direction, veering south-west from our starboard quarter, enabling us to make very good time out of the danger zone, now, of course, in broad daylight. Slightly to my surprise, the Args made no attempt to counter-attack us as we cleared the northern waters off East Falkland. We decided, anyway, to send in a Harrier group to bomb the Port Stanley airstrip and to take advantage of the broken cloud to acquire some new recce photographs of Fox Bay, Goose Green and Pebble.

Upon our return to the main Battle Group we heard that, amazingly, the stricken *Glasgow* was back in business, patched up with full power on two turbines, all weapons working and computers back in good shape, with only marginal manoeuvring restrictions at low speed. That was rather a weight off my mind because it restored some of our long-range radar capabilities around the Battle Group and brought (hopefully) another Sea Dart system back into our defensive network. We all knew Argentina's Navy Day was on 17 May – forty-eight hours hence – and our general belief was that they would strike against us from the air on that day, if not sooner. I was now just beginning to believe their ships really had gone home for good.

I retired to my cabin for a while that afternoon, having been up most of the night, and tried to sleep. But I ended up instead wrestling with the guided missile problem, the now dreaded Exocet. The air-to-surface Exocet, that is, the one they fire from the French Etendards, the one that finished *Sheffield*. I endeavoured, as I always do, to deal with inescapable facts and with regard to this particular missile, I had only very limited information:

a) the Args had fired two of them at us;

b) one of them had missed us completely;

c) despite all of our defensive systems, one had got through and demolished one of my three Type 42 destroyers without even exploding;

d) the Exocet's remaining fuel had ignited the most terrible fire, with burning electrical cables causing dense smoke as it spread through the ship, slowly turning a very bad situation into a fatal one, in which twenty men died;

e) the Ops Room crew of the departed *Sheffield* had been unable to do *anything* about it, not even fire their chaff.

Those were the facts. Which meant that Exocet was achieving a fifty per cent success rate. I understood that Exocet might not do as well next time, and that we might do better, but I was not there to act as a bookmaker, watching the odds and awaiting the outcome. I was there to do something about it.

Now, our intelligence said that the Args had started this war with about five of these particular missiles, which meant that, if they fired the other three, on form to date I would lose one, perhaps two more ships. What would prove much worse was the possibility that they might manage to find another supply of missiles – indeed there were rumours abroad in London that they were negotiating for as many as forty more. With an arsenal such as that, even if their success rate dropped by a half, it could rapidly prove fatal to this entire operation. The fact was, we had to stop them. The question was, how?

Well, there are only a few ways to tackle such a problem (in the absence of an inexhaustible supply of utterly foolproof chaff). The best course of action is, naturally, to catch and kill the incoming Etendards which carry the missile. For this we really only had Sea Dart, which had not yet proved itself to be even reliable, far less infallible. What's more, the way the Argentinians seemed to fly their Etendards, Sea Dart was not all that likely to catch them even when it was working well. There just wasn't the necessary warning – only AEW aircraft could give that and we had none.

In sum, you will agree, we faced a considerable challenge, since we plainly could not just sit there, waiting for them to attack, hoping for their known strike rate to decrease, praying that our (as yet) unproven chaff procedures work, and trusting that Sea Dart would suddenly become reliable for no obvious reason. Generally speaking, those are fairly sound ways of getting a lot more ships sunk and people killed. But there really did not seem to be much choice.

They were worried at home, and all of my conversations with Northwood reinforced this anxiety – not so much at the remaining few Exocets, but at the prospect that they might very shortly have more. While the French assurance that they would not supply additional missiles was a considerable comfort, we feared there were other less reliable sources about, not least Libya.

I am not sure who came up with the idea, but I imagine it originated at Headquarters, if only because political clearance would have been fundamental. However, over several long conversations with David Hallifax, it all gained momentum. There was no military choice other than to catch the Etendards at their home base of Rio Grande, on the island of Tierra del Fuego, and destroy them on the ground. I am sure the overnight success of our SAS raid on Pebble Island did much to encourage the powers-that-be of the feasibility of a second such operation. As a matter of fact I thought it sounded pretty good too.

We were very aware that a British attack on the Argentinian mainland might well have its detractors in the political arena. There are always people who cannot recognise the difference between a barren, treeless island like Tierra del Fuego, and the teeming Plaza de Mayo nearly 1500 miles north in the middle of the city of Buenos Aires. There was, of course, an enormous difference. The Rio Grande base of Argentina's 2nd Naval Fighter and Attack Squadron was the home of the Etendards, the only type of aircraft which could fire Exocet at us. It was a purely military base. Everyone who worked there was engaged in some way in the single objective of defeating the British Task Force. The most junior aircraft mechanic was as much a part of this battle as I was, and we were clear enough that it was a proper and fair target for us. The Etendards could not claim 'sanctuary' in Rio Grande, any more than the *Belgrano* could, outside the TEZ.

Also we had no intention of wasting our time blowing up buildings, much less killing people, unless, of course, they got in the way. Our aim was very specific – to take out those Etendards, all of them, with the same efficiency we had demonstrated at Pebble Island.

Nevertheless, this operation was always going to be a political minefield. Prior covert reconnaissance was essential and okay. But the overt destruction of Etendards on the Argentinian mainland, coupled with subsequent possible embarrassment for Chile was quite a different matter. Whatever the political arguments, I was eventually asked to consider how we might get a reconnaissance team in, and make my recommendations to Northwood. As it happened, the planning took place over the next several days, but for clarity, I shall recount it as a single event. In reality it was rather more disjointed than that.

For all the reasons rehearsed before the raid on Pebble Island, the first assumption was, naturally enough, that this was another job for the SAS. But just to get such a team to the Battle Group, we would have to fly them all the way from the UK and then have them parachute into the ocean to be picked up by one of my destroyers or frigates. This was not a route I would have been crazy about myself, but the SAS treat it, more or less, on a par with 'going to the office'.

It seemed to us that it called for a fairly small team. We would take them in, part of the way by ship – no closer to mainland Argentina than absolutely necessary – and then fly them on in a Sea King 4, landing a few miles up the coast from Rio Grande.

The recce team would go in, ascertain the lie of the land, and report back. Because the journey would have to be one-way (not enough fuel for the helicopter to get back to the launching ship – not enough time for the launching ship to get back to the Battle Group before dawn), they would have to burn or ditch the chopper, or even give it to the Chileans. Burning it seemed less politically awkward, if militarily wasteful. Then the three man aircrew would have to give themselves up to the Chileans.

The recce team had a different problem. Whether or not their surveillance report was favourable, and we subsequently obtained political permission for direct action, they might face a one-hundred-mile walk to the comparative safety, we hoped, of Chile – possibly with some very angry Argentinians in hot pursuit. Alternatively they might be taken off by submarine from a point along the coast. Either way, it was not a comfortable prospect.

That was more or less my Plan A, and, of several fairly desperate possibilities, I reckoned it was easily the best. Or perhaps I should say it was easily the least bad. It did seem to offer the maximum eventual gain (the Etendard force) for the minimum risk (the SAS team, three aircrew and one Sea King).

However, my views were not received with instant acclaim. For a start the Royal Marines took a remarkably poor view of the entire thing, on the basis that they laid claim of ownership to the Sea King 4's, along with their special lighting and equipment geared for this kind of operation. The Marines are of course apt to forget that they are actually a part of the Royal Navy and that we provide them with their aircraft. They are also apt to forget the old aphorism that: 'He that giveth, may also taketh away.'

I am told, although I confess it to be only hearsay, that a

'very senior Marine', on hearing of my plan, expostulated: 'Has Woodward finally gone out of his mind? Our lovely brand new helicopters cost over £8,000,000 each, and he wants to send one on a one-way ride to Chile and set it on fire? Well, tell him that if he really wants to burn a helicopter, he can burn one of his own b*****ds!'

I was quite surprised to be told from Northwood, by Admiral Hallifax himself, that Plan A was a non-starter. 'Let's have your second option, Sandy', he said. So, with all the frustrations of the twenty-four-hour time loop it took to get a decision through Head Office, I settled down to refine the infinitely inferior Plan B.

For this option I proposed to send the 22,000-ton fleet replenishment ship *Fort Austin*, under the command of Commodore Sam Dunlop, in company with two frigates, south, and then west along the Antarctic Circle, to creep into Chilean waters on the Pacific side of Tierra del Fuego.

From here they could slide through into the wide channel at the end of the Magellan Straits, and a helicopter could ferry the SAS swiftly to the Rio Grande area, drop them, and then return to pick them up, much as we had done at Pebble Island.

What was the balance of advantage? We posed the same threat to the Etendards at Rio Grande, but we increased our 'forces at substantial risk' factor by two frigates and a large replenishment ship. Also it would require a very 'blind eye' on the part of the Chileans. The prospect of British military operations on this sort of scale (or indeed any sort of scale), from inside Chilean waters, was probably another political non-starter. Also, *Fort Austin* was an extremely valuable ship, which as well as being crammed with food, ammunition and mechanical spares, carried nearly all our stock of replacement Sea Dart missiles. Whichever way we played this one, she was going to have go out and come back in daylight. If she was caught anywhere near the Argentinian air bases, her loss would become all too likely. I still very much preferred Plan A.

Despite this, I spoke to Northwood and laid out Plan B. Several hours went by, and back came David Hallifax's reply: 'Sorry. Don't like it.' Not surprisingly, I thought, but if you don't like stealth and burning helicopters, and neither do you want to risk *Fort Austin*, which is the only kind of ship, apart from the Carriers, from which you can operate a Sea King 4, well, I suppose you are going to have to go for a full-scale battle. So I suggested they may prefer to send in *Hermes*, with two Type 42s and two Type 22s in company, and try a strike using as many Harriers as we'd got, hoping to hit the Etendards before the Args sank one, some, or all of us.

Northwood did not think much of that either. And so, in some exasperation, I suggested an even bigger sally, for which we would take the entire Battle Group and try to flatten the place. I had gone from quiet, proven SAS economy of effort to mindless desperation on the grandest possible scale – albeit still not all that grand. And of course, they did not think much of that either.

So I got on the line to Northwood once more and told them as politely as I could that I was unsurprised they did not like Plans B, C and D. Neither did I, much; they were after all my second, third and fourth choices. Plan A remained my preference out of a collection of not very cheerful possibilities. I was pretty sure it also *had* to be theirs, so what was the problem?

'The Ministry keeps on turning us down,' said David. 'I'll do some checking to see what's going on up there.'

Twenty-four hours later, Plan A was approved, now some four days after it was originally put forward. I asked David how on earth this could have come about. He told me – at length. In essence, it turned out that my first signal had been misread, and/or badly drafted at my end. A sentence within it which said that the SAS team would be dropped several miles from Rio Grande had been taken by the Director SAS (then Brigadier, later General Sir Peter de la Billiere – our Commander in the Gulf Operation against Iraq in 1991), to mean that they would be dropped in the water several miles off shore and invited to swim in! He had, understandably not approved the plan therefore.

Inwardly I groaned the groan of the deeply misunderstood. Maybe my signal had been unclear and understandable probably only to myself? Even if this were so, what I found slightly irritating was that the SAS were somehow able to remain outside the full military chain of command, allowing a relatively simple misunderstanding to go unquestioned for four whole days. But their Director, who had the ear of certain people in high political places, was able to murmur his disapproval very quietly, and very privately, without having to face the full searching questioning that befalls the rest of us wartime commanders. I resolved that sometime, some day, I would put a stop to that. And did, but not until 1986.

The revelation that I was not planning to unload the SAS men into the freezing South Atlantic and then make them swim for it, solved our impasse. 'Plan A accepted', I was told. And so, after four long days of time-wasting, I was told to proceed.

At the end of 15 May I filled in my diary for both of the two preceding days – and since the lines form a kind of bridge from one SAS raid to the next, I shall reproduce them here:

May 14th: Then it started, a gale from the west ... spent evening speeding into the teeth of it for a Direct Action job on what looks like a very ripe plum – 11 aircraft plus all the stores for a major 'Nasty' against us on D-Day. And most of the spare time organizing a 'blind-eye' operation on the mainland. It will probably come to nothing, but, if it goes wrong, will have me court-martialled: if it goes right, no one is going to know.

Very quiet in filthy weather until Pebble Island raid late pm [in fact early am 15th]. Absolute cliff-hanger. And delays, due to Force Nine gale and minor incompetence, lost us 55 minutes in a tight programme. We were within five minutes of cancelling the whole thing. Eleven Arg aircraft destroyed on ground, no casualties, back out of main Arg air threat by midday (15th).

Continuing saga over Rio Grande looking a bit more settled now. I can do as I please!

May 15th: Fairly busy air day for us. Args not in evidence at all. It is weekend of course, and they're either saving up for the 'Big Push' or just wrapping their hand in. Rio Grande saga re-opened with further illogical/incompletely-thought-out plan from Northwood. Not doing so well, and making it very difficult to do what is actually needed. If only they would just leave it alone. By very late, it began to transpire that the Brigadier of SAS had interpreted 'Ditching SK4' [as in getting rid of it] as dropping the whole lot into the water, off the target, and expecting everyone to swim ashore. What an utter twit the man must be!

I hope it's sorted out now, anyway. Still getting half-assed suggestions from people at home – more now, what with this SAS bit, Flag Officer Submarines inventing new capabilities but refusing to change his stereotyped operating patterns – and even C-in-C starting to make suggestions as to how to do my business – none of which we hadn't already considered and discarded.

I was getting more than a bit ratty, as you can tell. Of course the Director, SAS, wasn't a 'twit' – we should have spoken directly to each other four days ago, but he was not in the chain of command.

I pressed on with the myriad of tasks which kept the Battle Group buzzing away like a big mobile city out here in the Atlantic, our main propulsion turbines running twenty-four hours a day, the generators driving without rest to give us light and heat and hot food, and the incessant twinkling dials and screens of the Ops Rooms doing their best to tell us what was going on around us.

The morning of 15 May dawned brighter, with the wind now much decreased and the sea blue and calm under sunny skies. We had two arrivals scheduled for today – that of my old nuclear-powered submarine, the 3,500-ton HMS *Valiant*, which was of course largely indifferent to the weather, and the SAS teams for Rio Grande, who were due to parachute into the ocean beside us during the late afternoon, and whose entire mission depended on reasonably calm sea for their splashdown.

I was thus in the Ops Room very early to check the forecast and did not especially like what I was told. There was a big front heading right towards us, slowly, but nonetheless likely to be over the island of Tierra del Fuego within thirty-six hours, doubtless covering it with a thick damp blanket of fog and rain and low cloud.

I quietly allowed myself an expletive and then tried to find a way around the tiresome fact that I was going to have to fish the SAS out of the sea, dry them off, feed them and fire them straight on in to the mainland that night. That would be, I surmised, a request not absolutely guaranteed to enhance any popularity I might still enjoy with either the men or their commanders. But I was just as sure that *Hermes* should start moving towards the mainland immediately they arrived on board, because the approaching bad weather would otherwise abort the mission. It's bad enough flying over a dark, unknown, and hostile coastline in clear conditions, but to attempt to do so through thick fog, cloud, strong winds and without radar would practically assure the pilots of getting thoroughly lost, while running out of fuel by the minute. I muttered 'Oh dear!' – or words to that effect – to myself once more, not looking forward one bit to the inevitable forthcoming argument with the SAS Commander.

Meanwhile I ordered *Fort Austin* to detach from the Group to rendezvous with the RAF Hercules which was due very soon, and to organise the recovery of the airdrop of SAS men, and their equipment, from the ocean.

While this was happening we sent *Brilliant* and *Alacrity* back into Falkland Sound to sweep the area once more for mines and/or Argentinian ships. And just to keep the Args' minds focussed throughout the night, we sent *Glamorgan* back into her old familiar position in the gun-line off Port Stanley to launch yet another long bombardment of the area around the airstrip. We also sent up Harriers to photo-recce the areas of Darwin, Camilla Creek, Moody Brook and, once more, the Stanley airfield. Throughout all of this I was conducting some kind of a running debate with the SAS management as to whether the Rio Grande operation was on or not.

Basically these well-armed chaps were going to land on a deserted shore from an expensive helicopter, and then make their way across virtually empty countryside for a couple of days and then, if militarily viable and politically acceptable, quietly set about estimating the feasibility of blowing up a few aircraft with state-of-the-art British military equipment. We all thought the job could be done. We were not agreed as to when to set off.

The Royal Marines continued their custodial concern over the Sea King 4's, causing my temper to shorten further. Echoing his general, one colonel RM again suggested using 'A naval SK5 rather than one of our valuable SK4's for the job', and tried such comments as 'Have you considered working from a landing site in West Falkland', as if we hadn't been thinking this operation through, over and over again for the best part of a week.

I reminded him, reasonably politely, that we had no landing site anywhere on the Falklands yet, and that Sea King 5's cost a good deal more than Sea King 4's, quite apart from being markedly less well suited for the task. My diary simply said in reference to our discussion – 'I could have strangled him!'

Finally, reason prevailed and the SAS management accepted, with much reluctance, that the original plan – adapted incidentally from an idea of several days ago from Lin Middleton, Captain of HMS *Hermes* – should now proceed.

Late that afternoon the RAF Hercules made contact with *Fort Austin* which guided it down into the area we had selected for the airdrop – about a hundred yards off her port beam – and the SAS men, zipped into their survival suits, parachuted into the freezing Atlantic and were picked up very quickly by the Navy helicopters. We were getting rather good at this type of thing, and we were blessed with a perfect day for it – blue skies, westerly zephyrs and no swell, which was a good augury for a difficult task.

In my opinion it also accentuated the need to go now, while the weather held, rather than wait for it to deteriorate into the kind of clag which can shut down modern airports like Heathrow, London, or JFK, New York, never mind some blasted rock on Tierra del Fuego.

The SAS team, led by a major, finally assembled on board *Fort Austin*, and she turned south-west to join us. This new team of 'Talking Trees' would have been better described as a smallish, cold, wet forest. Their equipment was also soaked; they were very tired after a twenty-eight-hour flight from England, and they had had little sleep.

When they arrived in *Hermes* it was already dark, and I told the major I wanted them to get dry, get rested, get a sandwich, get briefed, get ready and then get going. I told them that *Hermes* was already running in towards the mainland and that I intended to launch the night-flying specialist SK4 at 0300 the following morning. 'It won't be easy but we should be able to put them down in the right place,' I said. 'They can then rest, before they walk in to begin their detailed observations and assess the feasibility of taking out the Etendards.' The major told me he understood, but that they were not quite ready to go yet. They were all still much too travel-weary. I pointed out that they still had five or six hours to get into a hot shower, and after eating and briefing, still grab three hours of sleep, adding: 'As far as I can see, it's now or never.'

I explained that the pressures to go were very great. This recce was absolutely critical, what with the landing likely in a few days time and the prospect that the weather front coming in from the west would be right over their target area by late tomorrow afternoon. I told him that in my opinion it would be damned nearly impossible to get the helicopter down at all, never mind with any geographical accuracy, in the kind of weather the forecasters were giving for the Rio Grande coastal area tomorrow night.

The major replied that as far as he and his men were concerned we could forget about the meteorologists. 'I am afraid,' he said, 'that we must delay for twenty-four hours while the men recover from their journey.' I had no alternative but to agree, I hope with adequate good grace. I ordered *Hermes* to be brought about and to return to the main group. As the carrier made her turn, I felt somehow the success of the project was making an about turn with us. Unfortunately, I was correct.

I told them they would have to go in the following night from *Invincible* as both I and *Hermes* would be otherwise engaged. And this in fact was what they did. However the bad weather came in and they had to ditch the helicopter, eventually landing on a sand spit ten miles to the east of Punta Arenas, some fifty miles from the selected landing site. For all I know, they had got hopelessly lost in the fog and were lucky not to have been drowned.

They presumably then set fire to their Sea King, because it was found on 20 May by the Chileans, burned out and mysteriously abandoned. The aircrew walked out and found their way to the local authorities, who interrogated them and permitted the press to interview them.

The two pilots said, for all I know perfectly truthfully, that they had got lost while conducting a recce up the coast and had put down through lack of fuel. But since then there has been a great deal of speculation as to what they might have been doing, clattering around in the dead of night in Chilean airspace.

The three aircrew were deported from Chile to the UK, where they had a few days off before re-joining their squadron in the South Atlantic.

My diary's last mention of the whole event was: '*Hermes* set off for the launch area. But the operation was cancelled – the Trees are wilting after their journey and all their kit got soaked in the water. So we turned back. *Invincible* will have to try tomorrow . . .'

I did receive a letter from the Argentinian CO of Rio Grande in 1994 to say that they were ready at all times for an attack by us – but even that doesn't tell me anything much about how successful an SAS raid might actually have been, nor whether it would ever have received political approval.

As for the SAS team, I know absolutely nothing whatsoever. But that's the way they work. We never got so much as a short report. And in 2002 the Ministry of Defence wished me to add that nothing here written represents their own views – they quite properly and sensibly maintain a policy of 'Neither Confirm nor Deny' on such matters.

The following day, 17 May, was, as I mentioned, Argentina Navy Day and the weather suited Etendard operations. The Argentinians did try but failed to find the Battle Group – understandably enough since we had taken a variety of measures to suggest that we were somewhere other than where we actually were. We did get a sniff of them, but it *was* only a sniff and our best efforts to catch them with the CAP came to nothing. *Glamorgan* arrived home right after breakfast having done her deceptive bit along Choiseul Sound to the south-east of Port Stanley and we sent out a stream of Harriers to take recce photographs of key locations all over the islands. The landings (D-Day) were now just four days away and I was attempting to eliminate all surprises.

During the course of the day my involvement with the planning for the landing and the days that immediately followed it just about ceased. The plans were as near complete as they could be and, though they had to be reasonably flexible, we now had a simple lay-out. Firstly, a long supply line, which did not appear to be under great threat. We planned to minimize the air threat by only transiting in and out at night; to minimize the danger of submarine attack by steering well clear of the Port Stanley area and its environs; and to minimize the risk of attack by surface ships by judicious placement of the SSNs. Secondly, an easterly offshore assembly and operations area, from which we could mount missions for combat air patrol and close air support for ground forces, and from which we could despatch convoys and troops and supplies inshore. This area must of course be well outside the range of unrefuelled Mirage, Skyhawk and Etendard attack and east of the Battle Group, which would hopefully double the Argentinians' problems. And thirdly, the amphibious operating area (AOA), where the land battle would start from. In the very early stages this would lack good air defence and might cost us ships until the Rapier umbrella became effective.

I did believe that we could win this battle, but I also knew there were no guarantees, because so much can turn on chance, luck and the fortunes of war – as the *Brilliant/Glasgow* action had so starkly revealed just a few days ago. We had so little in reserve.

That evening I wrote home to Char. It was quite a long letter, so I have had to edit it a bit:

The *Sheffield* survivors have, I am afraid, set off for home without this. But Sam Salt has promised to give you a ring when he gets back, so you'll hear from him before me.

A copy of the *Daily Mail*, with pictures of you in it, fell out of the sky yesterday – I notice they caught you in your West End best beside the dustbins outside the garage, clearly about to nip round to the corporation rubbish dump! Seems a long way off from here.

We have just had our first beautiful Indian summer day since arriving (and it was a Sunday, so the Args didn't come out). I could actually see one of our Harriers at thirty-five miles through the binoculars – that's the sort of visibility you get in these latitudes, clear as crystal and no warmer.

We had a busy night doing the Pebble Island operation, which I was rather pleased with – removed about a fifth of their army air force at a go, which can't be bad.

But time will tell. I worry that the landing will go terribly wrong, but then I comfort myself that I worry that everything will go wrong. That, actually, is my job – to arrange things, carry them through and take the consequences. Hence, the more I worry, the better chance there is that we will have thought of everything. But, of course, you can't do much about luck, and there is a good deal more luck in this business than I care to think about.

As for the dangers, I think most of us have had to face up to a rather different set of values, with a lot of previously important things now seeming fairly trivial. For those who are looking particularly worried I say:

it's all a matter of percentages really. You have about as much chance of snuffing it out here as you have of dying of lung cancer if you are a smoker. The only difference is that out here it will be quicker and less painful. So count your blessings!

For those of us who have already given up smoking for fear of lung cancer, it can all begin to seem a bit much! But I haven't restarted anyway – and feel no need to.

Meanwhile, and this is why I am writing, most plans for the landing are made and, barring accidents, there's little left for me to do except aft the sheets and pick up speed for the starting line – hoping to catch the opposition on a port tack.

This analogy is not that good when you realize that the last thirty seconds before the start gun in a yacht race takes two days out here. And I have to judge the weather two days ahead . . . and we have to rely on South American weather reports . . . Well, fingers crossed and all the other platitudes . . .

I finished my letter, sealed it and went back to the Ops Room. At 2340z Captain Middleton turned *Hermes* on to an east-north-east course and, in company with *Fort Austin* and the 23,000-ton Royal Naval stores ship *Resource*, we set off into the night, leaving Captain Mike Barrow in *Glamorgan* in charge.

As we moved away from the TEZ there was, steaming towards us from out of the dark north-east, the British Amphibious Group of twenty-one ships. It was headed by the two 12,000-tonners *Fearless* and *Intrepid*, the vital hard-core of the group carrying the Brigade Headquarters. They would lead the rest in, packed with about six hundred and fifty Royal Marines each, ready to go ashore in their eight landing craft – four of which were small ones to be lowered over the side, four were larger LCUs to be floated out of the big ships' stern docks once they had flooded down. Behind them steamed fifteen Royal Fleet Auxiliaries and ships taken up from trade (STUFT). These included the 44,000-ton P&O passenger liner *Canberra*, now with two thousand men of the (reinforced) 3 Commando Brigade. She carried a Royal Marine Commando, the 3rd Battalion Parachute Regiment, the Commando Regiment of the Royal Artillery, the Commando Squadron of the Royal Engineers, the Navy's Surgical Support Teams, the 19th Field Ambulance, and the Blues and Royals (Royal Horse Guards and First Dragoons). *Canberra* was loaded to capacity with men, kit and supplies, a volume of such unprecedented weight that they had to shore up the sun-deck down aft to prevent the whole lot from collapsing under the weight of stores.

Escorting the heavily burdened little fleet to the Falkland Islands was *Antrim*, my old flagship from Springtrain, under the command of Captain Brian Young, plus three frigates, the Type 12 *Plymouth* under Captain David Pentreath, the Leander Class *Argonaut* under Captain Kit Layman, and the Type 21 *Ardent* under Commander Alan West. All four of them would be damaged in the forthcoming conflict, three of them would be bombed, and one of them would never leave the waters which surround the Falklands.

Within the first hour of our journey that night we nearly came to grief – one of our Sea King 5s, patrolling as a part of our anti-submarine screen, suddenly ditched. Captain Middleton took *Hermes* over to have a look at the floating helicopter while the crew was being picked up. The reason for the crash was a failure of the radio altimeter while in automatic hover close to the water and the pilot took the right action as per the manual. I could not quite see why he could not have got it up off the water, but then I wasn't driving the bloody thing. So there we stood high up in *Hermes* staring down at this nice shiny new aircraft worth millions of pounds, floating the right way up in calm water, apparently unharmed.

The temptation was too great. Lin Middleton thought we ought to try and lift it out with our crane, an unorthodox but possibly effective course of action. I agreed with his proposal. He nosed *Hermes* up to it until we were just yards away when the thought occurred to us that the Sea King had been on an anti-submarine patrol, and that it must be loaded with depth-charges in case they found what they were looking for. There was a very slight possibility that if any of those depth charges had been primed, it might go off, probably taking with it a fair proportion of *Hermes*'s bow. This would not have looked good on any of our records. Indeed, it could have ended Britain's war in the South Atlantic. Very, very gently we backed away and sent for *Brilliant* to come over and sink the Sea King. As it sank, now a couple of miles away from us, the depth-charges went off. It remains, to this day, a subject Lin and I do not discuss.

We made our rendezvous with the Amphibious Group in the desolation of the black South Atlantic night at 1100. There were fourteen Harriers, brought down by Cunard's massive transatlantic container ship the *Atlantic Conveyor*, and all of them had to be transferred to *Hermes*. There were also additional Royal Navy Wessex helicopters and four of the huge RAF Chinooks. They needed to get the Harriers off the *Conveyor* before there was room to start the long job of preparing the helicopters for flight ashore after the landings at Carlos. And, because we were now getting very crowded, some of the

Harriers had to be flown off *Hermes* and away to *Invincible* back in the TEZ. The complexities of such an operation, being conducted in the middle of the ocean, are, I promise you, considerable.

At 1230 the Commodore Amphibious Warfare, Commodore Mike Clapp and his staff flew from *Fearless* over to *Hermes*. I had known Mike Clapp for over thirty years, since we had been in the training cruiser HMS *Devonshire* together, and I had great faith in his judgement and steadiness. I personally believed that our 'partnership' was very well defined: I would have the final say as to when we go, where we go and indeed how we go; but once inshore, the landings would become *his* business, and the AOA *his* patch.

It was readily apparent that we could not land before the evening of Thursday 20 May and that we would want to land as soon as possible after that if we were to keep to the timetable. Right now, on a slightly overcast 18 May, in fairly calm seas, we were clearly not ready. Not least among our problems was the very lately arrived requirement (from the UK) to move all but one of the land force units out of *Canberra* and spread them around the rest of the force in case she was sunk. Tomorrow, if the fairly clear, calm conditions persisted, we should be able to complete the necessary cross-decking. Only then would we be ready to go.

I went on to explain to Mike and to the commander of the embarked troops, Brigadier Julian Thompson, that the Args had *never* yet attacked from the air at night and therefore I believed we could safely discount that possibility. We all agreed that the earlier we could get in the better.

The only altercation we had was a mild one: the land commanders would have preferred to get the men ashore in the early part of the evening in order to give themselves as many hours of darkness as possible for their troops to establish their beach-head. My own view was slightly different. First of all, I *knew* that the Args Air Force would pack up around dusk. I also knew that they would surely attack, with absolutely everything they had, any large group of British ships sighted steaming towards the northern entrance to the Falkland Sound in the late afternoon. Such a group, they would realize, would have to be the amphibious force. Thus, I reasoned, the critical time for this landing is in the few hours prior to sunset. Where the amphibians do not want to be during that time is in sight of any Argentinians. While I can't do much about a chance, patrolling aircraft, I can at least keep the amphibians well out of sight from observation posts on the shore. So the first landings needed to be delayed a few hours into the night, so that the final approach could be done entirely in darkness.

I realized that this course of action would lessen the hours of darkness the troops had to get ashore – but at least they would *be* ashore rather than on board ships fighting their way in. And was not Carlos Bay recommended *inter alia* for its good mountain cover against air attacks? I think I made my position clear to Mike Clapp and Julian Thompson, and I did so without having to remind them of the experiences of *Sheffield* and *Glasgow*. I did not have to utter the phrase 'Gentlemen, do you have any idea what it is actually like when a warship gets hit by a bomb or a guided missile?' And they in turn did not have to articulate the thought that must have been on their minds 'Well, we thought the Battle Group was supposed to have destroyed the Args Air Force in its entirety by now. What have you been doing these last three weeks, for ****'s sake?' There are times when I am very grateful for the well-mannered rituals of discussion with which we, in Her Majesty's armed forces, settle our differences.

Nonetheless they accepted my point of view about the landing times – and I think they also accepted the extreme difficulty we had had in fooling the Argentine Air Force into coming out to fight before they really needed to. Including Pebble Island, we had removed over a dozen aircraft from their inventory, but their formidable fighter/ground attack force was still more or less intact. On paper, they still had air superiority and for all we knew had been saving themselves up for the day when the British finally moved in to re-take the Falkland Islands. I did not know that to be a fact, but it seemed a reasonable explanation of their apparent reluctance so far in coming out to attack us.

But our destiny would also be governed by the great drifting weather fronts which stream across those unfriendly southern oceans. Mike knew as well as I did that all landings depend enormously on the weather. You have only to think of 1944 and the terrible problems General Eisenhower's armada encountered – the one month's delay and choice of the only few days that gave any chance of success in that dreadful June.

Even as we conferred in the Ops Room of *Hermes* I had still not been given the final word from my C-in-C to proceed with the landing – or 'Operation Sutton' to give it its trade name. We knew of course that there were still political forces urging the British Government to wait a little longer, to strive for the diplomatic solution that did not look much of a starter from down this end of the world. In Margaret Thatcher, however, Britain had a Prime Minister who was not going to allow peripheral circumstances to get in the way of grim reality. She knew she had the support of her High Command, she knew she had the support of the House of Commons, and indeed the House of Lords. And she knew she had the support of the British people, thousands of whom were writing sackloads of mail to the Task Force to wish us well. Each and every one of those letters meant a great deal to all of us.

Margaret Thatcher also understood the tyranny of our time-table, the fact that the Royal Navy would be effectively out of action in the South Atlantic winter of late June. She understood with total clarity that our deadline to land was 25 May. And she knew perfectly well that every day's delay thereafter was a day in favour of General Galtieri. Now she also knew the *earliest* time that we could be ready. She was faced with making the final, historically momentous decision to permit us to go in and establish the beach-head. Whatever may have been said about the irrevocability of the sailing of the Task Force back in April, and whatever she thought herself, I am clear that this was easily the biggest single military decision she had to take. A landing is likely to be expensive enough in men and equip-ment. But if it fails later, an evacuation is usually a disaster. There may have been a few politicians, ministers or even ser-vicemen who still doubted her resolve. But Margaret Thatcher never shirked a hard decision. And when asked for her verdict, just a few hours from now, she would not falter.

In my Ops Room, of course, we were not in much doubt that the decision to land would be given and, based on her track record to date, that it would be given in adequate time. Meanwhile we could only continue to go forward with our final plans. What pre-occupied my thoughts were the dispositions of the entire Task Force when the amphibians began to make their way inshore, perhaps only forty-eight hours from now. I had to provide enough air defence for the amphibious group, yet I had to protect the carriers, otherwise there might be no air cover for anyone.

Captain John Coward was inclined to station the two Type 42s *Glasgow* and *Coventry* well forward (west of West Falkland!)

with the combat air patrols flying forward of them in order to hit the incoming Arg bombers and fighter aircraft at the earliest possible opportunity. He then felt the amphibious group should steam in accompanied by the Type 22s *Brilliant* and *Broadsword* with their half-proven Sea Wolf missile systems. He considered the carriers *Hermes* and *Invincible* should bring up the rear some fifty miles back – though they would be virtually undefended in terms of close-in air defence.

I recorded all this in my diary, which then continued with,

> Jeremy Black [Captain of *Invincible*] obviously feels the same way about the Type 42s forward, but he wants the carriers well up too. This also smacks of 'all or nothing', and I like it even less [than Coward's plan]. Yet I can't help feeling I ought to do it – and I just might, if it weren't that the [Args' likely] submarine area is exactly where we would need to be to do the job.

My own plan preferred the Amphibious Group with the 22s and a combat air patrol, and the Type 42s well back with the carriers. I recognized the various merits of Captain Coward's thoughts, and I was very much torn between the two. I tried to sort the matter out further, in the process pin-pointing the critical part the weather could play. I wrote my notes thus:

> My problem is really, that if the weather is good for the opposition (i.e. good for low [flying] ship attack), then Coward could be right, because I am into a high-risk situation anyway. A bold move (which effectively assumes the enemy will concentrate, to the exclusion of all else, on the amphibious group) might be the only thing to carry the day.

The other thought, that I ought not to make it too easy for the Args to remove half of our air defence force at a stroke, also convinces [me] against. [I] Hope I'm right.

But if I get the weather right, then the safer [second] course will be best. Hence of course it all falls out [simply enough]. We are trying to judge the weather right and must at least trust their [the meteorologists'] judgment. Unlike the enemy, the weather is not malevolent, though it may be no more predictable.

We had already seen the ability of Argentinian bombers to fly straight through our defences . . . two Etendards on 4 May and *five* Skyhawks (against *Brilliant/Glasgow*) on 12 May. What might happen if they launched twenty or even thirty attack aircraft against us with *Hermes* and *Invincible* out on their own, prime targets? The land forces would be left with no air cover, that's what. And they would quite reasonably refuse to land. And we would have to go home. I was simply not prepared, deliberately, to run that kind of risk. I realized the plan depended on our weather forecasting, but on that I *was* prepared to gamble. The vagaries of the weather have always bedevilled military commanders and I too must accept that element of uncertainty even though I already have nearly three weeks experience of weather forecasting in this area now.

The luck of the Woodwards seemed to be holding. By the evening of the 19 May there was a front scheduled to arrive, bringing with it the welcome low cloud and poor visibility we needed. It should last through that night and possibly until after sunset the following day. This might let the amphibians in unobserved. Our longer-range forecast gave Friday 21 May as likely to be once more clear and calm, conditions which would remain for another two days, until the twenty-third or even the twenty-fourth of the month. You will remember that our last possible date for the landings, the day when we must either go or abandon the entire operation, was 25 May. This made my task dead simple, really: the Amphibious Group goes in under cover of poor visibility and starts the landing as soon after midnight as possible on Thursday night 20/21 May. The Battle Group remains concentrated to the east providing support as required. No risky expeditions out to the west. No undefended carriers.

How extraordinary that the single most important decision COMAW and I should ever be called upon to make in our entire lives should finally have made itself. Just as well, I suppose, otherwise we might have got it wrong. Every course of action involves guesswork and hope. But here we had a reasonably firm prediction for precisely the weather we needed. I'll sign up for that. No heroics, just stealth – that's the way in.

CANBERRA.

13

Night Landing

In the early hours of 19 May we were steaming slowly south-west, some two hundred and fifty miles from Port Stanley. We were making our way towards the perimeter of the TEZ, approaching the now well-established Battle Group patrol area from its easterly border. The wind was gusting up and causing an awkward sea, the long Atlantic swells splitting quite high up on the bow of *Hermes*. The moon and the stars were obscured by cloud, and one way or another you could not see much. Only the very dim deck lights on the two carriers betrayed our presence whenever they operated aircraft, and we were near enough invisible to an enemy eye.

Our aim was of course to proceed in the covert manner of the night prowler, but we all knew how thoroughly impossible this was. Our considerable presence could never really be disguised for several inevitable reasons – not least the endless hubbub of our radio circuits which were sweet music to the electronic ears which sought us. Our many radars probing the sea and sky around us were also an unavoidable signal to distant Arg operators. Even the hulls of our little fleet of ships were perfect to reflect incoming Argentinian radar. And no matter how carefully we regulated our turbines, the sound of our propellers driving the ships through the sea was audible, underwater, for many miles.

In addition to the tell-tale signs of our whereabouts, we faced a further difficult conundrum in that we had, at this moment, almost all of our eggs in one basket. Actually all of these eggs were soldiers, more than fifteen hundred of them and every one in the big white-painted basket of the liner *Canberra*. Northwood believed this ought to be corrected before sending the P&O flagship inshore. I thought so too, although it looked rather more tricky from where I stood than from where they sat.

There are three basic ways to undertake such a huge 'cross-decking' programme. The first method is by boat. This requires either small landing craft or some other much smaller boats to come alongside, load the men on board and ferry them away. But in a sizeable sea this is too dangerous because the little 'ferries' will rise and fall perhaps fifteen feet against the hull with every wave, while the soldiers, with all of their kit, are trying to jump aboard or clamber out at the other end of the trip. The second way is by helicopter. This is all right for smallish numbers, but for us the sheer scale of the operation would make it a very long drawn out affair, very expensive on engines, aircraft, pilots and mechanics. The third cross-decking option is by jackstay. This tried and tested naval process requires rigging steel hawsers between the ships and winching each man over in a special harness. This is not without its obvious hazards and anyway, for an operation as prolonged as this was going to be, it would be desperately slow, even by comparison with helicopters.

I did not really have to make up my mind how to proceed until daylight, when we could have another look at the weather, but it was beginning to look very much as though we would have no alternative but to do the whole thing with helicopters. This would entail hundreds of flights, with all of the inevitable delays, but at least it would be better than having men breaking their necks and legs, and falling into the sea, which is what tends to happen when you undertake ship-to-ship transfers by boat in bad weather. Some of Mike Clapp's staff believed the only way to get the job done was by going all the way to South Georgia, seven hundred miles away and completing the operation in the shelter of the harbour. But time was against that. Helicopters it would have to be.

However, we stuck to the traditional position that executive decisions should *never* be made until they absolutely have to be, particularly if circumstances could change in the meantime. So we elected to delay decision until dawn, when the weather might make it for us. Happily, when I stepped out on my little bridge in the half-light of that cold Atlantic morning, to my considerable surprise, I saw that the Atlantic had calmed down into a gentle swell and the wind had dropped. I walked quickly to the Ops Room to learn that *Fearless* and *Intrepid* would be able to launch their landing craft. These were the 75-ton Landing Craft Utilities which were powered by two diesel engines and would hold one hundred tons of cargo or a hundred and forty men. We also decided to use the helicopters as well and the staffs immediately put this massive cross-decking operation into action before the calm could give way once more to the prevailing rough conditions.

And so began the most extraordinary day's work: re-positioning, in the middle of the Atlantic, almost two thousand men, removing the majority of them from the single basket of *Canberra* and thereby spreading the risk of the damage the Args could do us, should they manage to hit her. It all went on until late afternoon, the LCUs banging their way across the one thousand yards of ocean to *Fearless* and *Intrepid*, with the weather worsening by the minute, the wind gusting at twenty-five knots and the spray soaking the men huddled on board.

The job was completed just in time and with everyone re-housed we swung on to a more westerly course in the early evening. I was beginning to think the majority of our problems for this day were over. But I am afraid they were not.

At 2144 a Sea King 4, loaded with men of the SAS and SBS, crashed into the sea for reasons unknown, but seemingly a mechanical failure. John Coward had *Brilliant* on the scene extremely quickly and Captain Peter Dingemans was equally swift with *Intrepid*, but the chopper sank too soon and only eight were rescued. Twenty-two men were lost, including twenty from the SAS, some of them veterans of the helicopter crashes on the glacier at South Georgia, some of them veterans of the Pebble Island raid. It was, I thought, one of the saddest occurrences of the whole war and I had some difficulty metaphorically pulling my battle commander's hat down hard and acting as if nothing had happened. Knowing that I, as usual, could not afford to dwell upon such dreadful human tragedy.

I said nothing. What *could* you say? But I did need to walk along to my cabin and isolate myself before I could wrench my mind away from the thought of those brave men drowning, uselessly, unnecessarily, in that cold, dark ocean out there.

Around midnight I left the Ops Room and wrote my diary thus.

> Further massive cross-decking *Canberra/Fearless/ Intrepid/Hermes*. Shifting over 1500 blokes around (out of *Canberra*) and hundreds of helicopter loads, at same time keeping some six Sea Harriers/GR3s airborne for Combat Air Patrol and familiarization.
>
> While the decision to move fifteen hundred soldiers from *Canberra* is, I am sure, right, the time at which it was taken could have been a lot more felicitous! *Canberra*, with her totally inadequate damage-control and fire-fighting arrangements, is a floating bonfire awaiting a light.
>
> Decision to go ahead still not received – if Cabinet stall tomorrow landing area could well be compromised, and ships lost/hazarded unnecessarily. Intention for tomorrow is basically to press on (unless told to stop) and try to maintain a low profile. The Amphibious Group might just get in unnoticed.
>
> I am fairly confident that we should bring this off, but zero *can* come up twice running and that would break this bank.

You will note that I did not even mention the crash of the Sea King 4, almost as if I was trying to strike the incident from my mind. Months later, back in England, I re-read this part of the diary and can only assume that I did not write down anything about the crash because I could not bear to think about it ... any more than I could really think about the *Sheffield* or the *Belgrano* and the sad deaths that accompanied those two sinkings.

Every death carries a heart-rending story of sadness and

grief which lives for years with families and friends. I will always remember the words of one wife and mother whose husband, a veteran seaman, had perished in the South Atlantic. 'I know that it was necessary to go and fight for our sense of honour and duty,' she said, 'But this family paid the most terrible price.' But no battle commander should allow himself to dwell upon such humanitarian matters or the entire job becomes impossible, clouding your judgement dangerously when there is still everyone else to think of. Too much pondering the moral issues involved, while bearing the ultimate responsibility for your men, is a likely path to mental breakdown.

For myself I have thought about the mental process long and often. For years I always considered that in the face of truth too awful to cope with, I would say to myself, 'Woodward, forget it. Turn away. Get on with your job. Waste no time grieving. Your job is to *stop it happening again*.' But I do not really think that completely describes the process any more. I have come to believe that to a large extent the mind does it for you, that it builds some kind of a wall, in self-protection. The process is automatic. Of course it does not always work, but it will probably work if you let it. And your training and experience should do the rest.

My own thirty-six years in the Royal Navy probably compelled me to act as I did. Only thus was I able to turn away, to ignore the horror and the terrible sadness. That perhaps is why I didn't even mention in my own diary the death of the SAS men and why even several months later I was still trying to rationalize it all on the grounds that I was too busy with more important things. My mind had simply locked it all out, and I had unconsciously but willingly allowed it to do so. Such self-analysis may be tedious, but I believe it important for all of us to try to understand how we get through the inevitable bad days of our lives.

Later that night I received my orders personally from the Commander-in-Chief, Fleet, Admiral Sir John Fieldhouse. As expected they were succinct. He gave me permission to proceed with the landing, using my own local judgment as to the day chosen. I learned years later that he said almost exactly the same thing quite separately to Mike Clapp, with the consequence that we each thought at the time that we had the sole responsibility for the final decision.

Fortunately for us both, the weather could scarcely have suited better at this very moment. My forecasters in *Hermes*, the nearest any of us came to 'local experts', were still predicting poor visibility during the daylight of tomorrow, 20 May, and an indefinite clearance thereafter. This might very well be the only opportunity to make the final approach, unobserved, for some time. The C-in-C seemed to have left the decision on timing to me alone. And I decided to go. Tomorrow. Sharing the same information, not something either of us could always rely on, Mike Clapp inevitably came to the same conclusion.

With the cross-decking providentially complete, we moved slowly through the night into the old Battle Group area out on the eastern edge of the TEZ. The landing group would travel at about twelve and a half knots which meant they would leave around midday, with a journey of some one hundred and eighty-five miles or fifteen hours before them, most of it to be covered in mist and low cloud, with the last part also under cover of darkness. In the past twenty-four hours this natural camouflage from the heavens had become even more important to me because our cover had been blown by the Ministry of Defence, who had released the information that the Battle

Group and the Amphibious Group had now joined up, and the BBC, who had broadcast this on the World Service. Probably some clown in the MOD had told them, sharing the impenetrable stupidity engendered by 8,000 miles distance from the front line.

I had hoped that this particular rendezvous at least could have remained a military secret until after the actual landing, but as ever the British media were more interested in the truth than in the consequences for our own people. We were infuriated. The information could not be kept from the correspondents among the Task Force, but we did hope that someone, somewhere, would have the common sense to put a censoring delay on release of this kind of information. There were those who said that if we got hit on the way in and lost a lot of men, the Director General of the BBC should be charged with treason. This does sound rather extravagant, though maybe less so if you consequently happened to find yourself swimming in the South Atlantic as a result of your ship having been blown in half. On the same theme, it ought to be recorded, perhaps, that the commanding officer of 2 Para, Lieutenant Colonel H. Jones, also wanted to sue John Nott, the Prime Minister, the Defence Ministry, the BBC and many others, charging them with manslaughter. Colonel Jones was killed leading his men towards Goose Green shortly after telling reporters that he wished to undertake the legal proceedings himself, after the BBC broadcast the fact that an attack on Goose Green was imminent – that 2 Para was within five miles of Darwin. There are still some who believe that BBC report was directly responsible for the Argentinian 'ambush' in which Colonel Jones and many others died.

Standing in the Ops Room of *Hermes* on the day the BBC effectively informed the Args of our position and bearing, I am sure we all felt very much the same. We just had to hope the Args were too slow, too frightened or, most likely, too confused to act on the information of their assistants in the UK. Either way, we just got on with our overwhelming amount of work. The air warfare plan was, of course, now finalized, but since it was slightly unusual, it encountered some opposition when first suggested.

As far as I could see, one of our main problems was that of the dreaded 'Blue-on-Blue' (shooting your own people by mistake). The Args had already done it to their own aircraft – once to our certain knowledge, and possibly twice. I was quite determined that we should do our very best to avoid making the same mistake despite the all-too-real difficulties, particularly during the very complicated business of an amphibious landing, the time when the most terrible errors are easily made. The lines between opposing forces are anything but clear, and the fog of war rapidly descends even when matters are proceeding more or less as intended. With all three services involved, and plans changing by the hour – not to mention the disruptive attentions of the enemy – it is never easy.

I had thus devised the simplest possible plan, which, if not making a 'Blue-on-Blue' an impossibility, would certainly ensure it being a rarity. We initially designated an area which covered the eastern waters of Falkland Sound from North-West Island to Fanning Head and the land all around Carlos Water and Carlos Bay. I knew that inside that area would be virtually all of the British troops, landing craft, warships and transports. I set a ceiling of ten thousand feet above it to form a kind of massive 'box' made of fresh air – roughly ten miles across and two miles high. Into this box, I declared, our Harriers *must not go*. Inside it, our choppers could ferry anything to and from the beaches and ships, but they would 'duck' whenever enemy aircraft came in. And into this box, the enemy's fighter/attack aircraft would *have* to fly if they were to be any threat to the landings.

It would be far better, I decided, to give our own troops and ships complete freedom to fire at any 'fixed-wing' aircraft they saw *inside the box* because those aircraft *must* be Args. Meanwhile the Harriers would be waiting high above, knowing that if anything at all flies into or out of the box it *must* be Argentinian, because our fixed-wing aircraft are not allowed *in* there and our helicopters are not allowed *out*. The last thing we needed was for a Mirage to enter the box, with a Harrier in hot pursuit, only to get our own aircraft shot down by one of our own frigates. Bad luck, or even bad timing, I can deal with – bad planning is unforgivable. Remember that, to traverse the box at four hundred knots, an Arg Mirage may have only ninety seconds in there before he's out the other side, with a Harrier swooping on him like a falcon . . . I trust.

There might have been better plans, but that was ours. It also might have seemed a bit primitive, but simplicity is the only sensible policy when fast reactions are required in confused situations involving three different services. This was reasonably safe and dead simple; the more likely, therefore, to work. There was a bit of a family discussion, with one commander quoting me the rules under which such matters were normally conducted. I smiled and explained the matter thoughtfully for a bit and ended, not entirely uncharacteristically by saying, 'I don't give a damn about your bloody rules, this is how it is going to be done.' Which, when you think about it, was a lot kinder than 'Sod off'. Mike Clapp reduced the 'ceiling' over the AOA to three thousand, five hundred feet without bothering to tell me. But the pilots knew better and stayed high over the AOA – they had already lost one Sea Harrier to missile fire from the ground at nine thousand five hundred feet over Port Stanley.

By the very early hours of the morning *Hermes* and *Brilliant* had led *Resource*, *Fort Toronto*, *Elk* and *Atlantic Conveyor* to join *Invincible* and the Battle Group which would now move towards the west, in order to be up-threat of the amphibians should the Args try to put in an air attack. At 0400 this carrier Battle Group began to move slowly south. It comprised the following ships: *Hermes*, *Invincible*, *Glamorgan*, *Alacrity*, *Arrow*, *Glasgow*, *Coventry*, *Olmeda*, *Resource*, *Regent*, *Tidepool*, *Pearleaf*, *Elk*, *Fort Toronto* and *Atlantic Conveyor*.

The Amphibious Group was made up of the following: the command ship *Fearless*, with Brigadier Julian Thompson and Commodore Mike Clapp on board; her sister ship *Intrepid*; and the rather smaller landing ships logistic *Sir Galahad*, *Sir Geraint*, *Sir Lancelot*, *Sir Percivale* and *Sir Tristram*. They each carried four hundred men and, with a full load, weighed a little over five thousand five hundred tons as compared with the twelve thousand tons of *Fearless* and *Intrepid*, with six hundred and fifty men on board each, plus full supplies and four LCUs apiece. In addition there was the big sixteen-thousand-ton stores ship *Stromness*, now a troopship under the command of Captain J. B. Dickinson; *Fort Austin*, with a full complement of helicopters; and the big ships taken up from trade, *Canberra* and two converted roll-on-roll-off ferries, the *Europic Ferry* and the *Norland*.

I had detached seven warships as escorts to the convoy: *Antrim*, the six-thousand-ton County Class guided-missile destroyer, which carried anti-aircraft guns, Seaslug and Seacat missile systems, plus four Exocet launchers. She was a newer but still eleven-year-old sister ship to *Glamorgan* and she was commanded by the veteran Captain Brian Young, who was due to retire later in the year.

The second escort was *Argonaut*, a smallish three-thousand-ton Leander Class frigate armed with Bofors 40mm guns, Seacat missile systems, ASW torpedoes and Exocet missiles. She was commanded by the grey-haired, gently spoken but rather stern-mannered Captain Kit Layman, whose ships' companies I always suspected would be highly efficient if not exactly light-hearted. This forty-four-year-old Scotsman from Argyll, married to Katherine, with a young son, was another captain I had complete confidence in, capable of dealing with whatever came his way. He was the son of Captain Herbert Layman, who commanded the destroyer *Hotspur* in the first sea battles in the Med during the Second World War, and Kit was also the grandson of a rear admiral. The Navy was in his blood.

Third was *Ardent*, a Type 21 frigate armed with the 4.5-inch Mark 8 gun, 20mm AA guns, Seacat missiles and Exocet. Her captain was Commander Alan West, of Yeovilton, at thirty-five the youngest frigate captain in the Royal Navy. He was married to an extremely attractive red-haired artist named Rosemary and they had three small children under seven.

Fourth, *Plymouth*, a 2800-ton Type 12 frigate, nearly twenty years old and commanded by the tall ex-aviator Captain David Pentreath. She carried a twin 4.5-inch Mark 6 gun mounting, 20mm AA guns, Seacat and a Mark 10 anti-submarine mortar. Like all RN frigates, she carried a small helicopter on her stern deck.

Fifth was *Yarmouth*, sister ship to *Plymouth* and even older. Her captain was Commander Tony Morton, another ex-aviator but rather new to surface ship command. At first, not unreasonably, he tended to over-react to events – it is sometimes said of such people, 'If a shrimp farts, he'll drop a bomb on it.' But while initially he had a lot to learn, he learned it – fast.

Sixth, *Brilliant*, Captain John Coward's Type 22 Sea Wolf frigate, displaced four thousand four hundred tons fully loaded and also carried 40mm AA guns, Exocet missiles and ASW torpedoes. I have already recounted some of this captain's adventures. Suffice to say he seemed to have lived all of his life to fight this forthcoming battle. For all of his pushy attitudes, though, Coward was pretty sound. An ex-submariner, he had been on my first 'Perisher' when I was Teacher. I do not, offhand, recall a more canny submariner among all of those who followed him.

Seventh and finally, *Broadsword*, sister ship to *Brilliant*, was commanded by the vastly experienced professional seaman Captain Bill Canning. This smiling, always-cheerful officer from Hampshire was the complete master of his trade and I had a great regard for his steadfastness. Actually I always thought he would go further in the Navy than he did. But he was something of a straight talker and may have trodden upon a few of the wrong toes.

The weather, just as it had been for the cross-decking, was tailor-made: low clouds, with maximum visibility of about three miles. This was very good indeed for us, since it meant that an Argentinian attack aircraft approaching at four hundred knots would have at most only twenty-seven seconds to see the convoy, line himself up on the target and get his bombs away. That's if he was actually looking in exactly the right spot from the start. If he was looking even slightly 'off' – which is very likely when you're flying low and fast in poor visibility – he would be lucky to get more than twelve seconds before he's over and past . . . if Sea Wolf didn't get him first. Under such circumstances, every advantage was ours.

The two groups split up at 1415. The amphibians with their escort of the seven warships leaving me behind to conduct the war as best I could from the Ops Room of *Hermes*. It was a strange moment for me, because for the first time I was not effectively in charge of the front line of the battle. Mike Clapp would now take over and my own role would slip into that of secondary commander, providing the ships and the troops inshore with all of the back-up and support that I could. I did not particularly like it. I was used to being the man in charge out there. Now I had to allow Commodore Mike Clapp to go ahead and run the Amphibious Operating Area (AOA) as we had planned. All on his own. If, of course, he wished to stray from that which we had agreed, then he must clear it with me. But he had to be able to manage the landings himself, and I would not interfere if I could possibly help it.

In any case I had other things on my mind. As the Amphibious Group headed westward without me, I was still mildly astonished that the Argentinians had not yet come in force to attack *Hermes* and *Invincible*. Indeed I was sure that they *must* soon make an all-out effort to eliminate our two floating airfields – it surely could not have escaped them that the carriers were absolutely critical to our success.

So while I can't say that I entirely envied the amphibians their task, I felt anything but safe out here and, to make matters worse, I had sent our two 'goalkeepers' *Brilliant* and *Broadsword* in with the rest of the 'landers'. For the next few days the carriers would be more vulnerable than ever before.

I wrote home to Char that night, 'And this morning we are heading for the beaches – not your actual Blackpool. The weather is grey and grim: so are we. The next forty-eight hours are the *most* critical ones, I suppose, and things can go wrong at any time. My problem is less one of not being able to do the job than that if the Argentinians get a break (like two 'zeros' running at roulette) then we'll be done for. Not very likely, but we have all seen it happen.'

Meanwhile the amphibious force steamed on, with the wind building and the sea getting up. As usual, my task was temporarily done: the plans were made, in every tiny detail. My doom-watcher's job was just to wait – to wait for it to go wrong – and then try to put matters right quickly, with whatever might be required . . . perhaps more Harriers, more helicopters, more ships, more stores, more support or even more diversions. There could of course also be some major change in the plan consequent upon some disaster – like the loss of the amphibious headquarters ship, which would completely disrupt the whole landing for vital hours. For me, this was 'hands off' management, with hands standing by to go right back on if suddenly need be.

Tension was high in the Battle Group as the amphibians went in. We found ourselves speaking almost in whispers, afraid that somehow the Argentinians would hear us, afraid that somehow our own heartbeats would give the game away. I think I did absolutely nothing that long afternoon. Silence and stealth seemed the only requirement that day. As the light faded into welcome darkness, we knew, because we heard nothing, that all was well; that the ships were continuing, undetected, towards the Falkland Sound.

On this night, an important one in terms of the history of the Royal Navy, it was perhaps significant that I wrote only a couple of lines in my diary, as if I were unconsciously trying to reflect the instinctive wish of us all to do the absolute minimum to attract attention to ourselves. My two and a half lines stated simply, 'Moving towards the AOA. Fingers crossed and hoping not to be noticed. Deliberately no flying, any more than usual. *Glamorgan* doing her usual deception thing.' So on this, the single most dangerous day for the whole operation, I had little to do. For the amphibians, however, it was a quite different story.

At 1900 *Antrim* and *Ardent* detached from the main group, as we had planned, to make the run-in to Falkland Sound. Each ship had a key mission to undertake, both concerned with the stealthy business of making the Args think the landings were taking place elsewhere, not in Carlos Water. We had already sent *Glamorgan* on her nightly deception task in the Choiseul Sound, the long bay which divides East Falkland almost in two – it runs west from the open ocean, all the way up to Goose Green and Darwin. Captain Mike Barrow's orders were to do his best to stage a 'one-man amphibious landing', using his guns with star-shell and high explosive to simulate a softening up bombardment, while his helicopter tried to be in twenty places at once – all designed to convince any right-thinking Arg commander that the filthy British were coming in, right here in Choiseul Sound. Later, *Ardent*, from her position in the Sound – more or less diagonally opposite from *Glamorgan* – would also open fire in support of an SAS diversionary raid on Darwin. All of this was intended to increase the Args' confusion factor as much as possible, to buy time for COMAW to get the real landing force on to the beaches of Carlos Water.

The Amphibious Group with its escort force continued on its way towards the northern coast of East Falkland. The weather was still holding out for them, very moderate visibility, with low cloud and the wind getting up to Force Six. We were in the last stages of launching Britain's first wartime amphibious landing in years. How *could* the Args not know that all of these ships were coming in to the shores of the Falklands? On this, of all days, the lack of reaction by the Argentinians had to be the biggest stroke of luck we enjoyed throughout the entire war.

Now it was night, 2200 our time – but, don't forget, only seven in the evening for the Argentinians. Off Fanning Head, the Wessex helicopters of *Antrim* began to ferry parties of Marines of the SBS ashore to launch an assault on the Args' strong outpost which was dug in on the 770-foot peak of the great headland, guarding the entrance to Falkland Sound and to Carlos Water. Plainly they were not guarding anything terribly well, because they apparently did not hear the choppers and neither did they use the special night-viewing equipment we subsequently discovered them to have. They remained completely unaware of our presence, even as *Ardent* hurried through the entrance to the Sound at just about 2300.

By 0130 *Antrim*, too, was well into the Sound, steaming slowly, taking up her position six miles from Fanning Head, ready to provide gunfire support to the SBS teams at the appropriate moment. The rest of Mike Clapp's force now divided into three separate columns scheduled to arrive in the Sound in separate waves, inside a time-frame of five hours. Column One was formed of *Fearless* and *Intrepid*, escorted by Tony Morton's *Yarmouth*. It was essential to get the two assault ships in first because it would take some time to dock down and float out the eight LCUs ready to take the troops ashore. This must all be going smoothly before David Pentreath, on the darkened bridge of *Plymouth*, led the big troop transporters *Canberra*, *Norland* and *Stromness* into the Sound forty-five minutes later and began to disembark their contingents into the LCUs. Bringing up the rear of this group would be *Fort Austin*, loaded with helicopters, and *Brilliant* for close anti-aircraft protection, her radars and Sea Wolf systems doubtless on top line under the direction of John Coward.

Four hours later the smaller landing ships *Sir Galahad*, *Sir Geraint*, *Sir Lancelot*, *Sir Percivale* and *Sir Tristram*, plus the *Europic Ferry*, were scheduled to follow Bill Canning's *Broadsword* and Kit Layman's *Argonaut* into what I fervently hoped would still be the quiet undisturbed waters of the entrance to Falkland Sound.

I told myself that it must surely come out all right at least until dawn because the Args would not attack by air at night. Certainly they never had so far. But then again, faced with the desperation that must surely grip their commanders when they see our final irrevocable commitment to the landing, they may just order their attack aircraft to go for us by night as well, on the basis that anything is better than nothing. They *should* throw *everything* at us once they have decided we are there for real, and not just another deception. My best hope was that their air force would prove no braver than their navy, which *still* had not been sighted outside twelve miles from the mainland since we removed *Belgrano* from their Order of Battle.

At 0145 on the morning of 21 May Captain Jeremy Larken, his Ops Room alert as perhaps never before, steamed *Fearless* into Falkland Sound, one mile ahead of *Intrepid*. High up on Fanning Head the Argentinians never stirred, never fired, never even noticed, as the twelve-thousand-ton British assault ship, with the whole of 40 Commando on board, slid quietly past Jersey Point a couple of miles out and almost eight hundred feet below their guns. Behind her, Captain Peter Dingemans brought *Intrepid* through in direct line astern, the men of 3 Para huddled below decks finishing off some Navy stew, in pretty sharp contrast to the haute cuisine to which they had become accustomed on the journey south in *Canberra*.

Still nothing stirred. The two British captains made their way down the Sound, close to the western shore, before swinging past *Antrim* with Chancho Point close ahead. A little before 0230 the stern gates of their flooded docks opened and the landing craft, one at a time, pushed out into the sea, now beneath a starry sky, for the weather had cleared, though the moon had not risen to act as a floodlight.

Around this time we received in the Ops Room of *Hermes* the first signal that the Amphibious Group was in and proceeding smoothly so far – twenty minutes behind time but hoping to catch up in the now calm, clear weather. By now the second wave of ships was through to the Sound, entering in single file. Protected by the guns of *Plymouth*, one of the most spectacular-looking ocean liners in the world the *Canberra* steamed through the narrows, ghostly white beneath the southern stars, and took up her position with *Stromness* and *Norland* at the gateway to the inlet.

David Pentreath then swung *Plymouth* into her allotted place, with her guns facing south-east ready to fire straight over Port San Carlos to the east or straight down the more southerly bearing of the much wider San Carlos Water directly in front of her, whichever way an incoming attack showed up. *Brilliant*, bringing up the rear of Group Two, cleared the narrows just before 0300 (midnight local) and took up position close to the shore of West Falkland, her Sea Wolf missile directors alert to deal with an air attack from any direction.

On board *Canberra* the troops of 42 Commando made ready for the landing. In *Norland* Colonel H. Jones spoke quietly to the men of 2 Para, whose task it would be to hit the beach, climb six hundred feet to the uppermost ridge of the Sussex Mountains and fight to take them if necessary. In *Stromness*, 45 Commando, the last of the units of the reinforced 3 Commando Brigade, prepared to embark in the landing craft.

With *Fort Austin* now anchored inshore, half a mile south of Chancho Point in the Sound, and *Yarmouth* positioned south of *Brilliant*, bang in the middle of Falkland Sound, there was a total of eleven British ships now deployed around the north-western shores of East Falkland. It is still well-nigh unbelievable that the Argentinians appeared to be utterly unaware of this large force, the rightful proprietors of the place – especially as the Args also had a second high look-out position on Mount Rosalie which stares out across the Sound from the north-east corner of West Falkland. How could they possibly have missed seeing or hearing *something*?

But miss it they did and, incredibly, by 0330 it was still all quiet in the Sound, as *Antrim* waited silently over to the east, near Cat Island. In her Ops Room, radio signals from the SBS spotters six miles north, up on the freezing heights of Fanning Head, were being logged and recorded, the men in charge of her 4.5-inch guns making final adjustments. At 0350 they were ready. Captain Brian Young quietly ordered his operation to commence and the guns of HMS *Antrim* opened fire, thudding dully above the black waters, the shells screaming into the granite headland far above them. I expect the barrage finally awakened the Args, as they crouched in the freezing wind at the top of the cliff. *Antrim* plastered the area with more than two hundred and fifty shells in less than thirty minutes – sufficient, probably, to flatten something the size of Windsor Castle.

On the landward side of Fanning Head the SBS men kept their heads down until Captain Young's gunners had done their work. Then they stormed the Argentinian position and found twenty-one dead or wounded, with at least that number having fled down the hill to safety – yet another chance of war had run in our favour. The entrance to the Sound was safely in British hands, clear for the rest of our convoy of the five smaller landing ships and their escorts *Argonaut* and *Broadsword*. These were all scheduled to enter Carlos Water at around 0600.

By now the LCUs from *Fearless* were heading south down Carlos Water, packed with the men of 40 Commando. The landing craft of *Intrepid* moved away empty, running south down Carlos Water to the *Norland*, the thirteen-thousand-ton P&O roll-on-roll-off ferry in which 2 Para waited quietly in the dark. Colonel Jones had his men ready and they clambered aboard, dragging their heavy packs with them, crammed tightly into the confined utilitarian space of the landing craft. This was the landing we had come eight thousand miles to achieve. We were, if you judged us harshly, a day late. I had hoped very much to get in on 20 May, but the bright weather and the need to get all the 'cross-decking' done had ruled that out. In my cabin in *Hermes* I opened my diary and wrote gratefully, '0740 – still a deathly hush – extraordinary.' For all these hours we had waited offshore for bad news and, incredibly, there was none.

What I also did not know was that exactly ten minutes ago, the LCUs which carried 2 Para to the south end of Carlos Water had surged into the shallows and that, even as I wrote, H. Jones's men were splashing their way forward on to the beaches of the Falkland Islands. Minutes later the troops of 40 Commando hit the beaches slightly to the north, wading ashore and, soon after, running up the flag in San Carlos Settlement, which was, I suppose, sound thinking, even if you couldn't see it in the dark – this was, after all, more or less what we were here for.

Within half an hour the moon would rise out of the Atlantic to deliver cold judgement upon us all. We saw it, out in the Battle Group, as we prepared to launch the supporting Harriers. It was odd, really, but ever since we arrived here that moon had seemed to me to be strange, somehow alien, maybe Argentinian, but very different from the one seen through the street lights of Kingston-upon-Thames. But this morning, after the landings, with the Union Jack flying in the cold breeze in San Carlos Settlement, that seemed to have changed. Somehow, the moon was, once again, friendly. And we could still see it, quite pale and very high, long after the sun had risen.

CARLOS WATER

14

The Battle of 'Bomb Alley'

I suppose I knew that on the morning of 21 May 1982 the Royal Navy would be required to fight its first major action since the end of the Second World War. I do not often admit this, because my reply to any formal question on the subject is always, 'We did not have the slightest idea *what* was going to happen.' Nonetheless one pretty simple fact dominated my thoughts: on this day the Argentinians are going to have to fight. They cannot simply sit there, wait for the British forces to get organized and trust that they will win the inevitable land battle some time later. No commander in his right mind – particularly an Argentinian, on their record to date – will choose to fight a well-organized enemy later if he can catch him off-balance now.

So, today the Args had no option but to come out and make some kind of a fight of it, unless they should choose to take this as an opportunity to give in gracefully, which, sadly, did not look very likely, not least because they seemed to have little idea what was happening. Indeed, by dawn, they had already proved to be so profoundly slack that the entire British landing force, eleven ships plus escorts, had sailed straight past their 'guards' apparently unnoticed and was in the process of establishing a firm beach-head ashore in the Carlos Water area.

But now it was light. They still had a navy and a substantial air force, which had not tried to come at us in any strength since 1 May, when they last thought we were landing. They, at least, must surely come again. It was inconceivable to any person of normal learning that they would *not* attack the amphibious ships while there were still so many men and so much material to go ashore. So it had to be done, from the air, sometime today, starting very soon.

Out in the Ops Room of *Hermes* we waited, largely cut off from the Amphibious Group. We were much too far away to pick up their short-wave radio signals, which were effectively only 'line-of-sight' and well over the horizon. Long-haul communications, of course, remained available, but these are not much used for detailed battle management. Any communications between the inshore forces and *Hermes* would have to be by the less immediate process of satellite link or the HF circuits, which would be of pretty variable strength from among the hills of the Falklands.

Today they would fight without me. My job was to ensure they had as much protection from the air as we could possibly provide and we were ready to back them up in any way which might become necessary with supplies or reinforcements. But on this morning, with the Army and the Marines not yet ready for combat, and the Rapier missile systems not yet in place, the battle was going to have to be fought by the ships and aircraft of the Navy alone.

It was curious how relaxed I was, but I reckoned I knew how they would fight, how resolute they would be under fire and what gallantry they could be relied on to show under pressure. They would fight as the Royal Navy has always fought, down all the years, and it never crossed my mind, nor, I am certain, the minds of any of my commanders, that today's men would be much different from those of the often glorious past. The *big* difference was, that unlike Jervis, Nelson, Hawke, Hood, Jellicoe, Beatty and Cunningham, we would have to defeat an air force as well as a rival navy, and the Navy's record at surviving concentrated air attack was not one to inspire confidence.

I had had to surrender my ringside seat for one at the back of the arena. The battle itself would rest in the capable hands of COMAW and Captains Layman, Coward, Young, Canning and Pentreath, Commanders Morton and West, and, most critical as it was to turn out, the Sea Harrier pilots.

The story of 21 May has been told many times, by others who were there and by many more who were not. I don't much enjoy being yet another of the latter group, but this book would clearly be incomplete if I did not relate to you yet another version, from the point of view of the Royal Navy, even though I was a satellite signal away from the action. In the years since, opinions and assessments have been considerably refined, and some 'facts' have been cast in stone when they probably should have been cast on the rubbish tip. I can only do my best to tell our story as I understand the facts to be, as they have been told to me, by my colleagues and friends, who fought with such high courage on that frightful day. Throughout this book I have endeavoured to stay as close as possible to those situations in which I was directly involved. In this way I hope I have been able, thus far, to acquaint you with the interior workings of the mind of a battle commander. However, it is essential that I keep the events not only in context, but also in perspective. As such you ought to understand the full ferocity of the air–sea battle that was fought on this day in order to follow my thoughts and actions in the tense and sometimes dreadful days that followed.

I have tried to reconcile my own records, particularly the assessments of losses we had inflicted on the Argentinians, with those of other chroniclers of this war. But they are usually slightly different; I tended to err on the side of scepticism at the naturally enthusiastic claims of aircraft shot down. It was the same during the Battle of Britain; optimism often getting the better of harsh truth. But I am also trained not to exaggerate. I am trained, if such a thing is possible, to be accurate, to accept only hard facts and to distinguish folklore from reality. I am also trained to avoid becoming too involved with individuals and their problems. I have to count the attrition of both sides, to assess how much longer we can reasonably go on before I call home and tell them we are coming out on the wrong side of this particular conflict – and that in my judgement we had better either pack it in or get heavy reinforcements. To some, this could seem like 'bureaucratic book-keeping' from the comparative safety of the Battle Group – for me, it was simply an essential part of overall battle management. In any event, I will spend the rest of this chapter recording my analysis of what went on on the real opening day of the air–sea war.

D-Day, 21 May, did not start terribly well for either side. After weeks of watching for them, two of our Harrier pilots finally discovered an Argentinian helicopter area on Mount Kent – probably only because they now needed to come out of their 'hides' – and very quickly wiped out three of them on the ground: believed to be two army Pumas, and a big army Chinook. Forty-five minutes later Flight Lieutenant Jeremy Glover's GR3 Harrier was shot down by ground fire from Port Howard and at about the same time we lost two of the Royal Marines' Gazelle choppers just east of the landing area.

The early combat air patrols of the day came under the control of *Antrim*, who stationed herself roughly in the middle of the AOA, on the eastern side of the Falkland Sound. Most of them would be back on board the carriers before anything much happened, for it remained uncannily quiet, in terms of Argentinian attack, for more than two hours after sunrise. Then it began. An Argentinian light attack two-seater jet aircraft, the Italian-built Naval Macchi 339, flying at wave-top height along the northern coast, swung suddenly into the narrow entrance to Falkland Sound, going as fast as he could. The first ship he saw was Kit Layman's *Argonaut* and he fired all eight of his five-inch rockets at the frigate, coming on in low and raking the decks with 30mm cannon shells. One rocket hit the Seacat missile deck area and injured three men – one of whom lost an eye; another, the Master-at-Arms, took a piece of shrapnel one inch above his heart.

The attack had been so swift and sudden that the raider was making his escape away to the south-east before any kind of hardware could be aimed at him. As it was, they had a shot at him with a Blowpipe missile from the deck of *Canberra*; *Intrepid* launched a Seacat missile and David Pentreath opened up with the 4.5-inch guns of *Plymouth*. But the Macchi got away doubtless to stagger his High Command with the tale of what he had just seen spread out below him in Carlos Water.

Five minutes later we evened the score when the SAS, with a Stinger missile, hit a turbo-prop Pucara which had made the error of flying too close to their mountain lair. Then a couple more of these same light attack aircraft managed to dodge the bombardment of *Ardent* and got off the ground from Goose Green.

Commander West's Ops Room moved quickly. His two young Principal Warfare Officers, Lieutenants Mike Knowles and Tom Williams, were about to become used to switching from attack to defence in their very exposed position far south of the other ships. But their Captain, himself a former frigate PWO, had coached them both personally and now they ordered *Ardent*'s 4.5-inch gun into action, firing at the raiders and launching a Seacat missile, which went close and drove the Arg pilots away without achieving anything.

The first major attack of the day swept in about half an hour later at 1235. Three Israeli-built Daggers, capable of supersonic speed, came in over West Falkland behind the cover of Mount Rosalie. They dropped to a height of only fifty feet above the water and raced across the Sound, flying straight for the gap between Fanning Head and Chancho Point, no doubt intending to attack the many amphibious ships beyond.

This time we were ready. *Argonaut* and *Intrepid* had their Seacat missiles away before the incoming Args were within two miles of Carlos Bay. But it was *Plymouth* which scored the first hit, blowing the aircraft on the far right of the trio out of the sky with a Seacat. The pilot never had a chance. The second Dagger swerved right, away from the missiles now flying through the gap, and the next ship he saw was Bill Canning's Type 22 *Broadsword*. He pressed home his attack, coming in close and strafing the frigate with 30mm cannon shell – and hitting with twenty-nine in all. He wounded four-

teen men in the hangar area and damaged the two Lynx helicopters, but missed with both of his bombs, thankfully.

The third Dagger swung to the south, making a bee-line
for Brian Young's *Antrim* which was positioned less than a
mile off the rocky shore of Cat Island, three and half miles
down the coast from Chancho Point. The Argentinian bomb,
a thousand-pounder it later transpired, hit *Antrim*'s flight deck,
bounced through the flash doors at the aft end of the Seaslug
missile magazine, catching two of these big missiles a glancing
blow, and ended up, appropriately enough, in a lavatory space
– known as the 'heads' in naval jargon. Miraculously, neither
the bomb nor the two missiles went off. A major explosion in
Antrim's missile magazine would almost certainly have finished
the ship. As it was, several fires broke out and *Antrim*'s crew
were hard-pressed to contain them. Captain Young made all
speed to the north, to join *Broadsword*, for both cover and
assistance. But she didn't get there before the next Argentinian
raid was on its way in, only six minutes later.

This was another wave of three Daggers, flying on an almost
identical course to the first group, fast and low over West
Falkland. They were coming straight for the battered *Antrim*,
whose crew was now trying to jettison the Seaslug missiles in
case the fire reached them. In desperation, *Antrim* fired a Seaslug missile, completely unguided, in the general direction of
the Daggers, hoping to put them off a bit. Their Seacat system
was already out of action, but they had the 4.5-inch guns
working and every machine gun they had was blazing away at
the attackers.

One, however, made it through and strafed the burning
destroyer with cannon shells, wounding seven men and causing
further fires to break out. The situation in *Antrim* was now
serious. The second Dagger elected to go for *Fort Austin* which

was very bad news for us, since the big supply ship was almost defenceless against this type of attack, but Commodore Sam Dunlop ordered his two machine guns into action and there was a volley of small-arms fire from the twenty-four riflemen on the upper deck. But it was not going to be enough and Sam must have braced himself for the impact of a bomb when, to his amazement, the Dagger blew apart one thousand yards out, hit by a critically timed Sea Wolf missile from *Broadsword*. But the last one came on in, strafing *Broadsword* once again and just missing Bill Canning's frigate with a one-thousand-pound bomb.

The guns of *Ardent* were still firing as the surviving Daggers made their getaway and it was now becoming clear that *Antrim*, quite badly damaged, was in no condition to direct the Harriers on to their targets from their waiting positions high overhead. At this point in the battle, Captain John Coward of *Brilliant*, informed of the plight of Brian Young's ship, immediately took over the task of fighter director for the CAP. He assumed command, as I would expect any Royal Navy officer to do, without so much as a 'by your leave', reacting instantly to the changing situation. We could hear them on the high-frequency nets in *Hermes*, suddenly directing the Harriers.

Our aviation controllers interrupted and advised *Brilliant*: 'Now you be very careful with our aircraft.'

To which they replied, 'Of course we'll be very careful. Don't worry.' And, fairly typically for that ship, they finished with a flourish – 'We know what we're bloody doing.'

And, of course, they did know what they were bloody doing. Coward had in his Ops Room a first lieutenant who was a real expert in this field, a former instructor in the Navy's Aircraft Direction School. They evolved a plan combining two radar systems which would enable them to 'see' over the land, clearer than most others, both the Harriers and the incoming raiders. In their brand-new Type 22 they had the latest radars and were rapidly learning new ways of using them. John Coward swung *Brilliant* around and hurried north-east into Carlos Water where he seemed most needed. Coward had already come to the conclusion that our defences were too spread out and now he was proposing to concentrate them, on his own. His basic plan was to position *Brilliant* bang in the middle of the entrance to the bay and treat the entire operation like a pheasant shoot, blasting the Argentinian raiders out of the sky with his trusty Sea Wolf as they came in.

For many years colleagues had heard Captain Coward quote a well-known naval phrase which is considered by some to date back to the eighteenth century, by others to be the invention of the Navy's legendary turn-of-the-century First Sea Lord, Admiral Fisher: 'The essence of war is violence; moderation in war is imbecility.' That was his philosophy for better or for worse, and now he would have the chance he had always longed for, to put it into stark and belligerent practice. While his Sea Wolf reaped havoc among the incoming raiders, he planned simultaneously to direct the Harriers on to their targets as the Args flew out of the 'box' and attempted to get home.

And now, as the two Daggers fled away to the south, *Brilliant*'s Ops Room directed the CAP on to them, but they were slightly too late. Undaunted the captain returned to the screen, refining the electronic process with his first lieutenant, confirming to everyone in his Ops Room, 'Look here, I know damned well we can really take charge of this operation, and that's what we're going to do.'

He was very clear in his own mind as to the merits of the various ships. He knew that the long-range radar in ships like *Antrim* and *Glamorgan* was never going to be effective in the enclosed waters of Carlos Bay, and he also knew that the equipment of the two older frigates *Yarmouth* and *Plymouth* would be inadequate for this particular kind of warfare. Actually his phrases were slightly different – 'Clapped out old ships, bloody useless radar' – but Coward's heart was in exactly the right place, and so was his brain.

His general plan was to catch the incoming aircraft on his radar as early as possible, hopefully in time to vector Sea Harriers onto them. Failing that he'd try to lock on with Sea Wolf and call up the Harriers again, letting them know in the following seconds exactly where the Args could be expected to burst out of the 'box' – if they were lucky enough to escape *Brilliant*'s Sea Wolf.

Meanwhile *Ardent* blew up a Pucara before it got off the runway at Goose Green – 'quite by accident, actually,' said Commander West. And *Antrim* made her way over to *Fearless* in Carlos Water where she was boarded by a bomb-disposal team and a squad of engineers.

The following couple of hours were fairly quiet, which gave the ships time to tend to the wounded and put out the fires. It also allowed the massive landing programme to continue – more than one thousand tons of kit during that day, including the parts for Rapier and the big 105mm guns which would help to defend the beach-head against Argentinian counter-attack.

At 1345, the Args Air Forces came again – two Pucaras nipping in from West Falkland down to the south. *Ardent*'s gun swung on to them, driving them off with the 4.5-inch shells, and launching another Seacat missile, which failed to hit. Shortly after 1400 they returned, determined, apparently, to get *Ardent*. But this time *Brilliant* caught them early, vectoring in the Harriers, whose leader Lieutenant-Commander

Sharkey Ward instantly destroyed the front-running Pucara with cannon-fire. The pilot ejected, walked home.

One hour later the Args sent in another wave and these four Skyhawks coming in very low across the land were not spotted until they were two miles away. *Ardent*'s guns were not quick enough, but the bombs were not accurate enough either. They hit the sea and bounced majestically right over the frigate. One of the Skyhawks was so low he hit *Ardent*'s 992 radar aerial with his underwing fuel tank.

It looked rather as if all four of them might get safely away, but Coward's Ops Room was very fast in calling to the new CAP, which had only just arrived, the range and bearing of the fleeing Args. The two *Hermes*-based Lieutenant-Commanders, Mike Blissett and Neil Thomas, brought their Harriers lancing down from fifteen thousand feet, fired their Sidewinders and blew two of the Skyhawks apart, killing both pilots.

Back in Carlos Water another hour went by before the Argentinians sent in their most lethal and sustained air raid of the day. It would last for just over half an hour and it did great damage. The opening assault was made by six Skyhawks flying extremely low along the north coast, out of sight of all of our radars. As swiftly as any of the opening attacks, they came through the narrows at more than five hundred knots. There they found Kit Layman's *Argonaut*, from which the crew was desperately trying to evacuate their wounded by helicopter over to *Canberra*. At the last moment the *Argonaut*s saw them and opened fire with everything they had, but they had no hope whatsoever of stopping all six. Five made it through, dropping a total of ten thousand-pounders, eight of which exploded in the water close to the embattled Leander Class frigate. The other two hit her, but mercifully failed to explode. The first one hit forward, going through a diesel fuel tank and coming to rest in the Seacat magazine, starting a fire and causing considerable structural damage. By the most extraordinary bit of luck, the escaping diesel fuel was cold enough to put the fire out without itself igniting and adding to the fire instead. The second bomb rammed through the bulkhead between the engine room and the boiler room, wrecking the steering mechanism and the reverse gearing.

Argonaut was perilously close to the rocks around Fanning Head and still going ahead with effectively no brakes and no steering. With remarkable presence of mind, Sub-Lieutenant Peter Morgan raced off the bridge, collecting a couple of ratings as he went, and managed to let go the anchor, which dragged the three-thousand-tonner to a halt, just short of the shoreline. Seconds later they lost all power, there was almost total devastation in certain parts of the ship and, with two men killed in the magazine, *Argonaut*'s war was almost over.

Beyond her, the battle was increasing in pace. Joining the Skyhawk attack was a formation of three Daggers – there had been four but *Brilliant* had directed the CAP on to them a few minutes earlier and Lieutenant-Commander Fred Frederiksen had hit and destroyed one with a Sidewinder out over West Falkland. Now they ran into the Sound, right behind the Skyhawks, and as they did so all the British ships opened fire, *Antrim*, *Plymouth* and *Intrepid*, all with Seacat missiles, all of which missed. *Fort Austin*'s machine guns hit but failed to down one of the Daggers, but another of them drew a bead on *Brilliant*, by now positioned firmly in the middle of the anchorage.

Once again the computerized limitations of John Coward's Sea Wolf system were exposed. His radar would not lock on, would not recognize the target, approaching fast, diagonally, because it was programmed to fire straight. John knew what had happened but was powerless at present to fix it.

Bill Canning's men, however, did get a Sea Wolf away and very nearly hit the Dagger which was threatening *Brilliant*, possibly causing it to miss with its bomb. But its 30mm cannon was effective, one shell smashing through one side of the Ops Room and exiting through the other. I am afraid my history of the day does not record Captain Coward's precise words at this interruption, but I understand they were not terribly complimentary.

At this time they were also busy directing the Harriers, and a metal splinter hit the vitally important aircraft director, Lieutenant-Commander Lee Hulme, in the back – quite a nasty injury. But when you fight for John Coward, minor problems like that tend to fade into the background. Lee Hulme faltered for just three seconds, with the words, 'Just a moment, please.' Then, discovering he could still walk, and talk, he pressed on with his task, instructing the Harriers precisely which end of the 'box' to watch for the homeward-bound Arg fliers.

By now another formation of Skyhawks, this time navy aircraft, had made a big swing around the Sound, swept over the land and, having cleared the Port Howard area, were heading, at sea-level, straight towards *Ardent*. They were positioned right on Commander West's six o'clock (stern) away from the arc of his 4.5-inch gun, as the British frigate made its way up to the North-West Islands to join *Yarmouth*. Three of them made the attack together. *Ardent* could bring her Seacat to bear, but the launcher refused to fire. That left just his 20mm Oerlikon guns and two other machine guns to open fire.

Everyone who could help did. Lieutenant-Commander John Sephton, the Lynx helicopter pilot and his observer Brian

Murphy, were up above the flight deck, Sephton with a Sterling sub-machine gun and his assistant with a Bren gun, both blasting away at the Skyhawks. But the situation was hopeless. The Argentinians dropped nine bombs, three of them hitting *Ardent*, two exploding in the hangar, the third failing to explode after smashing its way into the after auxiliary machinery room. The bomb that hit the hangar wreaked havoc, blowing the Seacat launcher, which was positioned on top of the hangar, into the air, only to crash down on to the flight deck killing Commander West's cheerful supply officer, Richard Banfield. The blast also killed Lieutenant-Commander Sephton and Brian Murphy and one other crew member.

A large fire broke out in the stern section of the ship with the flooding that always takes place when a warship suffers bad fractures in its fresh water and fire-fighting systems. *Ardent* was still able to run on her Tyne engines and she could make over fifteen knots, but damage to her electrics had put the gun and Seacat firmly out of action. Commander West, with a great plume of black smoke pouring from his ship, ordered her to be turned to the north, to gain some respite for the firefighters and the medical teams.

Minutes after this, *Brilliant*'s Ops Room located the next raid, coming in from the west. Lee Hulme contacted the CAP which was circling over the Pebble Island area and vectored Lieutenant-Commander Ward and Lieutenant Steve Thomas down towards Port Howard. Below them, the two Harrier pilots saw three Daggers making a northward course towards the British ships. Anti-aircraft fire from the small arms of the Arg garrison in Port Howard came up towards the Harriers as they dived towards the sea at six hundred knots. Lieutenant Thomas's Harrier took three fortunately unimportant hits, but they pressed on, loosed off their Sidewinders and destroyed all three of the Daggers. More importantly, they both made it home to *Invincible*, Lieutenant Thomas now having hit a total of three Argentinian aircraft.

But back in the Sound, yet another formation of Skyhawks was already on its way over West Falkland, streaking across the land to the south of Mount Rosalie and crossing Many Branch Harbour, leaving themselves with the option of a swing north-east towards the anchorage. Unhappily the first thing they saw was *Ardent*, in which the fires were now just about out of control.

Once more Commander West swung his weapons on to the enemy. His 4.5-inch gun was now repaired, but even as they aimed it, the Arg pilots swung away, making a long two-mile circle back towards West Falkland. Everyone feared they would not be gone for long, but, though *Ardent* was in a poor way, they weren't giving up yet. One of her machine guns now had no one to fire it, so the ship's NAAFI canteen manager, John Leake, an ex-regular Army man, ran through the carnage on the decks to take it over.

In less than a minute the Skyhawks were on their way back. John Leake hit one of them in the wing – it later crashed trying to land at Port Stanley, after the pilot ejected – but nothing *Ardent* possessed could possibly have stopped this attack. She was hit by seven bombs, one after the other, the force of the blasts lifting the ship almost out of the water, blowing men who were lying prostrate on the decks more than three feet into the air, blowing three more into the sea. One of the five-hundred-pounders that hit the stern killed or wounded the entire fire-fighting team. By any standards of any sea-battle, from Cape St Vincent to Jutland, it ranked as one hell of a hammering.

The Args might have got away with it too, except that, high

above it all, was a CAP from 800 Squadron, Lieutenant-Commander Clive Morrell and Flight Lieutenant John Leeming. They had both been told by Sharkey Ward and by *Brilliant* of the presence of the Skyhawks, and now they dived down to make the intercept as the Argentinian bombers banked away from the mortally wounded *Ardent*. Leeming hit and destroyed the leader with two bursts of 30mm cannon shells. Morrell coming in behind him hit and wiped out the second Arg with a Sidewinder. His next missile refused to fire, but he had time to shoot at the remaining aircraft, hitting it in both wings, blowing the undercarriage away and forcing the pilot to eject.

These three 'kills' helped to even the score, but *Ardent* had twenty-two officers and men dead with thirty-seven more wounded. As the fire blazed they struggled to get the 4.5 ready to face the enemy once more, but *Ardent* could no longer steer, the fires were heading inexorably towards the missile magazines and ice-cold sea water was pouring in through a hole on the water line. *Ardent* was sinking and, with the greatest reluctance, Commander West, in conference now with Commander Morton who was alongside in *Yarmouth*, gave his last order as captain: 'Abandon ship.'

Yarmouth placed her stern on *Ardent*'s bow and the wounded were transferred. In the next half hour her remaining company of one hundred and forty-two officers and men also stepped across, many of them unashamedly crying, until finally it was the turn of Commander West himself. The last to leave his ship, he hesitated just briefly, glancing back at the terrible fire. And then, at 1755, he too stepped on board *Yarmouth*, tears of anger and frustration streaming down his cheeks. HMS *Ardent* burned all night and sank eleven hours later.

The final attack of the day took place with just ninety minutes of daylight left: five more Skyhawks of 5th Air Brigade

Captain John Coward (*above*), the aggressive, inappropriately named Captain of the new guided-missile frigate HMS *Brilliant*, had in a way been waiting all of his life to fight this war, and his motto was well-known: 'The essence of war is violence. Moderation in war is imbecility.'

Captain Bill Canning (*above, right*) of the Type 22 frigate HMS *Broadsword*. Hit by a bomb on 25 May and still under attack, his missile systems computer refused to function. Bill required every ounce of cunning and control he possessed after a lifetime in the Navy to hold his team together.

Commander Christopher Craig (*right*), Captain of HMS *Alacrity*. By late May the overworked 4.5-inch gun on this Type 22 frigate was just about worn out. 'I am proposing,' said Chris 'to stay here and fight until the bloody barrel drops off.'

Ian North (*left*), Captain of the *Atlantic Conveyor*, with Captain Mike Layard, the senior Royal Navy officer on board – '. . . Captain Layard took the steps to the bridge three at a time, and Captain North ordered a hard turn to port in an attempt to present *Conveyor*'s very strong stern to the incoming missiles'.

Commodore Mike Clapp (*left*), was in charge of the landings and all operations around Carlos Water.

Peter Dingemans (*below*) and Jeremy Larken, the two Captains of the British amphibious ships *Intrepid* and *Fearless*, respectively. On the night of the landings, they entered the narrows below Fanning Head, one mile apart, line astern, their ships crammed with British Commandos and Paras.

Captain Hugh Balfour (*inset, top right*) of HMS *Exeter*. To some he appeared to be a bit of a dandy, very smoothly turned out, but Hugh was an extremely modern thinker, an expert on satellites, an electronic warfare specialist, and the master of the newest Sea Dart system we had in the South Atlantic.

HMS *Exeter* opens fire at an oncoming Argentinian Learjet. And she hit it many miles away.

On 4 July 1982 Admiral
Sir John Fieldhouse, the
C-in-C, met me at Brize
Norton . . . this picture
shows us out of step for
the first time in one
hundred days.

Home again – Char, Andy
and Tessa issue me a short
pep talk before I faced
Fleet Street's finest.

came in on their now familiar route towards the narrows – but heavy fire from *Antrim*, *Intrepid*, *Plymouth* and *Fearless* drove them away. No one hit anything and everyone lived to fight another day.

Up to the north of the Sound, *Plymouth* now joined *Argonaut*, securing alongside and hooking up a power line which would help them weigh anchor and get the ship further into the shelter of Carlos Water. Captain Pentreath's galley was also active serving hot food for the crew. Bill Canning positioned *Broadsword* outside the bay – the only ship there – to guard the entrance off Chancho Point. At 1930 the survivors of *Ardent* boarded *Canberra*, from which 3 Commando were actually still disembarking to go ashore.

Over in *Antrim*, Chief Petty Officer Fellows and his team were in the final stages of removing the unexploded bomb by cutting out a 'tunnel' and lowering it into the water. The Chief would be highly decorated with a rare Distinguished Service Cross upon his return to England. *Argonaut* too was trying to return to normal life – with Lieutenant-Commander Brian Dutton and his team successfully removing that unexploded bomb from the Seacat magazine, an act of gallantry which would see him become the most junior officer ever to be awarded the DSO. While Brian Dutton worked, CMEM Townsend actually patched a four-foot steel plate over the hole near the water line, working only six feet or so from the bomb itself!

By now the full reports from what was rapidly becoming known as 'Bomb Alley' were beginning to arrive in the Ops Room of *Hermes*. With *Ardent* sinking, *Argonaut* and *Antrim* both severely battered with unexploded bombs in them and *Brilliant* and *Broadsword* damaged, it was clear that the Args were doing at least something right. It seemed to us that the first priority must be to get those troop ships out of there as quickly as possible. There had been a total of twenty-seven men killed on this day and unless we moved the big 'ferries' away forthwith that number could rapidly be increased.

We agreed a latest departure time of 0130 when *Antrim* would escort *Canberra*, *Europic Ferry* and *Norland* out of Carlos Bay to safer waters east of the Battle Group. Everyone was dumbfounded as to how the Args had come to miss the *Canberra*, the Great White Whale, as she came to be called. She had sat, gleaming white, bang in the middle of the bay all day and never been hit by anything.

The fact was, the Args had screwed this operation up very badly indeed. Not only had they failed to provide their bombers with any top-cover fighter escort which could take on the Harriers, they had also made the crucial mistake of going for our frigates and destroyers, rather than the amphibious ships and troop carriers, which were there for the taking, not to mention the three-thousand-odd men they carried.

By contrast, the Royal Navy had planned and carried out one of the most successful landings in military history. We had got our forces ashore, with most of their equipment, on the first day of the amphibious operation – always the most dangerous. Casualties to the land forces: Zero.

It was the Royal Navy which had taken the punishment in order that the troops should land safely, not that that had been in our gift. The Argentinians, possibly more by bad luck than bad judgement, had gone for the warships, but then I suppose if you are travelling at five hundred knots very low over the water, with only split seconds after you lift over a hill or swerve round a headland in which to make your decision, you may very easily be tempted to go for the first ship you can line up. If you hang about to give it more thought, you will have probably over-flown it before you decide. And you don't much want to come back for another pass; they will be ready for you next time. To operate these aircraft at all you need the reflexes of a Formula One Grand Prix driver – and the South Americans are traditionally pretty good at that – but they also hadn't been properly briefed, which is, I suppose, why our escorts took so much stick on 21 May, and not the troopships.

History has more or less accorded with our calculations for that day and shown that we had destroyed fourteen of their aircraft in return, plus the three helicopters on Mount Kent. Our list showed three Pucaras, six Daggers and five Skyhawks. Nine of them were hit by the Harriers, the SAS got one with a Stinger missile, *Ardent* got one of the Pucaras (on the ground) and the small-arms fire of John Leake accounted for a Skyhawk. *Plymouth* and *Broadsword* got one each with missiles. As far as we could tell the Argentinians had launched some fifty sorties at Carlos Water, almost all of them from the mainland, which, considering the amount of TNT we had dropped on and around Port Stanley airstrip, was scarcely surprising.

The part played by *Brilliant* was extremely important; but for them, at least eight more Arg bombers would probably have got through to the ships. Captain Coward and Lieutenant-Commander Hulme somehow set up *four* interceptions, the last of which brought such welcome revenge on those Skyhawks which had signed the final death warrant of *Ardent*.

The analysis showed another rather depressing feature. The warships had hit only two incoming aircraft with their missiles. I did not of course know how many missiles they had fired, but I was fairly sure our success rate was somewhere between dead-moderate and bloody awful. John Coward was particularly disappointed with Sea Wolf and its flat refusal to attack an enemy aircraft which was *not* coming straight at the launcher: the damned thing would not even recognize it as a possible target. In addition Captain Coward, in our newest ship, found out the hard way that his surveillance radar was nothing like as effective in the tight mountainous surroundings which bordered Carlos Water. Finally his forward Sea Wolf system had been damaged by enemy action.

By nightfall he realized that it would have been much better if he had stationed *Brilliant* just a little further out in the open water to give his radar a better chance. Knowing John he was privately berating himself for this ill-fortune, but, as ever, he had a plan. By some remarkable piece of chicanery, he still had on board *Brilliant* the specialist computer engineer from Marconi, the British company that made the Sea Wolf radar. He had not *quite* kidnapped him – the chap had been working on *Brilliant*'s electronics in Gibraltar before we set off to the south and then went home to England, but somehow, by the time we cleared Ascension on that April night, Mr David Brean – whom John describes as a 'deep expert' in missile computer technology – was ensconced in none other than *Brilliant*. 'A key player in my team,' said Coward briskly, as if it were the most natural thing in the world for a Royal Navy frigate to be heading into battle with various civilian technologists wandering around their Ops Rooms. Unusual, I thought, but not half a bad idea.

On this dark night, with the weather getting up, David Brean was wrestling with the problem of *Brilliant*'s Sea Wolf and the extensive damage to its wiring. The captain had ordered her out of the Sound by 2030 to go round to King George Bay, West Falkland, and insert SAS reconnaissance teams. As he did so, David Brean re-wired and re-programmed.

'The trouble is,' he said to Captain Coward, sometime after

midnight, 'we have a problem with the radar antenna up the mast.'

Without a thought for the knifing wind and the cold rain, not to mention that Mr Brean was not even in the Navy, John Coward replied: 'Better get up there then.'

David Brean, I am reliably informed, gulped. Then he said, 'Okay, sir,' and proceeded to go up the mast in the middle of the night to fix the antenna. 'First class man,' confirmed Coward. 'Best after-sales service you can imagine.'

The following morning, *Brilliant* reported one of her Sea Wolf systems was completely operable again, improved on yesterday's model, and that the man from Marconi was working on the other.

That day, 21 May, was a day which by any standards had tested once more the courage, the will to fight and the years of training of the Royal Navy. I reflected as I looked at the signals now coming in from Carlos Water that little had changed since the eighteenth century, except of course for the hardware and the speed of the conflict: the people were just the same, the spirit in the ships was just the same, the courage of the men was just the same. Was not the performance of *Argonaut* facing the incoming Skyhawks comparable with the best of Britain's naval traditions? What difference between *Ardent*, crippled and burning, still fighting and Sir Richard Grenville's *Revenge* all those centuries ago. Or between this and that October day off Cape Trafalgar as Nelson and Hardy walked the quarter deck of the *Victory* shortly after noon, her tiller ropes cut, her mizzen topmast on the deck and her sails in tatters, their casualty count very much the same as that of *Ardent*, twenty men killed and thirty wounded.

As I said, far back in my early training days in this book, we have all been taught that one day we may be asked to emulate the actions of the captains of *Jervis Bay* or *Glowworm*, to go on fighting the ship until the bitter end. You may have thought you joined the Navy in order to attend courses and to make yourself a comfortable career. But, whether you knew it or not, you actually joined for this day, the day of reckoning. And if that should be today – *then go do it*.

It was perfectly clear that on the opening day of our battle in San Carlos Water, the people had conducted themselves in the great traditions of the Navy with the highest possible professionalism. I was sure there would be many stories of heroism to come out of it and, of them all, I remain most impressed by the conduct of John Leake who manned the machine gun in *Ardent*. He was not really in the Navy, but, as we say, we are all of one company, the captain *and* the NAAFI man. And we all go together.

It is interesting to note how many of the officers came from Royal Navy families, whose forebears had fought such actions too. In addition to the First Sea Lord himself, Henry Leach, there were captains like Paul Hoddinott and Kit Layman. But there were also many, many others. Lieutenant-Commander John Sephton who died on the flight deck of *Ardent* was from such a family – his uncle Petty Officer Alfred Sephton vc was killed on another May afternoon, forty-one years previously just south of the island of Crete. Mortally wounded, the thirty-year-old gun director was credited with saving, 'very nearly single-handedly', a previous HMS *Coventry* from certain destruction by the Luftwaffe. Both of the gallant Sephtons were buried at sea. Yet another English family had paid yet another dreadful price.

But my job is in the price-control section and during the evening of 21 May I had a long conversation with Mike Clapp via the satellite to discuss the new placement of the warships in Carlos Bay. Clearly, with all the damage sustained we could not risk the troop and logistics carriers in there during daylight hours, and perhaps the initial dispersion of the frigates and destroyers needed a careful look too. We quickly came to a meeting of minds and I was careful to follow up our strangulated conversation with a hard copy signal as usual – a lesson I had already learned from experience, but not COMAW. He rather uncharitably put it down as 'yard-arm squaring' but it was perhaps my fault, I suppose, I should have told him about the dangers of DSSS. Anyway, I was very glad of the opportunity to do something constructive because, aside from the constant comings and goings of the priceless Harriers, all day long I had in my mind been rather kicking my heels out here on this otherwise historic day. My diary betrays my restlessness. Reading it now, it shows I was obviously filling it in, on and off, hour after hour. It is self-explanatory and gives some insight into my thoughts. I reproduce it thus, with just a little sharpening of the hasty punctuation:

> 0930. Dawn still an hour away and little sign of Arg activity from any source. The weather is fine and clear – not what I wanted for Day One at all, but at least it's fairly calm for the soldiers and the transfers. Today should therefore be critical not only for the land forces but also for the air forces. If the Args are going to fight, today is their best opportunity. We shall see.
>
> Meanwhile we are ready to put up as much Sea Harrier air defence as we can through the daylight hours, clear of the AOA itself, so that our ground-missile defence has a free hand against fixed wing.
>
> I am already finding that no longer being the core of the activity – and the reversion to 'support force

commander' – is a bit irksome this morning. No doubt I'll be too busy to think about this later.

1115. First indication that Args know we're in. Some local disturbance in the AOA. Can't be long now.

1300. They're beginning to come. So it wasn't 'long now'. Fairly continuous air attacks in near perfect weather have given us the punishment we were bound to have. *Ardent* sinking. *Argonaut* stopped. *Antrim* with no effective weapons. But at least the two Type 22s and the two Type 12s are fit. So the Args have hit the wrong ships.

Unfortunately the weather tomorrow will be no better, at least until the evening, if then. So until the army have their own AD [Air Defence] set up, I can't leave them to their own devices, not least because there are all the LSLs to unload yet.

Later. It turns out that the 22s are by no means fit. Indeed *Brilliant* has one end only, and radar and propulsion. By 2300 it seems that *Ardent* is sinking, *Argonaut* is stopped but has her weapons systems working. *Antrim* is floating and moving, but has no weapons and an unexploded bomb in her backside. *Broadsword* minor damage. *Plymouth* and *Yarmouth* unscathed. All the AW ships untouched, as yet.

I put down my pen sometime well after midnight but, unknown to me, there was one other Royal Naval officer still writing – Commander Alan West. Alone now in the vast dining room of *Canberra*, he sat with a legal tablet before him, wracking his brains to recall every last detail of the action which had finished his ship. He wrote the heading: Lessons Learned/ Re-Learned. Beneath this he listed in order of importance each aspect of the battle in which his own experiences might, possibly, in the coming days, help others to avoid the devastation he now felt. He pointed out yet again the great value of the anti-flash gear, how the hoods and gloves had saved men's hands and faces from burning when the bombs had exploded in *Ardent*. He outlined the fact that a ship which maintains heavy fire against incoming aircraft, as his had done, will have a very detrimental effect on the enemy's accuracy – 'Keep firing, no matter what,' was his message. And he pointed out that the closer to the shore a ship was positioned the harder it was for enemy aircraft to maintain low altitude, because the shoreline forced them to climb. Then, in the small hours, still trembling from his ordeal, Commander Alan West went to the Radio Room and sent his signal to me personally. After all he had gone through, with his ship still blazing out in the Sound, with one-third of his crew killed or wounded, he was still trying to help.

I doubt he slept that night. What captain who has lost his ship ever does? The events of that day had been too traumatic and I'm sure they live with him still. But, like so many others, and perhaps once more in response to the most famous Royal Navy battle signal of all, Alan West had done his duty, as was only to be expected.

15

Calamity For *Coventry*

It would be futile even to suggest that I was not worried by
the events of 21 May. We had been attacked fiercely by Argentinian fighter aircraft – sporadically during the morning and
almost continuously throughout the afternoon. You might say
we were entering the very heart of this treacherous chess game.
Of the seven warship escorts I had sent in with the Amphibious
Group the previous night, only *Plymouth* and *Yarmouth* had
escaped scot free. Our most modern short-range defensive
system, Sea Wolf, was showing distinct signs of temperament
and both of the ships that carried it – *Brilliant* and *Broadsword*
– were damaged. Of our probable 'kills', nine had been
achieved by the Harriers.

The war of attrition was laid out before me as follows.
Firstly, on the first day of the landings, they have sunk one
escort, put two others more or less out of action and, further,

knocked another two about. If the Args can go on like this just for another two days, my destroyer and frigate force will be wiped out. Question: can we live with that? Answer: obviously not, because if it went on for a few days after that, at the same rate of destruction, we'd lose all the early reinforcements as well – there would be no protection for the amphibious ships, or for the carriers, and the rest of the Royal Navy is weeks away. Secondly, our pilots and gunners are claiming some twenty Argentinian planes knocked out – by Second World War rules that will probably mean about fourteen, perhaps another seven seriously damaged. Question: for how long can the Args put up with that? Answer: I'm not sure, but if this goes on for another week I do not think they can tolerate the loss of another hundred-odd aircraft. That kind of attrition would cause even the Russians to take a pull.

In addition – including Pebble Island – we had already taken out some twenty-seven of their aircraft prior to the landing. Plus of course the massive volume of small arms fire from the British ships must also have taken its toll of enemy aircraft damaged or out of action more or less permanently. The only intelligence we had, suggested they started with some one hundred and ninety fixed-wing combat aircraft, and a rule of thumb says a country like Argentina would have only about one half of those immediately ready for modern combat. That means they really started with some eighty-five aircraft ready to go. We had removed about forty, and probably irreparably damaged another ten. That left them with forty-odd, plus whatever they could bring forward – perhaps thirty – plus a dwindling group of highly skilled pilots. In my view they were going to have to be bloody careful.

Not, however, as bloody careful as we had to be, since we already had less than twenty Sea Harriers, which, apart from providing air cover now, were going to have to provide air defence for the islands for months after the land battle completed. It was going to take a considerable while to get the Port Stanley runway up to the length and standards required to operate RAF Phantoms from it. We were also heavily reliant on our two battered Sea Wolf Type 22 frigates because with only one more Type 22 as yet in service in the whole Fleet, there were far too few replacements available.

The pattern was now clear. The war had developed, at this stage, into a prize fight between the Royal Navy and General Galtieri's Air Forces. Who's winning right at that moment? Not us, I fear. However, unlike the Args, I was about to send one of our pawns into their back line to give me a new Queen. Its name was of course Rapier, the land-forces' guided-missile system which I had been led to believe was well able to provide a real anti-aircraft 'umbrella' over the whole San Carlos area. Though only what was called a 'point defence system', it was similar in range and visual-guidance capability to Sea Wolf – pretty effective in a confined area like Carlos Water, I might reasonably hope. COMAW and I were relying on this to take some of the weight off the destroyers and frigates within three days of the first landing. All day, on the twenty-first, the soldiers had been battling to ready the launchers, as the helicopters ferried in the big heavy components and the lethal (I hoped) missiles themselves. It seemed to me that as the Rapier batteries were set up, the relative attrition rate would move dramatically in our favour. If the Args were to send in another fifty sorties today, we might expect to be more successful than we were yesterday. By Day Three we should have a safe haven for the ships in Carlos Water, or at least a 'death trap' for the opposition.

Which leads us to the question I had to ask myself, and

answer, on a daily basis: can I recommend that we continue to fight this war, that our losses are militarily acceptable? Right now the answer was, yes. But the outcome is as yet undecided, and the future contains reasonable hope of significant improvement, courtesy of Rapier. The Harriers are performing superbly, by any standards, and our technique of vectoring them in, guiding them on to the fleeing Args' aircraft from the Ops Rooms of the frigates, is also working very well, as long as the ships stay afloat – though I do wish that Sea Wolf would strike home more often. Our entire performance is rather hanging upon that of the Harriers, which have so far been excellent *only* because the Args do not seem to have sent in any high-level escorts to take them on while their bombers do their business below. Also we are fortunate that the Harriers 'airfields' are still unharmed. I still have to worry that the Args *must* soon come after *Hermes* and *Invincible* in a more determined way; and remember that the consequence of that could be the loss of half our fixed wing air force at a stroke – I am under the clearest instructions from my CTF not to put either carrier at serious risk of major damage. I also have to worry that they must surely soon wake up to the fact that fighter escorts engaging the Sea Harriers up above will cut down the losses being inflicted upon their bombers.

On Day Two, 22 May, COMAW and I had resolved to minimize the number of transport ships in the inshore area and to range our warships into a tighter defensive pattern concentrated in San Carlos Water itself. This was specifically to protect the landing beaches and such amphibious ships as had to remain. With plenty of conflicting advice, I also decided to send *Coventry* up front to form a 42/22 missile trap with *Broadsword* off the north coast of West Falkland. I edged the Battle Group further forward, trying to balance the risk of putting *Hermes* and *Invincible* well within range of Argentinian Etendard/Exocet attack against the advantage of gaining extra time for the Harriers on CAP over the AOA.

By now I was making notes in my diary for most of the day, rather than filling it out at night, and on 22 May I began as follows:

> Dispositions made and another critical day lies ahead. The Args lost fifteen or so aircraft yesterday, by having no escorts for their attacks. That policy [of theirs] could change today. Bearing in mind that their max effort [yesterday] . . . may have set them back at least for a day or so.
>
> Equally it may cause them to [start sending] escort against our Combat Air Patrols, which scored most of our successes. *Brilliant* and *Broadsword* accounting for two, possibly three, only, despite being frequently 'surrounded' by circling attackers. Meanwhile HMS *Exeter* [the Type 42 guided-missile destroyer under the command of Captain Hugh Balfour] will be with us before dawn.

By 0700 we had received word of an Argentinian shadower coming within eight miles of *Coventry*. Captain Hart-Dyke's Ops Room had not fired their missile, which confirmed once more that we could never really *count* on the effectiveness of this weapon. When we heard that *Coventry* had been unable to fire, I was moved to write in the diary the words, 'I despair. The GWS 30 [Sea Dart] system appears to be totally unreliable. Altogether we are in a fairly desperate situation until Rapier comes good. After yesterday's dusting we do have the capability and the will to continue. No vital part of our capability has been lost (yet). But we still have a very long way to go before we can be sure the back of the Arg air force is broken.'

A short while afterwards it did become apparent that *Coventry*'s Ops Room had spotted the Argentinian Boeing and had indeed 'locked on' efficiently, but disaster struck as the Sea Dart missiles were coming up from the magazine to the launcher: the flash doors jammed, crusted up with salt from the heavy sea which had been breaking over the destroyer's bow for most of the night. You will remember that when I recounted the saga of *Glasgow* being hit ten days previously, Captain Hoddinott's Sea Dart had failed because a micro-switch was crusted over with salt after a night in a big sea. You may also recall I said that tomorrow if not the switch, then it will be something else. Well, tomorrow it was . . . a flash door crusted up. *Why?* That's what I wanted to know. Type 42s cost close to £200 million to build. How come whenever they went out in a big sea for a period of several hours their main weapons system crashed immediately afterwards because water is rushing in where it plainly ought not to be? I knew from my own time in *Sheffield* that the 42s were not as fast as they should be, that they were unreasonably slow in a short swell, with their bows slamming into the waves rather than splitting them to each side cleanly. Even in those days, it had seemed to me the waves were landing on the foredeck too steeply and too short, breaking downwards, on to the top of the Sea Dart launcher system. But the consequences had not been obvious then – now they were. (I resolved to look into this further, if and when we got home. It transpired much as I feared: the bow had 'happened' rather than been designed – and the problem was eventually cured for future T42s with a completely new shape.)

*   *   *

By first light there were, according to our estimates in the Battle Group, five battalions of Marines and Paras dug in on the eastern shores of Carlos Water. There were batteries of Blowpipes and Rapiers ready to open fire on the incoming Argentinian aircraft. The weather was a bit gloomy, which we thought might discourage them from coming at all today, but we were ready for anything. A wandering Arg coast guard/ supply ship found this out when a Harrier swooped down from fifteen thousand feet, strafed it, started fires on board and caused it to run aground in Choiseul Sound.

During the morning, it cleared somewhat around the AOA, but it remained very cloudy over the mainland and I would guess the Args thought it was the same for us. They launched no serious attacks all day and we were very glad of the respite. The busiest spots in all of the South Atlantic must have been the flight decks of *Hermes* and *Invincible*, from which we launched a total of sixty combat air patrols, ten more than we did on D-Day. Also that morning we were glad to welcome some important reinforcements: the *Exeter*, a vital replacement for *Sheffield*; two Type 21s, HMS *Ambuscade* and HMS *Antelope*; and a despatch vessel from Rosyth, HMS *Leeds Castle*. By the end of the day, the final good news was that both *Glasgow* and *Argonaut* were also in much better shape.

During the night the wind swung south, cleared the clag off the Argentinian coast and at first light we sent up four Harriers to bomb one of their airstrips on West Falkland. They found no Args, but with a stroke of fortune they located a second helicopter base, blew up three Arg Pumas and burnt one Augusta 109 close to Shag Cove inlet. That just about cleared half the Args' serviceable helicopter assets in the Islands by Day 3. We were quite pleased with ourselves, too pleased perhaps. It seems we forgot to tell COMAW, so he thought we weren't even trying.

Nothing much happened until 1600 when they finally came at us with a formation of Skyhawks, flying very low and very fast off the coast of West Falkland. *Antelope*, under Commander Nick Tobin, took the brunt of this raid, the first of the enemy bombers hitting the newly arrived frigate with a thousand-pounder six feet above the starboard waterline right below the hangar. The Skyhawk hit *Antelope*'s mast in passing, but was then blown away by a Sea Wolf from Bill Canning's *Broadsword*, recently returned from her stint with *Coventry* up to the north-west.

The raid pressed on in, the second Skyhawk again hitting the luckless *Antelope* with another thousand-pounder which smashed into the frigate's port side, right below the bridge. Like the first, it did not explode, but it devastated the Petty Officers' Mess. Miraculously there was only one man dead and one wounded, but the fires were pretty nasty and one of the bombs had come to rest in the air-conditioning unit and was thus surrounded by dangerous toxic gas. Also the gyros had failed and the lighting system had gone, but *Antelope* could still move and she could still shoot.

In the next ninety minutes eight more Skyhawks came in. They attacked *Broadsword*, *Antelope* and *Yarmouth* to no avail. All the Args bombs missed and they came under withering fire from the ships and from the Rapier batteries ashore. I have no doubt that some of the aircraft were damaged but they all escaped.

Half an hour later three more Daggers came in, but a Harrier shot one of them down, which I noted, with some satisfaction, made a total of seven Daggers downed out of the twenty-one launched at us. That's a one-third casualty rate and I was reasonably sure they could not put up with that for long. We also had reports that they had sent in a couple of Super Etendards which had arrived at a point north of Stanley, strangely saw nothing of the Battle Group, which was up that way too, and went home to Rio Grande.

By the end of the afternoon, *Argonaut*'s boiler room bomb had been made safe and the two Royal Engineers bomb disposal experts, Warrant Officer Phillips and Staff Sergeant Prescott boarded *Antelope* to try to deal with the bomb in the air conditioner. It was a dangerous situation and the ship's company was ordered to gather up on the fo'c'sle and on the flight deck in the now freezing weather, while the work proceeded. At 2015 the two Sappers set and prepared to detonate a small defusing charge, but the whole bomb suddenly exploded, killing the Staff Sergeant and badly injuring Warrant Officer Phillips, who later lost an arm.

At this point *Antelope* became an inferno, the fire sweeping through all three of her decks, fanned by the near gale-force wind. The fire mains were ruptured, the blaze was totally out of control anyway, *and* there was still another unexploded bomb lodged in her hull. Commander Tobin and his first lieutenant ordered the ship to be abandoned and ten minutes after the last man left, the main Sea Cat and torpedo magazine blew up, providing one photographer with quite the most spectacular picture of the entire war. Commander Tobin, on board *Fearless*, watched her burn for much of the night, until finally the second bomb went off, blowing his ship in half. She sank into the icy waters with her bow and stern jutting skywards.

I suppose the day belonged to us – just – with four choppers, one Skyhawk and two Daggers on our score sheet, but I deeply regretted the loss of *Antelope*. I don't know quite why – perhaps because they had only just arrived, because somehow they never had a chance to show what they could do – but it upset me and I was feeling a bit low that evening. To cap my day of rain, it now came on to pour. Shortly after 2200 we launched four Sea Harriers to bomb Port Stanley and I stood on my little bridge to watch them go.

One by one they rushed off into the dark and I was still watching for a short while after the last had gone when I saw a ball of fire low down on the horizon. For a moment I thought one of the ships had been hit. I remember thinking, '*Christ! They've got Brilliant.*' Well, they had not done that, but the news was still bad. Lieutenant-Commander Gordon Batt's Harrier had gone in. He was one of the few Harrier pilots I knew. No trace was ever found of him or his aircraft, though John Coward searched all night for Gordon's Harrier. We owed him at least that – he had flown thirty missions for us. When the task became hopeless the Ops Room of *Brilliant* let us know the worst. John did not contact me himself because he did not want his staff or anyone else to see him that upset. He was a good friend of Gordon's – their children were at the same school back in England, eight thousand miles away from this miserable place.

I sat down to write my diary that night with much on my mind, almost all of it to do with the placement of the warships. We had been attacked by a total of fifteen Argentinian aircraft on this day not including the Super Etendards. Sea Wolf got one, a Harrier splashed another, Rapier hit nothing. Hmmmm. That was not exactly what I had planned for. It was now clear that I had to give the Harriers every possible chance with the carriers as far forward as I dared bring them. It also seemed to me that the missilemen in the Ops Room of *Broadsword* were critical to the safety of the landing forces and the burgeoning beach-head. And yet I had to provide them with some early warning, which meant putting *Coventry* out there in the open ocean with her long-range radar open to the south-west, from where the Args would come. But I could not leave her out there alone without a Sea Wolf frigate: *Brilliant* was still under repair, which left *Broadsword* badly needed in two places simultaneously. I tried to clarify things in my mind and cast aside the serious worry that Rapier might not work any better tomorrow than it did today – and my sorrow that Gordon Batt was dead.

I wrote my diary carefully:

> Feeling a bit hassled. Support of Amphibious Operating Area requires me well forward; long-term maintenance of carriers requires me well back; provision of in/out convoys requires me somewhere in the middle. This week, I guess I have to be up front and hope to get away with it, but I must get clear at the first opportunity. The only solution I can see is to get the AOA's missile defences on top line and then run the Sea Harriers from a forward base – *in* the AOA, as best we can. The aviators won't like it.
>
> Meanwhile another day of split aims faces me. Had to withdraw the missile trap and let COMAW keep *Broadsword* for another day. But don't know what to do for forward radar tomorrow, since I don't feel I can send a Type 42 destroyer up there [alone] with any real hope of avoiding a very big bang.

I then had a rather rambling gripe about spurious contacts causing a lot of wasted chaff and another about the carefree way certain officers were prepared to treat our aircraft. I finished by recording sadly, for posterity, 'A Sea Harrier (Lt Cdr Batt) low over water, burned bright orange for three seconds, then snuffed out.'

I went to bed and managed to sleep the sleep which descends mercifully upon a troubled mind. As I did so *Coventry* set off once more to rendezvous with *Broadsword* and to take up their highly dangerous position to the north of Pebble Island. It was a position which pleased no one. Captain David Hart-Dyke was another of my officers from a family with dark blue naval blood. His father Commander Eric Hart-Dyke fought the U-Boats in the Second World War destroyer *Gallant* – his personal telescope lived now in his son's locker in the Captain's cabin in *Coventry*. David's wife Diana bore the well-known naval name of Luce, both her grandfathers being admirals, one of whom in 1914 commanded the light cruiser HMS *Glasgow*, the only British ship to escape the German Far East Squadron under Vice-Admiral Graf von Spee at the disastrous Battle of Coronel. They fought him again at the Battle of the Falkland Islands a few weeks later, but this time with a far superior force which included our battle-cruisers *Invincible* and *Inflexible*. All but one – *Dresden* – of von Spee's entire squadron were sunk, with awful loss of life, including the German Admiral and his two sons. Diana's other grandfather Admiral Napier was the first Captain of Dartmouth, her uncle was Admiral Sir David Luce, and her brother Richard Luce, Minister of State of the Foreign Office, had resigned over the Falklands, with Lord Carrington, a few months before. And now Diana, with their two very young daughters Alice and Miranda, waited at home in Hampshire while David took *Coventry* out to what he believed was a 'suicidal' position in the turbulent waters to the north of West Falkland.

The trouble was, *Coventry* and *Broadsword* were trying to accomplish two distinct, and different tasks: firstly, to warn the inshore warships of approaching Argentinian attack aircraft and to guide the British Harriers on to them; and secondly, to take out the raiders with Sea Dart at long-range over the open ocean between the Argentinian mainland and the Falklands. *Broadsword*'s Sea Wolf was there to provide close-in cover for *Coventry*.

David Hart-Dyke would have preferred to stay well out where they had the best chance of hitting any Args that came at them, but then they would have been too far out for good radio contact with the inshore ships, which was one of their prime jobs and, worse, Sea Dart would not have been able to reach the Args on their way to and from the AOA. Bill Canning felt they should patrol about twelve miles off the coast, where they would be in good radio contact, but David's radar and Sea Dart systems would be far less effective in self defence. Bill was, however, confident that his Sea Wolf would do all that was needed to protect the two ships, leaving Sea Dart to shoot at 'passers by'.

This was no easy decision. My instincts were that if they were to be effective in defence of the AOA, as opposed to just bystanders awaiting attack at the enemy's leisure, *Coventry* and *Broadsword* must operate as best they could fairly close to the north coast, despite the very real risks. As I slept, that's where they were headed.

Dawn brought with it clear weather over Carlos Water and, unknown to us, the Argentinian High Command was planning a major blitz upon the landing area, still crowded with ships busily unloading. *Coventry* and *Broadsword* were on their dangerous station with lines already opened up to the Harriers which circled above. The radar operators in David Hart-Dyke's Ops Room were glued to their screens. Lieutenant-Commander Mike O'Connell, his senior Air Warfare Officer, was in near-perpetual conference with the Principal Warfare Officer Lieutenant Clive Gwilliam. Sub-Lieutenant Andy Moll, the Fighter Controller, was murmuring on his direct link to the British pilots above.

Altogether the Arg commanders were planning to hit us with seventeen fighter-attack bombers: two waves of Skyhawks, one of six, one of three, plus two waves of four Daggers apiece. Also they planned to change direction, sending the majority in from the south-east, over the land and straight down the narrow bay to the British anchorage. That of course is strictly hindsight, gathered from years of study by many people, but it will make it much easier for you to follow these air–sea actions if you understand precisely what was on the enemy's mind, as we most certainly did not.

The first formation of five Skyhawks (I am uncertain where the planned sixth was) came spearing across the Lafonia flat-lands in the south-east at 1245. The Paras up on the Sussex Mountains saw them first and sounded a warning, but there were only seconds left and the Args came tearing in, bombing *Sir Galahad* with a thousand-pounder, hitting *Sir Lancelot* with another, and putting a third straight through the upperworks of *Sir Bedivere*. None of those bombs went off; bad fusing again, fortunately.

Within fifteen minutes four Daggers came in the same way. The Paras again sounded the alert and the British ships met them with an onslaught of fire from every available gun in the fleet. Seacat and Rapier missiles streaked into the sky, but they could not stop the raiders. The Args strafed *Fearless* and *Sir Galahad*, in which fires had broken out under the vehicle deck. They again bombed *Sir Lancelot* where the damage-control teams were trying to fight the fires in the thankfully empty troop-accommodation area. *Fort Austin*, *Norland*, and *Stromness* were all near-missed by bombs which exploded in the water. All the Args aircraft were hit, three of them virtual write-offs, but despite the many subsequent claims by the British missile operators – Blowpipe, Rapier, Sea Wolf and Seacat – the Args all made it home and we were none the wiser.

The last formation of Argentinian Daggers, however, made a fatal mistake, swinging round and coming in from the north-west. *Coventry*'s Ops Room caught them on their radar, vectored the Harriers on to them and Lieutenant-Commander Andy Auld blew two of them out of the sky with his Sidewinders, as Lieutenant Smith wiped out another with his. Three more Daggers gone – that's ten out of twenty-seven. The empty places round the Argentinian mess table that night must have devastated morale.

The final Argentinian wave of three Skyhawks ran into another furious barrage of gun and missile fire from the British ships and land forces in the anchorage of San Carlos Water. *Norland*, from whose upper deck one thousand two hundred rounds of rifle fire were aimed, was certain a Rapier had struck home and the volume of fire from *Fearless*, under Captain Jeremy Larken, was as hot as usual. The three Arg pilots, however, did get away, which presented a rather confusing picture, given the certainty with which the British defenders reported their hits. As it turned out, one of the Skyhawks later crashed into St George's Bay and the other two were complete write-offs. But we of course did not know that. Neither did we know that as night fell over San Carlos Water the Royal Navy had already defeated the Air Forces of Argentina. The damage inflicted upon those sixteen aircraft which had pressed home their attacks was really unacceptable by any standards and their High Command would in the next few hours arrive at much the same conclusions that their naval colleagues had reached twenty-two days ago – that an out-and-out battle with the Royal Navy is not a particularly appealing idea ... that the price of the Malvinas is becoming too high. I subsequently learned that what we had called 'Bomb Alley' was now rechristened 'Death Valley' by the Argentinians. They would of course return to the attack, but never in great numbers, never as an air-armada as they had done today and yesterday and on 21 May.

We, in *Hermes*, were entirely ignorant of all this. Indeed we expected them back in full force tomorrow and the day after, and next week. But I think my diary gives some indication of my personal state of mind and my own doubts as to the wisdom of the Arg tactics. It also shows precisely what we *thought* they were doing at that time. These are extracts from the page which recorded the events of Monday 24 May:

Argentinian Air Force has to be in a bad way. They put up 46-odd aircraft on Saturday. Virtually nothing on Sunday, and some 23 or so (only 17 came into the AOA) today. They lost 15 or so on Saturday and nine today. I find it hard to believe they have many aircraft or pilots left. COMAW reported today's aircraft as real kamikazes – so they are probably young braves who don't know any better. Truly, a terrible business and I can only hope the Args stop soon.

It is increasingly apparent how easy it is to lose control. I was fairly desperate on the 21st, but yesterday's events were not quite so bad ... the basic facts are that the Arg Air Force has to be depleted by attrition. And the only force we have, which can afford it, is the destroyers and frigates.

The Args have got it wrong with their anti-escort

(if that is what it is – as opposed to a [simple] hit-what-you-see) policy.

By 1530 it begins to emerge that the Args have noticed they have got it wrong and they are now concentrating on the amphibious ships. Somehow they got a dozen aircraft together and sent them in. One empty LSL badly hit. The ammo LSL has an unexploded bomb on her stern – three Mirage and four Skyhawks splashed in the process [based on earliest reports].

Where are they getting the volunteers? What on earth do we do with this unexploded bomb after *Antelope*'s – the one that finally went off – killing the defuser?

I glanced at my watch and noticed it was coming up to midnight. Tomorrow would be 25 May – Argentina National Day ... perhaps the very day for a comeback for Admiral Anaya's men who had vanished, more or less, with the *General Belgrano*. I tried to think about the South American character and its reputation for exuberant behaviour, and what that might entail for us. Study of the psychology of your opponent is an essential part of war. Unfortunately South American habit is one of the many aspects of human psychology about which I am profoundly ignorant. But still, it would be a fine, daredevil counter-stroke for them to play – bringing out their carrier *Veintecinco de Mayo* and launching a co-ordinated attack on *Hermes* and *Invincible* to celebrate such an important day. Win *or* lose, it would go down in their history books as their 'finest hour'.

Yes, well, that's as maybe. So I had better make sure we are on top form tomorrow. I am horribly afraid that that is going to mean sending *Coventry* and *Broadsword* back out to their little missile trap, just twelve miles off-shore, ready to guide the Harriers, which had once more recorded the only definite 'kills' of the day, and they had done it working in tandem with *Coventry*.

I pored over the charts for a while longer, tried to assess where the Arg carrier might show, and eventually decided to leave *Coventry* more or less where she had been in order to guard the northern and western approaches. I also tried to assess what I might do, if I was wearing Argentinian boots, and generally I thought I might sneak the *Veintecinco de Mayo* right down south to act as a recovery platform for the Etendards, which could then strike at us from the south-east of the TEZ. Yes, that is what I *would* do ... try to skirt the British long-range radar and get in quick, from a new direction, without having the problem of in-flight refuelling. That would be a clever plan, one just bold enough to succeed.

You cannot play chess without a plan which takes account of the immediate future and as such I attempted to work out my response. The answer of course rested with the submarines. On the five per cent chance that Admiral Anaya was following my exact train of thought, I decided to signal Northwood with a request to move a submarine – my preference was for *Conqueror* – to guard those southern waters and to sink the Arg carrier if it came within range. The Flag Officer Submarines in London did not agree with what he felt was my over-reaction to an unlikely worst-case scenario. This further reduced my confidence in their ability to do what was required to win this war. They seemed so separate, so damned strategic. This was a subject in which I was well-qualified to have a view – so I stumped back to my diary and wrote angrily one last line: 'THERES JUST F*** ALL FLEXIBILITY THERE.'

I don't expect they cared much what I thought – as I said before, both the C-in-C and FOSM were ex-submariners, like I was, and they were both senior to me. As it soon turned out, they were proved right as well, which was doubly irritating. But it still remains the job of the man in the front line to plan to deal with the worst, as well as the most likely, things that can happen.

It also looked as if I had finally lost *Glasgow*, with her precious long-range radar. I had a signal from Paul Hoddinott telling me he had, at this moment, his head down in one of his two remaining engines. I decided that his war was, for the moment, over. I sent him a signal, thanking him for all he had done and instructing him to 'toddle off home' and get his ship into working order. With immense reluctance he agreed to do so. I would miss his steadfast professionalism from the moment he turned *Glasgow* north up the Atlantic the next morning.

Meanwhile there was a stream of new warships due to join us in the next couple of days – steaming in from the north-east were two more guided-missile destroyers, the 7000-ton Type 82 HMS *Bristol* with Sea Dart and under the command of Captain Alan Grose, and the Type 42 HMS *Cardiff*, commanded by yet another ex-submariner Captain Mike Harris. There were two Leander Class frigates, sister ships to *Argonaut* – HMS *Minerva* and HMS *Penelope*; plus *Andromeda*, the broad-beamed Leander armed with Sea Wolf and Exocet under Captain Jim Weatherall. There were also another two Type 21s coming in, HMS *Active* and HMS *Avenger*, plus another couple of big oilers, *Olna* and *Bayleaf*, accompanied by *Fort Austin*'s sister supply ship, *Fort Grange*.

From where I sat they were more than welcome, since at this stage we were losing warships at a fairly high rate – and I had no reason, at present, to hope for any improvement. By now I did believe that we were winning this war of attrition – just – but I would have felt a great deal happier about it if Rapier could have demonstrated a solid ability to knock Argentinian aircraft out of the sky, no ifs, ands or buts. But so far that had not happened. We were keeping the Args at bay with a combination of desperate gun and missile fire from anything that would shoot, together with the accuracy and reliability of the American Sidewinder missiles from beneath the wings of the Harriers.

All of which was not much comfort to Captain David Hart-Dyke and his men, arriving before first light, in company with *Broadsword* out in their exposed position twelve miles north of Pebble Island. By now this was undoubtedly the most alert British ship in the Fleet. Sailors are not stupid and they know true danger when it threatens. They can sense it, everyone in the ship can – in the commands that are broadcast inside the ship, in the speed with which people react, in the near-hypersense of urgency which exists, at all levels. Imminent risk of explosion, fire and death is a sure way of concentrating the mind. Each man has a different way of dealing with it: Captain Hart-Dyke was personally very realistic and very brave. He recognized the danger and *Coventry*'s possible helplessness under attack and he faced it all with a steely resignation. There was perhaps a shade of acceptance in his soul, given his and his wife's historic naval background, but perhaps that is the highest form of courage there is. David had been in the very front line of this war since the first day: *Coventry* had been out there in the same three-ship picket line when *Sheffield* was hit and they had essentially been there ever since. David knew that some of his men were frightened. He spoke to them often in his easy, slightly laconic way, encouraging them repeatedly, telling them that *Coventry* was a 'lucky ship' – that they'd always got away with it and within a couple of weeks it would all be over . . . 'Don't worry, we'll get through it . . .'

Just two days before, Petty Officer Burke, an Irishman who knew the captain, had presented him with an ancient, 2000-year-old prayer to Saint Joseph which, according to Gaelic legend, would keep safe from war and drowning those who carried it with them. Captain Hart-Dyke read it to *Coventry*'s ship's company at the church service on Sunday 23 May, then, superstitious like most sailors, he placed it in his pocket.

It was still there on the morning of 25 May which saw *Coventry*'s crew, as ever, in hard training, going over the routines and drills to deal with air attack. To David Hart-Dyke's great satisfaction his men were able to accomplish in four minutes flat '*Damage control – state one!*' (shutting and clipping home all doors and all hatches, and preparing ship's systems in readiness to fight major fire and flooding). This often takes twice as long. *Coventry* was good, no doubt about that. Good and battle hardened, with a captain and his team very much on high alert, because in the place they were operating nothing less would do, as the company of *Sheffield* had discovered.

During the morning there was once more discussion between the two captains David Hart-Dyke and the more senior Bill Canning as to whether *Coventry* ought not to move out into more distant waters in order to maximize the efficiency of Sea Dart. But Captain Canning agreed with me: the communications were more important – a fact accentuated by yesterday's performance when they had vectored the Harriers into making three brilliant 'kills' against the Arg Daggers. Bill added, in that calm, confident way he has, that he would ensure that *Broadsword* did all of the necessary fast manoeuvring and that *Coventry* could proceed, assured that the swift Type 22 would get into more or less the right spot for both attack and defence. 'Just make absolutely sure, David, that you do not increase speed when I'm trying to get by,' was Bill's careful instruction to the younger commander.

There was nevertheless, I believe, a slight feeling in the Type 42 that they were 'the forgotten ship' – left out there to accomplish a thankless task which might very well end in their being sunk. Not true. I was thinking of them constantly, trying to remain in touch whenever possible, but what Captain Hart-Dyke and his men really wanted was a major success with their Sea Dart system.

At 1130Z that morning (0830 for the Args), they got it. A small formation of Skyhawks was circling out over the Atlantic to the west in readiness for a run-in over West Falkland to attack the British anchorage. *Broadsword* picked them up and, working through the data link to *Coventry*'s computers, enabled Captain Hart-Dyke's Ops Room to 'see' the target. Moments later *Coventry*'s AWO confirmed the 909 radar was locked on, flashing 'VALID TARGET'.

'*Take it with sea dart!*' commanded Hart-Dyke, and the destroyer briefly shuddered as the guided missile blasted into the sky. Within the minute the missile reached its target. On the upper deck the missile gun director (visual) saw the Sky-hawk break up in the crystalline air and everyone in *Coventry* felt, as the captain later recalled, a great deal better about the world in general.

The next Argentinian raid came in three hours later, four more Skyhawks screaming in over East Falkland and rushing north up Carlos Water. Tony Morton's *Yarmouth* went into action instantly and destroyed one of them with his Seacat missile. The other three stayed on their course, dropped their bombs sufficiently clear of any of our ships and were picked up on *Broadsword*'s radar as they crossed the narrows. *Coventry* had them immediately on the 909 and once more Captain Hart-Dyke's men launched Sea Dart. Their second missile of the day destroyed a Skyhawk and understandably caused a feeling of confidence among the destroyer's 'forgotten men'. David Hart-Dyke spoke to the ship's company, telling them again what a 'lucky ship' they were, even though he was personally very worried about how hopeless his own radars were against aircraft coming in over the land – precisely the same problem Captain Hoddinott had experienced in *Glasgow* on 12 May. Nonetheless *Broadsword* was certainly doing her job and, after all, her Sea Wolf missiles had thus far proved very useful indeed with two, possibly three 'kills' of her own to credit.

At this stage it was beginning to seem as though the 42/22 missile trap was working, although I too was extremely conscious of the difficulties Captain Hart-Dyke and Captain Canning were having in spotting the enemy aircraft when they overflew the land. From where the Arg commanders stood they must have thought the Ops Rooms of *Broadsword* and *Coventry* were manned by the very devil. Between them the two ships had been responsible for the destruction of *five* aircraft in two days, in addition to their former successes. Which is why, I suppose, they made a formal decision to eliminate them both, once and for all, using whatever aircraft they had left. The Spanish-speaking officer in *Coventry* tuned in to the Arg radio frequencies actually heard them finalizing the plan. It was taken as rather a compliment that the Args thought it would take six Skyhawks to 'get that Type 42 out there'.

The captain told the crew with a natural drollness that it would take more aircraft than the Args had – 'Stay sharp, and remember again, we're a lucky ship.' Privately David thought it was entirely possible that this time *Coventry* might take a real hit. He also thought to himself, 'If we can just get through today, we'll survive the war.'

At 1700 six Skyhawks of 5th Air Brigade took off from Rio Gallegos, heading due east to make their rendezvous with their Hercules tanker to re-fuel. As usual this went slightly wrong for them and only four went on forward with full tanks. They risked flying, for once, in the 'middle air' and were picked up by Navy radar one hundred miles due south-west of Carlos Water. They must have known this because they immediately split into two pairs. Harriers were sent out to meet them, but they dived instantly, spearing up the south coast of West Falkland. They rushed low over the land and we 'saw' them again on the coast of the Sound. All the ships in the anchorage stood by to take the bombing attack, but the Args suddenly swerved again, heading *inland* over West Falkland.

Broadsword picked up the first two, but missed the second pair, as *Coventry* went to Action Stations at 1800. They alerted the Harriers from *Hermes* now heading in towards the narrows. Then *Coventry*'s AWO called out, 'We'll pick the raid up on 909 in a few seconds. They will already be within Sea Dart range!'

'*Call the Harriers off!*' ordered Captain Hart Dyke. 'They may be too far away, and Sea Dart will take them from here.'

But the 909, confused by the land, did not lock on. The first two Skyhawks, only twenty feet above the water, tucked behind Pebble Island, suddenly rocketed out from behind the headland into open water – some fifty seconds away from *Coventry* and *Broadsword*. Still the 909 did not acquire. On the upper deck *Coventry*'s visual gun director actually saw the planes and opened fire immediately with the 4.5-inch gun. In *Broadsword*'s Ops Room they had Sea Wolf locked on, ready to fire automatically, but the Arg aircraft were flying wing-to-wing. Sea Wolf's radar computer hesitated, deciding perhaps that two close targets were not its business and refused to fire. It swung away forty or fifty degrees, looking for a 'phantom target'. *Broadsword*'s AWO shouted to override the system, the missile director's fingers flew over the keys, but it was already too late. The scenario was just the same as it had been in *Brilliant* thirteen days previously. The Sea Wolf launchers had switched back to their stowed positions.

The aircraft swung away from the destroyer and made directly for *Broadsword* dropping four thousand-pound bombs, one of which fell short, with two others flying over the top, a few feet above the bridge. The fourth bomb ricocheted off the sea, smashing its way straight through the frigate's starboard side aft, five feet above the waterline. It crashed upwards through the flight deck, wrecking the Lynx helicopter before plunging over the side. The frigate's damage-control team hurried into action while a computer engineer wrestled frantically with the Sea Wolf software. How could they fight when the missile would not fire? Bill Canning required every ounce of cunning and control he possessed after a lifetime in the Royal Navy to hold his team together.

The situation in *Coventry*'s Ops Room was equally terrifying. They knew *Broadsword* was hit, but they also knew there were two more Arg aircraft out there, looking for *Coventry*. But they had no idea from which direction the attack would come. Or when. The captain likened it to standing in a pitch-black cellar waiting to be hit on the head. As it was, he watched the clock, praying for it to go faster, praying for the moment when night would fall, when he knew the Args would go home. There was a running commentary now going on in *Coventry*'s Ops Room as all of the operators searched for the tell-tale dots on the screens which would betray the Skyhawks.

Suddenly they had them – 'out of the north-west' – then

they lost them – then they had them again – 'now from the north-east'. The talk was becoming desperate. 'Where are they?' 'Which way? Which way? ... *for Christ's sake, which way?*'

And then there was a sudden, dreadful silence. Everyone had simply run out of ideas. And as the silence enveloped the beleaguered Ops Room of the Type 42, the two Argentinian Skyhawks hurtled out from behind Pebble Island, racing low over the water, coming straight at Captain David Hart-Dyke's ship. On the upper deck, even the cooks and stewards had been given small arms to fire at the enemy pilots.

Broadsword's Ops Room did not see them immediately, but a roar of '*Here they come again!*' echoed down the intercom from the upper deck.

Then, from the bridge, 'Aircraft – red two-zero!'

Simultaneously the engineer shouted, 'Sea Wolf working again.'

Bill Canning permitted himself a grim smile, as his AWO snapped, 'Sea Wolf locked on.'

The two Skyhawks were now less than half a minute out. *Coventry*'s 909s still would not lock-on – Sea Dart was impotent, it couldn't see the Skyhawks against the land behind. Captain Hart-Dyke ordered the bridge to alter course to starboard, trying to improve the situation. *Coventry* continued her turn, unaware that she was presenting her bow, not her beam, to the Skyhawks. I was on the line to Bill Canning, as he calmly told me what had already happened and called his temperamental Sea Wolf once more into action. Suddenly he said, 'Just a moment, Admiral.' Then I heard him quietly say, 'Oh my God!'

A missile director's most appalling dread had taken place. *Coventry* had slewed across the path of the Sea Wolf missile launcher. *Broadsword* was comprehensively 'wooded'. She could not fire without hitting the *Coventry*. And now it really was too late. Through the hail of hundreds of bullets from the upper-decks, the Arg pilots held a true line on *Coventry*'s bow. Taking hits from the small-calibre machine-gun fire as they came in, they released their four thousand-pound bombs in a dead straight line, just as the bombing manual instructs. Three of them went into David Hart-Dyke's ship and they all exploded, one of them in the Computer Room. Nineteen men were killed instantly.

David remembers not the impact, just the heat, and then he blacked out from the blast. Coming to, still in his Ops Room chair, he found himself in total darkness, in a room full of acrid choking smoke. Then he became conscious of light, flickering light, and to his horror he realized it was people burning, their clothes on fire, like screaming candles. 'I thought', he once told me, trembling again at the memory, 'that I had died and that this was, literally, Hell.' He was burned himself, his flash gear seared from his face and hands, and he struggled through the devastation of his 'office' to find a ladder. Clawing his way up, he ordered the ship to the north-east, unaware that *Coventry* was not going anywhere, never mind to the north-east. She was finished, her port side wide open, water rushing in, with an increasing list that would shortly cause her to capsize.

Most of the ship's senior command was either killed or wounded, and the evacuation was being handled by young sailors. 'I sat and watched them in complete amazement,' said the captain. 'They just went about their tasks sensibly and steadily. Some of them must have been scared out of their wits. And until the day I die those young men will always be my heroes.'

Finally with everyone taken off, Captain Hart-Dyke walked down the side of the ship and jumped into the sea swimming with his terribly burnt hands through the icy salt water. As he reached the life raft he felt big hands reach down and, mercifully, grab his wrists. And he found himself looking into the eyes of the keeper of St Joseph's prayer. 'There you are, sir,' said Petty Officer Burke with an Irish smile. 'It worked. I told you we'd be all right.'

On board *Broadsword* Captain Hart-Dyke reported to Captain Canning. Neither of them had had much luck in this engagement and the frigate captain spoke first. 'I'm sorry, David,' he said. 'I really am most terribly sorry.'

Neither of them had any wish to apportion blame. *Coventry*'s swing to her right had not, in hindsight, been very clever, but equally *Broadsword* was supposed to have been in charge. However, she had just been bombed, which ranks as a pretty serious distraction, and we have to put the loss of *Coventry* down to 'the fortunes of war'. She went down in three hundred feet of water within twenty minutes of the first hit, having capsized. Among many treasured possessions she took with her was Captain Eric Hart-Dyke's telescope which had survived Hitler's U-Boats. But over two hundred and sixty men were taken off and they left for England that night in *Fort Austin*. Twenty wounded men were treated in the hospital ship *Uganda* and in the field hospital at Ajax Bay.

I re-considered my earlier opinion that the 22/42 combination actually worked and decided that, upon reflection, it probably didn't. Not close to the shore anyway, and the tactic had now cost us both *Glasgow* and *Coventry*. And possibly *Broadsword*. But again, I could not allow myself to be affected by this dreadful loss of the last of the three Type 42s that had originally come south with me in April. After all, I thought, the Args just might decide that this was a pretty good time to have another shot at us and it was just as well that I reached this executive decision. Because they were not yet finished for the day, not by a long way. Even as I sat alone, reflecting upon the loss of *Coventry*, they were well on the way to hitting us again with the weapon which had destroyed *Sheffield* – Exocet.

ATLANTIC CONVEYOR

16

The Marines Will Have To Walk

The loss of HMS *Coventry*, the last of my original picket ships, weighed heavily upon me. I had lost an old and familiar friend. I stood once more alone in the glass-fronted Admiral's Bridge on that desolate afternoon staring out over the cold Atlantic, watching the always-busy deck of *Hermes* and cursing the world in general. Cursing specifically Argentina and her bloody National Day. It was *still* 25 May, as it had been, it seemed, to me, for about the last thousand hours. I glanced at my watch. It was a little after 1900Z, still another couple of hours of daylight left, and then several hours of uncertain darkness before it became, with any luck, 26 May.

I gazed at the sea, and pondered the many times I had stood here before; times when I had searched my own soul, wondering whether I should send the quietly spoken David Hart-Dyke into the most lethal spot on this most lethal southern ocean. Well, I suppose I had done it once too often and now the gallant *Coventry* was gone – small comfort for her captain to know that she had gone down fighting, in a manner which had conferred the greatest credit upon his crew and indeed had done his illustrious family proud. Doubtless as I stood there, he was resting in *Broadsword*, alone as he will always be, with the terrible visions of the last moments of his ship, of the fires, of the screams of the burning men, of lost friends, of the darkness and the helplessness. I doubt if it will ever be entirely erased from his sub-conscious, though in moments of sadness, he may perhaps find solace in the heroism and the selflessness demonstrated by the young men who fought with him, to the end. There is an aura of lasting, private glory about such disasters, understood, inevitably, only by those who were actually there.

In the last chapter I tried to concentrate the events of the day from the point of view of the ships which fought the action. But there is no doubt that from first light I had had a very distinct premonition that this was going to be an especially depressing few hours. I began my diary right after breakfast with an irritable diatribe about the weather, bemoaning our luck that since the landings, four days previously, we had been sitting out here under almost clear skies. Today we were in a slowly clearing fog, but it was bright over the mainland – the worst possible combination for us.

> The bad visibility around us should clear at about midday. The Args seldom arrive before 1300, so all may yet be well. Again though, the question arises of whether to take the carriers west into non-AAR range [Navy shorthand for an area where the Args fighter-bombers can reach us without having to refuel in the

air]. My answer, reinforced by our lack of escorts, is [again] no.

I have with us only two Type 21s, one Type 42, and one DLG [*Glamorgan*] (useless really), and *Brilliant* (not very fit). *Coventry* is up front in the missile trap with *Broadsword*. *Glasgow* is de-storing to the rear. *Bristol* won't be here till midnight and *Cardiff* is even further behind. COMAW is still unprepared to rely on Rapier and I can't say I blame him. Missile trap needed for better CAP direction meanwhile.

1200. This has all the signs of a disastrous day. COMAW has packed the stage with ships he can't possibly unload today, the 'missile trap' is in clear sky, and the carriers are in thick fog. Combat air patrol cannot be provided. The only thing to be thankful for is that this did not happen on Day One. And the only hope is that the Args have had enough for the moment, and perhaps their minds are on other things.

1300. It cleared and the CAP is up. Thank Heavens.

1600. The reports from the Amphibious Operating Area and the missile trap are various, but it sounds as though the Args have been into Carlos Water with A4s [Skyhawks] and Pucaras and lost several.

At about 1900 yet another bloody disaster. Three A4s apparently trundled in towards AOA over Pebble Island swerved north and bombed *Coventry* and *Broadsword*. *Coventry* badly hit and sinking. *Broadsword* probably not too badly, picking up survivors. No missiles fired – which is quite extraordinary and saps any faith we may have had in our modern systems, even against these previous-generation [Arg] aircraft.

Looking back all of these years later I realize that it was a terrible moment for me. One of those times when a commander has no one to whom he can turn, for fear of betraying uncertainty or wavering will-power. But I remember thinking to myself, 'Christ! Where are we? Are we actually *losing* this?' It was, without any question, thus far my lowest ebb of the whole operation. I walked back into my cabin and sat for a while alone. I opened my notebook and jotted down a few notes in the following coldly pessimistic mood:

1. The 42/22 combination does not work.

2. Sea Dart virtually useless against low fliers.

3. Sea Wolf unreliable.

4. Surface ships have to have Airborne Early Warning and Combat Air Patrol up-threat for survival in open water.

5. We must do much more rigorous multi-target trials of Anti-Air War systems.

6. Stick to night operations and/or bad weather.

7. They really must try to come for the carriers now!

That did not take me long and I went once more back out to the bridge, hoping that the view of the sea and sky would somehow clear my mind and allow my perspective and sense of clarity to return. I stood there for several minutes pondering our formation, pondering the likelihood of another Arg strike before dark.

At this moment *Hermes* was about four miles north of *Invincible*. John Coward in the improving *Brilliant* was keeping 'goal' for us and, ranged in a north–south line facing west, the fleet auxiliaries formed what I hoped was some kind of a 'chaff' wall in case of incoming threat. In the most brutal terms, I could afford to lose a big merchant ship, or even a tanker, a whole lot more than I could afford to lose a carrier – not that I thought very highly of either option. It was simply a matter of the lesser of two evils. Anyway, out in front I did have the newly arrived *Exeter* with her sharp Captain Hugh Balfour and her Sea Dart system with all the latest improvements.

The only area which I did find rather worrying was the position of the *Atlantic Conveyor*, stationed by me at the far north end of the line of the auxiliaries, on the 'disengaged' side from Rio Grande, home of the Etendards. This 18,000-ton Cunard roll-on-roll-off freighter was of incalculable value to us, for she still carried three of the big troop transport helicopters, the Chinooks (these priceless monsters can lift twelve tons) and five Wessex. She already had one Chinook and one Wessex in the air and had brought down the Atlantic from England fourteen Harriers wrapped in plastic bags and lashed down to her upper deck. They had been unwrapped, serviced and flown off as soon as *Conveyor* reached the Battle Group of course and were a critically important reinforcement for our dwindling Harrier force.

Atlantic Conveyor had two landing spots on her long 'flight deck'. Since her arrival several days ago she had been used virtually as a third aircraft carrier by the chopper pilots. She was still loaded to the gunwales with stores and ammunition including six hundred cluster bombs for the Harriers and *all* of the equipment we needed to construct an airstrip for Harriers in the beach-head area in Carlos Water. Her refitting, loading and preparation in Devonport had been a masterpiece of organization and in her cargo holds were most of the spares and support equipment for the land force helicopters. Her captain was a real old sea dog named Ian North, a York-shireman who had been twice sunk during the Second World War. All the way south from Liverpool he had made himself increasingly popular with the young seamen in his ship from both branches of the Navy, regaling them with stories of the sea and occasionally, late at night, to the delight of everyone, playing his trombone. When they 'crossed the line', the short, chunky Ian North, with his snowy beard, played the part, inevitably, of King Neptune.

The senior Royal Naval officer on board, Captain Mike Layard adored the old boy, for his humour, his complete professionalism and for his wisdom. He also admired him for his philosophical outlook, remembering that Captain North was probably the only senior officer who actually *knew* what it was like to be hit, possibly the only man in the entire operation who had no illusions about what to expect in the event of a bomb, missile or torpedo strike. Between them Captain Layard and Captain North made a just-about-perfect team. Indeed on a quick visit to *Hermes* a few days previously Captain Layard could not resist telling me of an incident which took place as they flew the tenth Harrier off the deck, vertically, for the short flight over to the carriers.

The pilot mistakenly had the jet nozzles facing slightly aft as well as down and when he opened up the throttle to lift off, the aircraft charged across the deck straight towards the guard rails. The pilot, with well-honed instinct for survival, slammed the nozzles to the vertical and the Harrier leaped into the air, clearing the guard rails with inches to spare. Men were already rushing for cover, but Captain North turned to Captain Layard and said, deadpan, 'Hmmmm. That's rather a novel way of doing it.'

We had deliberately retained the *Conveyor* back in the holding area until the very last moment, until the timing was exactly right for them to make a fast run into Carlos Water, unload as much as possible overnight with all speed, then get the hell out of there and back to the relative safety of the Battle Group. Well, tonight was the night and it had seemed reasonable to me to bring them forward into the Battle Group two hours early, exposing them to some small risk of air attack for a few daylight hours, but granting them more hours to unload in the dark. My alternative was to leave them in complete safety until dark, east of the Battle Group, and then let them run late into the AOA with the prospect of either a dangerous return trip in broad daylight or of spending the whole of the next day inshore in 'Bomb Alley'. Bearing in mind the fact that the Args had not launched a successful raid on the deep-water Battle Group out here since *Sheffield* was hit three weeks ago today, it seemed to me that the dark hours in Carlos Water were worth playing for ... especially as the *Conveyor* would be in ten times *more* danger parked in the Sound tomorrow morning possibly in bright sunlight – the quintessential sitting duck.

And so, earlier that morning I had ordered *Atlantic Conveyor* into the Battle Group, taking the precaution of stationing her at the likely 'safe' end of the line of auxiliaries while she waited for the light to fade before beginning her dark journey inshore. Captain North and Captain Layard had already ordered their white superstructure to be painted a dark matt grey for the hundred-mile voyage. Understandably, tension in the big container ship was extremely high; everyone preparing to make the last lap of the highly dangerous task with which they had been charged.

However, unknown to any of us, as I had pondered the world and made my notes, two Argentinian Etendards were making a long sweep north up from Rio Grande before heading slightly south of east for their final approach towards the Battle Group. They had gone a very long way out of their direct route in order to surprise us by coming in from the north-west. They had been refuelled and now, just as I returned to my cabin for the second time, shortly after 1830, they 'popped up' to look for us. They were about forty miles out. *Exeter* promply detected their radars on her UAA1 ESM, and issued a formal warning to the rest of the Battle Group. Within the minute, *Ambuscade*, the northern-most of our outer ring of escorts and pickets, picked them up on her own radar at twenty-four miles and *Brilliant*, further back, 'saw' them at twenty-eight miles. Roars of 'CHAFF!' echoed through the Ops Rooms. At 1838 the two Argentinians released their Exocets, both at the same 'blip', the first they came across – probably Commander Peter Mosse's Type 21 frigate *Ambuscade*, from which the chaff rockets had already been launched. The two French-built missiles appeared to swerve past her, through the chaff cloud, still looking ahead for a target.

Which they immediately found. They each adjusted course automatically to skim the water for another four miles straight towards *Atlantic Conveyor*. On board the freighter they had no chaff. Mike Layard, upon receipt of the 'Air Raid Warning Red' signal, had given the order to broadcast instantly *'Emergency stations! Emergency stations!'* The ship's siren was blasting out its deafening 'BAAHA ... BAAHA ... BAAHA' and everyone with a gun was heading for the upper deck. Machine-gun crews were at action stations on each wing of the bridge, complete with aimers, loaders and lookouts. All damage-control and first-aid parties took up their posts. Anyone without a specific task headed for the two dining rooms to act as man-power pools in case of serious damage. Everyone was pulling on life-jackets and anti-flash gear as they ran to their places of duty. Captain Layard took the steps to the bridge three at a time. Captain North had ordered a hard turn to port in an attempt to present *Conveyor*'s very strong stern to the incoming missiles. At 1841 Captain Layard demanded the threat direction, but even as he did so both Exocets crashed through *Atlantic Conveyor*'s port quarter – nine feet above the waterline – with an enormous explosion.

Sir Percivale and Christopher Craig's *Alacrity* were quickly on their way to help, and Captain North's fire-fighting crews were struggling with a rare desperation to contain the blaze. They activated the water sprinkler systems, tried to blanket the fires with carbon dioxide gas, shut down all the ventilation fans and pumped sea water through all the fire hoses they could find down into the cargo decks. But it was all hopeless. The ship rapidly filled with acrid black smoke, just as *Sheffield* had. The whole of the upper deck was becoming too hot to stand on and the fire was creeping forward towards thousands of gallons of kerosene and the huge consignment of cluster bombs. The *Atlantic Conveyor* was one massive explosion waiting to happen. Eleven men were already dead.

Captain Layard conferred with the Master of the merchant ship at 1920 and in Captain North's opinion there was no alternative but to abandon her. *Atlantic Conveyor* was doomed and so was her precious cargo of helicopters, as were the proposed landing strip at the beach-head and all the spares. The land forces were going to have to walk across East Falkland.

Meanwhile *Invincible* picked up yet another pair of solid contacts only twenty miles out, heading for *Hermes*. She launched *six* Sea Dart missiles in short order, adding to the confusion on the radar screens of the entire force, before it all turned out to be spurious. The consensus in *Hermes* was that *Invincible* had been shooting at chaff blooms – certainly the sky had filled with ordnance of one kind or another, little of it being of Arg origin.

Back in *Atlantic Conveyor* there was no good news whatsoever. One team of thirteen fire-fighters were cut off and trapped, but we got them off with a Sea King from *Hermes*. The remainder of the one hundred and thirty-four men would have to climb down the ladders and ropes into the life rafts, a task which would become nightmarish because of the explosions inside the ship. Parts of the hull were now glowing red hot in the gathering dark. But somehow they managed, and finally Captain Layard set off, the second last man to leave. Behind him, close to exhaustion, climbed Captain Ian North, who, at sixty-ish, was perhaps least able to cope with this awful physical test.

Mike dropped the last ten feet into the icy water. Ian North splashed in beside him. But something was wrong. He was floating too low in the water. The Royal Navy officer grabbed him by the life jacket, holding him up, but the *Conveyor*, with her rounded stern, was riding up and down in the long swell. As she rose, she sucked the men in, under the overhang, before falling down on top of them, forcing them beneath the surface. 'My God!' muttered Captain Layard. 'She's going to take us to the bottom with her.'

Within minutes the great heaving freighter had sucked in the life rafts which were squashing the men against the ship's side, a terrifying experience, especially for the several non-swimmers who found it difficult enough just to breathe. But Mike Layard hung on to Ian North until finally he got a hand on a life raft. He summoned all of his remaining strength and shoved the old captain in the small of the back, straight at the raft, but the sea broke over them. Captain Layard went under, grabbing for Ian North, but when the Royal Navy officer came up there was no sign of the Master of the *Conveyor*. With frantic courage Captain Layard dived after him.

But Ian North was gone, claimed by the great sea he had been plying all of his working life. Mike Layard surfaced again half drowned, grabbed at another man in trouble and swam with him to the raft, from which hands reached down and heaved them aboard. The captain passed out after that and it was several minutes before they could revive him. When he did regain consciousness he could only see the bright orange glow of the burning Cunarder and he sat with his head in his hands and wept for his friend, Captain Ian North. The trauma stayed with him for a long time too. Thirteen days later when he arrived back in England they had arranged a press conference, but it had to be delayed for half an hour because Captain Layard couldn't bear it, unable to speak for the lump in his throat. It's often that way with the bravest of men.

Meanwhile there was still enormous danger in the life rafts as the rising stern kept sucking them in towards her, then; falling again, threatening to squash them. Not for the first time completely regardless of his own safety, Commander Christopher Craig, minesweeper extraordinary, brought *Alacrity* right up to the floating time-bomb which was the *Conveyor* – she would surely have taken them *both* to the bottom if she had exploded – and fired lifelines over to the rafts. Then gently, he backed his ship away and towed them all clear.

By now I was back out on my bridge and I could see the *Atlantic Conveyor* burning on the horizon. I watched her, on and off, until she disappeared in the dark distance and wondered, without much genuine optimism, if they could save anything, if we could get a salvage party on board and reclaim some of her precious equipment. But the following morning she was just a dangerous, drifting hulk as another internal explosion blew her bow off. Her war had lasted exactly thirty days and, even without her final mission accomplished, we still owed her a considerable debt. Not least, I suppose, because she was in a dead line between *Hermes* and *Ambuscade*. If the *Conveyor* had possessed a chaff system and decoyed the missiles, they might have come straight on for the carrier. We may, or may not, have been able to divert them yet again.

Conveyor's loss left the Land Forces very badly placed for any means of transport other than walking to get from Carlos to Stanley. And it left me assailed by guilt – again. Was it all my fault? Had I just made a horrendous mistake? Should I have left her safely to the east of the Battle Group until dark? Who knows? I suppose if I had waited and let her go in late and the Args had blown her apart with bombs the following morning, everyone would have assumed automatically that I was off my head for not getting her in there earlier and on her way home by dawn. You can't win, as ever. Sad and troubled as I was, I resolved once more to put it behind me and to press on.

I sat down to finish my diary, and saw that it was still not quite midnight. 'Sod it!' I said to myself bitterly. 'It's *still* 25 May. Will this bloody day ever end?' In the late afternoon I had felt fairly certain this was the worst day of my life. Now I was sure of it. My diary paragraph, as always, reflected my despondency by being as dry as dust, as if I were trying to write the emotion out of it. 'Half an hour later two Etendards got in amongst the Battle Group – actually detected on radar in good time, like at twenty-four miles from *Ambuscade*, twenty-eight miles by *Brilliant*, and even in *Hermes*, visually by all. Seduced by *Ambuscade*'s chaff and went for *Atlantic Conveyor* – both hit, well aft. *Conveyor* a total loss, but eighty per cent of crew saved and one Chinook and one Wessex 5. Down goes another £100 million worth. The Etendards got away, having fired at the first thing they saw.'

As if my half-morbid, half-furious mood were not enough, there was yet another serious cause for anger circulating the Ops Rooms of Operation Corporate. You will doubtless recall that several of the bombs which hit the British ships in Carlos Water had, happily for us, not exploded, thus saving a considerable number of lives. Well, on the evening of 23 May – forty-eight hours ago – the BBC, in the light of information from the MOD, announced this. Not content with broadcasting it locally in London, for the ears of any Argentinian diplomat or military attaché, they actually put it out on the World Service for the entire South Atlantic to hear. Some of my officers were outraged and their anger was fuelled by the inescapable coincidence that all three bombs which had hit *Coventry* had exploded. Of course the Args *may* have sorted out the fusing problems on their own, but that could not stop much hostile comment about 'shallow, smug, half-educated morons who work at the BBC'. As you can imagine, since the BBC World Service was the sole source of media information to us, we were less than delighted.

I realized their self-appointed task as 'Fearless Seekers After Truth' was, to them, sacrosanct. But their 'ratings' that week just may have been paid for with the blood of Captain Hart-Dyke's people. This ought to have upset me too, but I couldn't allow myself to be put off balance by this sort of thing – for me, it could only be classified as 'spilt milk'. And, as the BBC told me years later, the information had been given to them by the MOD anyway. While it was clear that something *must* be done by someone about this sort of carelessness, it was unlikely to be me.

Finally, 25 May ended. The new early morning saw me, as I had been so often, sitting by myself in my cabin, putting yesterday behind me and trying to formulate my thoughts for the immediate future. I began by revising my 'Lessons' – they were fairly rough notes, so I have added occasional words for clarification here.

1. Radar *will* detect and track aircraft and missiles at reasonable range.

2. Chaff *can* seduce [Exocet], off small ships [*Ambuscade*] anyway.

3. Using merchant vessels as spare targets probably not such a good idea – unless they [also] have chaff.

4. Remember UAA1 distribution for the screen [picket line]. OK this time, but more by accident [. . . than design].

5. Keep escorts fairly well forward for early warning.

6. Do not have too many ships, in depth, down Anti-Air Warfare axis otherwise missile [Exocet] has too many chances to get it right.

7. Stay outside 460-mile circles [from Arg mainland air bases]; we'd had to creep inside for CAP [over AOA].

8. Turn towards [incoming missiles]. At least you present the strongest part of the ship that way.

9. [To find the escaping Etendards] Fire [send] CAP straight out along the initial bearing [of

Handbrake warning]. Opposition will be scampering low out along it.

10. Cross fingers.

Beneath these notes I wrote the words: 'And so the war will go on. Setbacks, yes. Defeat, no. But we are very much in need of a decent airfield ashore.'

In terms of actual air–sea combat, the following four days passed relatively quietly, in variously bad weather, fog, gales and big seas. The Args launched very few attacks at us. No ships were hit, although we did lose an RAF Harrier and a Royal Marine Scout over Goose Green – and a Sea Harrier slid off the wet deck of *Invincible*, as the ship heeled in a turn. We bombed the Mount Kent area and wiped out an army Puma, and *Fearless* and *Intrepid* downed a Skyhawk with gunfire in Carlos Water. The troops on land knocked out a couple of Pucaras, a naval Macchi 339 and a Dagger with Blowpipe and Rapier, and one Arg pilot drove into a hillside by mistake in yet another Pucara.

I was feeling a bit depressed on Wednesday morning 26 May, probably a bout of post-*Coventry* blues, exaggerated by continued strain and worry, which is never very easy to live with. As much as anything it was the waiting that sometimes got me down. Once it all started happening I often felt almost a sense of release, hoping somehow that it could all be decided soon – although I knew it would not, short of *our* suffering a really frightful disaster.

By now I was also beginning to experience a symptom which has afflicted just about every Navy commander involved in an amphibious landing in the history of the world – that of an unreasonable, obdurate, barely controlled feeling of frustration with your own forces ashore! What the hell are they doing? Digging bloody holes? Cleaning their little rifles? Looking at maps? Waiting for their nutty rations? My ships have now unloaded five thousand tons of kit for five and a half thousand troops – that's nearly a ton each! What more do they want? All these short-tempered thoughts were constantly in my mind. I wrote in my diary: 'The land force will probably bog down (because they always do)'. On another separate piece of paper I actually wrote the words in block capitals: 'THEY'VE BEEN HERE FOR FIVE DAYS AND DONE F*** ALL!' Thankfully that particular piece of paper no longer exists but I thought it worth recording as an illustration of Royal Naval irritation with their less-mobile land-bound colleagues. To us they always seem to act so *slowly*.

However, I was determined not to try to run the land-force commander's battle for him and hence resolved to confine myself merely to keeping him informed of our rapidly dwindling support capability. I wrote, to wrap it all up, in my diary, 'Conclusion: the battle is high risk at sea and in the air. It must now go high risk on land.' I felt strongly enough to pass this thought directly to the land-force commander together with a reminder that mid-June was the end date I had in mind. I got it wrong again – though he certainly did need to be kept informed what my situation was, the last sentence was interpreted as trying to run his battle for him. Having just lost most of his air transport force for him, it was not exactly well-timed.

The other thought that preoccupied me was the old and vexed problem of trying to stop Exocet. I did not yet know whether the missiles which hit and sank *Atlantic Conveyor* had been fired from an Etendard which had been refuelled. My opinion was that it had not – that it was at the maximum extent of its range – but that I could expect them to solve the refuelling problem soon enough. I was entirely wrong, as it happened. They had already solved the problem. It was also beginning to occur to me that they might yet find a way to refuel the Etendards *twice*, permitting them to come all the way round and in behind the Battle Group from the east, avoiding my carefully placed pickets twenty miles up-threat to the west of the carriers.

All the above thoughts were made worse by the realization that the Args might also find a way to replenish their supplies of Exocet. As it was we thought they had one, possibly two left, and that the Etendard range was still around four hundred to four hundred and forty miles. It would be extremely bad news if they improved both their supplies and their range, and I thought once more, just as I had done a couple of weeks ago, that we, somehow, *had* to remove the Etendards from the Arg Order of Battle.

Between my machinations over this ever-present threat, I did some careful stocktaking and that was not the happiest read you have ever seen either. British losses: Harriers (five); several SK4s and 5s; Chinooks (three); Wessex (five); *Ardent*, *Antelope*, *Sheffield*, *Coventry* and *Atlantic Conveyor*. Badly damaged: *Argonaut*, *Antrim* and *Glasgow*; LSLs (two); *Arrow* (defective). In return we had put something like seventy Argentinian aircraft out of action, destroyed or otherwise written off; we'd sunk their only cruiser, captured one very broken submarine and removed a few auxiliaries/fishing vessels. Both navies had taken a fairly comprehensive hammering, but the weather had been generally against us and helpful to the Args. But we *had* established our beach-head, firmly.

However, with the elements of surprise and manoeuvre by this time largely lost, we were into a strictly attritive war, but one where you have to 'rob Peter to pay Paul' – ships for aircraft, aircraft for soldiers, soldiers for time, and time for ships. And we were rapidly approaching the point where our biggest enemy was time. Just as that little bar-chart had insisted back at Ascension Island, failure by the land-force commander to win the land battle by mid to late June will cause him to lose it because the Battle Group will lose it for him. We will simply be unable to support and protect him. We will be unable to go on fighting. There'll be nothing much left out here to fight with.

During these four days, up until the night of the twenty-ninth, the Args did launch one serious raid, for the first time hitting targets on the land around Carlos Water. They blew up an ammunition dump and damaged a temporary field hospital in Ajax Bay. We in turn hit them with a diversionary cover of over sixteen tons of shells from five ships while the Paras took Goose Green. This was of course that amazing battle in which the troops in red berets ran into a surprisingly strong Arg defence, unhappily thought at the time to be a result of the BBC World Service announcement that 'the Paras are moving towards Darwin'. At least the soldiers thought so. I doubt if the Parachute Regiment will ever entirely forgive the BBC despite the BBC's best attempts to set the record straight.

But, again, I digress. By now we had been reinforced by HMS *Cardiff*, a three-year-old Type 42 guided-missile destroyer under the command of another ex-submarine officer Captain Mike Harris. Two elderly sister ships to our battered Leander Class frigate *Argonaut* had also arrived – HMS *Minerva* and HMS *Penelope*. Every night we sent our small supply convoys in to the AOA shepherded by the warships and every night we battered away at Arg positions on the islands, their bases and their airstrips.

On 30 May, however, the scene changed. The Argentinian High Command decided to fire what was their last remaining Exocet and again they made a firm decision to try to aim it at *Hermes* or *Invincible*. At their present Exocet strike rate they had an even-money chance of hitting something, but longish odds against hitting a carrier.

In our favour, apart from the lessons of the last two Exocet attacks, we now had the very latest version of the Sea Dart system in the Royal Navy – the one in *Exeter*, the Type 42 commanded by Hugh Balfour. He was a rather smooth chap really, a bit of a dandy, but a very modern thinker and, as a communications officer, he was an expert in satellites and electronic warfare. He was the type of man you associate with clean white handkerchiefs in the breast pocket, a bit upmarket, perhaps even a dilettante, and quite the opposite of the traditionally 'grimy submariner'. That said, however, Hugh Balfour was also the precise opposite of a dilettante – he was a sharp, professional warfare specialist and the master of that brand-new Sea Dart system in *Exeter*. It actually saved about fifteen vital seconds in engagement time compared with the best that *Glasgow* and *Coventry* could do due to brilliant new software.

Anyway, the Args elected to send up two Etendards, one with the missile, another for additional radar assistance. They would be accompanied by four Skyhawks of 4th Air Brigade, each armed with two five-hundred-pound bombs. Their brief was to use the Exocet as their guide to the carrier while the Etendards turned away for home. I of course was entirely ignorant of this 'Good night, Woodward' scenario of theirs. I was also unaware of the route they planned, which was to run due east for four hundred miles from Rio Grande and then turn north-west, hoping to catch us in the rear. As a serious attack mission, it was not badly thought out, even though it did require a very long round trip.

They took off and made their air refuelling rendezvous and then headed on in towards the British Battle Group, in which *Cardiff* and *Exeter* were out on the westerly picket line, with Captain Hugo White's Type 21 frigate *Avenger*, largely by chance, steaming twelve miles south-south-east of them. Twenty miles further back to the east were ranged the fleet auxiliaries and three and a half miles behind them were the two carriers, *Hermes* seven miles due north of *Invincible*. The Argentinians flew as usual below the radar, until they 'popped up' at 1631z for the Etendards to scan the sea with their radars, looking for the British Fleet.

As they did so, the most attention-getting Ops Room call in the South Atlantic was broadcast from *Exeter*: 'Handbrake! Two-Two-Five.'

Within seconds *Exeter* had a warning on the networks and *Cardiff*, *Avenger* and *Exeter* all swung around to face the attack from the south-west. The two Etendards 'popped up' once more three minutes later. All three British ships saw them on their radar screens and they all knew that an Exocet missile, fired at twenty-one miles range, was on its way – *and* that there were four aircraft coming in right behind it.

Captain Balfour ordered his first Sea Dart away. The missile travelled close past *Avenger* and, five miles later, obliterated the lead Skyhawk, killing the pilot Primer Teniente Vazquez. The other three pilots pressed on, but either *Exeter*'s second Sea Dart or *Avenger*'s 4.5-inch gun blew another of them away, killing that pilot too.

Meanwhile the Exocet, either poorly aimed or unserviceable, passed harmlessly mid-way between *Exeter* and *Avenger*, with several miles to spare on either side. With immense gallantry, the other two Argentinian pilots, feeling extremely lonely by now, continued to race forward, determined to press home their attack. They went for *Avenger*, now surrounded by smoke from the gun which was still blazing away at the Skyhawks. Their bombs, however, missed as they overflew the frigate and they shot through the smoke at over four hundred knots, banking away for home, the hair on the back of their necks doubtless standing on end as they imagined the Sea Harriers lancing down from the rear, Sidewinders at the ready. As it happened they made it home safely, to regale their commanders with just about the least accurate story of the whole war: that they had bombed *Invincible*, which had already been struck and set on fire by the Exocet, that they had seen the smoke, witnessed the damage.

Still, young men as brave as that deserve their fantasies and in the coming days I did not even begrudge them the front-page picture, deftly dressed up by an artist, in the Arg newspapers which showed *Invincible* burning fiercely in the South Atlantic. Actually she was a good twenty miles from the action and nearly as pristine and spotless as Captain Balfour's white handkerchief.

Personally, I ended the day with a smile of relief. As you will by now have realized, I try to deal only in 'facts' and my facts looked good to me. The Args started this game with five Exocets – five aces – and they had now, incontrovertibly, played them all, on 4, 25 and 30 May. Each time they let them loose at the first radar blip they saw – a set of three incompetent blunders which may very well cost them this war.

LSL

17

Port Unpleasant

During the course of my 'cruise' I had watched the ice and frost of winter fall away behind us as we worked our way down to Gibraltar. Spring was a season I had not often witnessed on land since my school days. It may seem surprisingly unobservant of me but I actually was never sure which bloomed first, the blossom of the pear or the apple, until my first staff appointment ashore at the age of thirty-nine. But there was no time for either this year. Running south, with the seasons cascading one upon the other, my spring gave way to a brief equatorial summer in April and then we hurried immediately into a southern autumn, as April turned to May.

Now, still staring out over *Hermes*'s busy flight deck at the cold, shifting grey-green waters, I saw May turn at last into flaming June, the summer season back home – of the Derby, of Wimbledon, of Royal Ascot, with the Round the Island

Race and Cowes Week to follow. I felt more than a little deprived. On the black night of 31 May I wrote, rather plaintively in my diary: 'Oh, for the peace of the Isle of Wight on a summer evening.' But realities, as ever, pressed. With Goose Green and Darwin back in British hands, after a bitter and dogged action fought by the Paras, the land-force commander was preparing to break out of our Carlos Water beach-head and establish two new operational areas from which to launch the main assault on the Argentinian positions around Port Stanley.

The first was Teal Inlet, a huge area of open country broken by many inter-connecting stretches of open water, with its twisting, narrow entrance leading in off the long northern coast of East Falkland – fifteen miles deep from northern entrance to southern shallows (and early on rejected as a possible landing site because the Arg Navy could too easily have bottled us up in there). The second area was that of Bluff Cove, which sits on the Atlantic side of East Falkland, about fourteen miles west-south-west of Port Stanley, in a small bay reaching north off Port Fitzroy.

The general plan was that the land forces could advance from both of these operational areas simultaneously, thus forcing the Args to defend their Port Stanley stronghold almost on two fronts. For the land forces this would mean splitting their advance and forcing an added element of confusion upon the enemy when they realized we were coming at them from two directions. For the Royal Navy it meant a period of unprecedented activity which was going to need a masterpiece of planning and compliance. For a start, we would be trying to cope with *five* different areas of operation, each with its own special requirements, yet each related to the others:

a) the Battle Group area itself, 'home' to the total of thirty-five warships fighting this campaign and positioned in the eastern sector of the TEZ;

b) the TRALA (tug, repair and logistics area), the mobile 'home' for any damaged warships making final preparations for the long voyage back north; and 'home' also for the Royal Fleet Auxiliaries not required to stay up with the Battle Group and for all amphibious and merchant ships not required inshore – it was a sea-bound base camp for fuel, stores and the not-so-fit, positioned outside and east of the TEZ;

c) Carlos Water itself, still the highly dangerous main land-force base and main 'harbour' into which the warships led the supply convoys every night and which we had to defend with frigates/destroyers at all times – renamed on 1 June 'TA' (transport area) as opposed to the old AOA (amphibious operating area);

d) Teal Inlet, our new base, into which we had to send at least one of the LSLs, packed with supplies for 3 Commando Brigade, and which would be a major build-up because this base took twenty-five miles off the sixty-mile overland journey from San Carlos to Port Stanley. In the coming week the Navy would make numerous journeys into Teal;

e) Bluff Cove, our second new base, would contain the troops of the Scots and Welsh Guards and General Moore's Headquarters – as at Teal, we had to get LSLs into the deep bay and protect them from air attack, but it was a much longer journey from the TA.

So there was no chance to stop and draw breath. Ships and tankers, laden with thousands of tons of fuel, stores and ammunition were arriving down the Atlantic almost daily and reporting to the TRALA. From there they awaited their warship escorts before being shepherded along the hundred-and-twenty-mile seaway into the TA for unloading. In addition, frigates steamed in from the Battle Group every night to form the now-familiar gun lines off the coast, pouring harassing fire into known Argentinian positions, in direct support of land operations.

Out in the Battle Group, it was the big City that never sleeps. The ceaseless hum of activity rendered the night hours little different from those of day, save for the roar of the Harriers, to and from the decks of *Hermes* and *Invincible*, which tended to die out at dusk and begin again at dawn. Those who worked in the tense gloom of the Ops Rooms, among the screens and the flickering lights of the computers, were of course cocooned from the cutting winds and rising seas of the southern ocean outside. But it was difficult, on a personal level, for any of them to keep track of the days of the week, never mind night and day. The bustle and babel of the watch-changes were about all that marked their calendar.

The loss of the *Atlantic Conveyor* also had its effect, for this ship had been, at the time of the missile strike, on station *in* the heart of the Battle Group. She was the first British ship to be so destroyed (*Sheffield*, when hit, had been a front-line picket ship positioned far out on the Group's most remote outpost). The double-Exocet hit which had sent the big freighter to the bottom of the Atlantic had shown all of us that the Args could actually get deep in among us with that confounded missile and it served to focus the minds ever more sharply.

It made me, if anything, rather crustier. I suppose I was, as often as not, trying to juggle and separate about two hundred different thoughts. One of them, however, represented my mainstream opinion: that if the land forces do not get their skates on, the Args are going to get in here again and it is a matter of time before they find a way to hit the British carriers and remove half our air force at a stroke. That preoccupied me above all else. Subconsciously it lurked behind all of my other considerations and I suppose it was magnified in my own mind by the fact that I felt I ought not to interfere with the tasks of the land commanders, least of all by carelessly halving their fixed-wing air support as well as half their helicopter force in *Conveyor*. We had, after all, landed a sizeable force on the beaches of the Falkland Islands, barely twenty-four hours late on a six-week crash programme. There had been *no casualties* during the landing and before achieving it we had frightened the entire Argentinian Navy back into their home ports. No one should be left in much doubt that the land forces were expected to perform with equal dispatch despite the difficulties. The trouble was, as we entered the month of June, I was having to live with the tyranny of that little bar-chart drawn up so long ago at Ascension. As forecast, the Battle Group was now well on its way to falling apart: aside from the losses, we were coping with daily breakdowns in equipment and, as the land forces prepared for the break-out from Carlos, we faced an almost overwhelming workload.

'The Glorious First of June' is a celebratory day in the Royal Navy when we are all invited to recall the famous victory over the French in the North Atlantic in 1794 by the sixty-eight-year-old British admiral, Lord Howe, known (I am told, affectionately) as 'Black Dick'. Students of naval history will know that the old boy battered the French battle fleet from dawn till dusk, sank one ship and captured six others as prizes. However, as that rather awkward-minded schoolboy back at Dartmouth I had wondered about the fact that Admiral Howe was actually supposed to be preventing a big consignment of American grain reaching France. For all the blood and thunder of British victory, that French convoy still got through. The failure to achieve the aim, in my youthful opinion, had been completely obscured by the glory of the battle.

Well, here we were again, at war, a hundred and eighty-eight years later, in a similar sort of situation, albeit with the roles a bit muddled up. I had a sort of 'grain convoy' to get through, in the form of the continued support of the land forces, and there could be no battles, glorious or inglorious, which put that at risk. The date 1 June 1982 saw everyone as jumpy in the Ops Room of *Hermes* as they doubtless had been in Howe's Flagship *Queen Charlotte* on this very day so long ago. A spurious call to '*Action stations*' saw everyone tearing around in a collective frenzy before the admiral had even finished his breakfast. A short while later we heard one of the Harriers had splashed a big Argentinian C130 transport aircraft near Carlos, which made us all feel much better. We'd been after them for weeks now.

Then I began to worry about the horrendous volume of signals required to keep the whole act together, not just locally in the south, but between the task groups and the UK. The whole communications system was already grossly overloaded and could come to a grinding halt if we had a major operational problem. Meanwhile the ever-present threat of Exocet was at the back of my mind. The weather was sometimes quite good enough for the Etendards and I could not get away from the fact that 'my frigates' were 'literally all over the bloody place', as my diary reminds me.

As a matter of fact 1 June was very like 2 June, and 3 June, and 4 June. We kept at it night and day, through varying degrees of fog, cold, wind and cloud. Fixed-wing flying was occasionally curtailed, but the ships, of course, kept going. *Active*, *Ambuscade* and *Cardiff* valiantly tried to keep up a nightly bombardment of East Falkland. *Avenger* had a go at deterring any return of Arg aircraft to Pebble Island, while the ever-aggressive *Plymouth* blitzed Port Howard on her way home from escort duties. Hugh Balfour's *Exeter* had the uncomfortable task of standing 'missile trap' off Stanley. *Brilliant*, *Avenger*, *Broadsword* and *Minerva* also undertook escort duties bringing the convoys inshore, and *Yarmouth* took care of *Sir Galahad* and *Sir Bedivere* on the back-up runs to Teal from the TA. *Sir Percivale* had paved the way through these tricky, hemmed-in waters, unloading three hundred tons on the first day. Her sister ship *Sir Tristram* began the opening up of Port Fitzroy and *Intrepid* transported 5 Brigade from the TRALA to the beaches. Somehow we brought *Canberra*, the Great White Whale, back into Carlos Water for the first time since 21 May and, more impressively, after one hundred chopper-unloadings, we got her safely back out again, escorted by *Plymouth* and *Minerva*. *Argonaut*, repaired as well as she could be, transferred her stores and left for home on 4 June.

During these long and busy days I had made several rather telling notes in my diary, some of them concerned with my other preoccupation about getting a landing strip for the Harriers organized in the TA in order to take the endless pressure off the flight decks of the carriers. Also I recorded formally that in my opinion the intelligence people were moving into a total 'decline', forecasting 'last desperate efforts by the Argentinians'. I allowed myself the indulgence of adding:

> Am very impatient for the FOB (Forward Operating Base, Landing Strip) to come on to service for the SHARs [Sea Harriers] – then I should be able to unhook myself from this too-well-trodden patch of water.
>
> For myself, these days are not so easy. Some of the pressure – in terms of innovation and involvement – is off. We are faced with the need to act in an almost entirely defensive/supportive role, with little control of events. It is becoming more difficult to hold the act together as a result. While in no way wishing for a major upsurge in activity, we are not well adjusted to this phoney phase and probably need to be replaced soon by a new team, which can start afresh with new ideas.

During these quiet-ish few days I also took note of a piece of intelligence that suggested the Args had set up a land-based Exocet battery in the Stanley area and, not wishing to find out the hard way, I pulled the naval gunfire ships off early on the very first morning we had the information. I wrote in my diary: 'No doubt CLFFI [Commander Land Forces Falkland Islands] will be unhappy, but so would I be at the loss of another frigate or destroyer.'

Every few days we received bundles of newspaper clippings – a couple of weeks late – which I thought showed a remarkable breadth of support for this military action, resisted only by the more left-wing leaders. Even the trade unions seemed solid behind us. I nevertheless suspected that if, with typical British understatement, it was all made to look too easy – though exactly how that was to be done was not very obvious to me – the 'typically British' audience might start to see us as 'bullies'. Perhaps with this in mind I wrote on the night of 3 June: 'It is an extraordinary world. I am left more than ever convinced that this has been "nip and tuck" all the way, mostly on account of the Exocet threat and the poor showing of our missile systems, and the extremely determined attacks of the Argentinian Air Force.'

By now, the runs to Teal Inlet were becoming fairly routine. It seemed that only I was a bit edgy about it. I understood that we had only one LSL in there at a time and that the chances of detection by the Args were not high. So the achievements justified the risk. And yet . . . I could never be entirely happy with this sort of thing. Single ships in the middle of nowhere, particularly with no defence at all against air attack, were bound eventually to catch it – as both sides knew well enough from bitter experience now. I think I had it in my mind that CLFFI, who had only arrived in the Falklands after the actual landing, might not have fully taken in how thunderously lucky we had been on D-Day, putting the land forces ashore without loss to them and without even taking an attack of any sort on the troopships and supply ships.

CLFFI might, I feared, have missed the important point that the Args had gone for the wrong targets, attacking the escorts instead of the landing force. I knew of no guarantee that they would do the same if they found a heavily laden LSL sitting calmly in the still waters of Teal Inlet. Anyhow, landings were not my job and the smoother things went at Teal, the more confident we would all become. My concerns had to remain unvoiced – not least because the very last thing I wanted to do was to slow up the advance by being over-cautious.

As the days passed, the relatively peaceful build-up at Teal did indeed inspire CLFFI to want to repeat the dose on the southern flank, somewhere in the Fitzroy/Bluff Cove area. I was asked for my view on the possibility of taking in an LPD, *Fearless* or *Intrepid*, and several LSLs rather than having 5 Brigade walk from the TA or Darwin the forty-odd miles overland. The land force commander was, not without reason, concluding that to take the troops round by ship would take five hours, whereas to walk would take at least two days. They knew well that speed was essential, if not 'at all costs'. They had been left in no doubt of that before they even landed.

But, despite this, their plan did not seem worth while. I knew that the prospect of an operation involving several amphibious ships, and their frigate and destroyer escorts, effectively another complete landing well clear of Carlos Water and its air defences, would hold little appeal back at Headquarters in Northwood. I recognized my own position in all this as 'on the fringe' and, though I could of course have stopped it, I did not really wish to do that – after all I had already done my utmost to get the land forces to press on. It was no use blowing 'hot and cold'. So I cravenly decided to allow Northwood to do it for me. Which they did.

In my diary, on the night of 4 June, I wrote the following:

And CLFFI is proposing a mini D-Day all over again at Bluff Cove on the 6th. Perhaps they still do not understand how fortunate we were on D-Day when the Args went for the wrong targets, and perhaps they have forgotten that, when the Args finally corrected their mistake on D+3 and 4 [24 and 25 May], the Rapier batteries were in action. Above all they appear to have forgotten that Bluff Cove is in open country and not a bit like Carlos Water.

It seems daft to take this size of risk for the sake of a two-day march. [You could] send the War Maintenance Reserve by LSL – probably get away with that, if the weather is bad. But don't put two battalions back into such hazard, just because the opposition seems to have taken a day off. [This is] all very difficult. I don't want to cramp CLFFI's style, nor do I want to slow him up. Nor yet do I wish to be seen to tell him his business. *But . . .* !

The essence of the problem is that such a move could blow the entire operation. Unless it is essential to success, it should not be undertaken.

1600. It emerges that Fleet also don't much like the idea . . . so it probably won't happen.

Underlying this whole calculation was a strange bit of misinformation. I had been told by my experts in such matters that land forces could 'move at two miles an hour' – I should have been more sceptical. Unlike ships which at two knots will cover twenty-four miles in twenty-four hours, what they actually meant but failed to mention, was 'two miles an hour for five hours a day if you're lucky, and less if there's any opposition'. Nevertheless, a four-day march would have been better than what finally happened. But how was anyone to know? And I *had* recommended the land force went 'high risk' even if they didn't like being told their own business.

The following morning, 5 June, things looked rather better all round. The thick fog was now only patchy, so we got the combat air patrol up early and it landed, at last, on the new strip on shore, which had been named HMS *Sheathbill* in the

Navy's tradition of naming such areas after sea-birds. This new 'airfield' did not solve all our problems at a stroke, but it was going to be a considerable help. As my diary said that day:

> I have taken *Hermes* out of the front line to do her boiler cleaning in order to have that out of the way before *Invincible* departs for her SMP/AMP. All this is necessary in case she never comes back. However, rather than retire 100 miles or so to go right down for maintenance, we need to keep flying to back up *Invincible* aircrew and provide GR3's. So it's OUT OF THE FRONT LINE, BUT ONLY JUST. The aim is quite simply to reduce the threat while we have a whole boiler room OOA [out of action].

Convoys were unloading in Carlos Water and during the morning the Scots Guards began to embark in *Intrepid*, bound overnight for Fitzroy. They did not get away until shortly before midnight and when they did David Pentreath's *Plymouth* sailed with them as close escort. Captain Hugo White's *Avenger* steamed in front of them to Fox Bay, West Falkland, into which she began a bombardment designed to avert Argentinian attention from the 12,000-ton British assault ship.

We had *Arrow* on picket duty at the north end of the Sound, with *Exeter* to the south in Grantham Sound, her Sea Dart system giving area air defence. *Cardiff* and *Yarmouth* were on their way in from the Battle Group to bombard the Port Stanley area. The sea was rising and a gale was beginning to build to the south-west. It was, to use an old Royal Navy colloquialism, coming on to blow.

I remember it all too clearly. At 0100 I was standing out on the wing of my bridge in full moonlight, thinking about the ships and their activities this night. Below me I could see the deserted flight deck, with a row of Sea Harriers silently waiting. Occasionally I heard the sound of a wave breaking as fitful cold gusts whistled around the island. There was nothing else, except the strange tiny clattering of the Harriers' little plastic wind vanes as they turned with the puffs. I even remember thinking what a very odd kind of a war we were fighting, after all we had been trained for – no real submarine threat, no serious air threat at night, little enough air threat by day now we have HMS *Sheathbill*. And no surface threat.

As the night wore on, the weather rapidly grew worse. *Intrepid* finally made Lively Island – the disembarking point some way out from Fitzroy at the mouth of the Choiseul Sound. She dropped her LCUs before heading rather too quickly back for the relative safety of Carlos Water. Some five hundred and sixty Guardsmen set off in *Intrepid*'s four LCUs on the thirty-five-mile one-way trip inshore. It was to be a horrendous journey, one which should have taken under three hours but in fact was to take seven, with many of the troops very seasick and all of them soaked through to the skin.

As *Intrepid* left them, strangely far short of their destination, to fight the waves in their little landing craft, *Cardiff* and *Yarmouth* arrived nearby to take up station for the nightly bombardment and the air 'blockade'. *Intrepid*'s Ops Room was especially worried about a possible threat to the LCUs from an Arg air strike at night, but *Cardiff* and *Yarmouth*, under the direct control of the Battle Group, did not know about the LCUs' activities, for the landing craft packed with the drenched Guardsmen were under the direct control of COMAW. And communications between the two groups had become heavily overloaded.

At 0400, *Cardiff*'s Ops Room was suddenly jolted into action when one of the radar operators detected an unidentified air contact moving slowly east across East Falkland.

Urgent voices were immediately heard rising in the gloom of *Cardiff*'s sleepless nerve-centre: 'What is it?' . . . 'An Arg Hercules heading into Port Stanley?' . . . 'Perhaps an Arg special forces helicopter coming back in?' . . . 'Or could it be one of ours?'

Captain Mike Harris's staff raced through their signals for the night. There was nothing to indicate the presence of *any* British air movement in that spot, no special signal to make any exception for any British aircraft doing anything that night. This contact had come *out of the box* unannounced – if it was one of ours, then it had broken the golden rule, which had been designed to prevent a 'Blue-on-Blue' in these precise circumstances.

With very little time to think, it *had* to be an Arg flying towards Port Stanley, or Fitzroy, or even out to sea. Mike Harris made the only possible decision open to him: he ordered his missile director to take the intruder out with Sea Dart. Moments later, away went the missiles, one of them knocking down the target at a range of eleven miles, a couple of miles short of Mount Pleasant. No one knew precisely what had been hit, simply an air target, detected on radar, which *should* have been Argentinian. Mike Harris told me the circumstances that very morning and mentioned his worry that it just could have been one of ours.

It was very soon known that one of our Gazelle helicopters was missing, though its final resting place was not discovered for days. Only when the wreckage was found was it revealed that all four of the crew and passengers had been killed and that the wreckage was very close to the spot that *Cardiff*'s missile engagement had taken place. As soon as practicable, after the war was over, a full-scale investigation was made. The forensic team, with no axe to grind, stated positively that no bits of a Sea Dart missile could be found among the wreckage or even near it. This exonerated *Cardiff*.

Continued pressure, apparently from the families but possibly with some political connection, eventually caused a second investigation to be started. This new forensic team reported, some three years on, that they were positive the wreckage included fragments which could only have come from a Sea Dart missile.

There was immense consternation in very high places. We were dealing with completely contradictory reports, after all this time. Could no one be trusted to get it right? I was there, in 1985, when the Ministry of Defence had to decide between letting that particular sleeping dog lie or telling the world. The basic arguments were that it made no difference in terms of compensation payments and pensions to the families, but that it would reopen, for them, all of the old heartbreak and trauma. The brand-new, now certain knowledge that your brother/husband/son was in fact killed by his own side is no comfort to anyone. But the pressure continued and, since the letters were signed by one of the parents, we ultimately accepted that these families did, indeed, really want to know. So, the information was released and widely criticized for its tardiness.

If, however, I were permitted to re-live the whole situation all over again, I would always be sure that Captain Harris had absolutely no alternative to the action he took in the small hours of 6 June 1982. And I would again try to protect the families from further heartbreak.

It is important to understand that this 'Blue-on-Blue' was

the *only* one between British air and sea forces throughout the entire war – which, however ghastly for relatives and friends of the dead, is nevertheless some kind of a world-record for safety, care and organization. Nonetheless, I regret it deeply and have often wondered in the still of other dark, sleepless nights whether it was not somehow my fault, as the designer of the Box. And, while on the subject of home truths, I may as well record formally that, with my usual need to consider the worst case as well as the most probable, I wrote in my diary immediately after the incident the words: 'Horrid feeling it was a Blue/Blue, but no clues yet.'

To return once more to that night, *Cardiff*'s activity was not over even after the missiles were fired. An hour later her Ops Room located several unexpected small surface contacts well offshore, at long range, coming up from the south-west. With the real possibility of these being Arg patrol craft making a bid for the history books, Captain Harris approached with sensible caution to within 4.5-inch-gun range. A few star-shell finally illuminated, in that doom-light they give, the unhappy Guardsmen in their four struggling little LCUs battering their way towards Bluff Cove. *Cardiff* was still working to the rule book, but here Captain Harris had both the time and the means to check before shooting.

Surprised and considerably relieved, *Cardiff* identified herself with a light signal and went about her business. I expect the poor, wretched Guardsmen had been wondering how soon the star-shell might be followed by high explosive. Rarely can there have been more heartfelt sighs of 'Thank God' than there were in those storm-tossed little landing craft – the age old phrase of the fighting soldier, 'Phew! It's one of ours.' As for the enemy ashore, they would have seen nothing more than a few starshell way out to the south and assumed we were up to our usual deceptive tricks. Another potential disaster avoided by quick thinking on the part of a sharp destroyer captain.

By the time dawn broke on 6 June, the LCUs were safe. *Sir Geraint* was loading for a journey to Teal, *Sir Tristram* was loading for Fitzroy, and the Welsh Guards were beginning to embark in *Fearless* which would sail at dusk for Lively Island. *Exeter* remained in the middle of the Sound, while *Invincible* and *Brilliant* went to the south to discourage Arg reinforcements. Commodore Sam Dunlop turned his gallant fighting workhorse *Fort Austin* north up the Atlantic, bound for home at last.

Out in *Hermes* our engineers were taking bets as to when our boilers would pack up altogether. They had been pressing me to take the ship out of the immediate front line to do essential and overdue maintenance for some while. We had been going without any discernible service for some twenty thousand miles and we had to have them at least cleaned. I had been resisting the engineers for over two weeks, since the pressure of events suggested strongly I should do so. Now, with the critically important FOB fully operational ashore, CAP effort increased, and response time considerably improved, I could give more serious thought to the longer-term pressures of the carrier *roulement* problem.

My first move was to get *Hermes* in best available condition before releasing *Invincible* for her own essential maintenance in turn. We would need to move about fifty miles further east into slightly less dangerous waters for the work to be undertaken. CAP and ground support effort from the carriers would not be significantly affected, since *Hermes* aircraft could be ferried through to the FOB via *Invincible* – meanwhile *Hermes*, presently with little more than half speed available, could quickly return to full operational mobility for the last few days/weeks of the land battle.

Successful completion of the land battle and the possession of two airstrips ashore should allow us to reduce to one carrier on station. Then *Invincible* could immediately go well clear of the area to do a three-week extended maintenance period (at sea) before relieving *Hermes* for a full base maintenance period back home before taking *Invincible*'s place again. In view of her comparative newness, *Invincible* was thought much the better bet to keep going for four or five months with only three weeks sea maintenance in the middle.

Successful completion of major work to make Port Stanley airstrip into an operational Phantom interceptor base should in turn, allow us to remove the single carrier altogether. That could take months, not helped by the onset of winter, and providing we had no further arguments from Argentina.

Illustrious was the 'joker' in this pack. Her accelerated building programme was by no means certain to hold, but if it did, it would greatly ease the pressures on this dangerously tight schedule for our two existing carriers. But in June, the *roulement* plan could not depend on her.

I have deliberately simplified a long, complicated bit of staff-work designed to guarantee a single carrier in support of the Islands for however long it might take to get Port Stanley airstrip upgraded to take the Phantoms. But none of it seemed a matter for my colleagues inshore to worry about, it wouldn't affect my sea/air support of their battle and they had more than enough problems of their own. Decision made, I wrote a few philosophical notes in my diary, pondering on the behaviour of people now that we have more time to ourselves. I might have mentioned my own, since my diary entries seem to have become longer and longer as I slipped into my support role. None of the old 'They blew my old ship *Sheffield* away last night'. . . end of note. I was now becoming a kind of Samuel Pepys of the Deep.

> I am beginning to find that the 'ageing Lieutenant-Commander' syndrome is making itself felt. People are beginning to find they have some time to spare and are busy organizing themselves to a complete standstill. At a certain stage, it remains my belief that the degree of organization and pre-planning has to be carefully balanced. Too little and there is chaos; too much and there is inflexibility.
>
> The principle of 'Command by Negation' [let your trusted men get on with it until they screw it up] should cope . . . provided they are kept fully informed of the situation as it changes. It will occasionally crumble. But these crumbles should not usually out-balance the very real advantages of flexibility, quick reaction, initiative and surprise that we gain. The essentially bureaucratic peacetime mind will, for the sake of avoiding a single Blue-on-Blue, cause Blue-on-Red [hitting the enemy] to cease!

So, while they cleaned the boilers, I put the world to rights. Meanwhile, around 0300 on the seventh, *Fearless*, in company with *Avenger* and *Penelope*, arrived off Lively Island to discover, scarcely surprisingly, that the LCUs which had taken the Guardsmen in the previous night had not yet arrived back. So they floated out their own two LCUs to take in some of the troops – yet another ghastly journey – and went back to Carlos with the remainder.

The morning essentially belonged to us. The Args sent out a photo-reconnaissance mission to fly very high over East

Falkland in a Lear jet. Hugh Balfour's Ops Room in *Exeter* was, as usual, bang on target, blowing it out of the sky with Sea Dart, killing all five occupants. While the Welsh Guardsmen embarked in *Sir Galahad* for the second attempt at making Fitzroy/Bluff Cove, I had a good-natured altercation with Commander Chris Craig of *Alacrity*, in which the 4.5-inch gun now kept going wrong. Basically its barrel was worn out and the gist of our discussion went like this:

'Well,' I reasoned, 'I think you'd better potter off home and get it fixed.'

Commander Craig's predictable response being, 'No, it's all right, sir. I am proposing to stay here and fight until the bloody barrel drops off.'

'No, Christopher,' I continued patiently. '*Alacrity* has done well and is wearing out. Go and get her back in top-shape and then get back down here.'

'Well, sir, we could certainly fight a bit longer, for the next week or so,' he said.

'I don't think so. Transfer your stores, and off you go,' I said and falling helplessly into that rather stiff, formal tone which overtakes me when I attempt to speak from the heart, I added, 'Christopher . . . thank you very much for all you have done.' It was a pretty inadequate 'Goodbye' to a particularly courageous officer who had fought with us since the first day. I never have been much good at goodbyes.

That night *Sir Galahad* cleared Carlos Water, bound for Port Pleasant, that particularly wind-blasted stretch of Atlantic coastline. Port Pleasant is, essentially, one large jagged bay, five miles wide by six miles deep, except that right down the middle of it is a peninsula, five miles long, shaped like a great crocodile with his jaws open to the ocean. The bay thus formed to the north of the reptile is Port Fitzroy, with Bluff Cove tucked into an inlet on the north shore. The settlement of Fitzroy sits at the end of the crocodile's tail, mainly on the *south* bay, which is known as Port Pleasant.

COMAW's objective was to send *Sir Galahad* up into Port Pleasant to join *Sir Tristram*, disembark the Guardsmen at Fitzroy, where we now had a base, and have them walk north to Bluff Cove. They believed that the ships would be hidden from Arg eyes – which were in any case a long way off to the north-east – firstly by the weather, which was still very nasty, and by the shallow cliff at Fitzroy. This had my approval to the extent that I disliked it (as recorded in my diary entry of 4 June), but not enough to have *insisted* that it be stopped. I remember thinking they would probably get away with it, as long as they were swift, spent as little time as possible in unloading the LSL and the weather stayed favourable. This, by the way, did not require any colossal mental effort on my part: it is standard procedure to get any amphibious ship into an anchorage, unload it and get it out as fast as possible – preferably under the cover of darkness, fog, cloud or rain, but, in the absence of the above, certainly under full-power. Never, says the Royal Navy's rule book, hang around in your most vulnerable position.

With *Cardiff* and *Yarmouth* still bombarding over to the north-east, *Sir Galahad* steamed on, anchoring in Port Pleasant close to *Sir Tristram* (still there from yesterday's ammunition deliveries) shortly before 1000. By midday, the weather cleared. It became a bright sunny day, finally, and the two LSLs sat under brilliant blue skies in calm waters. A Sea King unloaded the Rapier troop and the Welsh Guardsmen stayed on board, waiting for the LCUs. There was some discussion between the Army commanders and *Sir Galahad*'s officers about the time factor and it was not until 1530 that one LCU arrived. It did, however, have a damaged ramp and at 1600 the Guards were still there, waiting under the mid-afternoon sun, which was glinting off the high point of their mast.

There was, I believe, further discussion, about the walk to Bluff Cove. The soldiers thought it was a sixteen-mile hike, because of a damaged bridge over the creek at the end of the bay – apparently they had not been told the Paras had repaired it. One way or another they preferred to wait in the ships for further LCUs to ferry them round, directly to their destination.

The afternoon wore on, painstakingly slowly for the unloading crews in Port Fitzroy. But a great deal quicker for the Argentinian troops dug in on the high ground up to the north-east, now enjoying a clear view of the activity around General Moore's headquarters and of the sun-lit masts of the LSLs, stark against a darker background, with the sun now almost due north. They reported the presence of the British ships to the Arg command centre at Port Stanley. Soon after, the message was received by Southern Air Command on the mainland and altogether the Args put up *six* Daggers loaded with thousand-pound bombs, plus a formation of *eight* Sky-hawks. I have no doubt they could scarcely believe their luck: 'Bluff Cove – no hills, no cliffs, no escorts, no Rapier – no problem. Excelente.'

They hoped to get fourteen attack aircraft in, but various fuelling and technical problems reduced this to ten. The two Argentinian formations made the journey separately with the five Daggers running north up the western side of Falkland Sound prior to making a hard right turn and coming in over-land to Port Pleasant. However, as they adjusted their course, flying very fast at wave-top height they suddenly saw HMS *Plymouth* steaming out of Carlos Water, close off Chancho Point. The Args chose to attack the warship.

David Pentreath ordered her hard to port, as they replied with everything they had. They got a Seacat away which damaged one of the Daggers and they blasted at the raiders with 20mm shells and machine guns, but there was no stopping all five. Four thousand-pounders hit *Plymouth*, not one going off, though the last blew up a depth charge being prepared for loading into a helicopter and started a major fire. It all happened terribly quickly and, as the Daggers made off, now pursued by a couple of 801 Squadron's Harriers, they left behind five men injured and a frigate smoking spectacularly, but not by any means fatally damaged.

The pity was that *Plymouth* had not had time to turn right around, because she was fitted with the new laser equipment known locally to us as 'Flasher' – which could well have stopped the attack in its tracks, because it literally forces any incoming pilot to pull up sharply during the forty-second period in which he cannot see. But still, Captain Pentreath, in his ageing twenty-one-year-old Type 12 frigate, did all that could reasonably have been expected. It was of course *Plymouth*'s last battle and, if I may, I will recall a rather crisp description of her war mentioned to me by Captain John Coward. His words were as follows: 'Of course *Plymouth* was always going to cop it. She did not really have the right kit to fight these kinds of action. But I'll never forget her in Carlos Water when we were under such serious attack – she just steamed round and round the other ships in a gesture to the Args of total defiance. She had comparatively little to fight with, just guns and an old Sea Cat – but she gave it everything. Pentreath? Bravest chap I've ever seen. Of course, I knew that one day we'd steam into Carlos Water and *Plymouth* would be not much more than a cloud of black smoke. And one day she was.'

After the raid the Daggers headed home and there were now just five Skyhawks left, flying very low off the coast of Lafonia, heading north up the eastern coast, looking for the ships' masts so plainly visible from the ground to the north in the afternoon sun. Shortly after 1610 the Argentinian lead pilot spotted them, ordered two Skyhawks to follow him in and they swung on to a westerly course, racing low up Port Pleasant towards the two British LSLs. I suppose it was a ground-attack pilot's dream – two sitting ducks with none of the risk of missile, shell and bullet defences to face. They even had time to climb to a correct height to give their bombs a better chance of exploding. They dropped two, possibly three five-hundred-pounders straight into *Sir Galahad*, strafing her as they came in. The other two, bringing up the rear, went for *Sir Tristram* anchored just over a quarter of a mile away, delivered two bombs which did not explode into her stern and another, which did explode, under her stern, blowing off the ramp.

Fortunately *Sir Tristram* was not full of soldiers, but *Sir Galahad* was, and at least one of the bombs detonated deep inside the ship causing dreadful carnage among the Guardsmen. The fires were quickly out of control and ammunition kept exploding making the situation more ghastly by the minute. Luckily there was much rescue equipment on hand – four Sea Kings, a Wessex helicopter, the LCU, a floating freight raft called a Mexeflote, two lifeboats from *Sir Tristram*'s and *Sir Galahad*'s own life boats and life rafts. It took only half an hour or so to remove those who could walk and within an hour, thanks to some extremely efficient winching-up of the stretchered wounded by the chopper crews, everyone had been evacuated from the blazing LSL.

In the end fifty men were either killed or officially listed as missing; another fifty-seven were wounded, almost all of them badly burned. Of these, thirty-nine of the dead and twenty-eight of the wounded were from the 1st Battalion Welsh Guards, a regiment which has traditionally recruited heavily from the old coal-mining heartland of South Wales, from Cardiff and Newport, along to Llanelli and up the valleys to villages in the Rhondda – Maesteg, Bridgend, Pontypridd. None of those little communities are strangers to sadness, but the bombing of *Sir Galahad* will be with them all for a very long time.

The Royal Navy lost seven dead and eleven wounded in the action and there was much gallantry during the rescue. I was particularly moved by the posthumous George Medal awarded to *Sir Galahad*'s Second Engineer Officer Paul Henry of Berwick-on-Tweed, who handed over the only breathing apparatus in the burning engine room to enable a junior officer to escape.

The one mildly bright spot during the whole hideous day came shortly afterwards when yet another formation of Skyhawks came in to attack the Fitzroy base, but was caught over Choiseul Sound by the Harriers, who took three of them out with Sidewinders.

It took a few days before most of the facts became known, but the moment I was told that two LSLs were at Bluff Cove – early on that awful day – I was extremely upset. However, I was mostly upset at myself. Because I *could* have stopped it. *Should* have stopped it. *Didn't* stop it. I was supposed to be the Senior Task Group Commander down here, I had seen threatening danger, and, in a sense, turned away. My hand-written diary provides incontrovertible evidence of this. But I feared that *any* landing was trouble. My entry for 4 June is a page I never wish to read again.

I must have asked myself a thousand times why I did not insist on stopping it. All I had to do was to say flatly, 'Forget it. I will not permit our ships to undertake the mission. Find another way.' Instead I had said nothing, at least not to those who were in command ashore. I'm fairly certain I said a few things to close colleagues out in the Battle Group and, when I get right down to some serious soul-searching, I am pretty sure I know, now, what rested at the root of my reluctance to interfere. It was I who had been urging speed, I who had been making it quite plain that the land forces *must* go soon and get this war over by mid-to-late June. Now that they *were* getting on with it, who was I to start complaining about the risks they were taking? If that was indeed the reason for my reluctance to intervene – then I am not proud of it. It is not my job to worry that I may seem to blow hot and then cold. I should have just told Commodore Mike Clapp and Major General Jeremy Moore that I was not having it and the hell with their reactions.

In so many ways, when I look back at that campaign, I realize that quite often I am a stranger to myself. Was that really me making those decisions? I suppose the only factor that brings us together, me and my other self, is a shared conscience. That, as for all of us, is omnipresent; the echoing, lonely and hopefully truthful voice of our own soul.

On the night of 8 June I let off steam, as usual, on the pages of my diary:

> My worries for the LSLs all too well justified. I could strangle that COMAW. After being told not to plan on putting *Intrepid* and the LSLs into Fitzroy, even with a frigate in daylight (but possibly given to understand he might consider one LSL a reasonable

bet to get by unnoticed – see remarks 4 June). And
what does he do but fire the troops in by two LSLs
in broad daylight with predicted good flying weather.

My concern and frustration urged me on: 'I should have
stopped him of course [i.e. on 4 June]. And it's my own fault
– if only I'd seen it coming in time. I just had not realized the
two LSLs were out on their own until mid-afternoon, when,
almost without thinking, I decided not to countermand; and
hope they'd get away with it.'

In my own defence I reasoned that even if I had counter-
manded it it would not have helped much, as the LSLs 'would
still have been exposed – albeit somewhere else [that is,
between Carlos and Fitzroy] with more kit/people on board,
and a good deal further to swim'. I suppose in the end history
may judge that the dramatic change in the weather was the
single most significant cause of the tragedy. And I later found
out that the prediction of a marked change for the 'better' had
not reached COMAW or CLFFI before the operation was
fully committed. After working for so many days under the
cover of mist and low cloud, suddenly everyone was unexpectedly out in the bright sunlight again, with the amazing visibility you get in those latitudes. That, as we know only too well,
changes things.

As for 'strangling that COMAW', how many times have I
said, 'I could strangle that cat,' when it knocks something over,
or doesn't quite make it to the garden in time after being given
too much to eat? I feel better when I have said it, without
necessarily blaming the cat for what has happened and certainly
with no intention of taking one of its nine lives.

One of my deep regrets about the 'Bluff Cove Disaster' is
that it will always remain some people's abiding memory of

the Falklands War – because television was there, filming hor-
rific live pictures of burnt and badly injured soldiers. As a
military disaster it was not, in context, so earth-shakingly
dreadful. The losses of *Sheffield*, *Coventry* and *Ardent* were
individually not quite so serious in terms of dead and wounded,
but collectively they were considerably worse. *Belgrano* was of
course worse than all of them. Indeed, a few days previously
I heard that a flood in Indonesia had killed more than two
hundred people. I suspect we all have to learn to live with the
fact that television magnifies drastically what is already awful
and somehow diminishes in importance that which it does not
see.

Later that night I heard of yet another delay by the land
troops and yet again returned to my diary to write, somewhat
helplessly:

> I now hear CLFFI is going to delay an extra twenty-
> four hours on top of the last seventy-two. His people
> will soon run out of steam, I'm afraid – the cold front
> is due in tonight. And there seems to be stuff-all I can
> do, except hope the Army get on with it and succeed
> before the Args nibble too much of our naval strength
> away. It *is* only a matter of time before they find some
> way to get at us effectively – be it by submarine, A4s
> plus Etendards for attack direction, Canberra or what-
> ever. Attrition is very difficult to cope with when your
> assets are both finite and critical to the operation . . .
> I still see no likely end to this war and the only
> comfort is that the Args possibly don't either.

The night passed quietly, too quietly, I thought, and was
followed by a cold bright day. The C-in-C, clearly less than
happy about Bluff Cove, was on the phone-link to me in the

morning. I am proud to confirm that we both managed to avoid saying to the land force commander 'I told you so'. But then neither of us *had* really told him so in the first case: he *had* been told that a full-scale landing was not on, but then we had got away with one LSL at Teal – two more at Fitzroy were not totally unreasonable, if the bad weather had held. Anyway, we didn't linger on it as the main topic of the conversation emerged: Fleet was clearly no longer planning to replace me down here with the Flag Officer of the Third Flotilla. 'Won't be coming as soon as we thought,' was Admiral Fieldhouse's throwaway last remark. It sounded like a life sentence to me. That's the main trouble with being more or less trusted by your superiors.

On a total digression, I learned from Mike Clapp's book in 1992 that it was at about this time that he received a signal from my callsign, recommending that we should send the LSL's straight into Port Stanley to bring the war to an early close. He sensibly ignored it, mentally filing it as either some kind of tasteless joke or more 'crass meddling' from offshore. Had I received such a signal from him, I would have felt much the same no doubt. I still wonder where on earth it actually originated from bearing in mind my clearly stated views on sending even one LSL forward on its own, and knowledge that this was no time, nor was it any subject, for joking.

Joke or no joke, by whoever, wherever, on 10 June *Yarmouth* battered the mountains, we flew forty-four CAPs, sometimes with as many as sixteen aircraft over the island and *Active* went in to the southern gun line in company with *Arrow*. Out in the Battle Group we waited and I spent much time alone in the cabin – writing ill-tempered little essays in my diary.

This waiting is awful. I believe even the Args are getting fed up with it and threatening to attack. If CLFFI gets to hear about that, he'll no doubt have to completely re-organize and delay for several more weeks. If I had behaved like the land forces, we'd never have bloody well landed! I just don't understand, and therefore can't accept, these interminable delays: the Navy gets prepared and goes in within a day [of our planned date]. These ceremonious duffers take two weeks for a recce. There seems to be no room for improvisation, initiative, or even real skill. It's straight 'left, right, left, right'. And most of it spent marking time. To my mind the idea of 'mobile forces' has been completely lost . . . and we must be as vulnerable to 'blitzkrieg' as we were last time . . . Absolutely appalling – they're even waiting for the NAAFI packs now, with cigarettes, soap and razors. The mind boggles . . .

The tide is setting in our direction as strongly now as it ever will. This may, or may not be, strong enough, but it's the best we'll ever get. Therefore *go now* and accept the risks.

Years later, as I began to prepare my records for the creation of this book, I was moved to write the following retraction in the space beneath:

Plainly not 'ceremonious duffers' as Brigadier Julian Thompson's book *No Picnic* makes abundantly clear to me now. Though no complaint was heard from ashore at the time, the loss of *Atlantic Conveyor*'s Chinook and WX5 helicopters (which could well be laid at my door) had a major effect on land-force mobility.

My impatience stemmed from chilling consciousness that the Battle Group was running out of steam
and from substantial ignorance of conditions ashore.
This kind of comment is an excellent example of reading too much into a contemporary diary. Having
written it, I felt a bit better and avoided sending an
offensive and probably counter-productive message to
CLFFI thereby.

I thus present both passages for your perusal and trust that
Jeremy Moore will understand my reasons for revealing my
lack of insight into his problems, but be gracious enough to
forgive me for so doing.

As it was the troops began their final main offensive
the following day, 12 June at 0100. By the time they began
to push forward we had seen *Active*, Commander Canter's
Type 21 frigate, blow up an Arg ammunition dump on
Mount Harriet, to the delight of the British troops. The
Harriers had attacked the Port Stanley garrison strongly,
the Args had blown up one of their own helicopters and more
Harriers had peppered the Arg positions up on the hills with
bombs.

I assigned four warships to support the British land forces
in the following way:

a) Captain Hugo White's *Avenger* to provide back-
up bombardment to 3 Para in their grim and
bloody struggle for Mount Longdon;

b) Captain Mike Barrow's *Glamorgan* to assist 45
Commando attacking the twin peaks of Two
Sisters;

c) Commander Tony Morton's *Yarmouth* to help

42 Commando take Mount Harriet ridge and then push on to Tumbledown;

d) Commander Paul Bootherstone's *Arrow* to be on hand for the Special Forces, should the need arise.

Between them my ships had nearly fifteen hundred shells for the night's work: *Avenger* alone fired one hundred and fifty-six of them with her 4.5-inch gun but the Paras nonetheless had to fight all night on Mount Longdon, losing among their eighteen dead the extraordinarily gallant Sergeant Ian Mackay who would be awarded a posthumous Victoria Cross.

Glamorgan had been detached inshore as usual at about 1700 to go to her gun line south of Port Stanley by 2330 – this meant making twenty-six knots, just to get there. As usual, the ship's company went to Action Stations before entering the threat area, on this occasion at 2315, and remained at full alert throughout the night. The ship was operating very close inshore, with *Yarmouth* and *Avenger* in company, providing artillery support for the various actions being undertaken by the land forces that night. Her guns were being directed from the high ground by a naval 'spotter' until he was wounded, and then by a bombardier. She fired fairly continuously as the Commandos went forward to Two Sisters. The guided-missile destroyer and *Yarmouth* between them sent in over four hundred shells before the ships began their withdrawal at 0515. They were, in fact, a bit late in leaving because the Commandos were having a tough time on the mountain. The ship's company of *Glamorgan* were stood down from Action Stations at 0530, conscious of a good night's work.

When finally they did break away from the Stanley gun line, I thought at the time that *Glamorgan* just miscalculated the edge of the 'envelope' we had designated as being within range of the shore-based Exocet launcher on the road at the back of Port Harriet. But it is likely that the Argentinians had managed to move their mobile launchers a shade further east along the coast. Either way, at 0536 the Args fired one. *Avenger* saw it ten miles out, sounding an alarm shortly after it had been sighted visually in *Glamorgan*. The helm was put hard over to turn away from the missile, quite possibly saving the ship by doing so. At one-mile range they fired Seacat and, with *Glamorgan* still heeling to her turn, the missile clipped the upper deck exactly where it joins the hull on the port side and blew up just short of the hangar.

It killed eight men instantly and wiped out the Wessex helicopter. Burning fuel poured through the hole in the deck and started a fire in the galley. Four cooks and a steward were killed in here and there were several other injuries. Smoke was sucked into the gas turbine room, but these engines were only temporarily put out of action by the blast effect of the Exocet explosion and by the water used for fire-fighting draining down through splinter holes, causing flooding. *Glamorgan* was, rather remarkably, still well able to steam and, after sorting out the immediate problems, soon worked up to twenty knots to rejoin the Battle Group. I expect the British troops on the mountains watched her go with some sadness. Mike Barrow's ship had been an exceptionally good friend to them that night and for many, many nights before.

My opinion at the time was that the ships had probably relaxed at just the wrong moment, and my diary note read: '*Glamorgan*, in a hurry to get back before dawn, cut the corner of the Exocet danger area – and paid the price . . . they were unlucky to be shot at and lucky to be hit as they were. Meanwhile we feel we know a lot more about the opposition.'

Thirteen of *Glamorgan*'s gallant company died, nearly as many as 3 Para in their grim fight for Mount Longdon. And so, while they built a small memorial to Sergeant Mackay up on the frozen heights of Mount Longdon – just his rifle, a Para's helmet and a small jam jar of daffodils on the spot where he fell – we once more buried our dead at sea. Among the Royal Navy coffins which slid into the endless silence of the Atlantic depths one hundred and sixty miles east of the Falkland Islands that evening, was that of twenty-five-year-old Lieutenant David Tinker, who was killed in the hangar. He was a sensitive, intelligent young officer, with a love of literature and poetry and for this he will be remembered, for his father published a truly poignant book of his letters and writings later that year.

Essentially, this widely read book is a hymn against war and all that it stands for and in subsequent years has been recognized as a kind of cry, from beyond the grave, of a young man who understood the wickedness of it all. Almost with each letter he grew more certain of the foolishness of the conflict. He felt that Margaret Thatcher had Churchillian delusions of 'defying Hitler', that John Nott did not understand what war was like, that I 'seem to have no compunction about casualties at all'. He wrote of 'the military fiasco', the 'political disgrace', and wondered 'if I am totally odd in that I utterly oppose all this killing that is going on over a flag'. He even mentioned the rate of fuel consumption perpetrated by his own ship *Glamorgan* as she made her escape from the waters around Pebble Island on 14 May ... 33,000 gallons, six yards a gallon, was his assessment.

Nonetheless his was a voice which ought not to be ignored. It presents a point of view far removed from mine, but it was still a valid point of view. A well-written one too. Indeed some of his assertions – for instance, that the British government had been planning to 'leave the islands totally undefended and take away the islanders' British citizenship' – were a bit too close for comfort. And what, you might ask, was a chap like this doing on the flight deck of a 6000-ton British destroyer in the middle of a war? It's a good question. The truth is that David Tinker was what is known as a VOLRET, a man who had applied to resign his commission in the Royal Navy (voluntary retirement). He had made his application some time before the Falklands problem arose. He was not a chap who was just trying to get out, at the prospect of having to go and fight. I think he was sincere in his belief that a career in Her Majesty's armed forces was not for him and that having been married for a couple of years he wished to lead a more settled life ashore. There is nothing wrong with that. Indeed the whole sad story of David Tinker has always caused me to recall my own position back in the 1950s.

I was serving as first lieutenant to Captain Brian Hutchings in the 2300-ton newly designed patrol submarine *Porpoise*. Suddenly, with some major crisis looming before us, we were ordered to return to port from our deep-water exercises off Iceland and 'store for war'. Remember that was only just over ten years on from the end of the Second World War and war was still very real to us, even if I hadn't actually experienced fighting in one. I vividly remember thinking to myself, 'Now, wait a minute. Is this what I joined the Royal Navy for? To go to war? Over the question of who owns what, a long way from home? Start blowing people up? Maybe get killed myself? Now, hold on a moment.' It wasn't difficult for me to realize that this was indeed what the Navy had been training me for, that I might indeed have to face action one day, and, having thought carefully about it, I found no quarrel with the idea of military action in such a cause, nor with my involvement in it. At the time I was twenty-seven, two years older than David Tinker, and I had just realized that a career in dark blue was not merely one of comfort, adventure and good company. It may be fraught with great danger, we may all be called to account, should deterrence fail.

Thus, at a similar age, David and I had both looked at what was involved and made our own decisions. We simply arrived at different conclusions about our careers ... mine under the pressure of impending war, his under no such pressure. The trouble was, for David, that it takes about eighteen months to get out of the Royal Navy and the Falklands crisis blew up during his spell in that no man's land of being a naval officer whose heart was elsewhere. I would like to repeat that there was nothing wrong with his decision – only with his timing.

With *Glamorgan* effectively out of action, and a lull in activity off-shore, I had time to do some homework. I wrote up this attrition list: 'Two destroyers sunk, three seriously damaged; two frigates sunk, two seriously damaged; one container ship sunk; two LSLs sunk, one seriously damaged.' That night we planned to send in four frigates for the night-bombardment programme, but two of them, *Yarmouth* and *Ambuscade*, had to be recalled with mechanical defects. That left *Active* and *Arrow* to batter away at the Arg positions on Sapper Hill and Moody Brook. The fact that *Arrow* was still there, still firing shells, was a bit of a miracle really – very early in the campaign, we had had serious worries about cracks in her hull. Now there were only two warships from the original group of escorts which had escaped damage: she was one, *Yarmouth* was the other.

You may remember that I mentioned that Commander

Tony Morton, new to command of a ship, was a bit hyper-active in the early engagements, raising alarms when I thought no real danger threatened. Well, he had learned fast and by the end of the conflict had a truly outstanding record. To have brought *Yarmouth* through, thus far unscathed, was a memorable achievement. Tony had been in the thick of it for a long time. By now they had patched up *Plymouth* and she steamed back to join the Battle Group, while battered *Glamorgan* took charge of all the ships in the TRALA, safely further out to the east.

It was Sunday 13 June, yet another bright clear day, which eventually gave way to the most unbelievably lovely sunset, and you could see all the way to the clouds on the horizon, over one hundred miles I would guess. There was no swell on the ocean, a soft six knots of breeze, with the sky and the sea dissolving into a harmony of brilliant purples, oranges, blues and Payne's grey. The ships were starkly silhouetted, like bits of black cardboard on the flaring western skyline.

With some reluctance I turned my back on this wondrous evening seascape and fired off a short signal to CLFFI relating the Task Force's tale of woe. This was recorded, at greater length in the diary.

> We are now on the cliff edge of our capability, with only three ships lacking a major OPDEF [Operational Defect] (*Hermes*, *Yarmouth* and *Exeter*). Of the destroyer/frigate force, forty-five per cent are reduced to near zero capability. Of the 'goalkeepers', *Andromeda*'s Sea Wolf is u/s; *Brilliant*'s entire systems are hanging by a variety of Coward-type threads; *Broadsword* has one and a half [weapons] systems, but one [propeller] shaft fairly permanently locked. None of

the Type 21s are fit: *Avenger* has a screw off; *Arrow* is cracked and has an OLY [Olympus gas turbine] down – you name it. They're all falling apart.

This afternoon, I was left on this most beautiful day for Etendards with one channel of Sea Dart fire. The convoys I run in/out nightly are 'escorted' by one half-crippled frigate (doesn't need to go faster than his charges, does he?). The gun line started with four ships and reduced to two from defects. The TRALA is 'protected' by poor old crippled *Glamorgan* and South Georgia is valiantly defended by poor old crippled *Antrim* and the redoubtable battleship *Endurance*.

Frankly, if the Args could only breathe on us, we'd fall over! Perhaps they're the same way: can only trust so, otherwise we're in for a carve-up.

In the small hours of the following morning several Arg aircraft were spotted along the southern coastline of the islands, most of them heading north. One of them, however, a Canberra bomber, being tracked by *Cardiff*, began to head across the land to the north of Port Stanley and as it did so was struck by the Type 42's Sea Dart missile. The troops on the high ground waiting to begin their dawn attack watched it spiral in.

Shortly thereafter, the British land forces began to move forward. A massive bombardment from *Yarmouth* and *Ambuscade* preceded 2 Para as they pushed the Args off Wireless Ridge sometime around 0300. *Avenger* and *Yarmouth* then set about the Arg AA guns – capable of use against ground forces – on Port Stanley racecourse, while *Active* pounded Mount Tumbledown in support of the Scots Guards. Here on this ridge the Guards were pinned down for three hours by a well-trained battalion of Argentinian marines, but they were eventually softened up by the infantry's mortars and by a renewed shelling bombardment from *Active* and *Avenger*.

By the time the frigates made their escape before first light they had, between the three of them, poured over five hundred shells into the Args' entrenched positions. The only casualty was one of *Avenger*'s propeller blades, which had sheared off, but this was no time to try to find out why.

A little later in the morning we sent the RAF Harriers up from *Hermes* for one final laser-targeted bomb strike on an Argentinian artillery battery on the Stanley side of Tumbledown and thereafter things began to crumble for General Galtieri's men. With the big Sea King 4s now flying reinforcements from 40 Commando up to Sapper Hill, General Menendez was faced with many hundreds of his beaten troops pouring back off their vital positions in the icy hills surrounding Port Stanley. General Galtieri, their Commander-in-Chief, ordered them to fight on, but, true to form, his timing was hopeless. At 1405 General Menendez very sensibly sent a message to General Moore asking for terms for a ceasefire.

We heard the news out in the Battle Group pretty much in the form of rumours at first, and I have to admit that I hardly dared believe it. But, as the news hardened, we felt it would not be tempting providence too much to accept it.

And so ended the war. But really, only for the land forces, not the rest of us. Out here in the Battle Group, the electronic City still cannot sleep: the nightwatchmen remain alert. The combat air patrols are still required. The eyes and ears of the Fleet must continue to be tireless, indefinitely. I have no guarantee the Args won't come back at us tomorrow by air or sea. It is Menendez who has surrendered, not Galtieri. I don't trust dictators.

18

Welcome Home

I am fairly sure it was Napoleon who originally named him, the terrible Old Warrior who drove the Grande Armée of France from the gates of Moscow. 'I was not beaten by the Russians,' growled Bonaparte. 'I was beaten by General Winter.' And I have no doubt that one hundred and thirty years later, Adolf Hitler, perhaps with slightly less sang-froid, thought much the same when the tide turned on the German armies at Moscow and Stalingrad. But for us, down in the Falklands, the General was late. He turned up, sure enough, just as we had known he would, but he missed the six-week action by about seven hours, arriving on the evening of the surrender of the Argentine land forces.

The wind had been building from the Antarctic all afternoon, an icy chill cutting across the waves. It had started in the middle of the day, around the time General Menendez was asking for terms. By 2200z, General Winter was in full cry with his opening blizzard. The wind by now was gusting one hundred miles per hour – the Falkland Islands were being swept white with slashing snow and hail. I could actually hear the sleet pelting against the side of my cabin up in the island of *Hermes*. The sea was rough, the night was moonless, and the cold across the deck was nearly unbearable, with a wind-chill factor reducing the temperature to something like sixteen degrees below freezing. These are not the kind of conditions you meet nearer the Poles, where the waves break over the bow and freeze instantly on the ship's upperworks. This is the kind of cold inflicted mainly by the wind and which produces a rawness which would make the Scottish lochs in January seem like Honolulu.

But the sleet against my cabin bulkhead couldn't much distract me from tonight's main problem: how on earth to deal with the immediate problem of the thirteen thousand Argentinian prisoners of war, many ill-dressed for such conditions and many ill-fed, we believed. I thought then, for the first time, about the arrival of General Winter. If he had been here ten days ago, he would not have been much of a help to the Args, dug in on the heights with no chance of their High Command getting their air force into the skies. But I think he would have finished us. Ships are just as vulnerable as the marching armies of Napoleon and Hitler were in Russia. Everything goes wrong more often at sea when the weather is especially bad. In particular, the salt spray attacks electrical circuits and the salt crystals clog mechanical systems. Ice and snow don't help either. These difficulties had been forecast since mid-April, putting the pressure on us all to get on with it before the bad weather arrived. But now, seeing it right before me for the first time, the stark reality of a howling winter gale in the South Atlantic was no less formidable.

As it happened, we had been rather lucky with the weather throughout the war. It was nothing like as bad as we had expected, and certainly not as bad as certain sections of the Press kept saying it was. They of course have a rather overdeveloped sense of amateur dramatics. Indeed we had been working in cold, bright sunlight for almost the whole of the last nine days. Naturally, we had had our moments – a few storms and some ferocious seas – but nothing like that which arrived on the night of the capitulation of the Args' land forces. For the record, we logged that storm at Force Twelve at around midnight (that's a gale of 120mph), which was a bit draughty on the flight deck of *Hermes*, but much more unpleasant if you are bouncing about in a small frigate.

Still, I would far rather have been in my steel home out at sea than huddled ashore with not much cover, as so many of the soldiers of both sides must have been on that wild night. I found myself thinking of problems of hypothermia, trench foot and pneumonia, and how on earth we were going to cope with the colossal administrative problem of clearing up the tattered remnants of Galtieri's beaten army.

What I was not considering was the possibility of any serious celebration of victory, though I did allow myself the luxury of my first cigarette in eight months. As a matter of fact I did not really believe we *had* a victory yet – even though there were reports of white flags in Port Stanley and that the Union Jack was flying once more above Government House. I was by no means certain that we had beaten their air force, which could perfectly well reappear at four minutes' notice, in exactly the same way they had when they sank the *Sheffield*. And though their navy did seem to be staying firmly in harbour, it was still physically capable of coming out to fight.

What was clear was that the Arg soldiers in the Falkland

Islands had had enough and that their commander was surrendering. But that could only be taken as a 'local surrender', no more. No one had said anything about surrender from Buenos Aires, no one was telling me the entire Argentinian military machine was surrendering unconditionally to us and that the war was over. And the specious argument that because war had never been declared, there was no way it could be 'undeclared', did nothing to convince me that we could drop our guard. For all I knew they could be waiting for *Hermes* to enter Port Stanley harbour in triumph before they came again, this time in real force, with their Skyhawks, and turned the balance of power upside down by lunchtime.

I *was* being advised that the Arg commander had signed something – but that gave no guarantees. A piece of paper is still only a piece of paper (as in Neville Chamberlain) – and what's more, it was only a local piece of paper. For all I knew General Galtieri was demanding some last desperate effort, along with the resignation of Menendez. There were some pressing reasons, on that first evening of 'peacetime', encouraging me to take *Hermes* right inshore tonight. For a start, her flight deck would provide a vastly better helicopter operating base than Navy Point in Port Stanley – a single deserted, bare house and a few bits of concrete hard-standing for non-existent Nissen huts. But there was absolutely no chance that I would do it – without *Hermes* and the Harriers, the Task Force would have been virtually defenceless and we were eight thousand miles from home. I did not trust the Args so much as half an inch.

So *Hermes* remained hove-to out in the TEZ while I played it safe and worried. We were facing what was essentially a 'disaster relief' operation involving the repatriation of thousands of Argentinians, but this one had to be conducted under

474

immediate threat of major attack. I even asked Northwood to approach the BBC to air the problem in international circles so that we might avoid too much blame for the inevitable casualties of this far-from-orderly take-over of the Falkland Islands.

Like so many things in this world, it proved less difficult than we had feared. And on the morning of 17 June I felt I could leave my Flagship, the centre of all operations at sea, for a day ashore. I was very keen to have a look around these islands for which we had sacrificed the lives of eighty-seven men of the Royal Navy, including thirteen officers. I flew the eighty miles inshore by helicopter and landed on the deck of *Fearless*, anchored in Port William, shortly after dawn. There, over a quick cup of coffee, we settled the plans for the day. In passing, I was asked if I would like to meet General Menendez, who was being held on board. I chose not to. My reasons were simple: I was so bloody angry with him, I could not trust myself to observe the full requirements of the Geneva Convention.

The way I felt that day, he seemed to have caused us more damned trouble than any enemy commander since Erwin Rommel; in terms of obstinacy, that is, not military talent. I really felt the man should have packed it in the day he found out the British had landed. It is quite remarkable how clear I am in my mind about my feelings that morning. All these years later, however, I am not quite so certain of the accuracy of my assessments. Perhaps I should have simply been grateful for the incompetence of his defence, along with his lack of perseverance. It would not have taken much effort on his part to spin the land campaign out another ten days – and that would have finished us, not him.

Anyway we went on to Government House where I had a long chat with Jeremy Moore, whom I had not seen since he left the Battle Group for the beaches some weeks ago. Then he and I, in company with a driver and an armed guard, set off in a captured Argentinian staff car to go to Port Stanley airfield. This area, a prime target for our bombs for weeks, was now virtually a prisoner of war camp – a fine-sounding name for a near-featureless isthmus, with absolutely no 'facilities', not even tents, and almost completely surrounded by Arg minefields and freezing water. About the only things it had in common with a POW camp were defeated inmates and the difficulties put in the way of their escape.

Most of the way to the PSA we were passing groups of Argentinian POWs in their dark, drab green battle kit, coming in to be disarmed. I wound up my window and locked the door, in case a group of them suddenly changed their minds about the surrender. When, however, we arrived at the airport runway I really saw Major General Jeremy Moore in his true colours as the commander of the victorious British land forces. To my horror he jumped out of the car and, with total disregard for the thousands of Arg soldiers milling about – some of whom, I felt sure, could still be carrying personal weapons of one kind or another – strode purposefully off down the tarmac. Faced with an instant decision – shall I remain cravenly locked in the car and keep my head down until he returns, or do I go with him? – I narrowly decided I'd best follow. With not a few sidelong glances at this half-armed, ugly-looking South American rabble which flanked us, I reluctantly got out and joined him.

As I did so, there came towards us a detachment of presumably surrendered Argentinian marines in their distinctive black-and-white camouflage uniforms, looking as smart as if they were on parade, marching briskly – left-right, left-right, left-right, in perfect time. There must have been fifty of them

– seemed like a hundred! – forming a firmly disciplined body of hired, hard men.

'Christ!' I thought. 'Would it not be the supreme irony to be literally trampled to death by this lot, after all we have done?' I kept moving along, about two inches from Jeremy, as I remember, and the defeated marines marched on by, not ten feet from us. When they had passed, I nudged Jeremy and told him that I was not feeling too happy about this unnecessary fraternizing with the enemy. What if a couple of them decided to kill us?

The General, however, was unperturbed. 'Sandy, old chap,' he said. 'Don't even think about it. When an army surrenders, they are completely demoralized, right down to the last man. They don't have an ounce of fight left in 'em.'

Of course he was right and I was wrong. Soldiers were his business, after all. But I said again, 'That last lot didn't look completely demoralized.'

'No,' said the General. 'Perhaps not. But they were. They always are.'

I think at that very moment I realized how much of a thoroughgoing professional military officer this man was, a man who had led his troops with bravery, care and skill to victory on the ground against all the odds. He had not asked of anyone more than he was prepared to give himself. I don't know how much he frightened the Argentinians, but he certainly did a good deal more than just impress me.

Anyway, I came away from there a wiser man, lunched on board *Fearless* and then went off in a Sea King 4 to tour the places which had been, until now, just names on the chart to me. We started off by overflying the dark waters of Teal Inlet, its narrow entrance looked little wider from the air than it did on the map. Then we clattered our way west past the great

477

bulk of Fanning Head and I tried to see the marks of the shells from *Antrim* on the night of the landings. Some eight hundred feet below were the waters in which Captain Kit Layman's *Argonaut* had so nearly been lost.

We flew down the length of Carlos Water which I had seen in my thoughts so often, but now saw in broad daylight for the first time. We shuddered our way out over the Sound and I looked down to the south to the slate waters where Commander West's men had fought with such gallantry and beneath which *Ardent* now rested, not so far from the undersea grave of *Antelope*. These were the waters where John Coward had rallied his team on that dreadful opening day when they had bombed *Antrim*, where later *Plymouth* had been hit, *Brilliant* herself bombed and strafed. It all looked peaceful enough from up above.

We flew on over West Falkland, stopping off at Pebble Island to examine the eleven dead aircraft, seemingly untouched until we got close. I looked out to the north to the choppy grey Atlantic waves which now flowed over the wreck of the *Coventry*. Here too was where they had so nearly sent Bill Canning's *Broadsword* to join her. I felt, reasonably enough, anything but elated. We went down and looked at Port Howard, Darwin, Goose Green and finally to Fitzroy, the little bay of such distressful memory. Far to the south I could just make out Sea Lion Islands, upon which one day would be erected a memorial to the men who went down in the *Sheffield*. And so, back to *Fearless*.

That night, I tried to write down my impressions of the place, thinking perhaps I might find some poetry in my soul to describe it. But, curiously, my emotions recorded in my diary were flat.

Very north of Scotland. Dark, cold, windy, but patches in the weather. Wood smoke and clear air, but crystal visibility and mist. Many sheep and few cattle. Fewer people – square miles of rough turf, granite rock fields, tussock grass, nearly all of it soaking.

Twenty degrees warmer and it would be the yachting centre of the world. As it is, bloody awful ... definitely not a jewel in the Queen's crown.

I remember just as vividly the journey in the helicopter back to *Hermes*. We had just taken off when I happened to glance back towards the rear seating area, from which we were almost cut off by a large sonar set in this anti-submarine Sea King, and I spotted three or four strangers, all dressed in 'Talking Tree' outfits. All with rather tanned faces. All with sizeable and slightly droopy dark moustaches. All armed to the teeth. None of them speaking.

This, I surmised, is definitely odd. Unannounced 'passengers' do not usually travel with the Admiral – and no one asked *me* if they could hitch a lift. Also these people looked uncomfortably like Argentinian Special Forces would. Was Jeremy's belief in the demoralizing effect of surrender so totally reliable?

I sat very still, and very quiet, and scribbled a note to my Marine colonel sitting beside me, to the effect of, 'Don't on any account look aft, but just check with the pilot who his friends in the back are, will you?'

He read it and went forward to the cockpit. I could see the pilot shrug in answer and a minute later a scribbled note came back: '*Fearless* has absolutely no record of *anyone* on this aircraft except yourselves.'

I immediately instructed: 'Check with *Hermes* also.'

Back came a signal from the carrier's Ops Room: 'Absolutely no record of any visitors expected on your aircraft.'

Sod it, I thought. What a way to go. I scribbled a new note instructing the pilot to inform *Hermes*, 'I have four unwanted guests on board. Prepare reception for possible Arg SAS on landing.'

Down through the dusk we came, hovering over the flight deck of *Hermes*. We flopped down very fast. My two staff officers and I broke cover, piling out of the door forward on the port side. The helicopter was surrounded by our own SAS, each man with an automatic rifle levelled at the rear doors. We headed for shelter, confident that no enemy was getting out of that SK5 alive. But these four did. No bullets flew – only words. I was 'reliably' informed the conversation went roughly as follows:

'''Allo, Charlie. Fancy seeing you!'

'Wotcha, Sid. Just sneaked a ride 'ome with the brass. Had a lovely day on the beach. 'Bout time we had a look round after all this bloody hangin' about. And tell you the truth, it ain't really worth a carrot, full of f***ing sheep, innit? What're you all doing up 'ere on the flight deck then? Havin' a tea party?'

There was, I expect, plenty of laughter, most of it at my expense. I muttered something about 'Silly buggers – they should at least have told *someone*.' But that's the trouble with the SAS: they never tell anyone any more than they feel they absolutely have to. That tends to be very little, and it doesn't include a run-ashore in the Admiral's helicopter, it seems. But then I suppose it all goes with the job, along with their ability to merge into the background, to go anywhere in the utmost secrecy. I did just wish they had chosen someone else's transport, I'd had enough frights for one day, thank you.

As a result of that little incident, we always required incoming helos to show who they had in the back before landing on *Hermes*'s flight deck. It was a sobering thought how much damage half a dozen Special Forces men could have done on a carrier's flight deck, where the main concern is the safe handling of aircraft, not defence against a well-trained team of hard-men. You could almost hear the stable door slamming!

The following two weeks were busy but not really worthy of note. I had to write my personal report to the Task Force Commander, the Commander-in-Chief, Fleet, Admiral Field-house, most of the contents of which I have related a great deal more fully in this book. I was, however, struck some years later, re-reading the report, by the way the gentler habits and attitudes of peace had had to be ditched as the harsher realities of war pressed upon us. On the *Belgrano* sinking, I had drafted: '. . . the destroyers accompanying *Belgrano* had been deliber-ately spared – albeit against my strictly military judgement.' I had added that a hardening of attitudes is a natural process of war and, in referring to our discovery that the Argentinians intended to sink any ship coming to the aid of *Sheffield*, I went on: '. . . certainly it stripped away the last vestiges of any real determination on our part to let chivalry stand in the way of success . . .'

I also let loose on matters of Government policy; even I realized this was not strictly my business, but I proceeded anyway, with the following:

> I cannot resist a review of this whole affair. Were
> I Galtieri I would have observed the Malvinas negoti-
> ations of the last few decades and found little hope of

early satisfaction. I would also have observed that, over the same long period, there had been a progressive withdrawal of, and reduction in, British overseas military capability. In the General's boots, I would have concluded that, at some time in the not-so-distant future, British policy on the Falklands issue would become *all* shadow and *no* substance.

When the cuts in the Royal Navy were announced recently, the way ahead must have seemed clear to Galtieri, and he only needed a half-reasonable excuse. Señor Davidoff's scrap-dealers and our indignant reaction to them provided that excuse. Galtieri attacked. His reasoning was as impeccable as his timing was previous. All he had to do was wait another six months, when *Hermes, Invincible, Fearless* and *Intrepid* would all have *gone*...

If the Argentinian government, or others similarly minded elsewhere, are to be deterred from this kind of military adventurism, we shall need to provide not only the mark of our resolution on the spot [a flag, a ship, a platoon]. But also the obvious wherewithal to reinforce it [mobile forces, at short readiness].

We would not again wish to repair our mistakes the hard way. But it was the last Defence Review that was the problem. After the needs of the strategic nuclear deterrent and the defence of the home base had been met, they decided in favour of the short-term, politically expedient, continental European commitment. This was to the detriment of Britain's long-term, long-established, worldwide, national interest. This was plainly evident to Galtieri, and I doubt he was alone.

Whatever I may have thought before, the Falklands

experience has given me a new insight into the capacity of non-democratic governments for immorality and dishonesty. That capacity is apt to be too common in this turbulent world. What, if any, should be Britain's role in all of this? It is clear enough that our traditional global policy has long suited our geographic and political interests. That is a matter of history. And this war has once again demonstrated that it also suits our professional military capability – air, land and sea.

Our Defence budget, of course, can only buy a certain amount. But I am convinced that it ought to be spent where it can influence both European *and* world affairs. It *must* be a mistake to place it where it can affect – and in a very limited way at that – the policies of our European neighbours only.

I do not find that my views of 1982 have changed significantly almost twenty years years later, only that national defence policy now seems to have turned in the same direction. But at the time of writing that piece, I was essentially preparing to leave. I had been at sea now for three months since sailing from the UK, Ascension being the only other land I had seen, back in mid-April. How the time had run away. And now I had to prepare to meet a new challenge, the popular Press of England, who, I was sure, were just longing to make a fool of me, if I didn't manage to do it for them. I was well aware that the only time during the whole of this campaign my superiors had been deeply upset with me was because of what they had read the Press said I had said. Again I resolved not to drop my guard.

I set about rehearsing myself to deal with the opening Press conference I was certain I would face upon arrival. Quite frankly I dreaded the entire thing, because I am simply not trained to tackle it professionally. My diary assessed what their first question would be and listed my possible responses:

'Whose fault was the Bluff Cove disaster?'
A1 Mine, if anyone's.
A2 It was no disaster.
A3 The Argentinians'.
A4 CLFFI's? COMAW's?
A5 Don't know.
A6 No comment, on the grounds that if it was a culpable disaster I should not prejudice it; if it wasn't, then the question of fault does not arise.

Beneath this I wrote: 'Obviously, I prefer A1, true or not. A2 – A5 are either wet or criminal. A6 is patently a neat evasion.'

Next question, I guessed, would be a reference to the veiled accusation in the Press that I had kept *Hermes* out of bombing range through personal cowardice rather than strategic necessity:

'It has been said frequently that you commanded the South African Task Group (or should be awarded the South Africa Star). What have you to say to that?'

A1 Not a lot.
A2 South *Atlantic* would be more correct.
A3 Who said it, how often, and for what reason?
A4 You should not believe all you hear.
A5 Next question.

I then prepared myself to field the inevitable:

'What have you to say to Mr Nott about his cuts in the Navy?'

   A1 Nothing. He has not invited me to give my views.

   A2 I am a Naval Officer. I would regret them.

   A3 That would be between Mr Nott and myself, since I am a public servant.

Then might come:

'What was your first thought on getting back?'

   A1 Shit, it's still raining.

   A2 Oh, Gawd, I've got to face the Press again.

   A3 England, my England . . .

And so on, and so on . . . The days dragged by until 1 July when my old friend Admiral Sir Derek Reffell arrived to take over the continued defence of the islands. To this day, I remain mildly astonished that he was not given the job in the first place, since he was very much better qualified than I, in just about every respect. We spent a pleasant couple of days together until on the morning of 4 July 1982 I prepared to go home. I wrote my last signal and had it transmitted to all the front-line authorities in the South Atlantic under the command of General Moore and myself – to all of the thirty-one warships, the twenty Royal Fleet Auxiliaries, the five minesweepers, the forty-three merchant ships and thirteen air squadrons directly involved. It read:

As I haul my South Atlantic flag down, I reflect sadly on the brave lives lost, and the good ships gone, in the short time of our trial. I thank wholeheartedly each and every one of you for your gallant support, tough determination and fierce perseverance under bloody conditions. Let us all be grateful that Argentina doesn't breed bulldogs and, as we return severally to enjoy the blessings of our land, resolve that those left behind for ever shall not be forgotten.

They arranged a superb fly-past of some eighty aircraft, the Harriers and the Sea Kings forming a magnificent aerial Victory Parade. I stood alone in the pale sunlight, in my working rig, my Navy blue sweater and beret, up on the Gun Direction Platform right at the top of *Hermes*'s bridge. It was very impressive and served also as a reminder to anyone else that we still had serious air power here should the Args consider changing their minds about that surrender.

Then I ordered my flag to be hauled down and a helicopter flew me, Commander Jeremy Sanders and several of my personal staff to Port Stanley airfield – my two GWOs Captains Andy Buchanan and Peter Woodhead had left some time before. My war had lasted exactly one hundred days – one hundred days since I had said goodbye to Commodore Sam Dunlop, captain of *Fort Austin* in Gibraltar harbour on the evening of 26 March. A lifetime in one hundred days.

We took off in a Hercules c130 transport, with its long-range fuel tanks taking up a large part of the hold where we sat, bound for Ascension. From there we made a very quick turn-round into an RAF vc10 up the coast of Africa towards the Royal Air Force station at Brize Norton in Oxfordshire. We banked along the southern edge of the Cotswolds in pretty poor visibility and touched down at Brize in the middle of a dull, grey English summer day. The weather was not much different from that in the Falklands, except it was not quite so cold. The media's welcome, however, made up for that.

I was met by Char and the children, Admiral Fieldhouse,

and a good few others. It should have been a very emotional meeting, but a part of my mind was picking away at the next event. I was about to be taken into a hall to face thirty or forty of Fleet Street's finest.

'Welcome home, Admiral,' said the first of them. 'Right, then. How do you account for the disaster at Bluff Cove?'

Pusillanimously, I presented them with answer A6 – the skilfully worded evasion and I remember wondering to myself: 'Christ! I suppose it's a good thing we didn't lose the war, if it's like this when you win it.'

The rest of the day is rather a blur really. I had not had a day off since early March, I had been at a full level of concentration day after day for all of those months, and I just found it extremely difficult to deal with all of this. I had hardly met anyone outside my immediate tight working circle for such a long time – I had not even seen a proper television programme since February. Now I was faced with this seemingly hostile group in the full glare of publicity. I did not like it one bit.

But I got through it, took a week's leave and shuffled off in my little yacht with Char for a few days, pottering around the Solent. Then I returned to the office at Portsmouth trying to think of various ways to avoid all forms of public appearance, particularly when *Hermes* arrived home.

This took place on 20 July when she anchored at Spithead, outside Portsmouth harbour, for the night. The following morning, before they came in for their tumultuous welcome in that great naval dockyard, I went out privately to meet them, making the fifteen-minute journey in the barge of the Queen's Harbourmaster. I climbed up the starboard after gangway, pipes and bugles going as naval ceremonial and age-old tradition required. But so familiar were these sounds to me that I hardly heard them as they echoed out over those historic waters upon which so many greater commanders than I had sailed. The Quarterdeck was quiet and secluded under the flight deck above, and there the entire team of ship's officers I had known and worked with were fallen in, from captain to midshipman.

In that moment I felt pleased to my very heart to see every one of them. These were my companions in adversity – there was so much between us that could not be said, so much that would never be said. Yet we were bound to each other in mutual trust as only men who have faced danger together can ever be. I suppose it is always so after a battle has been fought, whether you win it or not – and quite often, I suspect, in this very place, in sight of England yet not quite home.

I believe that, somehow, I managed to say something intelligible to most of them, but even as I wrote this, eight years later, my throat tightened and the words got difficult. My original plans to deliver a few stirring words to them all as a group fell apart and I left with tears in my eyes, to hurry back to Portsmouth, leaving them to *their* triumphal, tearful return.

As my 'barge' took me away back to my offices in the dockyard, I could not help looking up at that great, grey, sea-stained warship, my home for the most comfortless three months of my life. And as I looked I could not help wondering whether it had all been worth while.

That is not a question to be answered by a simple 'Yes' or 'No' and left at that, although the underlying need to show that we, as a nation, very strongly disapprove of military takeover bids is clear enough.

So much for the *need* to do something concrete. What about the cost? What are we prepared to pay? My cold-hearted assessments of relative attrition should not have blinded you to the human price of standing up for a principle. The death rate among British forces in the Falklands War was roughly the same as it was on the roads in Britain over the same period. Which is the more wasteful, the less worthwhile? On a slightly larger canvas, the official figures tell us that the casualties, on both sides together, exceeded the number of residents in the islands. How much sense does this make? For there can be no real comfort for those whose close relations never came home or, at least if there is, I certainly seem unable to give it, however much I may wish to. And the mentally and physically injured are most unlikely to feel any better for their experience, even those who have not suffered permanent disablement.

As to the cost in cash – we lost two destroyers, two frigates, a large container ship, an LSL, twenty-four assorted helicopters and ten Harriers. We expended considerable quantities of ammunition, missiles, torpedoes, depth charges, spares, fuel ... the list is almost endless and all of it was required to be replaced afterwards. There is also an hard-cash cost, year by year, for the continued defence of the Falklands. Thus, while I may have my own personal views, the question of whether it is worth while spending X millions on the Falklands as opposed to Y millions on Gibraltar, or Z millions on the National Health Service, can only be for the Government on behalf of the electorate.

But anyway, the real question is, was it *right*? Not, was it was worth while? We must ask ourselves, was it right that we should have gone to the South Atlantic and fought for the Falklands almost as if we were defending the coast of Hampshire? It will always come down to a point of principle. Our response was a fundamental part of the British character. Those who die in battle always pay too high a price, but in the South Atlantic, as in so many other wars, they died for the ideas we stand for.

Expressed more formally, they died because we believe in the rule of law for the guidance of human behaviour. But they also died because we, as a nation, wherever we may be, take a perverse pride in that dogged streak of British truculence. And so, in a sense, they died for the very Britishness of us all.

Thus, for the final time, was it right to fight that grim battle down in the South Atlantic? I expect, before I am finished, I will be asked that question many times more. And each time the memories of lost friends stand before me. But the answer will always be, yes.

EPILOGUE

In the years since the cessation of hostilities in the South Atlantic I have often been offered the phrase, 'Nasty little war, wasn't it?' How often one heard about how much worse it was in Ulster, Malaya, Korea, Kenya and so on, where casualty figures reached the eight hundred level rather than the two hundred and fifty British men who died in and around the Falkland Islands in 1982. The difference was that we lost those two hundred and fifty men in six weeks flat, not over a period of years. During that time I lost nearly half of the destroyers and frigates I started with. The killing was at a particularly high rate, more than ten times worse than anything our Services had had to take since the Second World War.

Comparisons with other British conflicts of the previous forty years rarely do justice to the bravery of the people who served in what was one of the bloodiest fights in a long while, with the Navy taking much the worst of it. More than half of all the dead were from either the Royal Navy (eighty-seven), the Royal Marines (twenty-six), the Merchant Navy (nine) or the Royal Fleet Auxiliary (seven). Nasty it most certainly was. Little? It did not seem so to those who faced the waves of Argentine bombers streaking in over Falkland Sound. Nor indeed to those who fought the fires, patched up the ships, rescued the wounded, buried the dead, and later waited in tense, silent acceptance of the next incoming attack. The only thing 'little' about our war was the total number of British servicemen directly involved, some twenty-five thousand, and of course, the time span of the fighting, only six weeks. But those weeks had days, and occasionally hours, which seemed like eternity itself to those who fought there.

I suppose it will always carry the inference of being a 'push-over war' – the mighty Brits crushing the ridiculous Args. But even those wars usually bear a close comparison to a heavily backed odds-on favourite running in a classic horse race: about half the time the favourite wins and everyone says, afterwards, 'no trouble', ignoring the ever-present spectre of defeat which will become reality should the four-legged hero produce anything less than his absolute best on the day. Politicians similarly are too much inclined to take it for granted that Her Majesty's armed forces will do what they almost always have done in time of war, whether or not they are given the necessary equipment. The cuts in our surface fleet proposed in the Defence Review of 1981 would have rendered us impotent by late 1982. It was only the timely occurrence of the Falklands War that saved the Royal Navy from them and I have a strong suspicion the British public is grateful for that. When the battles around the waters of the Falklands were at their height, we kept receiving sackloads of mail from ordinary people wishing the Navy well, and when the ships returned to Portsmouth the welcomes were overwhelming.

There were other worthwhile aspects to emerge from the war, not least that it demonstrated to the Eastern Bloc that the West, if seriously challenged, was not in any way as decadent as they thought. The South Atlantic showed that we would fight fiercely under bloody conditions, take losses of men and equipment, and come back fighting. The Americans were also full of admiration and proud of their critical 'special relationship' assistance to us. Caspar Weinberger, the former US Defence

Secretary, winds up the chapter on the Falklands in his far-seeing book *Fighting For Peace* with these observations: 'Our allies, who were also Britain's allies, were uniformly admiring and re-assured that America was a far more reliable and helpful friend than they had thought ... Most important of all, the British success in the Falkland Islands told the world that aggression would not be allowed to succeed; that freedom and the rule of law had strong and effective defenders.' Remember this all took place when President Reagan and Mr Weinberger were in the process of a massive military build-up which saw them increase spending after the Carter years by 13.3, 11.5 and 7.9 per cent between 1981 and 1983. One year later President Reagan was re-elected by one of the biggest political landslides in American history – which I believe is a pretty sharp lesson to any government trying to find large savings by cutting defence.

There were of course other, less obvious advantages for both the Navy and the Army. The experience naturally toughened and battle-hardened men who had essentially been at peace for all of their careers. It sharpened all Service attitudes to education and preparation. Indeed Commander Craig of the *Alacrity* emerged as a Commodore, the front-line commander of the British Naval Task Group in the Gulf War. Perhaps also it ought to be remembered that when the Iraqis finally tried to launch a couple of Exocets at the allied Fleet it was the traditionally ultra-sharp Ops Room of a British warship which spotted the incoming aircraft and arranged their destruction. An Iraqi Silkworm missile, aimed at a big US warship, was also taken out with a British Sea Dart.

I will not attempt to go through the subsequent careers of my captains, save to mention a few, whom, like Chris Craig, you came slightly to 'know' through the pages of this book. At the time of writing in 1990, Paul Hoddinott, Sam Salt,

John Coward, Mike Harris, Kit Layman, Hugh Balfour, Jeremy Black, Lin Middleton, Jeremy Larken, Peter Dingemans, Hugo White and Mike Layard had all become admirals. There were more to come as the years went by. To my regret, Mike Clapp, Bill Canning and David Hart-Dyke left the Navy virtually unrewarded. This was no doubt as a result of the edict from the MOD which stated – after it was all over – that promotion boards should take no account of reports of officers' service in the Falklands. The belief at headquarters was that it would otherwise be unfair on those who had been unable to attend the action for whatever reason and had therefore missed their opportunity to shine. My personal thought on learning about this was that it was a complete disgrace and as well they hadn't told us on the way south or the outcome could well have been different. But this was not before Navy divers searching for highly-classified documents in the wreck of *Coventry*, recovered David's father's telescope from the captain's cabin. They also found the historic Cross of Nails which David and former colleagues formally presented to Coventry Cathedral. Others too were promoted and rewarded, but I shall not pursue the careers of those you hardly met. Neither will I open the Pandora's Box of honours and awards. This is a subject which invariably causes dissension, often acrimonious. I've had enough of that!

However, I would like to tell you about one of the first official letters I received on arriving back at my office. It was from the Director of Naval Pay and Pensions and had been mailed to me five days before my return from the south. It pointed out that the department had been conducting its quarterly review of my expenditure on entertainment and noted that in the last quarter – during which time I had been a bit busy – I had spent a total of £5.85. In the light of this,

... we have accordingly revised your entertainment allowance down by £1.78 per day. Furthermore we have backdated this revision to that of your promotion in July of 1981 last year. As a consequence you have been overpaid £649.70.

We should be glad to receive payment of this, in full, at your earliest convenience.

For a brief second, I actually thought it was a joke. But I quickly realized that it was no such thing and, being a bit pressed for cash, I wrote back and asked if I could have time to pay. I suggested £100 a month and, considerately, they agreed. I suppose I should have thrown a lavish Victory Party in *Hermes*, then it would not have happened. Serves me right for not entering into the spirit of things.

But at least that letter brought me down to earth with a considerable thump. This country really does have its own wonderful way of ensuring that *no one* gets too big for his boots. Perhaps that has preserved us from a home-grown Hitler, or a Mussolini, or a Stalin, or even a Galtieri or a Saddam Hussein.

But, anyway, who am I go on about such philosophical matters? As the Director of Naval Pay and Pensions was so swift to remind me, I was just another naval officer, the prisoner of my own experiences after a working life-time in dark blue ... a mere product of what the Navy blandly refers to as the System.

The Romans always employed a half-naked slave to stand behind conquering generals upon their triumphant return. At the 'Grand March Past' he would quietly remind the Caesar of the moment: 'Hominem te memento' – remember you are only a man. We, of course, do not require a half-naked slave for the job. We have civil servants instead, better dressed but just as necessary. Even for my small part, two thousand years later, the message was unchanged. Hominem te memento.

INDEX